From empire to exile

Manchester University Press

Studies in
Modern French History

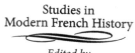

Edited by
David Hopkin and Máire Cross

This series is published in collaboration with the UK Society for the Study of
French History. It aims to showcase innovative short monographs relating to
the history of the French, in France and in the world since c.1750. Each volume
speaks to a theme in the history of France with broader resonances to other
discourses about the past. Authors demonstrate how the sources and interpretations of modern French history are being opened to historical investigation in
new and interesting ways, and how unfamiliar subjects have the capacity to tell
us more about the role of France within the European continent. The series is
particularly open to interdisciplinary studies that break down the traditional
boundaries and conventional disciplinary divisions.

Titles already published in this series

*Emile and Isaac Pereire: Bankers, Socialists and Sephardic Jews
in nineteenth-century France*
Helen Davies

*Catholicism and children's literature in France:
The comtesse de Ségur (1799–1874)*
Sophie Heywood

Aristocratic families in republican France, 1870–1940
Elizabeth C. Macknight

The republican line: Caricature and French republican identity, 1830–52
Laura O'Brien

The routes to exile: France and the Spanish Civil War refugees, 1939–2009
Scott Soo

The Society for the
Study of French History

From empire to exile

History and memory within the *pied-noir* and *harki* communities, 1962–2012

CLAIRE ELDRIDGE

Manchester University Press

Published by Manchester University Press
Altrincham Street, Manchester M1 7JA, UK
www.manchesteruniversitypress.co.uk

British Library Cataloguing-in-Publication Data is available

ISBN 978 0 7190 8723 3 hardback
ISBN 978 1 5261 2716 7 paperback

First published by Manchester University Press in hardback 2016

Typeset by Out of House Publishing

To Peggy and Nora, for all the happy memories

Contents

Acknowledgements

In the many years it has taken to research and write this book I have in-curred innumerable debts. One of the largest of these is to my supervisor, Stephen Tyre. Had he not turned up at the University of St Andrews in my final year of undergraduate studies, my academic career might have taken a very different path. As a supervisor and in the years since I finished my PhD he has been unfailingly encouraging and generous with his time. I was equally lucky that my first job at Keele University introduced me to Malcolm Crook whose kindness and guidance made my transition from postgraduate student to lecturer far smoother than it might otherwise have been. Both have been formative influences on me as an academic and I cannot thank them enough.

At the University of Southampton working in the interdisciplinary environment of Modern Languages taught me many things, while the History department there generously included me their activities. Scott Soo, Chris Prior, Julia Huettner, Laurence Richard, Julia Kelly, Jaine Beswick, Tony Campbell, Patrick Stevenson, Aude Campmas, Vivienne Orchard and Kelly Reynolds all made my time at Southampton that much more enjoyable. Adrian Sewell deserves a special mention for helping me with my many translation queries, especially the more obscure ones, and for being a generally lovely human being. Any mistakes that remain in the text are, of course, entirely my responsibility. I would also like to thank Tony Chafer, Natalya Vince, Joanna Warson, Walid Benkhaled and Ed Naylor down the road at the University of Portsmouth for putting on so many stimulating events and for always inviting me along. Supportive colleagues make a huge difference and are something I have been particu-larly fortunate to find in all the places I have worked. My new home at the

University of Leeds appears to be no exception to this and I look forward to getting to know the History staff there better. The ideas in this book have benefited enormously from being presented and discussed in a variety of forums. These invaluable intellectual opportunities, particularly those afforded through conference attendance and research trips, were often only possible thanks to the generous financial support I have received over the years. I am therefore extremely grateful to the Arts and Humanities Research Council, the University of St Andrews, the Roddan Trust, the British Academy and the Leverhulme Trust, the University of Southampton and the Society for the Study of French History, all of whom have funded aspects of my work.

These opportunities also brought me into contact with a range of scholars in the fields of French and Algerian history resulting in many thought-provoking and enjoyable conversations. For their insightful comments and questions, and, in many cases, for their friendship, I would particularly like to thank Rabah Aissaoui, Sam Kalman, Fiona Barclay, Akhila Yechury, Martin Evans, Christoph Kalter, Jan Jansen, Manuel Borutta, Martin Thomas, Jim House, James McDougall, Todd Shepard, Andrea Smith, Jeannette Miller, Yann Scioldo-Zürcher, Sung Choi, Ethan Katz, Daniel Gordon, Cari Campbell, Alison Carrol and Louisa Zanoun. I also want to express my appreciation to Emma Brennan and the MUP team who have been very patient with me, as well as highly efficient.

Of the many things to come out of my time at the BnF, friendship with Sara Barker and Katie Edwards is something I am particularly grateful for. I could not have asked for better company as this project began to take shape and in the years since. Sarah Howell exemplifies the fact that true friendship always survives, irrespective of distance and other distractions, but it is even better when you find yourselves together again in the same city. Emile Chabal has been unstintingly generous to me, both intellectually and on a personal level. For this and for organising many French history-related adventures, including a memorable trip to Carnoux-en-Provence, I thank him. Jackie Clarke, Joan Tumblety, Jennifer Sessions and Rebecca Scales have all been invaluable to the completion of this book. Not only have they read and commented on various chapters, but with kindness, good humour and a good quantity of wine have helped me to emerge relatively sane from this whole process.

Spending so long thinking and writing about memory, identity and belonging has inevitably prompted me to reflect on the roles these things have played in my own life. Whether looking back on happy moments shared with people who are, sadly, no longer here or having the chance to create new memories with my niece and nephew, I am constantly reminded of how important family is to me. I owe an enormous amount to my parents: my father's creativity has inspired me to always look for new perspectives on the past, while my mother through her constant love and support ensured that I grew up to have both roots and wings. Their influence on me and therefore on this work is indelible.

And then there is Owen, who has brought me endless cups of tea and so much more besides. He has been my bookmark for this chapter of my life and, I hope, for many more chapters to come.

Abbreviations

AAE	Amicale des Algériens en Europe
ACHAC	Association pour la connaissance de l'histoire de l'Afrique contemporaine
ADIMAD	Association amicale pour la défense des intérêts moraux et matériels des anciens détenues politiques et exiles de l'Algérie française
AGEA	Amicale gardoise des enfants algérois
AJIR	Association justice, information et réparation pour les harkis
ANPNPA	Association nationale des pieds-noirs progressistes et leurs amis
ANFANOMA	Association nationale des Français d'Afrique du Nord, d'outre-mer et de leurs amis
AOCAZ	Amicale des oraniennes du Côte d'Azur
BIAC	Bureaux d'information, d'aide administrative et de conseils
CDDFA	Centre de documentation des Français d'Algérie
CDHA	Centre de documentation historique sur l'Algérie
CEPN	Centre d'études pied-noir
CFMRAA	Confédération des Français musulmans rapatriés d'Algérie
CLAN-R	Comité de liaison des associations nationales de rapatriés
CNFA	Coordination nationale des Français d'Algérie
CNFM	Conseil national des Français musulmans
CNLH	Comité national de liaison des harkis
ENA	Étoile nord-africaine
FLN	Front de libération nationale

FN	Front national
FNACA	Fédération nationale des anciens combattants en Algérie
FNFANOM	Fédération nationale des Français d'Afrique du Nord et d'outre-mer
FNR	Front national des rapatriés
FNRFCI	Front national des Français rapatriés de confession islamique
FPA	Force de police auxiliaire
FSNA	Français de souche nord africaine
FURR	Fédération pour l'unité des rapatriés, réfugiés et de leurs amis
GAD	Groupes d'auto défense
GNPI	Groupement national pour l'indemnisation des biens spoliés ou perdus outre-mer
HCR	Haut conseil des rapatriés
HLM	Habitations à loyer modéré
JPN	Jeune pied-noir
LDH	Ligue des droits de l'Homme
MADRAN	Mouvement d'assistance et de défense des rapatriés d'Afrique du Nord
MNA	Mouvement national algérien
OAS	Organisation de l'armée secrète
ONASEC	Office national à l'action sociale educative et culturelle
PCF	Parti communiste français
PPN	Parti pied-noir
PS	Parti socialiste
RANFRAN	Rassemblement des Français d'Afrique du Nord
RECOURS	Rassemblement et coordination unitaires des rapatriés et spoliés
RNFAA	Rassemblement national des Français d'Algérie et leurs amis
RPR	Rassemblement pour la République
SAS	Sections administrative spécialisées
SFIM	Service d'accueil et de reclassement des Français d'Indochine et musulmans
UMP	Union pour un mouvement populaire
UNACFCI	Union nationale des anciens combattants français de confession islamique
UNC-AFN	Union nationale des combattants en Afrique du Nord
USDIFRA	Union syndicale de défense des intérêts des Français repliés d'Algérie

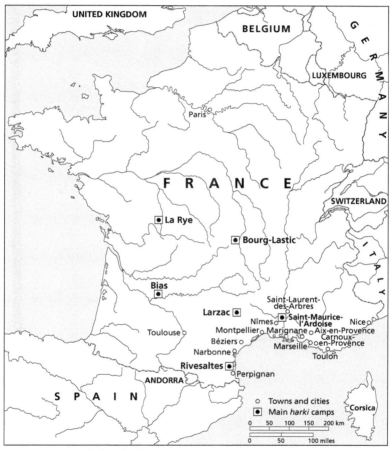

Map 1 France including *harki* camps

Map 2 Colonial Algeria

Introduction

On 23 February 2005, following an ordinary session of parliament, the French state passed an extraordinary law. Sponsored by a group of right-wing politicians from the ruling Union pour un mouvement populaire (UMP) party and framed by France's history as a colonial power, the law combined national recognition of those who had participated in the imperial endeavour with a series of financial measures in favour of those displaced as a result of decolonisation, the *rapatriés* (repatriates). Reflecting the centrality of Algeria in France's colonial past, the law's provisions were aimed primarily at *pieds-noirs*, the former settlers of that territory, who had been instrumental in lobbying for the measures, and *harkis*, Algerians who had served as native auxiliaries with the French army during the War of Independence (1954–62). Of the thirteen articles that comprised the law, Article 4 stood out through its stipulation that French school curricula should 'recognise in particular the positive role of the French presence overseas, notably in North Africa.'[1]

Reactions to the law were swift and vehement, as various groups mobilised to decry what they viewed as an attempt to impose a partisan, official reading of history upon the educational establishment. Historian and long-standing anti-colonial activist Claude Liauzu led the charge, denouncing Article 4 as an attack on the principles of freedom of thought and educational neutrality, and thus on *laïcité* (secularism) itself. '[A]n official lie' that denied the reality of crimes committed under empire, including slavery and 'genocide', and their contemporary legacies, such as racism, Liauzu argued that the law would worsen the already considerable divisions within postcolonial French society.[2]

Liauzu's concerns were partly or wholly shared by a range of other groups and individuals, including the Ligue des droits de l'Homme (LDH), trade unionists, schoolteachers, academics and the Parti socialiste (PS), whose leader, Jean-Pierre Ayrault, described the party's initial lack of opposition, which had allowed the law to pass, as an 'oversight'.[3] Even key *harki* organisations, like Harkis et droits de l'homme, voiced their opposition to specific clauses, including Article 4, within a law that had been devised partly for their benefit, stressing their refusal to allow themselves to be manipulated in accordance with the ideological agendas of others.[4] Further afield, the Algerian president Abdelaziz Bouteflika took time out of his re-election campaign to condemn Article 4 in the strongest terms as 'mental blindness bordering on Holocaust denial and revisionism'.[5]

Calls for the abrogation of Article 4 provoked bitter exchanges with those who had lobbied hard to get the measure onto the statute books in the first place and who were now determined to keep it there. Campaigning for the retention of Article 4 was conducted primarily by the political right and far right, with strong support from the *pied-noir* community. Wheeling out lists of France's contributions to the colonies – railways, sanitation, health care, education – defenders of Article 4 denounced the contemporary climate of 'political correctness' that would have the French deny these accomplishments out of a misguided sense of guilt and repentance.[6] Although opponents of Article 4 sought to dismiss such opinions as belonging to an anachronistic and irrelevant minority of colonial 'nostalgics', a survey conducted in December 2005 revealed that 64 per cent of French people approved of Article 4, suggesting that the narrative of benevolent colonialism continued to exert a certain appeal.[7] Sustained by a series of public petitions and Web-based polemics, the effects of this furore rumbled on throughout 2005, even prompting the cancellation of Interior Minister Nicholas Sarkozy's planned visit to France's overseas departments of Guadeloupe and Martinique.[8] Having privately admitted the law to have been 'a big screw up' [*une grosse connerie*], on 9 December President Jacques Chirac publicly announced the creation of a commission to evaluate the action of parliament in the domains of history and memory.[9] Less than a month later, Chirac made the following declaration: 'The current text divides the French. It must be rewritten.' By 25 January 2006, he had gone against his own party and abrogated Article 4, using his presidential veto powers to avoid a new parliamentary debate on the matter.[10]

'Memory wars'

Ostensibly centred on the right, or otherwise, of the state to impose an official and legally binding interpretation of the past upon the education system, the issues at stake in these debates were, in fact, much broader. More
than just a difference of opinion over how the past should be represented
in the present, this was a controversy about national identity. It exposed
the ongoing struggles of the Republic in trying to formulate a consensual
narrative about one of the most divisive periods in its history that would
be capable of satisfying the competing claims of the myriad postcolonial
peoples and perspectives now contained within its metropolitan borders.
The debates surrounding Article 4 furthermore constituted a particularly
high-profile manifestation of the 'memory wars' deemed to be sweeping
France. This problematic but increasingly commonplace phrase refers to
the fierce competition between different groups for control over the representation of the past in the public sphere as it pertains, in this instance,
to both the Algerian War and French colonialism more generally. The
French have a long history of formulating strikingly different interpretations of foundational historical events premised on what Jim House and
Neil MacMaster call 'competing myths of national identity'.[11] The French
Revolution, the Dreyfus Affair, the Vichy years, May 1968 – to name but
a few – have all been the subject of passionate and polarising debates
that revolve less around what did or did not happen, and more around
who possesses the right to speak about and thus define the contemporary
meaning and significance of these events.

   In recent years, these conflicts seem to have accelerated, an impression owing in no small part to the heightened visibility accorded to
them by a technologically sophisticated, globalised and instant media
culture.[12] In addition to the methods of debate and dissemination, what
has also changed is the composition of and cleavages between the people
fighting these 'wars'. The presence of a wealth of postcolonial minorities within France has placed the republican model of integration under
severe strain, as evidenced by the controversial comments of the Front
national (FN) regarding the racial composition of the 1998 World Cup
team, the debates surrounding the wearing of Islamic dress in public,
and the violence that periodically wracks the deprived *banlieue* sub-
urbs where France's ethnic minorities are heavily concentrated. Coming
hard on the heels of the 23 February law, the spate of urban unrest in
November 2005 was so severe that a state of emergency was declared in
metropolitan France for the first time since the Algerian War. France's

colonial past looms large in all of this, and it frames current social and political debates in ways that raise uncomfortable questions for a nation which has always promoted itself as a harbinger of progress and a bastion of equality.

Yet, in spite of its historical precedents and contemporary salience, the 'memory wars' phenomenon remains understudied from an academic perspective, particularly its present postcolonial incarnation. Beyond media commentaries, of which there are many, the little scholarly work that has been done has tended to focus on enumerating manifestations and the vectors of transmission that facilitate the appearance of commemorative conflicts.[13] In examining the symptoms, the underlying causes have been neglected, creating the impression that the current 'memory wars' over colonialism appeared suddenly towards the end of the 1990s with their battle lines already drawn, rather than evolving over time as a result of a series of changing contexts and interactions. The label 'memory wars' also risks creating a self-fulfilling prophecy, encouraging the various groups involved to see themselves as engaging in a 'battle' whose outcome is framed in terms of 'winners' and losers'. Rather than accepting them as simply 'a reality of our time', we instead need to critically probe the forms, functions and content of the current debates concerning colonialism, particularly the ways in which these have been packaged for public consumption by the media and the groups involved.[14]

In contrast to existing studies, this book argues that the current situation is the culmination of protracted processes of negotiation and contestation conducted, for a long time, beneath the radar of public attention by those with a personal investment in the empire and its legacies. Historicising the present situation by exposing its full gestation process allows for a better understanding of the nature of the conflicts themselves and of the agents involved, including their complex motivations and expectations, and their entangled relationships with each other. In using the Algerian War of Independence as its case study, this book seeks to reconceptualise the ways in which this conflict has been debated, evaluated and remembered in the five decades since it ended. The intention is to demonstrate that the current competition for control over the past, epitomised by the Article 4 controversy, is not a recent development, but merely the public culmination of long-running processes. To ignore this backstory is to ignore the diverse and dynamic historical contexts in which these debates are embedded and thus to potentially diminish our understanding of the present situation and its implications.

The 'war without a name'

At first glance, the vociferousness of contemporary debates over France's colonial past is a far cry from the obscurity in which this subject languished for many decades. Key to understanding the silence in which French society, but also French scholars, shrouded the colonial era is the Algerian War of Independence that sounded the death knell of the empire. Lasting from 1954 until 1962, the conflict pitted the independence-seeking forces of Front de libération nationale (FLN) against a French government and army determined, in the wake of the Second World War and Dien Bien Phu, to avoid another humiliating military defeat and under pressure from a settler population of just over one million to maintain the French flag in Algeria. Crucially, Algeria was not merely a piece of the empire; since 1848 the colony had been legally incorporated into the nation, making Algiers, Oran and Constantine France's southern-most *départements* (administrative regions). Consequently, while the neighbouring protectorates of Tunisia and Morocco gained independence relatively peacefully in 1956, Algeria was a different matter.

Noted for the brutality of tactics used by both sides, including the systematic use of torture by the French army, the conflict is estimated to have cost the lives of 250,000 to 300,000 Algerians, almost 25,000 French soldiers, and approximately 60,000 native auxiliaries.[15] Violence was, furthermore, not confined to the colonial periphery. The bitter struggle between the FLN and Messali Hadj's rival Mouvement national algérien (MNA) for the loyalty of the Algerian diaspora in France,[16] the terror tactics of dissident soldiers and settlers within the Organisation armée secrète (OAS),[17] and the ferocity of police repression of Algerian demonstrators on 17 October 1961 all brought bloodshed across the Mediterranean to the shores of metropolitan France.[18] The war fatally weakened the Fourth Republic, facilitating the controversial return to power of Charles de Gaulle and the creation of the Fifth Republic in 1958. Although ostensibly ending hostilities, the signature of ceasefire accords at Evian in March 1962 actually led to an escalation of certain forms of violence, while the declaration of Algerian independence on 5 July 1962 came amidst the exodus of almost the entire settler population. Widely deemed to have been a conflict won militarily but lost politically, the end of French Algeria was a major blow to national prestige that de Gaulle sought to assuage through recourse to the idea of an inevitable tide of history and by turning the nation's attention to modernisation, consumerism and Europe.[19]

The decision by de Gaulle to turn the page on this ingloriously conducted and concluded conflict manifested itself in a potent state silence. This was compounded by a series of amnesties granted to participants on both sides, combined with a lack of official commemoration either of the war or those who fought in it. Even the term 'war' was to be avoided in favour of euphemisms such as 'the events', while historians wishing to investigate these years were hampered by restricted access to state archives.[20] Consequently, the events of 1954–62 were not inserted into the nation's official memory. Instead, they were effectively forgotten in what appeared to be a troubling case of national amnesia. Historiographically, this situation was reflected in the dominance of the theme of absence in works concerning the memory of the war, epitomised by the evocatively titled *La Gangrène et l'oubli* [gangrene and forgetting] written by the Algeria-born historian Benjamin Stora and published in 1991. John Talbott's pithy phrase 'the war without a name' came to serve as an equally useful shorthand for the perception of a conflict that had been buried under a mound of shame and silence 'like a dark treasure of guilty family secrets'.[21] State-sponsored occultation furthermore meant that there were few popular cultural representations of the war in stark contrast, as is often noted, to treatments of the Vietnam War in America, particularly cinematically. Yet, this image of absence needs to be reconciled with the reality of multiple texts, almost 3000 by the end of 1997, dealing with the war across a range of genres, but especially personal testimony and historical fiction as the lack of public discourse left those involved in the conflict no alternative but to look to writing as a 'private substitute'.[22]

The juxtaposition of absence from above with proliferation on an individual level from below persisted until the 1990s, when a combination of social, political and cultural changes led the war to 'return' to public consciousness in a range of guises. Following Robert Frank's observation that 'in matters of memory as in strategy, the French are often a war behind', this development was prompted in large part by the renewed attention being devoted to another 'dark' historical episode, the Vichy years, which sensitised the general population to issues of memory and silence with respect to traumatic pasts.[23] Between the broadcasting of the widely viewed and hotly debated documentary series' *La Guerre d'Algérie* (Peter Batty) and *Les Années algériennes* (Stora) at the beginning of the decade,[24] and parliament's acknowledgement in 1999 that 'the events' in Algeria had in fact been 'a war', the conflict was rarely out of the public spotlight. These developments were framed internationally by a series of conflicts involving Arab nations, including the first Palestinian Intifada (1987–91), the first Gulf War (August 1990 to February 1991) and Algeria's decade-long civil war, all of which were closely followed in France, not least by the country's growing Muslim population.[25] Domestically, the continued prominence of immigration and integration on the social and political agenda led to wide-ranging debates concerning the ability of the republican model to adapt to the challenges posed by the changing composition of the French nation.[26] From an academic point of view, the 1990s witnessed a renewed interest in colonialism and postcolonialism, particularly with reference to Algeria. Initially, much of this scholarship appeared in large edited collections whose short but wide-ranging chapters were designed to enhance knowledge at a time when the war was still a relatively unstudied area.[27] By the early 2000s, improved archival access and a new generation of scholars unconnected to the conflict led to a series of landmark monographs that defined or redefined the ways in which events, institutions and communities during the War of Independence were understood. Both Francophone and Anglophone academics, such as Raphaëlle Branche, Sylvie Thénault, Jim House, Neil MacMaster and Todd Shepard, have been at the forefront of what is today a dynamic and rapidly expanding field of research.[28]

'A kaleidoscope of splintered memories'

By 2004, these developments meant that Stora and the FLN militant turned historian Mohammed Harbi felt confident enough to proclaim 'the end of amnesia' with respect to the Algerian War.[29] Going further, Henry Rousso argued that the 'end of amnesia' had, over the course of the 1990s, evolved into a state of hyper-memory characterised by 'a continual and almost obsessive presence in contemporary public space'.[30] This broadly parallels the evolution of Rousso's 'Vichy syndrome', whereby the 'duty to remember' came to undermine the legitimacy of the 'right to forget', leading to a state of 'obsession'.[31] But while the 'dark years' of the Second World War were a broadly national experience, the Algerian War replaced universality with 'a multitude of solitudes'.[32] More than simply dividing France into those who supported the continuation of colonial rule and those who advocated Algerian independence, the conflict produced fractures that messily criss-crossed the boundaries of race, class, gender and politics.

At the extreme ends of the spectrum were those whose convictions had led them to break the law. *Porteurs de valises* (suitcase carriers), such as the Jeanson Network, actively aided the independence struggle by smuggling documents, money and, sometimes, arms across borders, while the terroristic apogee of the OAS saw them resort to the indiscriminate targeting of civilians in their desperate attempts to keep Algeria French. Ranged between these poles were outspoken anti-colonial intellectuals such as Jean-Paul Sartre and Pierre Vidal-Naquet, whose views differed radically from those of the pro-*Algérie française* lobby. Even within supposedly cohesive bodies, divisions were to be found. In the army, for example, seasoned career soldiers determined to hold Algeria at all costs in order to prevent the fall of what they saw as another communist domino fought a very different war to the thousands of *appelés* (conscripts), most of whom were simply focused on reaching the end of their tour.[33] Equally, the approximately 350,000 Algerians who found themselves in France at the end of the war included those who had supported the FLN, those who had rallied to the MNA, and the *harkis* who had fought for the French against their compatriots.[34]

The result was a 'kaleidoscope of splintered memories', whose edges were sharpened by the fact that they stemmed from passionately held convictions and choices, which, in many cases, had had far-reaching impacts on the lives of these 'committed minorities'.[35] In examining these divisions, Stora coined the phrase 'cloistered remembering' to denote the phenomenon of partial memories carried by specific groups connected to the war, who, he argued, tended to seek out cultural representations and social interactions that affirmed their own experiences and perspectives.[36] While cloistered memories are a potential problem for all societies, they pose particular issues for the French whose assimilationist model of citizenship views group identities, especially those predicated on race, religion or ethnicity, as a threat to the integrity of the Republic. *Communautarisme* is the term most frequently used to describe the detrimental fracturing of the nation-state into competing factions, often cited as the destructive end point of Anglo-Saxon multiculturalism. Pierre Nora is only one of many to warn of the dangers of *communautarisme*, stating: 'Things begin to go awry when history, which belongs to no one and whose purpose is to make the past available to everyone, starts to be written under the pressure of groups with a shared past who want their particular reading of it to dominate.'[37] Within the heightened commemorative climate following the 'return' of the war to public attention, the French state, so its critics say, has been unable to create unifying official discourses and consensual commemorative gestures capable of transcending these entrenched divisions to the detriment of the national historical narrative and to the unity of the nation.[38]

This is the standard framework through which the history of the memory of the Algerian War of Independence is discussed and understood. There have been some attempts to nuance the absence/presence dichotomy, with Rousso arguing for a four-stage evolution from amnesty to amnesia to anamnesis and finally hyper-memory.[39] Yet, even this periodisation is predicated on a pivotal shift, whereby a lengthy period of forgetting gave way to an era of recollection. Such conceptualisations are problematic in several respects. First, they assume that the silence imposed by the state was all encompassing. Yet, as Luisa Passerini argues, the key point about silence is not simply to note that it exists, but rather to explore 'its limits, its context and its references'.[40] In other words, just because the state was not talking about the Algerian War, we cannot assume that no one else was talking about it. This presumption nonetheless took root within the academic literature because of an equally problematic equation between silence and forgetting, whereby the 'amnesia' attributed to the state was deemed to have affected all constituent parts of the nation. A situation owing, in large part, to the focus on memory within the public domain. Looking only in one place, previous studies reached only one conclusion: that the Algerian War was effectively forgotten until the state came to remember it during the 1990s.

But if we shift the focus away from the public realm and the state as the principal actor, a different picture emerges. If, instead of concentrating on official memories, we investigate the group memories that Nora and others are so critical of, a much richer history emerges; one that challenges not only the absence/presence paradigm, but many of the other assumptions upon which histories of the commemorative aftermath of the Algerian War have previously rested. Two memories that illuminate the shortcomings of current interpretations are those carried by the *pied-noir* and *harki* communities whose postwar experiences and activities do not fit the established chronology. *Pieds-noirs* and *harkis* were connected by the fact that they heralded from the same place, in spite of having lived very different lives there, and by the fact that they felt compelled to leave this land to migrate to France at the conclusion of a war in which they had both been on the losing side. These connections strengthened but also evolved after 1962 as activists within both communities organised in order to compose, codify and articulate memories of the recent past. Examining the fruits of this labour, this book rewrites the conventional periodisation of a 'forgotten' war that made a dramatic return to public attention during the 1990s by revealing a continual presence of memory and commemorative activity within these communities. This in turn attests to the establishment of a particular kind of postcolonial civil society and to the development of new forms of participation.

Adopting a comparative focus makes it possible to trace how the mobilisation and transmission of memories by *pieds-noirs* and *harkis* reflect and have been informed by the actions and discourses of each other, as well as by the behaviour of a range of additional actors connected to the War of Independence including veterans, Algerian migrants, academics and the media. Inevitably, the French state plays a crucial role and it is not the intention of this study to deny this, but, rather, to question the idea of the state as the sole agent and point of reference. Instead, identity politics are understood here as a creative dialogue between claims coming from below and a particular kind of republican culture that frames these from above. As Alon Confino reminds us, 'The history of memory should place the articulation of a particular perception of the past within the context of society as a shared symbolic universe.'[41] In foregrounding the interactive nature of these communal memories, this approach challenges the notion that cloistered memories are isolated memories, demonstrating that, although they may generally be created for and speak to particular constituencies, such representations are strongly influenced by external discourses and events.

Bringing to light the continuous activism within the *pied-noir* and *harki* communities enables the standard dichotomous absence/return timeline of the war to be replaced by a more nuanced chronological framework, which, in particular, fills the supposedly silent space of the pre-1990 era with a multiplicity of voices. The failure of these voices to reach the public ear does not invalidate them, but rather draws our attention to the power dynamics that determine which voices are heard, which are not, and what causes these categories to change over time. It is important because 'Silence, like memory and forgetting, has a life history, and – when new pressures or circumstances emerge – can be transformed into its opposite very rapidly.'[42] More than simply the fundamental changes brought about during the 1990s, the importance of which this study does not underestimate, silence, memory and forgetting have been subjected to constant processes of reframing as the many contexts which informed and shaped them have developed since 1962.

Framing memory

The concern of this book is therefore to understand the processes, contexts and agents that produce social and collective memories within particular communities connected to the War of Independence, and to trace how these have evolved over time. Focusing on acts of commemoration and their associated discourses, it explores the multiple ways in which narratives about the past are used to construct communal identities and what these reveal about how groups and their members have negotiated their

place within French society.[43] In line with the majority of theoretical scholarship, the memories traced and analysed here are understood as socially
framed, present-orientated, relational and driven by specific agents.[44]
Rather than an abstract entity floating somewhere in the cultural atmosphere, memory takes shape within the societies it concerns. As such, it has
'no existence beyond our politics, our social relationship and our histories'.[45] Memory is also considered to be social, representing the 'process(es)
through which a knowledge or awareness of past events … is developed
and sustained within human societies' and through which people 'are
given a sense of a past that extends beyond what they themselves personally remember'.[46] Although a composite phenomenon, social memory is
still only articulated through the actions of individuals. Just as there can
be no individual memory without social experience, so there can be no
social memory without individuals participating in forms of communal
life; the two are, as Geoffrey Cubitt puts it, 'always crossweaving'.[47] Today,
the term, 'social memory' is increasingly favoured over 'collective memory'
because of the latter's essentialising and reifying implications.[48] Cubitt is
right to point out that collective memory is an 'ideological fiction' when
used to imply that certain entities possess 'a stable mnemonic capacity
that is collectively exercised' and which casts representations of the past as
the 'natural expressions' of that capacity. Nonetheless, given that many of
the organisations and individuals featured in this study claim to speak in
the name of the collective memory of particular groups, it is necessary to
employ the term, especially in probing the extent to which there is an identifiable correspondence between the codified version of the past articulated
by representatives of the group and the lived experience of its members.

In addressing the link between memory and identity, Paul Ricoeur
noted 'we are what we tell ourselves'.[49] Recounting experiences gives
them coherence and comprehensibility, both to us and to outsiders.
This echoes Alistair Thomson's argument that 'Memories are "significant
pasts" that we compose to make a more comfortable sense of our life
over time and in which past and current identities are brought more into
line.' Such processes are particularly important when the lives in question
have undergone dramatic and often traumatic changes, as happened with
the *pieds-noirs* and *harkis*. In such cases, the affirmation of memories
by a particular public assumes a heightened significance as communal
remembering serves to 'compose a safe and necessary personal coherence'
out of the unresolved and painful fragments of the past.[50] By supporting
the restoration of identity continuity in this way, memory cultures create
unity and a sense of community with shared cultural scripts helping to
establish the nature and boundaries of belonging to a group. People are

then tied into the collective by their endorsement of the representations offered, even if these are not based on directly shared experiences.[51]

A concept rather than an object, memory has no agency in its own right. It requires individuals to select, organise and articulate narratives; memory is therefore always mediated. Memory is also performative, brought into existence at particular moments in time by specific actors.[52] Borrowing from anthropology, Jay Winter labels these agents of remembrance 'fictive kin'.[53] Operating as part of civil society in the liminal space between the individual and the national, the tasks of collation and enunciation undertaken by these 'fictive kin' are vital, since it is they who pick from the range of available individual memories those that are best suited to the creation and codification of a cohesive collective memory for the group.[54] Such memories, which are strategically chosen, reflect an awareness of the need to organise the past in order to achieve certain objectives. The way in which individual recollections are connected in order to create a 'collective consciousness' via an ongoing process, involving 'inscription and re-inscription, coding and recoding', is thus as important as the content of the memories themselves.[55] Memory should therefore be conceptualised as a relational nexus of competing, even conflicting, representations, in which hegemonic interpretations are the temporarily prevailing results of constant contestation and negotiation.[56] It is this process of agency-driven, interactive creation that this book seeks to capture, and which concurs with Winter's pronouncement that 'multi-vocality' is the order of the day when attempting to convey the richness and complexity of memorial practices and cultures.[57]

'French memory is full of Algeria'

Winter's concept of fictive kin is particularly interesting because of the way in which he applies it to the 'dense networks of filiations' that emerged following the First World War, often in the form of associations. Dedicated to providing assistance, support and forums through which to campaign for recognition, recompense and respect, Winter views these networks as the 'hidden prehistory of many, more visible, forms of collective remembrance'.[58] In the context of the War of Independence, it could equally be argued that the absence of public commemoration and the attention this attracted worked to conceal a rich 'undergrowth of non-official activity' that preceded the state-sponsored statues and plaques now being unveiled across France. As Stora argues, 'the real memory of this war ... has never ceased to function ... No people, no society, no individual can exist and define its identity in a state of amnesia; a parallel, individual memory always finds places of refuge when the powers want to render it captive or to forget it'.[59] Just as *War and Remembrance in the Twentieth Century* (Winter's collaborative project with Emmanuel Sivan) was partly inspired by a desire to correct Nora's 'premature and misleading obituary' of popular memory by providing evidence of its vibrancy and ongoing relevance, so a similar corrective seems necessary with respect to the War of Independence.[60] By bringing to light the neglected wealth of commemorative activity behind official occultation, it becomes possible to at least begin to respond to Confino's call for greater account to be taken of memories 'produced away from the corridors of political, cultural and entertainment power' and to consider instead 'the construction of popular memories ... and their links to the everyday level of experience'.[61] Moreover, it demonstrates, in the words of Robert Frank, that 'French memory is full of Algeria' and always has been.[62]

Such a project is particularly important given that many of the groups affected by the war – *pieds-noirs* and *harkis,* but also Algerian immigrants and veterans – have experienced extreme dislocation, have been denied social legitimacy and, consequently, do not feel part of the national symbolic heritage catalogued by Nora in his seminal multi-volume meditation *Les Lieux de mémoire* (published in English as *Realms of Memory*).[63] Indeed, while recognising the great potential in Nora's concept of a history of the 'second degree' and the attention it draws to the diverse and fluctuating processes through which representations of the past are created, disseminated and digested, this book echoes the concerns of other scholars about the limits of Nora's paradigm.[64] Instead, this study, through its engagement with empire as a central part of national history, its emphasis on private groups and their memories as contributors to a form of active civil society, through its acknowledgement that history and memory are distinct but closely interrelated, and through its grassroots focus offers a different perspective. Rather than *lieux de mémoire,* it situates itself closer to the idea of *nœuds* or 'knots' of memory. Formulated by Michael Rothberg as a conceptual antidote to Nora, this approach focuses on the 'knotted intersections' that Rothberg feels more accurately characterise the multi-directional nature of memory by deliberately cutting across national, ethnic and temporal boundaries to reveal a complex intersection of continually shifting elements and agents.[65]

Sources, conduits and reception

In addition to agents of remembrance, memories need conduits to ensure their dissemination.[66] In tracing these conduits, this study adopts Wulf

Kansteiner's belief that memories employed in the public realm are 'multimedia collages' and has therefore explored multiple source bases. Throughout, the intention has been to foreground outputs created by *pied-noir* and *harki* memory activists. The *pied-noir* community in particular has produced a vast amount of material pertaining to the history of French Algeria and to the war. Their activities include publishing testimonies, organising reunions and exhibitions, erecting monuments, launching law suits, diffusing their own press and propaganda, producing their own television documentaries and even building their own town; all of which testifies to 'a memorial dynamism independent of the state'.[67] However, with the exception of *pied-noir* literature and some limited work on film, very little has been done with this embarrassment of riches, particularly compared to works dealing more generally with cultural representations of the War of Independence.[68] In the same way as academics for many years have tended to regard the *pieds-noirs* as relics of a bygone era, so they have often dismissed their cultural production as nothing more than expressions of unassuaged colonial nostalgia. Yet, this material provides invaluable insights into how memory activists conceived of themselves, how they sought to construct and sustain a collective identity, what they were hoping to achieve, and how this has altered over time; painting a picture that, while heavily imbued with nostalgic hues, is more interesting than has previously been acknowledged. Similarly, with regard to the *harki* community, while there is a growing body of collected testimony and autobiographically informed fiction in the public domain, analysis of this corpus from a historical perspective remains limited.[69] Devoting more attention to these bodies of cultural work can, furthermore, act as a corrective to trends within social movement theory that privilege abstract conceptualisations over empirical studies of what those involved in these movements actually do and say, and why.[70]

Associations have been among the most visible vehicles for *pied-noir* and *harki* memories. This is in keeping with traditions of popular organisation and expression in a nation whose revolutionary lineage helped establish dissent as 'a national way of life', signalling not a breakdown of the system, but, in fact, healthy social and political participation. According to social movement theorists, the collective actions undertaken by associations enable 'ordinary people' to speak for themselves and to dictate the terms of their participation, rather than allowing others to speak for them. The importance of these bodies therefore lies in their ability to 'tell us a different story' to that of establishment institutions and actors;[71] therefore they can be especially useful for minority groups who are seeking to establish legitimacy with respect to public powers and society.[72]

Associations have been particularly important to the *pied-noir* community. As with all clichés, there is some truth in the saying 'when two *pieds-noirs* meet and start reminiscing, they create three associations'.[73] In the absence of commemorative discourses generated from above, these bodies, some of which have been continuously active since the latter stages of the War of Independence, have played a key role in the creation, codification and transmission of grassroots collective and social memories. It is, however, notoriously difficult to calculate the precise number of *pied-noir* associations in existence at any one time and few have attempted it. Dating from the 1990s, the most widely cited statistics put the number of associations at between 400 and 800, with 15 per cent of the total *pied-noir* population deemed to belong to one or more organisation.[74] Unfortunately, the source of the data on which these estimates rest is not clear; nor is any sense given of how these figures compared to previous years. More recently, Jean-Jacques Jordi has stated that approximately 5 per cent of *pieds-noirs* belong to an association, although, again, no indication is given of the origin of this figure.[75] Aside from such holistic assessments, all that exists are discrete and isolated snapshots of the size and strength of individual associations in particular regions at certain moments. In 1992, for example, Jordi claimed that the Cercle algérianiste had thirty-three local branches and 5000 members overall. Two years previously, Joëlle Hureau reported that the same association possessed 3500 adherents, in comparison to membership figures of 200,000 and 50,000 for the Association nationale des Français d'Afrique du Nord, d'outre-mer et de leurs amis (ANFANOMA) and the Rassemblement et coordination des rapatriés et spoliés d'outre-mer (RECOURS) respectively.[76] Such assessments sit alongside a limited number of small-scale case studies, usually based on a single association, such as Andrea Smith's excellent anthropological investigation of the Amicale France-Malte in the Bouches-du-Rhône.[77] Empirical data is even scarcer when it comes to *harki* associations. Although generally less established than the *pied-noir* lobby, such bodies, particularly those with a national reach such as the Association justice, information et réparation pour les harkis and Harkis et droits de l'Homme, have played a significant, though not unproblematic, role in shaping the public image and commemorative agenda of the wider *harki* community, particularly in recent years.[78]

As legal entities, associations possess an official status and visibility which makes them easy to find by the likes of journalists, filmmakers, government officials and academics.[79] This can lead to associations being accepted as representative even when such assessments are not supported by their membership statistics.[80] According undue weight to the pronouncements of such bodies is therefore something to guard against. There clearly has to be some degree of common ground and sense of connection among members for an association to form and remain active, sometimes over decades as in the case of numerous *pied-noir* groups. Nonetheless, it is equally clear that neither all *pieds-noirs* nor all *harkis* subscribe to the positions of the associations that claim to speak in their name, not least because these entities have different agendas, memberships and target audiences. A further distinction must be made between the activists who create and direct associations and the members who belong to and participate in the activities of these bodies with fluctuating degrees of commitment, consistency and motivation. Yet, irrespective of these caveats, it cannot be denied that *pied-noir* associations have been one of the primary vehicles through which a public collective identity has been constructed and disseminated over the past fifty years, and this identity, rightly or wrongly, has been taken as representative by the general public and government officials. It has furthermore been the success of lobbying by *pied-noir* associations in obtaining recognition and concessions – initially financial but more recently commemorative – from the state that has prompted other communities connected to the Algerian War, including the *harkis,* to adopt similar forms of mobilisation. In terms of their impact upon the commemorative landscape with respect to the war, associations, as conduits of memory, therefore merit a prominent place in this study.

Also distinctive in this study is the extensive use made of television programmes featuring, and sometimes produced by, *pieds-noirs* and *harkis.* As an important vector of memory, particularly following the end of the state monopoly in 1982, television offers a different medium through which to trace the construction and diffusion of representations of the past. While conceding that the correspondence can be uncertain, Isabelle Veyrat-Masson argues nonetheless that the small screen provides a way of 'envisaging the nation, the past, identity and history'.[81] This point is echoed by Tamara Chaplin, who states that in seeking to understand fully how ideas and images become 'invested' in national histories, 'we ignore the medium of television at our peril'.[82]

Since the 1960s, the number of programmes dedicated to the Algerian War has risen steadily.[83] Whereas only fifty-two programmes relating to the conflict were broadcast between 1962 and 1974, the following decade saw this number rise to ninety-seven, while in the five years from 1987 to 1992 a further ninety-seven programmes aired. During this time, there was a shift from a unifying discourse strongly influenced by the state's control over the media, to more independent programmes determined to investigate the war in all its complexity following the break-up of the Office de radiodiffusion télévision française in 1974. As well as diversity in terms of subjects approached, the 1980s and 1990s witnessed a growing plurality in terms of the voices and viewpoints represented. It was in this spirit that *Les Années algériennes,* Stora's 1991 documentary, brought together multiple, non-consensual perspectives to create a 'mosaic' of representations, rather than a single linear or authoritative narrative.[84] There was also a move away from 'official' spokespeople, such as former politicians and senior military figures, towards the inclusion of 'ordinary' French and Algerian people, who had lived through the years 1954 to 1962. Memory activists who were keen to engage with television as a powerful and wide-reaching medium welcomed such developments. In particular, panel discussions and live broadcasts allowed community representatives the opportunity to voice their own opinions and to actively contest what they regarded as inaccurate representations of themselves and their history. In this way, television provides a unique and under-explored lens through which to study interactions between different memory carriers over time.

Although a greater range of actors and voices was being given air time in the 1990s, there nonetheless remained a certain hierarchy. Association spokespeople or famous *pied-noirs,* such as the singer Enrico Macias or the actor Robert Castel were generally preferred over anonymous individuals. The same small cast, including well-connected spokespeople like Jacques Roseau of RECOURS, tended to appear again and again. Looking at who was able to gain access to studios and who featured in what capacity in various kinds of programmes represents one way to gauge shifting power dynamics within and between the different communities and associations over time. Thus, although *pieds-noirs* were regular contributing voices to television programmes up to the late 1990s, since that point their representation has declined. In contrast, the presence of *harki* spokespeople has risen in line with the public profile of the community.

Occupying an equally central place in this book is testimony. In keeping with other studies of memory, personal narratives and reflections have been used extensively as evidence of the experiences, thoughts and feelings of a range of different actors connected to the War of Independence or affected by its legacies. However, no oral history interviews were conducted for this project. This was partly a product of logistical factors and partly owing to issues of access, particularly with respect to the *harki* community, both of which posed considerable challenges in terms of generating sufficient data for a meaningful analysis. But the decision not to gather oral histories also stemmed from the core aim of the book, which is to explore changes in collective commemorative activities and discourses since 1962. This requires studying a broad array of narratives across a range of genres produced and transmitted by and on behalf of the *pied-noir* and *harki* communities at different moments over the last five decades and thinking about the impact of contemporaneous *cadres sociaux* [social frameworks] on these. Oral history interviews would have provided an insight into how certain *pieds-noirs* and *harkis* thought about themselves and their histories in the first decade of the twenty-first century. But they would not have offered the same potential to track evolutions in these narratives over time and to anchor particular representations in the historically specific contexts that produced them. Nor would they have provided the same scope for thinking about the ways in which different types of discourses have been packaged and disseminated by activists in the service of their respective political, cultural and commemorative agendas.

Taken together the nature of the sources used means that this is less a study of individual memories and more an exploration of the ways in which these, alongside other forms of evidence about the past, have been moulded by a series of memory activists and associations to create and legitimate public and collective discourses about the *pied-noir* and *harki* communities, and about the War of Independence more broadly. Consequently, although it does try to acknowledge the ways in which personal recollections may differ from the picture offered through associations and other collective conduits, this book cannot do justice to the range of different perspectives and experiences that exist within the diverse *pied-noir* and *harki* populations. Instead, it concentrates on those aspects of the past that have secured a place within the publicly proffered narratives about these two communities and on understanding why these particular elements were selected at specific moments over and above other available representations. It is therefore a study of memory in the public domain as opposed to private, familial memories, even as it recognises that these are by no means mutually exclusive arenas.

The *pied-noir* community

In order to contextualise the genealogies of memory and memory activism under discussion, it is necessary to establish the history of the communities within which these representations of the past have been created, circulated and consumed. *Pied-noir* has become the dominant term used to denote the settler community of French Algeria who made up approximately 10 per cent of the territory's population by 1954. Coming from a wide range of European countries and for an equally diverse array of reasons, these men and women arrived in Algeria from the 1830s onwards, as France's newest possession was 'pacified' and settled. In 1889 and 1893, naturalisation laws unilaterally conferred French citizenship upon the settlers, placing them firmly at the top of the colonial hierarchy. Although bestowed rather than requested, Frenchness quickly became a key part of the identity embraced by the settler community.[85] At the same time, the colonial context complicated the nature of the relationship between the settlers and their 'motherland', creating what Ali Yedes terms an 'inferiority complex' that manifested itself in a desire to be close to and yet simultaneously distinct from the metropolitan French.[86] Distinction was achieved through the creation of an *Algérianiste* identity in the early twentieth century, which was voiced through the works of men like Jean Pomier and Robert Randau.[87] In harking back to the Roman presence in North Africa and seeking to construe Algeria as a vibrant Mediterranean melting pot of cultures and peoples, their intention was to create a historical narrative that would root the settlers in Algerian soil and legitimate their presence at a time when indigenous nationalist currents were gaining strength.[88]

Intimately entwined with France's colonial project in Algeria, the settlers considered themselves and their land to be integral parts of the French nation. *Algérie française* was not simply a phrase to them, but an indisputable reality. It was also a reality they wished to see perpetuated; hence their opposition to the FLN. When, in July 1962, after almost eight years of bitter and bloody conflict, Algeria ceased to be part of France the settlers were faced with a dilemma: should they stay or go? Ultimately, the rapidly escalating violence that followed the signing of the Evian Accords, including the scorched earth policy of the OAS, led the settlers to conclude that their lives would be untenable in an independent Algeria. As a result, over 90 per cent chose to depart, with the vast majority heading for France. The bulk of this movement took place within a highly compressed time frame: 1,064,000 people arrived in France from Algeria in 1962, with the months of May through to August comprising the peak transit period. Of these, 421,000 returned to Algeria, at least temporarily, leaving more than 650,000 in France at the end of the year. This was in addition to over 100,000 who had departed prior to 1962 and the further 200,000 who would leave between 1963 and 1967.[89] This migratory wave also encompassed 120,000 Jews, who, having been naturalised via the 1870 Crémieux Decree, opted at the end of the war to place their French citizenship above their historical, cultural and emotional ties to Algeria. Distinct from both *pieds-noirs* and *harkis,* the experiences of the Algerian Jewish community

once in France and their resultant collective mobilisation are unfortunately beyond the scope of this study.[90]

The settlers believed that France had been victorious militarily and
therefore they regarded the Evian Accords as an act of incomprehensible
capitulation that unnecessarily sacrificed French Algeria; thus the pre-
dominant sentiments among them in 1962 were betrayal, abandonment
and anger. The hasty and improvised nature of departures, which took
place amidst ongoing FLN and OAS violence, as well as the sheer volume
of people leaving, rendered this a deeply traumatic experience, and one
that transformed 'exile' into the defining characteristic of the displaced
settlers. In this way, the death of French Algeria coincided with the birth
of the *pieds-noirs* as a population. The origins of the term *pied-noir* are
much debated. Evidence suggests that although the term existed prior to
the War of Independence, it only entered regular usage during the latter
stages of the conflict. Today *pied-noir* is primarily associated with the
postcolonial incarnation of the settler community. Although initially
perceived as pejorative, it has been progressively reclaimed by the settlers and used as a positive marker of their cultural and historical specificity, even if the phrase has never fully shed its negative connotations
among the wider French population. Officially, however, the *pieds-noirs*
were designated as 'returning citizens' or *rapatriés*. Given that most were
'returning' to a land they had never previously lived in and, often, to a
land from which their ancestors had not originated, this label was problematic. But it did at least capture the uncomfortable sense of being both
French and yet somehow different that was common to many *pieds-noirs*
at the time. Similarly dualistic monikers such as the 'French of Algeria'
and the 'overseas French' were also employed, albeit less frequently.
The most apt term for the settlers, according to Yann Scioldo-Zürcher,
is 'national migrants', since this recognises the violence of the rupture
from Algeria experienced in 1962, but equally the protection offered by
the state to its own citizens; a combination of circumstances that will be
explored further in the first chapter.[91]

The racially hierarchical nature of colonial society meant that, in comparison to Algerians, the settlers led highly privileged lives prior to 1954.
Yet, while there were certainly some fitting the stereotype of the rich and
exploitative *colon* (large-scale farmer/landowner) who 'made the natives
sweat', the European population as a whole was socio-economically
and culturally diverse, not least because of their transnational origins.
Overall, the standard of living in Algeria was lower than that in mainland France, while incomes varied between urban centres such as Algiers
and the countryside or *bled*. Location further affected the nature of

relationships between the settlers and the other inhabitants of Algeria, with interactions generally considered to be more frequent in rural areas, where proximity between the different ethno-religious communities was greater and the number of settlers much lower. In the postcolonial period, much of this diversity was bleached out by *pied-noir* spokespeople, who, for strategic reasons, emphasised the notion of a cohesive and homogenous *rapatrié* identity that revolved around the foundational moment of 'exodus' from Algeria. Finding unity in adversity, this shared experience bound the disparate settlers together, forging a new and distinct sense of community. By destroying the sense of security that had accompanied the dominant position of the settlers during the colonial era. Algerian independence jettisoned the *pieds-noirs* not only into an alien country, but also into an alien social and economic position. The trauma of this rupture produced a preoccupation with an idealised Algeria, the lineaments of which became more vivid and more perfect in direct proportion to the turmoil and distress of the present.[92]

The *pieds-noirs* therefore arrived in France in 1962 with few worldly possessions, but a long list of grievances. These were compounded by the lack of facilities initially available to assist with their installation, with the French having anticipated an exodus of 400,000 over four years, not one million in the space of a few of months. This difficult situation was further exacerbated by a lack of familial or kinship networks to help in easing their transition into their new world, and by the fact that the *pieds-noirs* felt themselves and their history to have been misunderstood by their metropolitan cousins. The settlers' imagined national community made it clear that they not only blamed them for the war and its associated violence, but also that they resented their presence with all the cost and disruption it entailed. Finding no wider community open to including them (indeed many considered the metropolitan French to be actively closing ranks against them), the *pieds-noirs* turned inwards. This propensity was further nurtured by their powerful sentiment of victimhood and by the range of perceived injustices they wished to see rectified. One of the principal ways in which *pieds-noirs* sought redress for their grievances was through associations which served as effective channels for a broader mobilisation rapidly instigated by a series of community leaders, As will be documented in the following chapters, this mobilisation focused initially on the material needs of the *rapatriés*, although by the mid-1970s efforts were being reorientated to the cultural realm, which remains the dominant sphere of activism today.

Pieds-noirs have always been prolific chroniclers of their own community. It took less than a year for memoirs of the war and its conclusion to appear in print, forming the first waves of what would become a veritable tide of personal accounts that are still appearing.[93] Those unable to secure publishing contracts have found platforms and audiences for their recollections within the pages of association newspapers, magazines and periodicals, alongside their photographs, poems, cartoons and recipes. There have also been regular attempts by leading activists, such as the Cercle algérianiste's Maurice Calmein, to produce broader histories and collections of testimony aimed specifically at transmitting knowledge to future generations.[94] Academic interest was, however, slower to materialise. The most noted *pied-noir* historian is Jean-Jacques Jordi, whose extensive knowledge of national and departmental archives has produced a body of work that offers a factually detailed and sympathetic portrait of the community, particularly with respect to their arrival and early years in France.[95]

Since 2000, Jordi's work has been supplemented by more critically engaged scholarship that has focused on the relationship between the state and the *pieds-noirs*. Offering a welcome empirical rebuttal to the stereotype that all *pieds-noirs* vote for the far right, Emmanuelle Comtat has revealed a more nuanced picture of electoral politics and how these have evolved since 1962.[96] Similarly grounded in concrete data is Yann Scioldo-Zürcher's magisterial study of the 'politics of integration' put in place by the state in the 1960s, which underscores the extensive and innovative nature of the support that was made available to 'returning' citizens from Algeria. Scioldo-Zürcher is at his strongest when chronicling the provision of material aid, including financial compensation, in the twenty-five years following 1962, with findings based on a deeply impressive breadth of research. However, the focus on archival documents limits the presence of perspectives from within the *pied-noir* community itself.[97] Valérie Esclangon-Morin pays greater attention to the role of *pied-noir* associations in *Les Rapatriés d'Afrique du Nord* which explores the extent to which activists were able to influence policy and how that policy was then received by the *rapatriés*. Although primarily focused on vertical interactions between the state and the *pieds-noirs*, the book nonetheless gives a welcome flavour of the horizontal relationships between various associations, which this study aims to expand upon.[98] Esclangon-Morin is not the only academic to have focused on associations, although much of this work, particularly that by Clarisse Buono, has revolved around establishing chronologies and typologies of different organisations.[99] In contrast, this study seeks to capture the fluidity that characterises associational allegiances. It is therefore less concerned with mapping structures than the relationships between associations and the influence of these upon the creation and circulation of particular narratives.

Analysis of memory within the *pied-noir* community has been led by the political scientist Eric Savarèse and by the anthropologists Michèle Baussant and Andrea Smith, all of whom have collected extensive and invaluable testimony as part of their research. Savarèse was the first to engage, in 2002, with the ways in which *pieds-noirs* have strategically reinterpreted the past so as to construct a particular image of themselves. His work also emphasises the fundamental role of associations as vehicles for such endeavours.[100] Through their studies of the annual *pied-noir* Ascension Day pilgrimage to Nîmes and the activities of an association of *pieds-noirs* with Maltese heritage, Baussant and Smith respectively provide real-world examples of how the processes theorised by Savarèse operate in specific environments.[101] What remains to be done is to historicise memory creation and mobilisation by linking its evolution more closely to changing political and social contexts in the years since 1962 and by embedding it with reference to a broader source base.

The *harki* community

Harki derives from the Arabic word *harka*, meaning movement. Ethnologist Jean Servier created the first *harka* in the mountainous Aurès region, but it was the minister resident, Robert Lacoste, who, in February 1956, regularised and institutionalised their use as mobile units to undertake offensive military operations. By September 1957, there were approximately 10,000 *harkis*. This figure then rose to 61,600 in January 1961, before dropping back down to 5000 by April 1962.[102] As the conflict progressed, *harki* increasingly became a generic term signifying a range of native auxiliaries employed in both military and civilian capacities. These roles included the *moghaznis* assigned to protect the soldiers of the Sections administratives spécialisées (SAS), who were charged with winning the hearts and minds of the Algerian people;[103] the men who comprised the Groupes d'auto défense (GAD), who were tasked with guarding isolated villages; the Groupes mobiles de sécurité of the rural police force; and finally the *assas* or guardians. It is in this broad sense that the term *harki* will be used in this study. The number of *harkis* so defined fluctuated throughout the war, peaking at 210,000 in 1958, but falling considerably in the final months of the conflict as France demobilised its auxiliaries.[104] *Harkis* were enrolled on short-term contracts – either military or civilian depending on the kind of activities they were being recruited for – that allowed the men to be let go when no longer required. The terms of employment for soldiers of Algerian origin engaged in the regular army were different in terms of duration, pay scale, promotional structure and benefits, such as pensions. In particular, being a soldier rather than an auxiliary guaranteed a transfer out of Algeria as part of the withdrawal of regular French units at the end of the war. Principally of rural origin, illiterate and unskilled, the status of *harkis* was also very different to the indigenous Muslim elite of colonial Algeria, who consisted of locally and nationally elected representatives, notables such as *caïds, bachagas* and *aghas,* members of the liberal professions, as well as career soldiers and officers. The support offered to the French cause by such men was often motivated by conviction rather than compulsion or necessity, indicated by the fact that many of them had obtained citizenship prior to 1958 when it was granted to all Algerians.

When the ceasefire was proclaimed, *harkis* were generally given three options: engage in the regular French army, which would mean going wherever the army went, resign with a small financial payment, or sign up as a civilian contractual agent for six months.[105] There was demonstrable disquiet among *harkis* at this time, most famously captured in a *Cinq colonnes à la une* interview with an auxiliary who feared that he would face reprisals for having 'worked under the French flag'.[106] Yet, with their lives and families in Algeria, *harkis* were understandably reluctant to leave. Reassurance that such a drastic act would not be necessary came from FLN tracts promising to 'forget' and 'pardon' the past, alongside guarantees from the substantial number of French troops still present that they would protect anyone who felt threatened. Furthermore, although the Evian Accords did not make a specific reference to the *harkis,* they did contain clauses stating that no one would be punished for actions undertaken during the war.[107] Consequently, 21,000 *harkis,* or 81.2 per cent of those still in active service, felt sufficiently reassured to accept their final pay and hand over their uniforms.[108]

Never having wanted to get caught up in the war in the first place, these men were keen to return to the lives they had been forced to suspend. 'I preferred to stay in the hope of finally living in peace in my country with my family', explained one *harki,* 'so I handed in my weapon and my kit'.[109] Such hopes were, however, quickly shattered as waves of terrible violence broke across the country. This bloodshed is often attributed to the so-called *marsiens,* last-minute FLN recruits who joined after the ceasefire on 19 March 1962, and who therefore felt it necessary to prove overtly their commitment to a cause to which they had rallied late in the day. Although compelling in their logic, such theories are, as François-Xavier Hautreux argues, hard to prove, not least because of the problems in identifying *marsiens.*[110] Equally difficult to determine is the exact role of the FLN leadership in the violence. Public documents claiming to forgive and forget were often accompanied by verbal threats and instructions to isolate the *harkis* and their families from the wider populace, while the punishment of 'traitors' was a long-standing FLN practice. However, much violence seems to have been spontaneous and the chaos within the FLN leadership at the time, owing to its own bitter and bloody internecine struggles for power, must also be borne in mind.[111]

There is no agreement on how many *harkis* and family members were killed. Violence began in April 1962, but the intensity of the massacres varied from region to region and also chronologically, with July and August constituting the most acute months. The earliest casualty estimates came from *Le Monde* journalist Jean Lacouture who advanced a figure of 10,000 on 13 November 1962. Thirty years later, he revised his calculation upwards to 100,000. This is also the statistic quoted by the majority of *harki* and *pied-noir* associations, although some claims go as high as 150,000 – an inflation that demonstrates the symbolic weight and thus strategic claims being advanced on the back of such statistics. Academics tend to congregate around the lower figure of 60,000 to 75,000, although Charles-Robert Ageron always refused to be more specific than 'several thousand'.[112] The scale and ferocity of this violence pushed many, but by no means all, *harkis* and their families to attempt to migrate to France. This was contrary to what the French government had envisaged and, as will be discussed in Chapter 2, there was considerable anxiety about both the number and the nature of the people seeking to cross the Mediterranean.

Taking charge of the processes of protection and transfer in May 1962, the army placed *harkis* under armed guard in a series of holding camps in Algeria to keep them safe while transport to France was arranged. However, the numbers seeking refuge quickly overwhelmed these facilities. The same was true of transport vessels that, in any case, were being used for settlers and regular French troops as a matter of priority. A concern to 'maintain order' and to filter out undesirable elements or 'false refugees' produced a series of administrative controls that have often been interpreted as an active attempt to prevent the *harkis* leaving Algeria, fuelling claims that the French 'abandoned' their auxiliaries in 1962. Particularly damning are telegrams sent by Louis Joxe, the minister for Algerian affairs. The first, on 16 May, reminded officers that it was forbidden to bring auxiliaries to France outside of official channels in response to a number of SAS units who were using their own networks to secure passage to France for 'their' *harkis*. This was followed on 15 July by a confidential directive stating that any such auxiliaries would be 'sent back to Algeria'.[113] Yet, while highlighting the deep inadequacies of the

French response and the consequences of restrictive transportation criteria, both Hautreux and Chantal Morelle have argued that it is nonetheless
important to acknowledge that measures were, in fact, put in place by the
government and army in relation to the threats faced by *harkis* in 1962.
The French authorities thus cannot be accused of having done nothing,
even if they could have done a lot more.[114]

As with the numbers killed, statistics vary with regard to how many
harkis came to France. William Cohen claimed that government organised repatriation programmes brought 25,000 *harkis* and their depend-
ants to the French mainland between 1962 and 1967, while a further 68,000
entered the country by unofficial means, frequently with the assistance of
their former officers.[115] This is broadly in line with figures provided by
Hautreux, who lists 12,000 transferred to France by July 1962, rising to
20,000 by December, with a further 6600 arriving in 1963.[116] Such estimates are complicated by the fact that there was more than one wave
of arrivals. Although 1962 saw the largest disembarkations, there was a
steady stream after this with spikes in 1965 and 1968 when many *harkis*
who had been taken prisoner by the FLN were released. In the light of
this, the most commonly cited figure is drawn from the 1968 census,
which listed 138,458 'French Muslims', the contemporary administrative
label for *harki*s and former Muslim notables, of which 88,000 had been
born in Algeria.[117]

Since the French government had not anticipated an arrival en masse
of *harki*s, neither strategies nor structures were in place to provide for
their accommodation. At least half of those who made it to France, and
certainly the vast majority of those who came through official channels, were initially placed in a series of hastily constructed or modified
camps, several of which had recently housed suspected FLN and OAS
militants.[118] Isolated rural sites such as Larzac, Bias and Rivesaltes were
conceived of as temporary expedients that would gradually become
obsolete as the *harki*s assimilated into French society. Indeed, some of
the estimated 42,500 people who passed through the camps between
1962 and 1969 remained there only briefly before being dispersed into the
wider populace.[119] Others, however, were not so lucky and were simply
transferred to other forms of government-allocated accommodation or
became long-term camp residents after being deemed incapable of integrating into French society.

The camps have become emblematic of the experience of *harki*s and
their families in France, and have come to stand as a symbol of the wider
process of marginalisation and forgetting to which the auxiliaries were
subjected.[120] These processes were compounded by the fact that, in spite

of the intensity and magnitude of their experiences, a *harki* memory of the war and its immediate aftermath was, for many years, notable by its absence. The reasons *harkis* were so reluctant to speak of their past were multiple and worked in varying combinations. Powerful external narratives, linguistic and cultural barriers, physical isolation, economic and social disempowerment, mixed with a potent sense of fear and exacerbated by the difficulty of articulating a past many were themselves still struggling to come to terms with all played their part in depriving the *harkis* of a voice in the years following their arrival in France. This situation persisted until the 1970s when a generation of *harki* children matured and mobilised to demand, amongst other things, the rehabilitation of the history and identity of their community.[121]

It took several decades for scholars to turn their attention to the *harkis*. Like memory activism within the community itself, this was also a development that owed much to the impetus of *harki* descendants such as Mohand Hamoumou, whose 1989 EHESS thesis was published in 1993 as *Et ils sont devenus harkis*.[122] Hamoumou is also representative of the dominance of sociological studies of the *harkis*, particularly during the 1990s, that tended to focus on the difficulties the 'second generation' have had integrating into France.[123] Continuing this trend, anthropologist Vincent Crapanzano maintains that even today the 'unhealed wounds' of the parental past over-determine the lives of current generations, trapping them within a politicised collective narrative of suffering.[124] In contrast, works by the ethnographer Giulia Fabbiano and the social scientist Rosella Spina present a more complex and nuanced picture. Both women point, in particular, to evolutions in the nature of relationships between children of *harkis* and Algerian immigrants, leading to what Fabbiano has termed a 'post-Algerian' generation for whom the war and the experiences of their ancestors are but one part of their identity and culture.[125]

In the light of the silence that for a long time prevailed within the community, considerable efforts have been made in recent years to collect and publish testimony from *harkis*, primarily by their descendants.[126] As will be explored in Chapter 6, this has led to an inverted process of memory transmission whereby the activism of younger generations, including making public their own experiences, in combination with broader changes in the way the Algerian War was discussed and understood, gave parents both the desire and the confidence to speak out in order to preserve a record of their past. Yet, although memory and its expression within the *harki* community is now a popular topic of academic research, to date there has been little attempt to historicise this growing body of testimony. One of the aims of this book is therefore to begin to redress the balance by focusing on the processes through which representations of the history and memory of the *harki* community have been constructed and reconstructed over the years.

Archival-based histories of the *harkis* is another area in need of additional scholarly attention since there remains much that we do not know about the actions of auxiliaries during the war and about their lives in France in the years immediately following 1962. While few can rival the archival knowledge, built up over decades, of General Maurice Faivre, his many publications present a particular ideological reading of the *harkis* informed by his own service during the war.[127] This underlines the importance of the work of scholars with a greater critical distance, including Hautreux, Tom Charbit, Jeannette E. Miller and Sung Choi, whose studies offer the kind of empirical knowledge necessary to complement and properly contextualise the array of first-hand accounts to which we now have access.[128]

International comparisons

In seeking to situate historically the *pieds-noirs* and *harkis*, it is important to connect their respective experiences to the broader international currents of which they were a part. French Algeria may have been one of the largest, but it was by no means the only settler colony. Across Africa and Asia, places such as Kenya, Rhodesia, Angola, Mozambique, Suriname and the Dutch East Indies all contained sizeable European minorities. As the empires of the European powers progressively came to an end from the Second World War onwards the men and women who had made their lives in these imperial outposts were faced with the same decision as the *pieds-noirs*: should they stay or go? Responses varied. Some opted to remain and were able to maintain their existence under new ruling regimes, as evidenced by the continued presence of European farms in Kenya's White Highlands. In other cases, especially within the British Empire, settlers moved but not very far, crossing borders into African territories such as Rhodesia where white rule still prevailed in an, ultimately futile, attempt to preserve a particular way of life. However, for the majority of settlers the advent of independence proved an insurmountable obstacle to their continued presence abroad. This was especially the case when independence had been achieved through violent struggle such as in Angola, Mozambique and the Dutch East Indies. The one million *pieds-noirs* who left Algeria in 1962 therefore need to be seen as part of a broader migratory wave that saw five to seven million Europeans 'repatriated' in the thirty-five years following the Second World War.[129] The French of Algeria thus joined 800,000

Portuguese *retornados* (returnees), 300,000 Dutch citizens, 100,000 British from Africa and 120,000 from India in 'coming home' to lands that were often unfamiliar and to which they possessed varying degrees of ancestral connection and kinship networks.

To this number might also be added the 12–14 million ethnic Germans expelled from Eastern Europe and the 3.2 million Japanese civilians abroad in 1945 when these two powers were defeated in the Second World War.[130] Known respectively as *Vertriebene* (expellees) and *hikiagesha* (literally 'a person who has been lifted and landed') the contexts in which these men and women were forced to migrate were somewhat different, not least because the empires of which they were citizens ended as a result of defeat within a much larger global conflict.[131] Nonetheless, connections can be made with *pieds-noirs* and other post-colonial European populations, particularly at the experiential level where all had to contend with the sense of being 'internal strangers' and had to navigate metropolitan populations who were at best suspicious and at worst actively hostile to their presence.[132] These communities are furthermore linked by the fact that they all came to serve as central sites of negotiation as their respective metropoles were forced to grapple with the questions surrounding the meaning and legacy of colonialism, notions of belonging and exclusion, and the role of state and non-state actors in managing diversity.

Case studies comparable to the experience of the *harkis* are harder to find. All the European imperial powers had recourse to indigenous auxiliaries, who were used regularly to help maintain order in the empire. The fates of these men and their families upon decolonisation varied, but many were subjected to retributive violence like that endured by the *harkis*. However, very few wanted or were able to leave and, even when this was an option, no other group of a comparable size ended up in the metropoles of their former colonial rulers. The closest parallel would probably be the Moluccans, an ethnic group from Ambon and the sur-rounding islands of the Dutch East Indies, who made up a significant proportion of the recruits of the Royal Dutch Indian Army and thus became obvious targets for nationalists when the Republic of Indonesia was created in 1949. Unsure of what to do with this last remnant of their colonial army, the Dutch government eventually brought these men and their families, approximately 12,500 people in total, to the Netherlands. Initially seen as temporary residents who would ultimately return to the Moluccan islands, they were placed in rural camps where their daily lives were managed by a special agency, the Commissariaat Ambonezenzorg. Echoing the two-tier approach adopted in France, while repatriates from the Dutch colonies were provided with a range of benefits designed to ensure their swift integration, the Moluccans endured many years of state-managed marginalisation resulting in a series of socio-economic problems similar to those faced by the *harkis* and their children. This bred significant frustrations which manifested themselves in a series of terrorist campaigns in the 1970s. In response, the government, having acknowledged that Moluccans were in the Netherlands permanently, undertook measures to enhance their participation in Dutch society. Educational and employment policies were combined with symbolic recognition of the community's history and identity. Since they were introduced in late 1970s, these initiatives have had considerable success. As with the *harkis,* although they have not resolved all the problems, government actions have significantly improved the situation of younger members of the community and resulted in a greater degree of integration for the Moluccans as a whole.[133]

Therefore, although distinctive in many ways, the fates of the *pieds-noirs* and *harkis* were not unique. Rather, they were shared to differing degrees by a range of populations caught up in some of the most significant historical episodes of the twentieth century. Yet, in spite of the appearance of several high-quality edited collections in recent years,[134] there remains much work to be done in order to bring the fates of what Andrea Smith terms 'Europe's invisible migrants' – and indeed case studies that fall outside Europe's borders – into a productive scholarly dialogue that balances acknowledgement of national particularities with an awareness of the international connections between these groups.

Structure of this book

Returning to this specific study, *pieds-noirs* were one of the most vocal memory carriers to offer interpretations of the *harkis* and their history during the period when this community was not speaking for itself. By no means a disinterested act, *harkis* were invoked by *pieds-noirs* in order to accentuate their own plight as marginalised and mistreated victims of decolonisation. Yet, these discourses also reflected the links between the two communities that developed initially in French Algeria but continued after they crossed the Mediterranean in the 1962. Exploring the similarities and differences in their memorial activism over time enables us to appreciate the continually evolving nature of social and collective memories, as well as to analyse the impact of changing broader social, political and cultural contexts upon these. By bringing together the histories and memories of the *pied-noir* and *harki* communities in the decades since 1962, this book aims to transcend the atomised nature of much existing scholarship where detailed studies exist for almost all groups from the OAS through to the Jeanson network, but not on the relationships between these actors.

The benefit of examining the War of Independence from this new perspective is that in place of the previously dominant absence/return paradigm, a more nuanced picture of memory formation is revealed. This comprises a four stage chronology moving from emergence between 1962 and 1975, consolidation between 1975 and 1991, then acceleration from 1991 as the war became a publicly prominent topic again, culminating in the present heightened 'memory wars' state. The book is accordingly structured around these key phases, with each of the four main sections containing chapters charting developments within the *pied-noir* and *harki* communities respectively. Although presented in parallel for reader clarity, the chapters nonetheless stress the points of connection and interaction between the two groups. A final section, 'Memory Wars', builds on these prior links, its thematic structure offering a fully integrated comparison. Dividing the book into two halves, 'The Era of "Absence"' and 'The "Return" of the War', indicates the ways in which this new periodisation relates to and intersects with the previously dominant paradigm of memory evolution. A genealogy of memory is therefore provided that serves to historicise the present commemorative situation while simultaneously drawing attention to the actors involved, and their complex motivations and expectations. In so doing, it reveals that competition for control over the past does not date from the 1990s and the return of the War of Independence to the public spotlight. Rather, it is part of a larger process of contestation and reappropriation that has been maintained within and between groups such as the *pieds-noirs* and the *harkis* since 1962.

Notes

1 www.legifrance.gouv.fr/affichTexte.do?cidTexte=JORFTEXT000000444898& categorieLien=id [5 November 2014].

2 Claude Liauzu, Gilbert Meynier, Gérard Noiriel, Frédéric Régent, Trinh Van Thao and Lucette Valensi, 'Colonisation: non à l'enseignement d'une histoire officielle', *Le Monde* (25 March 2005), p. 15.

3 Out of a possible total of 577 deputies, fewer than forty were present for the two readings of the law on 11 June 2004 and 10 February 2005. On the day the law was passed by the lower chamber, there were only four left-wing deputies in attendance. Valérie Esclangon-Morin, François Nadiras and Sylvie Thénault, 'Les Origines et la genèse d'une loi scélérate', in *La Colonisation, la loi et l'histoire*, ed. by Claude Liauzu and Gilles Manceron (Paris, 2006), p. 47; Valérie Morin, 'Quel devoir de mémoire pour les rapatriés?', *Confluences méditerranée*, 53 (Spring 2005), 115.

4 'Appel "d'enfants de harkis" contre les articles 4 et 13 de la loi du 23 février 2005', 8 January 2006. www.ldh-toulon.net/spip.php?article1679 [25 January 2016].

5 Gilles Manceron and François Nadiras, 'Les Réactions à cette loi', in *La Colonisation*, p. 72.

6 Indicative of this genre is Daniel Lefeuvre, *Pour en finir avec la repentance coloniale* (Paris, 2008).

7 G. Perrault, 'Deux français sur trois saluente le "rôle positif" de la colonisation', *Le Figaro* (2 December 2005), p. 8.

8 The trip was cancelled after Aimé Césaire announced that he would not receive the Minister of the Interior, Nicolas Sarkozy, in Martinique because of support given by Sarkozy's UMP party to the 2005 law and amidst plans to stage public protests to coincide with the visit.

9 Esclangon-Morin et al., 'Les Origines', p. 31.

10 Previous parliamentary debates had been noted for their highly acrimonious nature. See, for example, www.assemblee-nationale.fr/12/cra/2005-2006/081. asp [20 May 2014].

11 Jim House and Neil MacMaster, *Paris 1961: Algerians, State Terror and Memory* (Oxford, 2006), p. 10.

12 For links between 'memory wars' and the media, see Pascal Blanchard and Isabelle Veyrat-Masson (eds.), *Les Guerres de mémoires: la France et son histoire* (Paris, 2008).

13 One of the only book-length studies is Blanchard and Veyrat-Masson's *Les Guerres de mémoires* which aims to expand on and systematise previous observations published in *Vingtième siècle* during the 1980s and 1990s. See Jean-Pierre Azéma, Jean-Pierre Rioux and Henry Rousso, 'Les guerres franco-françaises', *Vingtième siècle*, 5 (January–March 1985), 3–6; Daniel Lindenberg, 'Guerres de mémoires en France', *Vingtième siècle* 42 (April–June 1994), 77–96. For discussion of 'memory wars' in relation specifically to the French empire, see Benjamin Stora and Thierry Leclère, *La Guerre des mémoires: la France face à son passé colonial* (Paris, 2007); Raphaëlle Branche, *La Guerre d'Algérie: une histoire apaisée?* (Paris, 2005); Eric Savarèse, *Algérie, la guerre des mémoires* (Paris, 2007).

14 Pascal Blanchard and Isabelle Veyrat-Masson, 'Les Guerres de mémoires', in *Les Guerres de mémoires*, p. 23.

15 For a discussion of casualty figures for different groups and the various controversies surrounding these estimates, see Martin Evans, *Algeria: France's Undeclared War* (Oxford, 2012), pp. 336–8.

16 The so-called 'café wars' left 3889 dead and 7678 wounded in 11,567 separate attacks between 1955 and 1961 as the FLN consolidated their supremacy over the MNA in France. During the same period, nationalist rivalries in Algeria left 6000 dead and 14,000 wounded. Benjamin Stora, *La Gangrène et l'oubli: la mémoire de la guerre d'Algérie* (Paris, 1991), pp. 143–4.

17 Formed in 1961 by dissident soldiers and members of the settler community, the extreme violence used by the OAS in an attempt to derail the

independence process included a failed assassination attempt on President Charles de Gaulle at Petit Clamart. See Rémi Kauffer, *OAS: histoire d'une guerre franco-française* (Paris, 2002); Olivier Dard, *Voyage au coeur de l'OAS* (Paris, 2011).

18   On 17 October 1961, the metropolitan branch of the FLN mobilised thousands of Algerians for a peaceful march through the streets of Paris in protest over a curfew recently imposed by the Prefect of Police, Maurice Papon. The savage repression of the demonstration by police and *harkis* of the Force de police auxiliaire (FPA) left up to 200 dead and many more wounded. The best historical account of this night is House and MacMaster, *Paris 1961*.

19   For an extended discussion of this idea, see Todd Shepard, *The Invention of Decolonization: The Algerian War and the Remaking of France* (Ithaca, NY and London, 2006).

20   The reluctance to term the events in Algeria a 'war' stemmed from the fact that this would entail admitting either that Algeria was a separate entity to France, thus giving credence to the FLN's claims for independence, or that the two sides were part of the same whole, which meant that what was occurring was a civil war, a phenomenon that sat uncomfortably with a population still trying to heal the domestic divisions of the Second World War.

21   John Talbott, *The War Without a Name: France in Algeria, 1954–1962* (London, 1981); Mike Mason, 'Batailles pour la mémoire', *Journal of African History*, 35 (1994), 305.

22   Philip Dine, *Images of the Algerian War: French Fiction and Film, 1954–1992* (Oxford, 1994); p. 7. See also Benjamin Stora, *Le Dictionnaire des livres de la guerre d'Algérie, 1955–1995* (Paris, 1996); Benjamin Stora, *Imaginaires de guerre: les images dans les guerres d'Algérie et du Viet-nam* (Paris, 2004); Philip Dine, '(Still) *A la recherche de l'Algérie perdue*: French Fiction and Film 1992–2004', *Historical Reflections/Réflexions historiques*, 28:2 (2002), 255–75.

23   Branche, *La Guerre d'Algérie*, p. 99.

24   *La Guerre d'Algérie* (five episodes), dir. Peter Batty, aired 12, 19 and 26 August, 2 and 9 September 1990 (FR3); *Les Années algériennes* (four episodes), prod. Benjamin Stora, aired 23 and 30 September, 7 and 8 October 1991 (A2).

25   In December 1991, elections in Algeria were cancelled after the first round at the army's behest when it appeared that the fundamentalist Front islamique du salut (FIS) were poised for victory. This plunged the country into almost a decade of violent civil war as the military-backed government fought a variety of Islamist groups, leading to the loss of 200,000 civilian lives. See Martin Evans and John Phillips, *Algeria, Anger of the Dispossessed* (New Haven, CT and London, 2007); Hugh Roberts, *The Battlefield Algeria 1988–2002: Studies in a Broken Polity* (London, 2003).

26   For an overview of these debates, see Emile Chabal, '*La République postcoloniale*? Making the Nation in Late Twentieth Century France', in *France's Lost Empires: Fragmentation, Nostalgia and la fracture coloniale*, ed. by Kate Marsh and Nicola Frith (Lanham, MD, 2010), pp. 137–52.

27 Jean-Pierre Rioux (ed.), *La Guerre d'Algérie et les français* (Paris, 1990); Charles-Robert Ageron (ed.), *La Guerre d'Algérie et les algériens* (Paris, 1997); *La Guerre d'Algérie au miroir des décolonisations françaises* (Paris, 2000); Jean-Charles Jauffret (ed.), *Militaires et guérrilla dans la guerre d'Algérie* (Brussels, 2001).

28 Raphaëlle Branche, *La Torture et l'armée pendant la guerre d'Algérie 1954–1962* (Paris, 2001); Sylvie Thénault, *Une drôle de justice, les magistrats dans la guerre d'Algérie* (Paris, 2001); House and MacMaster, *Paris 1961;* Shepard, *The Invention of Decolonization.*

29 Mohammed Harbi and Benjamin Stora (eds.), *La Guerre d'Algérie: 1954–2004, la fin de l'amnésie* (Paris, 2004). Ideas of amnesia and absence have nonetheless retained a strong hold on the popular imagination, fed by a media and publishing industry that continue to present the conflict as a perpetual site of rediscovery, claiming that their latest contribution will be the one to 'break the silence' by revealing some 'hidden' aspects of the conflict for the 'first time'.

30 Henry Rousso, 'Les Raisins verts de la guerre d'Algérie', in *La Guerre d'Algérie (1954–1962),* ed. by Yves Michaud (Paris, 2004), p. 139. Patricia Lorcin advances a similar proposition when she writes that the silence surrounding the war 'fissured' before being officially broken in the 1990s. Patricia M.E. Lorcin, 'Introduction', in *Algeria and France 1800–2000: Identity, Memory, Nostalgia,* ed. by Patricia M. E. Lorcin (New York, 2006), p. xxv.

31 Eric Conan and Henry Rousso, *Vichy an Ever-Present Past,* trans. Nathan Bracher (Hanover, NH and London, 1998), p. 4. See also Henry Rousso, *The Vichy Syndrome: History and Memory in France Since 1944,* trans. Arthur Goldhammer (Cambridge, MA, 1991).

32 Philippe Labro, *Des feux mal étients* (Paris, 1980), p. 354.

33 For further insight into the perspectives of the conscript troops, see Claire Mauss-Copeaux, *Appelés en Algérie: la parole confisquée* (Paris, 1999); Patrick Rotman and Bernard Tavernier, *La Guerre sans nom: les appelés d'Algérie, 1954–1962* (Paris: 1992); *Guerre d'Algérie, guerre d'indépendance: paroles d'humanité* (Paris, 2012).

34 Benjamin Stora, *Ils venaient d'Algérie* (Paris, 1992), p. 144; William B. Cohen, 'The *Harkis:* History and Memory', in *Algeria and France,* p. 169.

35 Charles-Robert Ageron, 'Conclusion', in *La Guerre d'Algérie,* p. 623; John Talbott, 'French Public Opinion and the Algerian War: A Research Note', *French Historical Studies* 9 (Fall 1975), 361.

36 Stora, *Imaginaires,* p. 190; Benjamin Stora, *Le Livre, mémoire de l'histoire: réflex-ions sur le livre et la guerre d'Algérie* (Paris, 2005), p. 196; Stora, *La Gangrène,* p. 249.

37 www.lph-asso.fr/index.php?option=com_content&view=article&id=152& Itemid=182&lang=fr [31 May 2014].The website belongs to the association Liberté pour l'Histoire. Nora set up the site with René Remond and Françoise Chandernagor in protest over the 2005 law which they viewed as the culmination of a series of misguided 'memory laws'.

38 See, for example, Stora and Leclère, *La Guerre des mémoires*, p. 28.

39 Rousso, 'Les Raisins verts', pp. 127–51.

40 Luisa Passerini, 'Memories between Silence and Oblivion', in *Contested Pasts: The Politics of Memory*, ed. by Katharine Hodgkin and Susannah Radstone (New York, 2003), p. 249.

41 Alon Confino, 'Collective Memory and Cultural History: Problems of Method', *American Historical Review*, 102:5 (December 1997), 1399.

42 Jay Winter, 'Thinking about Silence', in *Shadows of War: A Social History of Silence in the Twentieth Century*, ed. by Efrat Ben Ze'ev Ruth Ginio and Jay Winter (Cambridge, 2010), p. 5.

43 James Fentress and Chris Wickham, *Social Memory* (Oxford, 1992), p. 117; Savarèse, *Algérie*, p. 46.

44 Amidst the vast array of work on memory, see, in particular, Maurice Halbwachs, *On Collective Memory*, trans. Lewis A. Coser (Chicago, 1992); Jeffrey K. Olick, 'Collective Memory: The Two Cultures', *Sociological Theory*, 17:3 (1999), 333–48; Geoffrey Cubitt, *History and Memory* (Manchester, 2007), pp. 1–25; Wulf Kansteiner, 'Finding Meaning in Memory: A Methodological Critique of Collective Memory Studies', *History and Theory*, 41 (May 2002), 179–97.

45 Jay Winter, 'Forms of Kinship and Remembrance in the Aftermath of the Great War', in *War and Remembrance in the Twentieth Century*, ed. by Jay Winter and Emmanuel Sivan (Cambridge, 2000), p. 40; John R. Gillis, *Commemoration: The Politics of National Identity* (Princeton, NJ, 1996), p. 5.

46 Cubitt, *History and Memory*, p. 14.

47 Cubitt, *History and Memory*, pp. 14–15.

48 For a critique of this aspect of collective memory, see Kerwin Lee Klein, 'On the Emergence of Memory in Historical Discourse', *Representations* 69 (Winter 2000), 127–50. For a summary of the different position on the collective memory debate, see Cubitt, *History and Memory*, pp. 13–20.

49 Cited in Andrea Brazzoduro, 'Postcolonial Memories of the Algerian War of Independence, 1955–2010: French Veterans and Contemporary France', in *France and the Mediterranean*, ed. by Natalya Vince and Emmanuel Godin (Oxford, 2012), p. 277.

50 Alistair Thomson, *Anzac Memories: Living with the Legend* (Melbourne, 1994), pp. 8–11.

51 Barbara A. Misztal, *Theories of Social Remembering* (Maindenhead, 2003), p. 52; Nancy Wood, *Vectors of Memory: Legacies of Trauma in Postwar Europe* (Oxford and New York, 1999), p. 2; Confino, 'Collective Memory', 1390.

52 Wood, *Vectors of Memory*, p. 2; Cubitt, *History and Memory*, p. 6.

53 Fictive meaning, in this instance, constructed rather than imaginary or untrue. Winter, 'Forms of Kinship', p. 41.

54 Winter has been criticised for focusing too much on the grassroots level while ignoring, or at least under-conceptualising, the role played by the state. See T. G. Ashplant, Graham Dawson and Michael Roper (eds.), *The Politics of War, Memory and Commemoration* (London, 2000), p. 12.

55 Michael Rothberg, 'Between Memory and History: From *lieux de mémoire* to *noeuds de mémoire*', *Yale French Studies*, 118 and 119 (2010), 8; Nathan Wachtel, 'Introduction', in *Between Memory and History*, ed. by Marie-Noëlle Bourget, Lucette Valensi and Nathan Watchel (Chur, Switzerland, 1990), p. 14; Roger Bastide, 'Mémoire collective et sociologie du bricolage', *L'Année sociologique* (1970), 85.

56 Victoria Best and Kathryn Robson, 'Memory and Innovation in Post-Holocaust France', *French Studies*, 59:1 (2005), 2.

57 Jay Winter, 'In Conclusion: Palimpsests', *German Historical Institute London Bulletin*, Supplement 1 (2009), 171.

58 Winter, 'Forms of Kinship', p. 47.

59 Stora, *La Gangrène*, p. 319.

60 Jay Winter and Emmanuel Sivan, 'Setting the Framework', in *War and Remembrance*, p. 3.

61 Confino's observations are particularly pertinent to the French commemorative context since they were made in relation to Henry Rousso's *The Vichy Syndrome* and its focus on narrowly political and official memories. Confino, 'Collective Memory', 1394.

62 Robert Frank, 'Les Troubles de la mémoire française', in *La Guerre d'Algérie*, p. 604.

63 Pierre Nora (ed.), *Les Lieux de mémoire*, 7 vols. (Paris, 1984–92); available in English as *Realms of Memory*, trans. Arthur Goldhammer, 3 vols. (New York, 1994–98).

64 Among the many commentaries on Nora's work, some of the most trenchant critiques include Steven Englund, 'The Ghost of Nation Past', *Journal of Modern History*, 64 (1992), 299–320; Hue-Tam Ho Tai, 'Remembered Realms: Pierre Nora and French National Memory', *American Historical Review*, 106 (2001), 906–22; Nancy Wood, 'Memorial Militancy in France: "Working Through" or the Politics of Anachronism?', *Patterns of Prejudice*, 29:2 (1995), 89–103.

65 Rothberg, 'Between Memory and History', 3–12.

66 Joan Tumblety, 'Working with Memory as a Source and Subject', in *Memory and History*, ed. by Joan Tumblety (London and New York, 2013), p. 2.

67 Sylvie Thénault, 'France-Algérie: pour un traitement commun du passé de la guerre d'indépendance', *Vingtième siècle*, 85 (January–March 2005), 121.

68 For academics currently working specifically on *pied-noir* cultural output, see, in particular, Amy L. Hubbell, *Remembering French Algeria: Pieds-Noirs, Identity and Exile* (Lincoln, NE, 2015); Fiona Barclay, *Writing Postcolonial France: Haunting, Literature and the Marghreb* (Lanham, MD, 2011).

69 French studies specialists have undertaken the majority of research into *harki* cultural production. For a comprehensive collection of the most recent scholarship, see Keith Moser (ed.), *A Practical Guide to Harki Literature* (Lanham, MD, 2014).

70 Sarah Waters, *Social Movements in France: Towards a New Citizenship* (Basingstoke, 2003), p. 8.

71 Waters, *Social Movements*, p. 1.

72 Victoria Phaneuf, 'Negotiating Culture, Performing Identities: North African and Pied-Noir Associations in France', *The Journal of North African Studies*, 17:4 (September 2012), 673.

73 Jean-Jacques Jordi, 'Archéologie et structure du réseau de sociabilité rapatrié et pied-noir', *Provence Historique*, 47 (1997), 177.

74 Maurice Calmein, *Les Associations pieds-noirs* (Carcassonne, 1994), p. 15; Jean-Jacques Jordi, *De l'exode à l'exil: rapatriés et pieds noirs en France: l'exemple marseillais, 1954–1992* (Paris, 1993), p. 179; Jordi, 'Archéologie', 177.

75 Jean-Jacques Jordi, *Idées reçues: les pieds-noirs* (Paris, 2009), p. 138.

76 Jordi, 'Archéologie', 185; Joëlle Hureau, 'Associations et souvenir chez les français rapatriés d'Algérie', in Rioux (ed.), *La Guerre d'Algérie et les français*, p. 520.

77 Andrea L. Smith, *Colonial Memory and Postcolonial Europe: Maltese Settlers in Algeria and France* (Bloomington, IN, 2006).

78 One of the few pieces to discuss *harki* associations in detail is Abderahmen Moumen, 'De l'absence aux nouveaux porte-parole: évolution du mouvement associatif harki (1962–2011)', *Les Temps modernes*, 666 (November–December 2011), 159–70.

79 Under French law, associations are required to be registered, to have officers, to hold annual meetings for members and to possess a constitution. Phaneuf, 'Negotiating Culture', 673; Michèle Baussant, *Pieds-noirs: mémoires d'exils* (Paris, 2002), p. 47.

80 Phaneuf, 'Negotiating Culture', 673.

81 Isabelle Veyrat-Masson, 'Les Guerres de mémoires à la télévision', in Blanchard and Veyrat-Masson (eds.), *Les Guerres de mémoires*, p. 273.

82 Tamara Chaplin, *Turning on the Mind: French Philosophers in Television* (Chicago, IL and London, 2007), p. 7.

83 For a detailed breakdown of all programmes relating to the war broadcast on French television between 1962 and 1992, see Béatrice Fleury-Vilatte, *La mémoire télévisuelle de la guerre d'Algérie 1962–1992* (Paris, 2000), appendix.

84 For further discussion of this, see Fleury-Vilatte, *La Mémoire télévisuelle*, pp. 167–9.

85 Jean-Jacques Jordi, 'Les Pieds-noirs: constructions identitaires et réinvention des origines', *Hommes et migrations*, 1236 (March–April 2002), 19.

86 Ali Yedes, 'Social Dynamics in Colonial Algeria: The Question of *Pieds-Noirs* Identity', in *French Civilization and its Discontents*, ed. by Tyler Stovall and Georges Van Den Abbeele (Lanham, MD, 2003), p. 240.

87 For a flavour of the era and of the works produced by these men, see Jean Pomier, *Chronique d'Alger, 1910–1957 ou le Temps des algérianistes* (Paris, 1972); Robert Randau, *Les algérianistes* (Paris, 1911).

88 Peter Dunwoodie, *Writing French Algeria* (Oxford, 1998), pp. 125–75; Patricia M. E. Lorcin, *Imperial Identities: Stereotyping, Prejudice and Race in Colonial Algeria* (London, 1999), pp. 196–214.

89 Jean-Jacques Jordi, 'L'été 62 à Marseille: tensions et incompréhensions', in *Marseille et le choc des décolonisations*, ed. by Jean-Jacques Jordi and Emile Temime (Aix-en-Provence, 1996), p. 66.

90 For scholarship concerning the integration of Algerian Jews into France, see, in particular, Sarah Beth Sussman, 'Changing Lands, Changing Identities: The Migration of Algerian Jewry to France, 1954–1967' (unpublished doctoral dissertation, Stanford University, 2002); Michel Abitbol, 'La Cinquième République et l'accueil des juifs d'Afrique du Nord', in *Les Juifs de France de la Révolution française à nos jours*, ed. by Jean-Jacques Becker and Annette Wieviorka (Paris, 1998), pp. 287–327; Elizabeth Friedman, *Colonialism and After: An Algerian Jewish Community* (South Hadley, MA, 1988).

91 Yann Scioldo-Zürcher, 'Reflections on Return and the "Migratory Projects" of the *Français d'Algérie*', in *Coming Home? Vol. 2: Conflict and Postcolonial Return Migration in the Context of France and North Africa, 1962–2009*, ed. by Scott Soo and Sharif Gemie (Newcastle-upon-Tyne, 2013), pp. 53–71. The protection offered by the state to the settlers will be discussed in detail in the first chapter.

92 Jean-Jacques Jordi, *1962, l'arrivée des pieds-noirs* (Paris, 1995), p. 114.

93 Among the first and still best known *pied-noir* accounts are Francine Dessaigne, *Journal d'une mère de famille pied noir* (Paris, 1962); Anne Loesch, *La Valise et le cercueil* (Paris, 1963).

94 Calmein, *Les Associations pieds-noirs*; Maurice Calmein, *Dis, c'était comment, l'Algérie française?* (Friedberg and Bayern, 2002).

95 Among his many publications, see, in particular, Jean-Jacques Jordi and Emile Temime (eds.), *Marseille et le choc des décolonisations* (Aix-en-Provence, 1996); Jordi, *1962*; Jordi, *De l'exode à l'exil*.

96 Emmanuelle Comtat, *Les Pieds-noirs et la politique quarante ans après le retour* (Paris, 2009).

97 Yann Scioldo-Zürcher, *Devenir métropolitain: politique d'intégration et parcours de rapatriés d'Algérie en métropole (1954–2005)* (Paris, 2010).

98 Valérie Esclangon-Morin, *Les Rapatriés d'Afrique du Nord de 1956 à nos jours* (Paris, 2007), p. 18.

99 See, in particular, Jordi, 'Archéologie', 177–88; Clarisse Buono, *Pieds-noirs de père en fils* (Paris, 2004), pp. 103–13.

100 Savarèse, *L'invention des pieds-noirs*. Other relevant works from this prolific academic include Savarèse, *Algérie*; Eric Savarèse (ed.), *L'Algérie dépassionnée: au delà du tumulte des mémoires* (Paris, 2008); Eric Savarèse, 'Mobilisations politiques et posture victimaire chez les militants associatifs pieds-noirs', *Raisons politiques*, 30 (May 2008), 41–58.

101 Baussant, *Pieds-noirs*; Smith, *Colonial Memory*.

102 Claude Liauzu, 'Préface' in Fatima Besnaci-Lancou, *Nos mères, paroles blessées* (Léchelle, 2006), p. 14.

103 Despatched to rural parts of Algeria, soldiers in SAS units were given the dual mission of 'pacifying' the territories to which they were assigned, while also

providing administrative, social and medical services to the local population in a bid to win back their confidence in the French. See Jacques Fremeaux, 'Les SAS (sections administratives specialisées)', *Guerres mondiales et conflits contemporaines*, 208 (2002), 55–68.

104 Charles-Robert Ageron, 'Le "drame des harkis": mémoire ou histoire?', *Vingtième siècle*, 68 (2000), 3.

105 Ageron, 'Le "drame des harkis"', 4.

106 'Algérie: la fin de la guerre', *Cinq colonnes à l'une*, aired 6 June 1962 (Channel 1).

107 François-Xavier Hautreux, *La Guerre d'Algérie des harkis, 1954–1962* (Paris, 2013), pp. 306, 329.

108 Ageron, 'Le "drame des harkis"', 4. For the provisions made, see Accords d'Evian, Chapter II, Part A, Articles 1 and 2. Available at www.axl.cefan. ulaval.ca/afrique/algerie-accords_d'Evian.htm [20 December 2014]

109 Brahim Sadouni, *Français sans patrie: la reconnaissance* (Rouen, 1985), pp. 7, 97.

110 Hautreux, *La Guerre d'Algérie*, p. 357.

111 Hautreux, *La Guerre d'Algérie*, p. 329.

112 For further discussion of the debates concerning the numbers of people who were killed, see Cohen, 'The *Harkis*: History and Memory', p. 168; Charles-Robert Ageron, 'Les supplétifs algériens dans l'armée française pendant la Guerre d'Algérie', *Vingtième siècle*, 48 (October–December 1995), 12, 20; Hautreux, *La Guerre d'Algérie*, p. 345; Evans, *Algeria*, pp. 336–8.

113 Chantal Morelle, 'Les Pouvoirs publics français et le rapatriement des harkis en 1961–1962', *Vingtième siècle*, 83 (July–September 2004), 114. The minister of the armies at the time, Pierre Messmer, later claimed that Joxe's directives were never implemented and that no *harkis* were sent back to Algeria, but this is contested by both *pied-noir* and *harki* activists. See Pierre Messmer, *Les Blancs s'en vont: récits de décolonisation* (Paris, 1998), p. 175

114 Hautreux, *La Guerre d'Algérie*, p. 369; Morelle, 'Les pouvoirs publiques', 111.

115 Cohen, 'The *Harkis*', p. 169.

116 Hautreux, *La Guerre d'Algérie*, p. 374.

117 Mohand Hamoumou with Abderahmen Moumen, 'L'histoire des harkis et français musulmans: la fin d'un tabou?', in *La Guerre d'Algérie: 1954–2004*, p. 338.

118 For a full list of the camps and their locations, see Catherine Wihtol de Wenden, 'Harkis: le paradoxe identitaire', *Regards sur l'actualité*, 175 (November 1991), 36.

119 Wihtol de Wenden, 'Harkis', 36. Maurice Faivre advances a slightly different set of statistics, claiming that between 1962 and 1963, 41,000 passed through the camps at Rivesaltes, St-Maurice-l'Ardoise, Bourg-Lastic, Larzac and La Rye. In addition, 1800 soldiers were demobilised in the mainland and a further 1500 *harkis* who were released from FLN prisons in 1965 and 1968 were placed in the château de Lascours (Gard). Maurice Faivre, 'La Communauté des harkis', *Le Casoar*, 116 (January 1990), 39.

120 For discussion of these issues, see Jeannette E. Miller, 'A Camp for Foreigners and "Aliens": The Harkis' Exile at the Rivesaltes Camp (1962–1964)', *French Politics, Culture and Society*, 31:2 (Winter 2013), 37–9.

121 Claire Eldridge, ' "We've never had a voice": Memory Construction and the Children of the Harkis, 1962–1991', *French History*, 23:1 (March 2009), 88–107.

122 Mohand Hamoumou, *Et ils sont devenus harkis* (Paris, 1993).

123 See, in particular, Laurent Muller, *Le Silence des harkis* (Paris, 1999); Stéphanie Abrial, *Les Enfants de harkis de la révolte à l'intégration* (Paris, 2001); Emmanuel Brillet, 'A Remarkable Heritage: The "Daily Round" of the Children of the Harkis, between Merger and Villification', *Immigrants and Minorities*, 22:2–3 (July/November 2003), 333–45; Nordine Boulhaïs, *Histoire des harkis du nord de la France* (Paris, 2005); Régis Pierret, *Les Filles et fils de harkis: entre double rejet et triple appartenance* (Paris, 2008).

124 Vincent Crapanzano, *The Harkis: The Wound that Never Heals* (Chicago and London, 2011), pp. 178–80.

125 Rosella Spina, *Enfants de harkis et enfants d'émigrés: parcours croisés, identités à recoudre* (Paris, 2012). Of her many publications, see, in particular, Giulia Fabbiano, 'Mémoires postalgériennes: la guerre d'Algérie entre héritage et emprunts', in *La concurrence mémorielle*, ed. by Geoffrey Grandjean and Jérôme Jamin (Paris, 2011), pp. 131–47; Giulia Fabbiano, 'Mixité postcoloniale. Les unions des descendants d'émigrés algériens à l'épreuve de l'expérience migratoire parentale', *Diasporas*, 15 (2009), 99–110; Giulia Fabbiano, 'De l'indigène colonial aux générations postalgériennes: procès d'identification et de différenciation des descendants de harkis et d'immigrés', *Migrations société*, 19:113 (September–October 2007), 95–110.

126 Particularly prolific in this regard is Fatima Besnaci-Lancou, whose various collections of testimony will be discussed in Chapter 6.

127 See, in particular, Maurice Faivre, *Les Combattants musulmans de la guerre d'Algérie: des soldats sacrifiés* (Paris, 1995); Maurice Faivre, *Un village de harkis: des Babors au pays drouais* (Paris, 1994); Maurice Faivre, *L'action sociale de l'armée en faveur des musulmans, 1830–2006* (Paris, 2007).

128 This body of work includes Hautreux, *La Guerre d'Algérie*; Tom Charbit, 'Un petit monde colonial en métropole: le camp de harkis de Saint-Maurice-l'Ardoise (1962–1976)', *Politix*, 76 (2006), pp. 31–52; Miller, 'A Camp for Foreigners and "Aliens" ', 21–44; Sung Choi, 'Les Anciens combattants musulmans dans la France postcoloniale: La politique d'intégration des harkis après 1962', *Les Temps modernes* 666 (November–December 2011), 120–39; Sung Choi, 'The Muslim Veteran in Postcolonial France: The Politics of the Integration of Harkis after 1962', *French Politics, Culture and Society*, 29:1 (Spring 2011), 24–45.

129 Although some Europeans opted for fresh starts in places such as Canada or South America, the overwhelmingly majority 'returned' to their respective metropoles. Andrea L. Smith, 'Introduction', in *Europe's Invisible Migrants* (Amsterdam, 2003), p. 9.

130 Lori Watt, 'Imperial Remnants: The Repatriates in Postwar Japan', in *Settler Colonialism in the Twentieth Century*, ed. by Caroline Elkins and Susan Pedersen (New York, 2005), p. 244.

131 For further information on these two groups, see, in particular, Watt, 'Imperial Remnants', pp. 243–56; Manuel Borutta and Jan C. Jansen (eds.), *Vertriebene and Pieds-Noirs in Postwar Germany and France: Comparative Perspectives* (Basingstoke, 2016).

132 The term 'internal stranger' comes from Richard Werbner's 1989 framework for analysing strangerhood and is used very effectively in Stephen K. Lubkemann, 'Race, Class and Kin in the Negotiation of "Internal Strangerhood" among Portuguese Retornados', in *Europe's Invisible Migrants*, pp. 75–93.

133 For further information on the Moluccans, see Hans van Amersfoot and Mies van Niekerk, 'Immigration as a Colonial Inheritance: Post-Colonial Immigrants in the Netherlands, 1945–2002', *Journal of Ethnic and Migration Studies*, 32:3 (2006), 323–46; Gert Oostindie, 'Ruptures and Dissonance: Post-Colonial Migrations and the Remembrance of Colonialism in the Netherlands', in *Memories of Post-Imperial Nations: The Aftermath of Decolonization, 1945–2013*, ed. by Dietmar Rothermund (Cambridge, 2015), pp. 38–57.

134 In addition to the works already cited, see Dominik Geppert and Frank Lorenz Muller (eds), *Sites of Imperial Memory* (Manchester, 2015); Ulbe Bosma, Jan Lucassen and Gert Oostindie (eds.), *Postcolonial Migrants and Identity Politics* (New York, 2012); Panikos Panayi and Pippa Virdee (eds.), *Refugees and the End of Empire* (Basingstoke, 2011).

PART I

The Era of 'Absence', 1962–91

Emergence, 1962–75

1

Creating a community

For Manuel Gomez, the summer of 1962 represented 'the end of a world':

> It was the end of everything that made up our memories, the house where
> we grew up, surrounded by a loving family, the street where our eyes were
> opened to the world, the school where we wore out our first pair of short
> trousers ... the shadowy corners that sheltered our first rendez-vous, our
> first kisses, the sun, the trips, the excursions, the sporting events from
> which we returned exhausted, with no voice left, but happy.

All these memories crowded his and the minds of his fellow settlers as
they bade farewell to their homes. Whether departing by boat or plane,
their eyes lingered for as long as possible on 'what was for us the most
beautiful view in the world ... right until the moment when, eyes burned
by the sun, or full of tears, we had to lower our heads'.[1]

Such nostalgia-laden evocations of a painful 'exile' from the unique
and irreplaceable land that was French Algeria are, today, widely regarded
as the hallmark of the *pied-noir* community in France who are known
for their vocal mobilisation in the fields of memory and commemoration. Determined to secure space within the national narrative for their
particular vision of themselves and their history, the community and the
associations that represent them have become prominent players within
the 'memory wars' deemed to be currently surrounding the Algerian
War and France's colonial past more generally. Yet, when the former
settlers first arrived in France in 1962, their concerns were much more
practically orientated. Preoccupied with rebuilding their lives following
their abrupt and traumatic departure from French Algeria, they looked
to the small number of newly founded *rapatrié* [repatriate] associations

to press the government on their behalf for assistance with resettlement. The lynchpin of such demands was the French citizenship possessed by the *rapatriés*, a status which, associations argued, entitled them to a particular kind and level of support from the French government in order to ensure their successful integration into the body politic. Framed as statements about the 'Frenchness' of the former settlers and the extent to which the state was willing to recognise this through their actions, these material demands enabled *rapatrié* associations to define a set of common interests and goals and thus to begin to develop a sense of community among the French from Algeria, who were now dispersed throughout the Hexagon.

In exploring this early phase of *rapatrié* history, this chapter will trace how the link established by associations between material support and acceptance into the national community became a potent mobilisation tool that was used to bind individual *rapatriés* together into a constituency with a strong sense of common purpose and entitlement. The chapter will go on to consider how, as material demands became progressively less acute, the activities of associations increasingly turned towards the cultural realm. At this juncture, rather than continuing to insist on their similarity to the rest of the nation as a way of obtaining practical concessions from the state, associations instead began to stress what they claimed were the distinctive elements of *rapatrié* culture and identity, which were now to be proudly proclaimed and actively defended against the assimilationist pressures of French society. The result was the creation of a 'meta-memory',[2] premised on a canon of historical and cultural narratives relating to the unique patrimony of the former settlers that laid the groundwork for the kind of postcolonial identity politics so prevalent today.

The hand of the state

The migration of almost one million people to France in the summer of 1962 as a result of Algerian independence overwhelmed the largely unprepared French authorities. It furthermore took time for the government to concede the magnitude and significance of this population movement: as late as 30 May, the Secretary of State for *rapatriés* told his cabinet colleagues that the current number of recorded arrivals in France was in line with figures for the previous year, implying that it was a question of annual 'holidaymakers' rather than a permanent displacement.[3] Ultimately, however, the French government acknowledged and responded to this mass migration in ways that proved innovative and enduring. This response was based on the fact that the population in question was clearly defined as neither immigrants nor refugees, but 'returning' French citizens or *rapatriés*. As such they should and would be protected by the state, irrespective of their sympathies and actions during the War of Independence. Yet, although the principle of protection on the basis of nationality remained consistent with previous eras, in almost all other respects the support extended to the *rapatriés* from French Algeria broke with tradition. The unprecedented nature of the situation facing the authorities in the summer of 1962 brought forth a raft of measures that cumulatively represented a new and consciously interventionist approach from the state, which was centred on receiving, housing and employing the *rapatriés* as rapidly and as comprehensively as possible.[4]

In line with this goal, the resources made available to the settlers from French Algeria were far more extensive than those offered to previous waves of *rapatriés*, or to non-French migrants in the same era. The legal cornerstone of this new approach was law 61-1439 relating to the 'welcome and resettlement of the French from overseas', more commonly known as the Boulin Law after the recently appointed secretary of state for *rapatriés*, Robert Boulin. Coming into effect on 26 December 1961, the law recognised the need to codify the state's response to the rising number of citizens being displaced as a result of decolonisation, which had already affected French inhabitants of Egypt, Indo-China, Morocco, Tunisia and Guinea. Previously, acquiring *rapatrié* status, and thus the right to some financial assistance, had depended on a variety of factors including conditions of departure and the assessment of embassy or consular officials. The Boulin Law simplified and broadened the definition of those able to benefit from state aid to all Frenchmen and women 'having or expecting to have to leave, as a result of political events, a land where they were settled and which was previously placed under the sovereignty, protectorate or administration of France'. The law also expanded the type of aid available. In place of emergency aid, the state now promised 'a collection of measures' to 'integrate French *rapatriés* into the social and economic structures of the nation' in conformity with the principle of 'national solidarity' as specified in the 1946 constitution.[5]

In drafting the law, politicians had the French of Algeria uppermost in their mind. Paradoxically, however, in creating generous repatriation provisions the government's intention was to encourage the settlers to remain in Algeria, reassuring them that 'because they would be welcome in the metropole, they did not have to come'.[6] Amidst ongoing negotiations with the FLN and in order not to agitate further the *Algérie française* lobby, officials sought to conceal the unique scenario posed by Algerian independence and its potential implications by subsuming it within the larger processes of repatriation and decolonisation. They were preparing, as one official at the time noted, 'discreetly and immediately for the return of French Algerians under the guise of operations already under way for other territories'.[7] By anchoring the law in the concept of 'national solidarity', officials were able to convey the idea that this was something all citizens could expect from the state, rather than a specific set of measures directed at a particular group.[8] But by the following spring, events had moved on, prompting the government, on 10 March 1962, to extend formally by decree the provisions of the Boulin Law to the French of Algeria. The decree additionally clarified the nature of the support that would be made available.[9] Between this decree and 15 July 1970, when the first compensation law for the *rapatriés* from French Algeria was passed, the original provisions of the Boulin Law were supplemented by a further 323 legal texts as government agencies constantly adjusted their policies to meet the evolving needs of the substantial number of settlers now present in France.[10]

These provisions were unparalleled in their scale, but also in the way they reconceptualised the relationship between the state and its citizens. Rather than simply a question of 'welcoming' *rapatriés* as previous policies had sought to do, the state now envisaged its role as ensuring their holistic integration. This process began as soon as the *rapatriés* set foot on metropolitan soil, where welcome desks in airports, ports and train stations registered all new arrivals. Those who did not immediately have somewhere to go were offered temporary shelter, while longer-term solutions were sought via an acceleration of building programmes for social housing and the reservation of 15 to 30 per cent of these dwellings for *rapatriés*. The authorities furthermore requisitioned empty properties, incentivised private landlords to take on *rapatrié* tenants and offered funds directly to *rapatriés* at attractive rates to facilitate home ownership. All regular forms of social aid for the metropolitan French were made available to *rapatriés* without the usual stipulations regarding residency periods and documentation. A particularly significant innovation was the provision of a monthly cash subsidy of 350 francs, slightly above the minimum wage, for up to one year. This was designed to alleviate pressure on those seeking work, enabling them to search for employment commensurate with their skills and experience rather than being forced to take the first job that came along. Employment was a priority and, where possible, the government sought to reintegrate the *rapatriés* into the French labour market in the same positions and at the same levels as they had occupied in Algeria. Those whose professions were not transferable to the mainland were offered opportunities to retrain, while low-interest loans were made available to anyone wishing to purchase business premises or agricultural land. Those unable to work or in other vulnerable situations were given additional financial support. Above all, the authorities were concerned to protect the *rapatriés* from the negative socio-economic conditions usually associated with migration and to ensure that, as French citizens, they were not treated like any other immigrant population. The importance of nationality becomes particularly apparent when the treatment of French *rapatriés* is compared to the much more restricted aid that was available to the approximately 60,000 settlers from Algeria who did not possess French citizenship.[11]

This was not a social engineering project. The policies enacted were not intended to promote social mobility nor to erase socio-economic differences, but rather to ensure integration on comparable terms while countering the risks of pauperisation that mass displacement inherently carried. It was for this reason that, when drafting the law, Boulin insisted that the text should centre on the principle of 'national solidarity' as the best way to effect an equitable and global installation, rather than compensation, for which many *rapatriés* were pressing. For Boulin and other Gaullist officials, 'solidarity' was the most appropriate frame because it would allow a new category to be created – the *rapatrié* – to whom the government *could* extend assistance, in a manner of its own choosing, but without allowing this new status in and of itself to confer rights vis-à-vis the nation as the principle of 'compensation' potentially would.[12]

The timing of the *rapatriés'* arrival was fortuitous. The boom years of the *trente glorieuses*, which saw the French economy grow by an average of 5.7 per cent a year between 1955 and 1968, enabled the state to cover the high costs associated with integration. By 1970, an estimated 10 billion francs had been spent on monthly benefits and social aid, alongside another 12 billion francs on diverse grants and subsidies and a further 4 billion francs on aid loans.[13] Financial means were matched by political will as parliamentary deputies from all parties recognised the danger of leaving a population who had already demonstrated militant tendencies isolated and unsupported in the metropole.[14] The concern of the authorities was to prevent, as far as possible, socio-economic vulnerability fermenting discontent that could then be mobilised against the state. Journalist Philippe Hernandez, himself a *rapatrié*, was similarly conscious of this when he called on the metropolitan French to show solidarity so that 'any future associations made up of the French of Algeria have nothing better to do than to organise an annual cocktail party'.[15] Integration was therefore conceptualised as not only a duty owed by the state to its citizens, but also as a way of effecting national reconciliation, with the successful insertion of the *rapatriés* into French society enabling the page to be turned on the previous eight years of conflict.

It was not all plain sailing. In spite of major innovations, the state still found itself overwhelmed by the volume of demands being placed upon it in the early years of the 1960s. As much as there were notable successes, there were also inadequacies. The elderly and infirm, particularly women on their own, struggled to re-establish themselves, as did farmers and small shopkeepers. Although most *rapatriés* found housing within six to twenty-four months, others spent far longer crowded into *centres d'hébergement* or other forms of temporary accommodation.[16] Experiences also varied considerably according to geography. The government hoped that the new arrivals would settle throughout France, their movements regulated by differing levels of demand for labour. However, this geographical dispersion failed to materialise, in spite of various carrot-and-stick initiatives. Instead, heavy concentrations of *rapatriés* built up around Paris and in the south with an estimated 600,000 *rapatriés* choosing to settle in the twelve *départements* of the Midi.[17] Consequently, while those who headed north, primary civil servants and their families, were able to find work relatively easily, those who remained in the south faced fewer opportunities and greater competition. In Toulouse, only 820 out of 6000 employment requests were satisfied in 1963–64, while 'vagrancy' was a serious issue in Marseille where *rapatriés* aged over fifty represented 20 per cent of the unemployed. By this point it had also become 'impossible' to find lodgings in the city, underscoring the additional stresses this uneven distribution placed upon already inadequate housing stocks.[18] More generally, the sudden influx of one million *rapatriés* stretched resources and tempers to breaking point. The metropolitan French resented the disruption caused by the *rapatriés*, especially when these appeared to lead to rising prices and crime rates. Moreover, increased levels of crime across southern France were seen as proof that the *rapatriés* were serving as a conduit for OAS lawlessness, raising fears that their presence would create, as the Parti communiste français (PCF) put it, a 'reservoir of fascism' in the mainland.[19] The regular and vocal expression of these frustrations in local and national media left *rapatriés* feeling distinctly unwelcome, if not actively victimised. This was especially true when metropolitan hostility was framed with reference to the supposedly 'un-French' cultural and behavioural particularities of the former settlers. Yet, tellingly, as integration progressed, lessening the burden on local authorities while simultaneously revealing the economic contributions made by the *rapatriés*, relations improved.

The difficulties faced by *rapatriés* were highlighted in the national media through programmes such as *Cinq colonnes à la une*, a monthly news magazine which, in May 1963, revealed the plight of a fifty-nine-year-old widow reduced to living in a garage with her mother and son following the deaths of her husband and sister during the war. Back in Algeria, she and her husband had owned a bar, but she now found herself taking in washing in a bid to provide for her remaining family. When the interviewer asked her if she felt she had 'enough courage to start again when you have nothing', her response was a tearful but stoical 'you have to live!'[20] Although heart-rending, these and other tales of *rapatrié* hardship were placed within a narrative arc that, in line with the government's position, stressed integration as a work in progress, but one that was definitely moving forward.[21] Indeed, in spite of a few turbulent initial years, the socio-economic integration of the *rapatriés* proceeded steadily under the stewardship of an attentive state which could justifiably claim it had succeeded in its primary aim of preventing the marginalisation of its 'returning' citizens.

Associations and the mobilisation of the *rapatriés*

In June 1964, two years on from the height of the 'exodus' from Algeria, President de Gaulle used a visit to the Oise region to give his verdict on the whole process, proclaiming that 'in one year, a million French people established [in Algeria] have been repatriated without conflicts, without drama, without suffering and integrated into our national unit. This has never been seen before.'[22] This assessment did not, however, tally with the experiences of many former settlers, whose metropolitan trajectory had included plenty of conflicts, dramas and suffering. Not only did the state's efforts fall short of what the *rapatriés* deemed necessary, but their response to these perceived inadequacies was to mobilise collectively in precisely the manner the government had sought to avoid, leading to the creation of a series of associations dedicated to defending *rapatrié* rights. Several of these organisations pre-dated the Algerian conflict, having been formed to champion the cause of French people displaced by decolonisation in other parts of the empire. But the scale of the Algerian crisis and the numbers affected meant that this issue quickly came to dominate the focus of bodies such the Rassemblement des Français d'Afrique du Nord (RANFRAN), the Union syndicale de défense des intérêts des Français repliés d'Algérie (USDIFRA) and the Front national des rapatriés (FNR). Of these various associations, one in particular stood out: the Association nationale des Français d'Afrique du Nord, d'outre-mer et de leurs amis (ANFANOMA).

The association was created in 1956 by the Moroccan-born, Paris-based lawyer Jacques Reveillaud. But it was between 1958 and 1973, under the presidency of Colonel Pierre Battesti, who was also the parliamentary deputy for the Seine-et-Marne, that ANFANOMA established itself as the largest, most representative and most influential *rapatrié* association.[23] As such, it led the way in formulating and projecting a self-conscious *rapatrié* identity and agenda. ANFANOMA was particularly quick to highlight shortcomings in the state's reaction, claiming these were evidence that officials and the wider public believed the *rapatriés* were not full French citizens and thus not deserving of proper assistance. In this way, ANFANOMA made the provisions put in place by the government into a yardstick by which the wider acceptance of the *rapatriés* into the national community could be measured.

Solidarity and mutual aid: the activities of ANFANOMA

Prior to the Boulin Law, when the state conceived of its obligations towards *rapatriés* in much more limited terms, ANFANOMA offered itself as the voice of displaced French citizens from across the empire, claiming to be best placed to represent their concerns to the authorities and the French public. In accordance with these objectives, one of the earliest issues of the association's weekly newspaper, *France horizon,* demanded that the state afford all Frenchmen and women uprooted by decolonisation 'the right to return with dignity to the national community: not as diminished citizens but, on the contrary, conscious both of our duties towards the country and of the country's duties towards us'.[24] As committed supporters of the *Algérie française* cause, the association kept a close eye on the unfolding situation in French Algeria, proclaiming the territory's fate to be 'at the centre of our thoughts'.[25] When ANFANOMA's worst fears were realised with Algerian independence in 1962, one of the most immediate effects was a leap in the association's membership from 62,000 in April 1960, to 250,000 by 1962.[26] ANFANOMA could now claim to represent a formidable constituency and, as the exodus from Algeria gathered pace, one with myriad urgent needs.

In theory, the Boulin Law and the subsequent array of policies should have spelled the end for organisations like ANFANOMA who had established themselves in the gap between what they felt *rapatriés* deserved and what the state had been willing to provide. However, the government's strategy of using material assistance to deprive bodies such as ANFANOMA of the ability to make political capital out of *rapatrié* dissatisfaction proved ineffective; not least because ANFANOMA refused to explicitly acknowledge the vastly expanded levels of support now being supplied by the state. There was thus little change in the self-presentation of ANFANOMA pre- and post-Boulin as the association continued to promote itself as a vital middleman between a bewildered *rapatrié* community and an incompetent, apathetic administration. Retrospectively, the association even claimed that without its efforts 'there would certainly have been violent reactions against an overwhelmed and disorientated state ill-prepared to receive this avalanche of people'.[27]

Yet, behind such rhetoric, ANFANOMA did tacitly acknowledge the unprecedented nature of the state's response in a variety of ways. One of the key roles performed by *France horizon,* for example, was to inform *rapatriés* of their various welfare entitlements and to help them navigate the formidable bureaucracy that often stood between them and available assistance. ANFANOMA also kept *rapatriés* up to date with new legislative measures, providing digested accounts of parliamentary debates, including detailed breakdowns of the budget, so that *rapatriés* could see how much was being spent on them relative to previous years and to other groups within society. *France horizon's* coverage was painstakingly detailed, regularly including handy 'cut out and keep' sections which provided focused summaries of key topics like social security or housing benefits, or that targeted specific groups of *rapatriés* such as pensioners or civil servants. The fact that these functions took up such a significant proportion of every issue of *France horizon* testified to the vast array of state activities being undertaken on behalf of the *rapatriés.* Keeping on top of these developments was no small task, especially as additional measures were constantly being introduced, but ANFANOMA's dedication was unswerving. A few readers did write in to complain gently that this relentless focus on the practical side of integration was a little 'dry' and to suggest that perhaps more space could be devoted to providing cultural comforts to a community deprived of its 'sunshine'.[28] On the whole, however, it was by championing immediate concerns common to all *rapatriés* that ANFANOMA made itself a focal point for the displaced settlers and developed a wide base of support. In these early years, ordinary *rapatriés* may not have had much in common with the political and economic elites, like Battesti, who led the association, nor would many of them have been in a financial position to attend the association's annual conference with its star-studded gala dinner at which Enrico Macias regularly performed. But they could all relate to the campaigns waged on their behalf for decent housing, employment and standards of living, and to the association's commitment to ensuring their 'absolute, total integration' within the national community.[29]

In addition to pressing the state to deliver a comprehensive integration package, ANFANOMA also functioned as its own welfare and support network. Arguing forcefully that 'In the face of the misfortunes of the refugees and *rapatriés*, the whole nation should be mobilised',[30] ANFANOMA issued multiple appeals in the latter half of 1962 through its own publications and in the mainstream press, asking people to donate whatever they could – from money, food, clothing and furniture to spare rooms and jobs – to assist families who had lost everything. The association's regional branches served as useful collection points for donations. For those in better financial positions, *France Horizon* carried adverts for estate agents, removal firms, painters and decorators, and home furnishing companies who could help families as they rebuilt their lives. *Rapatriés* were also encouraged to advertise directly for services they required or that they could provide to others. These notices offer a glimpse into the everyday situations and priorities of the *rapatriés* from the practical – 'Frenchman, 65 years old, married, no children, very fit, WWI veteran, excellent references, seeking post as concierge or *gardien* in the south' – to the more personal – 'Marriage: *rapatrié*, 52 years old, prosperous divorcé, F4 apartment, wants to meet happy and kind lady, 45–48 years old. Teacher or civil servant preferred, very serious'.[31] As the years passed, these classified advertisements incorporated an increasing number of birth, death and marriage announcements, indicating the formation of a sense of community and connection among ANFANOMA's readers.

In this era, ANFANOMA was a highly masculine operation with exclusively male presidents and vice-presidents. Although the membership of the association was mixed, the delegates pictured speaking at the annual conference and leading other official occasions were invariably male, with occasional wives standing to the side. Men also penned the vast majority of articles in *France horizon*. Reflecting her prominent status within the *rapatrié* milieu, Francine Dessaigne, author of the popular memoirs *Journal d'une mère pied-noir* (1962) and *Déracinés!* (1964), was a rare exception to this rule, although it was primarily as a woman and a mother that she was called upon to express her thoughts.[32] In general, women featured only occasionally as a group in their own right and almost always in connection with charity or the home. In 1964, for example, ANFANOMA created a short-lived column entitled 'Madame Rapatrié s'installe' [Mrs Repatriate settles in], which advised female readers on some of the difficulties they might encounter establishing themselves in their new environment. As the column's anonymous author noted: 'Deprived, perhaps, of your friends and family, as well as your hairdresser, your dressmaker, your local cobbler and so many other suppliers closely linked to your life and personality, in all likelihood you feel a little disorientated.' To counter this potential malaise, the column offered a selection of advertisements for useful household products, suitable furnishing and decoration firms, as well as recipes for traditional yet simple-to-prepare culinary staples such as 'ramequins à la Provençale'.[33] Indicative of a wider post-1945 discourse in the feminine press that sought to educate and support women in their role as rational 'citizen consumers',[34] the nature of these particular home-making tips nonetheless highlighted some of the more serious issues facing *rapatriés* than whether their *Provençale* dishes were up to scratch. Acknowledging the gap that might exist between 'the white houses you had to leave in haste' and the 'impersonal (HLM style) flats' that she now found herself living in, Madame Rapatrié was enjoined not to succumb to nostalgia for her previous life. Instead, she should make the best of her current situation by envisaging 'the thousand and one possibilities available to you for personalising your interior'. Implicitly attesting to the difficult circumstances many *rapatriés* found themselves living in, these handy hints included how to turn your bedroom into a living space during the day, or how to construct a space-saving shelving unit on the back of an un-used door.[35] In combining the practical and the aspirational (shelves on the back of a door one day, but a beautifully furnished home full of the latest gadgets in the not too distant future), 'Madame Rapatrié' encapsulated the journey being undertaken by the former settlers as they sought to move beyond present material difficulties towards the full integration for which ANFANOMA ardently campaigned.

Alongside offering advice and practical assistance, ANFANOMA developed narratives about the *rapatriés* that emphasised the common denominator of their Frenchness. Proof of official recognition of this status by the government was then tied to the fulfilment of the association's demands. The representational tropes created in pursuit of these political goals in turn became the basis for a collective identity as individual *rapatriés* were encouraged to think of themselves as a culturally and socially cohesive community possessed of certain rights. Aware, for example, of the negative impression of the settlers held by the metropolitan French, ANFANOMA engaged in a careful re-presentation of the *rapatriés*, which was centred on their status as distressed victims deserving of compassion and assistance as part of a wider duty to national solidarity. 'Each day, each night, from boats, from planes, men, women and children disembark without money, without lodgings, without family', reported the association in June 1962, enjoining the French public to extend moral and material aid to those 'searching for sanctuary with Us, with You'.[36] The association also mirrored wider media discourses, which, as Todd Shepard has shown, employed the motif of the family to convey suffering and evoke sympathy on behalf of the *rapatriés*.[37] In February 1963, in the midst of one of the harshest winters on record, *France horizon*'s front cover showed a young couple with their baby and two young children huddled round a primitive stove in a sparse room. The caption made clear the 'intolerable' impact of such conditions upon these 'orphans of the sun' as they 'ask, shivering, if winter will ever end'.[38] Such depictions worked to distance the *rapatriés* from previous presentations that had connected them with the violence and disorder of the end of French Algeria. Domesticated by the presence of their wives and children, male *rapatriés* in particular were disassociated from the hyper-masculine, political fanaticism of the OAS in ways that meant they could be more easily envisioned as part of the national community.[39] That such an emphasis was placed upon being treated as a full part of the national community reflected long-standing settler anxieties regarding the metropolitan acceptance of their Frenchness dating back to the colonial era. This was further exacerbated by decolonisation and the belief among *rapatriés* that the government's decision to 'abandon' Algeria in 1962 signalled a rejection not just of the land, but also of them.[40]

The question of compensation

Through such tactics, ANFANOMA established a discourse whereby government measures designed to achieve integration became the criteria by which the state's willingness to recognise the *rapatriés* as true members of the nation could be judged. The association then applied the same logic in support of its other political goals, which went beyond immediate practical aid and into the domains of moral and material restitution. Granting amnesties to those convicted of political crimes during the Algerian War, many of whom were still incarcerated in the 1960s, was thus presented as a complement to broader campaigns for *rapatriés* to be treated the same as all other French people. Conscious of the sensitivity of such a topic, especially when the terrorist activities of the remnants of the OAS were still dominating the news, this regularly articulated demand made only vague references to why amnesties might be necessary, citing men whose sole 'crime' had been to love or believe in France and who were therefore true patriots.[41] Pointing out that amnesties had been issued after other major conflicts, particularly the Second World War, and had already been extended by the French state to FLN militants, ANFANOMA argued that it was only 'just' that the same principle should be applied to settlers involved in anti-government activities between 1954 and 1962. Without a general amnesty, the association claimed, 'a true national reconciliation' could not be achieved, leaving *rapatriés* unable to feel properly 'at home' in France.[42]

Equally central to being able to feel fully 'at home' in France was the question of financial reparations for land, homes, businesses and belongings lost or left behind in Algeria, including relief from any associated debts.[43] In spite of strong opposition from officials such as Boulin, the right to compensation had been written into Article 4 of the 1961 law, albeit in terms that allowed discussion and action on the matter to be postponed indefinitely. ANFANOMA, by contrast, insisted that, in addition to financial support for resettlement, monetary compensation should be immediately forthcoming. In making their case, the association deployed arguments drawn from a variety of realms. From the perspective of economic efficiency, for example, it was claimed that rather than a burden or risk, compensation would in fact be a financial gift to the French people as the money received would simply be re-invested within France, further stimulating an already flourishing economy.[44] Other arguments advanced by ANFANOMA reveal that the association regarded citizenship not simply as a legal category, but rather as something to be constructed in relation to other actors and groups as part of as a discursive terrain of struggle.[45] Thus by emphasising the moral dimension of indemnification, ANFANOMA asserted an understanding of 'national solidarity' that was much broader than the state's deliberately restrictive definition. From their tireless work establishing Algeria as a thriving imperial territory, to their willingness to lay down their lives in defence of their motherland in two world wars, ANFANOMA highlighted the consistent contribution of the *rapatriés* to the nation, often at great personal cost. It was therefore only right, the association argued, that in their time of need, France should repay this loyalty, especially given that decolonisation had been conceded by the government in Paris against the wishes of the French of Algeria. 'We have paid in advance', President Battesti declared at ANFANOMA's 1964 conference. 'We have paid with our misfortune, with our pain, with our misery ... with our tears and, sometimes, with our blood.' In the light of such sacrifices, only a 'total indemnification without restrictions' would demonstrate national solidarity and prove that the government was sincere when it proclaimed the *rapatriés* to be fully French.[46]

The association's most frequently iterated claim rested on the Declaration of the Rights of Man and the Citizen which established a 'sacred and inviolable right' to property; a right that no man could be deprived of unless in the service of public need and following a just indemnity. Aware that public support for compensation, particularly of colonial property, was limited, this historical precedent was used by associations to underwrite the claim that *rapatriés* were asking neither for charity, nor for preferential treatment, but simply for what was rightfully owed to them, as it would be to any French citizen. In a dossier submitted to parliament in July 1964, the Groupement national pour l'indemnisation des biens spoliés ou perdus outre-mer (GNPI) stated that 'the dispossessed demand what is owed to them. They are not making claims for fun'. This message was reiterated by the Rhône branch of ANFANOMA when they described financial recompense as 'not a favour but a right'.[47] Individual *rapatriés* who opted to take their compensation claims to court were offered support, including legal expertise, by associations like ANFANOMA and the GNPI. These cases received extensive publicity in *France horizon* because even when unsuccessful, as the majority were, they contributed to a process by which 'a legal and political articulation of repatriate rights was honed all in the name of their integral civic status'.[48] By framing compensation in universal terms and rooting it in a founding constitutional principle, ANFANOMA was able to divorce the issue from any discussion of the legitimacy, or otherwise, of the colonial enterprise, while also maintaining their wider position that there could be no difference in treatment between the *rapatriés* and other citizens.

The question of compensation had been central to the platform of ANFANOMA and other *rapatrié* associations from their inception, growing in importance as more immediate needs for housing and employment became progressively less acute. This was in no small part because, as an unresolved issue, compensation represented an effective way of ensuring the continued mobilisation of individual *rapatriés* and thus their adherence to the association. From ANFANOMA's perspective, one of the 'problems' with the *rapatriés* from Morocco and Tunisia had been that they very quickly succeeded in re-establishing their lives in France, at which point they lost interest in the association and stopped subscribing.[49] The determination of *rapatrié* organisations to ensure that compensation remained a national priority was matched only by the determination of the government to keep it off the political agenda. The state resisted demands for comprehensive and immediate compensation, claiming the cost was more than the treasury could reasonably bear. Officials also argued that releasing such sums would have significant inflationary and electoral implications for a nation already grumbling that too much was being done for the *rapatriés* at the expense of other French citizens.[50] Boulin maintained his opposition to indemnification on the grounds that it would aid the already wealthy while neglecting the most vulnerable. Responding directly to questioning from Battesti on the television programme *Faire face* in 1961, Boulin reiterated his belief that the government's strategy of 'integration', meaning financial support aimed at resettlement, represented the best and fairest way to ensure the collective assimilation of all *rapatriés* into the nation.[51] Such arguments did not impress ANFANOMA, which accused the government of being committed only to doing as little as possible as late as possible.

In spite of the government's clear preference for integration, acknowledgement of the right to compensation, contained in Article 4 of the Boulin Law, gave grist to the mills of *rapatrié* campaigns, which repeatedly referred to it, as associations continued to put pressure on the government over this issue. Faced with sustained lobbying by associations and with a growing perception that the *rapatriés* constituted an influential voting block, politicians recognised that, sooner or later, the subject of compensation would have to be addressed.[52] Once this principle was accepted, it then became a question of which party's solution would be best, both for the *rapatriés* and for their own electoral fortunes. Financial reparations, albeit within carefully defined limits, therefore began to be discussed as a necessary complement to the integration policies already in place. Georges Pompidou was the first to use the promise of compensation as a vote-garnering tactic during his 1969 presidential campaign, pledging that an annual sum of 500 million francs would be dedicated to indemnifying the *rapatriés*. Following Pompidou's election, the government of Jacques Chaban-Delmas (1969–72) was tasked with drafting the first law of indemnification, which appeared on the statute books on 15 July 1970. Presidents Valéry Giscard d'Estaing (1974–81) and François Mitterrand (1981–95) both followed in Pompidou's footsteps, resulting in further laws in 1974, 1978 and 1987. Even before the 1987 law came into effect, the collective cost to the treasury was already an estimated 28.7 billion francs.[53] The political rhetoric, from politicians on all sides, that accompanied these various laws evolved from endorsing indemnification as a necessary practical complement to existing integration policies, to conceiving of it as a symbolic right owed by the state to the *rapatriés* in recognition of their contribution to the nation as part of the colonial endeavour. This process witnessed the progressive blurring of the lines between national solidarity and indemnification (categories that Boulin had been determined to keep separate) and brought the position of the state ever closer to that of *rapatrié* associations for whom compensation had always been a moral as much as a material issue.[54]

The turn to culture

Coinciding with large-scale *rapatrié* mobilisations to commemorate the twenty-fifth anniversary of 1962 and therefore of the arrival of *rapatriés* in France, as well as the run-up to Mitterrand's re-election bid, the provisions of the 1987 compensation law were more generous than previous packages. Within the government, the hope was that the issue could finally be laid to rest and, indeed, no further major financial legislation relating to the *rapatriés* was passed until February 2005. In keeping with their reactions to previous laws, *rapatrié* associations focused on denouncing what they saw as the insufficiencies of the new measures, vowing to continue to fight for a 'just' compensation. The front cover of the December 1987 issue of *France horizon* featured Santa Claus reclining in a deckchair on a tropical beach under the headline 'Father Christmas is still on holiday. Compensation remains in his sack.'[55] Yet in spite of such rhetoric, the 1987 law, in combination with pre-existing measures, was substantial enough to neutralise indemnification as a burning issue for many individual *rapatriés*. This, in turn, made it a much less effective campaigning platform for bodies like ANFANOMA, leading the association to consider whether it was time to refocus their efforts in a different direction.

Although they were given a particular acuity by the 1987 law, such debates were already underway within ANFANOMA, prompted by the emergence, in the 1970s, of a new breed of culturally orientated *rapatrié* associations. Even prior to the first indemnification law of 1970, the exceptional array of support offered by the state had ensured the rapid integration of the majority of *rapatriés* who were no longer significantly distinguishable in material terms from the rest of the nation. Through its focus on economic reinstallation, the state had hoped to overcome cultural and political differences, erasing any sentiments of group belonging fostered by the experience of decolonisation and thus ensuring the complete assimilation of the *rapatriés*. Yet, ironically, the success of these integration policies had the opposite effect as socio-economic security provided associations with the time, resources and confidence to think of different ways to maintain the visibility of the *rapatriés* as a collective entity. As practical needs diminished in urgency, new issues were needed through which associations could engage the *rapatriés* and thus maintain their own memberships. Having spent years campaigning for material recompense from the state, associations now began pressing for symbolic recognition of the community and its place within the nation. This entailed creating a cultural and commemorative agenda centred on what was now presented as the unique patrimony of the former settlers.

The shift in priorities from practical to cultural was thus accompanied by a parallel move away from discourses anchored in universalism to arguments premised on the particularism of the *rapatriés*. This change in direction is usually dated to the founding of the Cercle algérianiste in 1973 by a new generation of self-styled 'young' *pieds-noirs*: Maurice Calmein was only twenty-six when he became the Cercle's first president, whereas ANFANOMA's president Battesti was sixty-eight at the time.[56] The Cercle algérianiste declared itself to be on a mission to 'give a new strength back to the "*Algérie française*" community', in order to 'restore [its] faith'.[57] This faith was to be propagated through the organisation's quarterly magazine, *L'Algérianiste*, which, in 1976, informed members:

> The era of *rapatrié* associations that we've known since 1962, which has been so useful in relieving miseries and defending the interests of our compatriots, will certainly be extinguished in the years to come and we'll be left alone, facing ourselves, with the enormous duty of preventing the soul of our people being swallowed up.[58]

As integration progressed, the danger, as identified by the Cercle algérianiste, was that assimilation would result in the loss of the specific identity and heritage they felt the *rapatriés* from Algeria carried within them. They thus conceived of their mission as 'saving a culture and a community in peril', which became the association's motto. Beyond the pages of *L'Algérianiste*, this goal was to be pursued through a range of culturally orientated initiatives including study groups, a literary prize and exhibitions, all designed to leave a paper trail for future generations. Meanwhile, cultural and memorial events brought individuals together as a community and established places of commemoration on French soil in lieu of being able to return to Algeria.[59] Underpinning these various activities was the desire to 'make the most beautiful pages of our history known, to denounce when necessary the lies and hypocrisy that surround it [and] to recount the daily life of our people ... preserving their language, their spirit, and their qualities'.[60]

The Cercle algérianiste fitted neatly into the post-1968 landscape of greater recognition for minority identities and cultures, which received further succour under Giscard's regionalism policies and his more pluralist conception of the nation. This broader context created a receptive climate for arguments being advanced by the Cercle that were premised on the unique cultural identity and heritage of the *rapatriés*. Echoing claims first made in the nineteenth century and prominent again during the 1930s, there was much talk of Algeria having been a 'province' of

France with Calmein arguing that 'In spite of the "geographical absence",
we carry within us all the constituent elements of a province. We are
provincials without a province, Algerian-French or simply Algerians
like others are Bretons, Corsicans or Basque.' Above all, what Calmein
claimed *algérianistes* like himself wanted was to 'integrate ourselves into
the heart of the French nation while having others accept our provincial identity'.[61] The growing importance of culture within the rhetoric of
rapatrié associations also acknowledged its utility as a unifying tool. In
searching for a new common denominator, history and memory, embodied in the notion of an endangered culture, provided an emotionally resonant, malleable and renewable resource. Consequently, where the Cercle
algérianiste led in the mid-1970s, others soon followed. By the 1980s,
rapatrié associations were numerous and diverse, grouping together former settlers on the basis of shared geographical origins, professions and
other facets of identity.

Initially, ANFANOMA resisted the shift away from practical issues,
regarding the Cercle algérianiste somewhat dismissively as merely a 'cultural complement' to its own work.[62] But as the popularity of the Cercle
grew, conflicts emerged between the two associations over the best way
forward for the *rapatrié* community that both were seeking to represent.
In 1983, ANFANOMA's then-president Paul-Emile Viard penned an editorial in defence of the association's strategies in which he opined that
for all it was good to remember the past, this should not be taken as goal
in and of itself, especially not in place of action centred on the practi-
calities associated with integration.[63] Responding on behalf of the Cercle
algérianiste, Calmein wrote an open letter in which he distinguished
between *rapatriés* who wanted only material compensation for their
losses, and *algérianistes*, such as himself, for whom 'the page cannot be
turned', no matter how many amnesties and indemnification laws were
passed. While acknowledging the value of ANFANOMA's work to defend
the rights and interests of the *rapatriés*, Calmein nonetheless argued
that now such 'priority' tasks had been accomplished, it was necessary
to 'organise our collective provincial life, to allow it to survive, even if
this displeases our detractors'.[64] More than just a question of whether to
privilege unresolved material issues over cultural demands, this debate
centred on the extent to which the *rapatrié* platform should continue to
be constructed on the bedrock of undifferentiated French citizenship, or
whether more emphasis should be placed on the cultural and historical
specificity of the community. In closing the exchange, Viard made clear
his position as a partisan of *enracinement* [rootedness], warning that the
logical end point of the approach advocated by the Cercle algérianiste

was a *rapatrié* 'ghetto'. He also pointed out the contradiction of having fought 'ferociously' to remain French during the Algerian War, only to now 'battle' not to be French in France.[65]

This debate reared its head again in 1987, when the combination of the indemnification law and the series of events marking the twenty-fifth anniversary of 1962 left ANFANOMA feeling the pressure as it sought to retain its place as 'the oldest, the most important, the most representative of the *rapatrié* associations' at this crucial historical juncture.[66] In June, at the height of both the parliamentary debates and the anniversary *rassemblements* [gatherings], ANFANOMA devoted a full page of *France horizon* to defending the utility of continuing to have *rapatrié* associations. In contrast to Viard's remarks four years previously, the article showed a marked shift towards the kind of cultural agenda championed by the Cercle algérianiste. Arguing that defending 'material patrimony' was, of course, important, the article also insisted on the 'intellectual, moral and spiritual' dimensions of such an endeavour, including 'the preservation of our cultural, literary, artistic riches and the conservation of our archives'.[67] Without ever renouncing its original goal of protecting the rights of *rapatriés,* ANFANOMA thus increasingly began to acknowledge the importance of culture as a mobilising force.

The emerging consensus on the importance of culture brought with it a consolidation of representational tropes developed in the 1960s and 1970s into a new collective identity. There remained some debate over what label to subsume this new identity under as revealed by the diverse suggestions collected as part of a Cercle algérianiste questionnaire, distributed between November 1977 and March 1978, which included 'French speaking Algerians', 'Franco-Algerians' and 'Algerianistes'. *Rapatrié* was widely dismissed by respondents as an inaccurate descriptor, while *pied-noir* was not included as an option owing to the Cercle algérianiste's aversion to it as an identifier.[68] Yet, this was ultimately the term that would emerge as the dominant designation for the community, especially in mainstream discourse. More than simply a label, *pied-noir* came to signify the collective identity created by associations who federated a number of ideas, images and narratives into a single stereotype. It fused notions of cultural specificity based on the most visible elements of settler popular culture in French Algeria with a common historical trajectory that moved from pioneering and patriotic contributions to the success of the French in Algeria, to the destruction of this paradise via the War of Independence, resulting in the forced migration of a million settlers to the metropole. As subsequent chapters will show, the precise shape of this new identity, which drew on a range of old and new sources, took several years to solidify. What is perhaps most striking about this process is the extent of the consensus established across associations and the durability of these codified tenets.

As they sought to integrate the French from Algeria into the nation as quickly and as comprehensively as possible, officials in the 1960s denied that what they were doing was exceptional in any way. Yet, while they were using the principle of national solidarity to claim that they were responding to the *rapatriés* as they would to any French citizen, in fact, state officials were creating an innovative and unprecedented programme of socio-economic support. In the same vein, ANFANOMA's early rhetoric was premised on ensuring that there was no difference in treatment between *rapatriés* and the metropolitan French. But in making these arguments, the association deliberately defined the *rapatriés* as a specific group with distinct common concerns and characteristics that needed to be addressed. By creating a sense of commonality among disparate and dispersed individuals, the association laid the foundation for the particularist collective narratives that the Cercle algérainiste would then parlay into a mobilisation tool to replace the dwindling efficacy of campaigns centred on material needs. Seen in this light, the turn towards cultural concerns in the 1970s represented less a change in direction, than the transfer of existing questions regarding identity and belonging to a new arena. One in which the *pieds-noirs'* perceived differences, this time cultural rather than material in nature, could be construed as an asset rather than an obstacle to the achievement of their ongoing demands for recognition and recompense.

Notes

1 Manuel Gomez, '3 ans… déjà', *Midi: le magazine pieds-noirs*, 2 (June 1965), 6.
2 Clarisse Buono, *Pieds-noirs de père en fils* (Paris, 2004), p. 100.
3 The term 'holidaymakers' was not actually used by the secretary of state himself. Rather it was the education minister, Pierre Sudreau, who used the term when pressing the secretary of state to clarify his remarks regarding the nature of the migrations from Algeria. Alain Peyrefitte, *C'était de Gaulle* (Paris, 2002), p. 152.
4 The best account of this overall process is Yann Scioldo-Zürcher, *Devenir métropolitain: politique d'intégration et parcours de rapatriés d'Algérie en métropole (1954–2005)* (Paris, 2010).
5 Loi 61–1429, *Journal Officiel de la République française (JORF)*, 27 December 1961, p. 11,959.
6 Todd Shepard, *The Invention of Decolonization: The Algerian War and the Remaking of France* (Ithaca, NY and London, 2006), p. 145.

7   G. de Wailly, Minister of State responsible for Algerian Affairs, cited in Shepard, *The Invention of Decolonization*, p. 146.

8   Shepard, *The Invention of Decolonization*, p. 234.

9   Since Algeria was considered a part of France, the settlers there were initially excluded from the Boulin Law's definition of *rapatriés* on the grounds that any movement by them would technically consist of migrating from one part of the nation to another, rather than 'returning' from an overseas territory.

10 Scioldo-Zürcher, *Devenir métropolitain*, p. 181.

11 The most detailed account of the assistance made available to the *rapatriés* is provided by Scioldo-Zürcher, *Devenir métropolitain*, in particular pp. 161–301.

12 Shepard, *The Invention of Decolonization*, pp. 148–9; Scioldo-Zürcher, *Devenir métropolitain*, p. 158.

13 Scioldo-Zürcher, *Devenir métropolitain*, p. 300.

14 Yann Scioldo-Zürcher, 'Des pratiques administratives inédites pour les français rapatriés d'Algérie (1961–1967)', in *Histoire de l'immigration et question coloniale en France*, ed. by Nancy L. Green and Marie Poinsot (Paris, 2008), p. 99.

15 Philippe Hernandez, 'Quatre pieds-noirs en métropole', *France-Observateur*, 623 (12 April 1962), p. 10; Shepard, *The Invention of Decolonization*, p. 222.

16 Scioldo-Zürcher, *Devenir métropolitain*, p. 242.

17 Anthony Rowley, 'La Réinsertion économique des rapatriés', in *La Guerre d'Algérie et les français*, ed. by Jean-Pierre Rioux (Paris, 1990), p. 349.

18 Rowley, 'La Réinsertion économique des rapatriés', p. 349.

19 Shepard, *The Invention of Decolonization*, p. 239.

20 'Où en sont les rapatriés?', *Cinq colonnes à la une*, aired 3 May 1963 (Channel 1).

21 See, for example, 'Un million de français: les rapatriés d'Algérie l'Île du Rhône', *Sept jours du monde*, aired 15 May 1964 (Channel 1); 'Naissance d'un village: Carnoux', *Cinq colonnes à l'une*, aired 7 October 1966 (Channel 1).

22 Guy Pervillé, 'Les Conditions de départ: l'Algérie', in *Marseille et le choc des décolonisations: les rapatriements 1954–1964*, ed. by Jean-Jacques Jordi and Emile Temime (Aix-en-Provence, 1996), p. 65.

23 Marcel Fenouillet, 'Naissance et histoire de l'ANFANOMA', in *Mémoires de la colonisation: relations colonisateurs-colonisés*, ed. by Régine Goutalier (Paris, 1994), p. 107; Jean-Jacques Jordi, 'Archéologie et structure du réseau de sociabilité rapatrié et pied-noir', *Provence Historique*, 47 (1997), 179.

24 Le Réfugié pied-noir, 'Apolitisme', *France horizon*, 2 (July–August 1957), 1.

25 *France horizon*, 16 (March 1959), 1.

26 Valérie Esclangon-Morin, *Les Rapatriés d'Afrique du Nord de 1956 à nos jours* (Paris, 2007), p. 155.

27 'En attendant le Parlement', *France horizon*, 283 (June 1987), 2.

28 'Tribune libre', *France horizon*, 165 (April 1975), 16.

29 Pierre Battesti, 'Editorial', *France horizon*, 50 (December 1962), 28.

30 'Face aux malheurs des réfugiés et rapatriés toute la nation doit être mobilisée', *France horizon*, 46 (June 1962), 12–13.

31   *France horizon,* 46 (June 1962), 21; *France horizon,* 79 (November 1965), 31.

32   Francine Dessaigne, *Journal d'une mère de famille pied-noir* (Paris, 1962); Francine Dessaigne, *Déracinés!* (Paris, 1964).

33   The ramequin dish contained a poached egg atop the classic *provençale* sauce. Given the emphasis on the Frenchness of the *rapatriés* across the rest of the publication, it is interesting that the column presumed *rapatrié* women would need instruction on the staples of French cuisine. The column only ran for a few months, perhaps suggesting that *rapatrié* women were better versed in the art of managing a 'French' home than *France horizon* had originally presumed.

34   For discussion of this, see Rebecca J. Pulju, *Women and Mass Consumer Society in Postwar France* (Cambridge, 2011), pp. 1–19.

35   The unused door probably linked to another room that had now become a separate dwelling space as houses and apartments were divided up in order to accommodate as many *rapatriés* as possible. Space limitations similarly explain the need for rooms to fulfil multiple purposes. 'Madame Rapatrié s'installe...', *France horizon,* 63 (March 1964), 13; 'Madame Rapatrié s'installe...', *France horizon,* 64 (April 1964), 11.

36   'Un cri d'alarme', *France horizon,* 46 (June 1962), 1.

37   Shepard, *The Invention of Decolonization,* pp. 223–7.

38   'Leur premier hiver en métropole', *France horizon,* 52 (February 1963), 1.

39   Shepard, *The Invention of Decolonization,* pp. 223–7.

40   For further discussion of the relationship between the settlers and France during the colonial period, see Ali Yedes, 'Social Dynamics in Colonial Algeria: The Question of *Pieds-Noirs* Identity', in *French Civilization and its Discontents,* ed. by Tyler Stovall and Georges Van Den Abbeele (Lanham, MD, 2003), pp. 235–49.

41   Roger Fenech, 'Réponse à M. Couste', *C'est nous les Africains* (February 1964), 7.

42   Fenech, 'Réponse à M. Couste', 7; 'Pourquoi allait-il crée *Midi le magazine pieds-noirs*', *Midi le magazine pieds-noirs,* 1 (May 1965), 7.

43   For a detailed discussion of the issues surrounding compensation for the *rapatriés,* see Yann Scioldo-Zürcher, 'The Cost of Decolonisation: Compensating the *Pieds-Noirs*', in *France since the 1970s: History, Politics and Memory in an Age of Uncertainty,* ed. by Emile Chabal (London, 2014), pp. 99–114.

44   *L'indemnisation des spoliations d'Outre Mer* (Paris, 1964), p. iii.

45   I am grateful to James McDougall for his insightful comments on this subject.

46   'Que revenons du congrès de Lyon', *C'est nous les Africains* (January 1964), 2.

47   *L'indemnisation,* p. ii; 'Pour l'indemnisation', *C'est nous les africains* (November 1963), 6.

48   Sung E. Choi, 'From Colonial Settler to Postcolonial Repatriate: The Integration of the French from Algeria, 1962 to the Present', unpublished doctoral dissertation, UCLA, 2007, pp. 184–98.

49   Choi, 'From Colonial Settler', p. 182.

50   Scioldo-Zürcher, *Devenir métropolitain,* p. 113.

51 'Les Rapatriés deuxième partie', *Faire face*, aired 8 December 1961 (Channel 1).

52 This perception was influenced by the strong showing in the first round of the 1965 presidential elections by the far-right candidate and former OAS lawyer Jean-Louis Tixier-Vignancourt in certain southern regions with significant *rapatrié* populations. The political lobbying and voting patterns of *rapatriés* will be discussed further in Chapter 5.

53 Scioldo-Zürcher, *Devenir métropolitain*, p. 354.

54 For further discussion of this process, see Scioldo-Zürcher, *Devenir métropolitain*, pp. 354–76.

55 *France horizon*, 287 (December 1987), 1.

56 In fact, Battesti died the year that the Cercle algérianiste was born. His death was not age-related; he was killed in a car crash.

57 'Manifeste', *L'Algérianiste* (1975).

58 *L'Algérianiste* (1976), 5.

59 Valérie Morin, 'Les "Pieds-noirs": des immigrés de la décolonisation', in Green and Poinsot (eds.), *Histoire de l'immigration*, p. 115.

60 *L'Algérianiste* (1975).

61 Maurice Calmein, 'Continuité et renouveau le phénomène algérianiste', *L'Algérianiste*, 9 (1980), 5.

62 'Création d'un "Cercle Algérianiste"', *France horizon*, 153 (December 1973), 7.

63 Paul-Emile Viard, 'Editorial: ils s'enracinent', *France horizon*, 241 (April 1983), 24.

64 'Lettre ouverte de M. Maurice Calmein', *France horizon*, 244 (July–August 1983), 2.

65 Paul-Emile Viard, 'Réponse à la lettre ouverte de M. Calmein', *France horizon*, 244 (July–August 1983), 24.

66 'En attendant le Parlement', 2–3.

67 Yves Sainsot, 'Notre légitime défense', *France horizon*, 283 (June 1987), 4.

68 The association sent out 2500 individual questionnaires. They also reproduced the survey in their own magazine, in *France horizon*, and in various local and regional newspapers including *L'Opinion indépendant*, *Sud-Ouest* and *L'Aurore*. Maurice Calmein, 'Appellation contrôlée', *L'Algérianiste* (1977), 4–5.

2

The sounds of silence

In the early 1960s, alongside its preoccupations with aid and compensation, ANFANOMA used the pages of its newspaper, *France horizon,* to evoke the plight of the *harkis.* Focusing on their current situation, this coverage emphasised the danger faced by *harkis* and the need for the French authorities to act promptly in order to guarantee the safety of 'these brave men who have always stayed loyal to us'.[1] In ANFANOMA's eyes, the faithful service of the *harkis* to France made it a question of honour and justice that the government take necessary steps to ensure the 'protection' and then 'integration' into France of men they referred to as 'our brothers'.[2] This demand was rendered all the more imperative because, as President Battesti reminded delegates at the association's 1963 conference, more than just 'brothers', the *harkis* were 'Frenchmen like us, often better than us perhaps, because in order to remain French they have paid with their flesh and their blood'.[3] Being French and having that status officially recognised and respected was thus integral to ANFANOMA's discourse concerning both European *rapatriés* and *harkis.*

Beyond the pages of *France horizon,* however, the Frenchness of the *harkis* was repeatedly questioned, not just in cultural and social terms, as was the case for the European settlers, but also at the political and legal level. The consequences of this were far-reaching, as *harkis* and their families found themselves subjected to an all-encompassing process of state control, which differed markedly from the government's response to other *rapatriés.* By placing many *harkis* into camps and other institutional environments upon their arrival in France, the state initiated a pattern of collectivisation, isolation and exceptional treatment that would continue for years, even decades. In contrast to the vocal mobilisation undertaken by members of the European *rapatrié* community, the reaction of *harkis* to this process was to turn inwards and seek refuge in silence. This left a space into which stepped a series of actors, including the French and Algerian governments, Muslim elites, French veterans, and *rapatrié* activists, all of whom offered their own representations of the *harkis*. Collectively, these overlapping and often mutually reinforcing discourses created a simplified, homogenised and politicised portrait of the community that would endure until the mid-1970s.

Citizens, repatriates or refugees? Defining the *harkis*

Battesti's claim that the *harkis* were French was, on the surface, unproblematic. All Algerians had been French citizens since 1944, while the 1958 Constitution of the Fifth Republic guaranteed the same rights and duties to all citizens, irrespective of whether they lived inside or outside the metropole.[4] *Harkis* who came to France were therefore entitled to the same levels and types of aid as any other repatriated citizen as per the terms of the Boulin Law. Yet, over the course of the summer of 1962, the French government deliberately muddied the waters around the legal reality of citizenship for the harkis.[5] After May 1962, for example, government documents increasingly used terms such as 'harkis' or 'refugees', as opposed to 'citizens' or 'rapatriés'. Todd Shepard regards this move as part of an attempt by the state to bring the legal situation into line with popular and official perceptions, which now took to be a matter of 'common sense' the notion that Muslims from Algeria could not be French.[6] Even de Gaulle himself stated, on 25 July 1962, that 'obviously' the term *rapatriés* did not apply to 'Muslims' since 'in their case, we are dealing only with refugees'; a statement that was contrary to both the Evian Accords and the Boulin Law. Such views also stood in direct opposition to long-standing assimilationist rhetoric proffered by the Republic which had insisted that inhabitants of the empire were, or could be, made French.[7]

More than just semantics, this new climate of opinion in which 'Muslims' from Algeria were viewed as irrevocably different had real ramifications for the *harkis*. The Evian Accords had guaranteed the right of all inhabitants of Algeria to keep their French citizenship following independence if they wished to. But realities on the ground rapidly undermined such principles, leading to Ordinance 62–825, which, as of 21 July 1962, differentiated between 'Français de souche européenne' (French of European Origin), or FSE, and 'Français de souche nord africaine' (French of North African Origin), or FSNA. The former were allowed to remain French following independence, while the latter were stripped of their citizenship and informed that to reclaim it they would have to make a formal request in front of a judge in France. Stipulating that the demand for citizenship had to be made in France posed considerable problems for *harkis* given that they could not easily obtain passage from Algeria to the metropole. Initially, applications also had to be made before January 1963, although this deadline was subsequently extended. The state reserved the right to reject the *harkis'* request at the point of registration or at any point for three years afterwards for 'reasons of unworthiness'.[8] Even if, in practice, the process turned out to be largely a formality, with 86 per cent of the approximately 70,000 applications made between 1962 and 1970 being granted, the effect of this law and the manoeuvres that preceded it was to cast the *harkis* as a group apart.[9] Rather than 'returning' citizens, the *harkis* were regarded and treated as 'outsiders whom the French Republic welcomed and assisted only out of charity and only in unavoidable circumstances'.[10] Such perceptions underpinned efforts by senior government figures, particularly the minister for Algerian affairs, Louis Joxe, and the minister of armies, Pierre Messmer, to control the flow of *harkis* into France. This included directives to ensure that those who came to France did so via official channels and were 'genuinely' in danger, as opposed to extremists, of either FLN or OAS persuasion, who might pose a threat to the security of the mainland.[11] Officials also reportedly took factors such as age, fitness and perceived ability to assimilate into account when deciding which *harkis* to admit.[12] The existence of any kind of selection criteria belies the ways in which the treatment of the *harkis* differed from that of European *rapatriés*. As Shepard pointedly notes, the authorities were much more concerned about OAS infiltration within the settler population than among *harkis*, yet there was never any suggestion that certain Europeans should be refused right of entry on grounds of national security.[13]

Cast to one side: the *harkis* in France

The 'otherness' of the *harkis* was confirmed by their treatment once in France. Comparing their fate to that of other *rapatriés*, *harki* descendant Boussad Azni observed: 'We took the same boats, we weren't put up in the same hotels.'[14] Whereas the goal of the state with respect to the European *rapatriés* was to integrate them into the wider French population as quickly as possible, *harkis* and their families were grouped together and funnelled through a series of institutional environments. Their state-directed trajectory included time spent in camps, *hameaux forestiers* (forest hamlets), *cités de transit* (temporary estates) and purpose-built social housing, known as *habitations à loyer modéré* or HLMs. Although each of these settings had different purposes and lifespans, all of them adhered to the principle of treating the *harkis* as a collective entity rather than as individuals.

It is true that not all 'FSNA' who fled Algeria passed through these facilities, nor were they all *harkis*, even using the broad definition of the term. Civilian elites, primarily those holding government positions and those who had obtained French citizenship prior to 1944, were often able to secure passage to France by purchasing plane or boat tickets in the same manner as European *rapatriés*. Upon arrival in France they largely dispersed into the wider population, as did many of the *harkis* who crossed the Mediterranean clandestinely. In contrast, *harkis* who came to France via official channels were kept together; first in Algeria where they spent time holding camps protected by the army while their transport was arranged, and then in France where they were initially placed in the Larzac military camp in the Aveyron department. Created by the army in 1902 as a summer instruction site, Larzac had served various functions, including a Foreign Legion training ground, a German POW camp and, most recently, the largest internment site in France for FLN prisoners.[15] As of 16 May 1962, Larzac's new purpose was to be a transit space for *harkis* and their families who were housed in the site's barracks where possible, but also under canvas on what came to be referred to as the 'plateau of a thousand tents'. Larzac quickly reached and then exceeded its capacity of 3200 places (3620 in exceptional circumstances), forcing the authorities to open an overflow camp on 19 June at Bourg-Lastic (Puy-de-Dôme).[16] Both sites were conceived of as temporary expedients while the authorities considered their next steps.

Overcrowding and the onset of cold weather prompted the creation that autumn of four *camps d'hébergement* (accommodation camps) located in Rivesaltes (Pyrénées-Orientales), Saint-Maurice-l'Ardoise (Gard), Bias (Lot-et-Garonne) and La Rye Vigéant (Vienne). Like Larzac, several of these sites had military origins and a history of housing those deemed 'undesirable' by the Republic at various points, including FLN and OAS prisoners. According to Jeannette Miller, the state used camps for three reasons. First, it was believed that the *harkis* needed time to adjust to the demands of life in metropolitan France and to be prepared adequately for integration. Second, grouping them together was felt to be the most effective way for the military to protect *harkis* from FLN reprisals. It was also thought necessary to exercise vigilance over the *harkis* lest they be recruited into the FLN or OAS, both of which were still active in 1962. Finally, on a very practical level, France's severe post-war housing crisis, exacerbated by the influx of European *rapatriés* whose needs the state prioritised, meant that there was nowhere else to put the *harkis*.[17] In total, an estimated 42,500 people passed through *harki* camps between 1962 and 1969.[18] Rivesaltes, the largest camp, saw approximately 20,000 *harkis* spend time there between September 1962 and its closure in December 1964. Both Saint-Maurice-l'Ardoise and Bias remained open until the mid-1970s, given longer lifespans to accommodate *harkis* deemed 'incapable' of integrating into metropolitan society on grounds such as age, infirmity or illness. In 1974, more than a decade after arriving in France, 16,000 people were still resident on these two sites.[19]

Although large numbers passed through these spaces, only a minority spent a sustained period of time in one or more camp. But departure from the camps often simply signalled a transfer to a different kind of institutional setting such as a forest hamlet. Created via consultation between the secretary of state for *rapatriés* and the ministries of the interior and agriculture, forest hamlets were located in rural areas, often in abandoned villages. They were intended not only to house the *harkis* and supply manpower for the forestry service, but also to stimulate local communities suffering the effects of rural depopulation. Part of the impetus for creating a forest hamlet in Ongles (Alpes-de-Haut-Provence) was that the local school was in danger of closing due to a lack of pupils. For the village's 236 inhabitants the impact of the arrival, in September 1962, of 133 *harkis* was considerable.[20] In total, seventy-five forest hamlets were constructed, although not all were operational simultaneously. The sixty-five in existence in 1965 housed 9720 *harkis* and their families; whereas a decade later both the number of hamlets and their population had roughly halved.[21] An alternative fate for the *harkis* was to be regrouped in one of forty-two purpose-built estates, located on the outskirts of towns such as Amiens, Dreux and Montpellier.[22]

An apprenticeship to France

The movement from camp to forest hamlet to social housing represented not only an improvement in material circumstances – HLM accommodation being superior, certainly at the time of construction, to that of either the camps or the hamlets – but was also taken as an indicator of progressive assimilation. The fact that the *harkis* would need time to become acculturated to life in France was considered axiomatic. Even ANFANOMA, who consistently reminded readers of the Frenchness of the *harkis* in terms of their nationality and loyalties, saw nothing wrong with initially placing them in institutional environments where the integration process could be taken in hand. Yet, although ostensibly geared towards integration, in practice, the organisation and administration of the camps isolated the *harkis*, while simultaneously subjecting them to constant surveillance and interference from state agents. This was reminiscent of the policies of *encadrement* (implying to frame or control) that were prevalent during the colonial era.[23] In both camps and forest hamlets, a director, usually with a military background and experience of the so-called 'Muslim mentality', was appointed to oversee a combination of military and civilian agents tasked with different aspects of the *harkis'* lives. For these men and women, prior experience of working with 'Muslims', preferably in Algeria itself, was a key employment criteria hence the preponderance of former SAS officers and *rapatriés*.

Equipped with everything from schools to medical facilities to post offices, the camps were self-enclosed worlds; 'a perfect example of a total institution' according to the sociologist Tom Charbit.[24] At Rivesaltes, a Bureaux d'Etat (registry) was even installed to enable various official administrative tasks, such as the registration of births, marriages and deaths, or the confirmation of requests for French nationality, to be processed, ostensibly to avoid overburdening local facilities.[25] Serving as a constant reminder of the *harkis'* lack of control over their daily lives was the military discipline to which they were subjected, which included being present for the raising of the flag in the morning, the fact that officials opened and read their post, the set times during which meals, showers and electricity were provided, or simply being housed in rows of identical barracks. For a period of time, some *harkis* were even denied the right to name their own children as social workers imposed French *prénoms* on newborns – the majority of whom were delivered in the camps, rather than in local hospitals – as an outward sign of assimilation.[26] Although the forest hamlets offered *harkis* more freedoms, they also had many features in common with the camps, including the presence of an ex-military or *pied-noir* 'boss' to oversee the lives of the inhabitants and a series of stringent rules to which residents were required to adhere or face immediate expulsion.[27]

Further underlining the differential treatment accorded to the *harkis* was the fact that although they were entitled to the same financial aid as the European *rapatriés*, the state, rather than distributing the money directly to them on an individual or family basis, instead used it to cover the costs of running the camps. The same was true of the forest hamlets where *harki* financial entitlements were used to build and then operate the sites, even though it was often the *harkis* themselves, working as unpaid labourers, who did the actual construction.[28] As a 1962 report from Comité des affaires algériennes explained, 'not being adapted to European life, it would not be appropriate to give to these Muslims the aid planned for *rapatriés* on an individual basis'. Instead, they should 'continue to benefit from a certain *encadrement* in terms of their work and housing' which would necessitate ring-fencing money to finance their collective settlement and integration.[29]

These resettlement costs also included social and cultural 'apprentice-ships', the end goal of which was to enable the *harkis* to discard their 'primitive' and 'archaic' customs in favour of French mores.[30] Press reports of women removing their veils on the boats that transported them across the Mediterranean in 1962 after being told that 'wearing the veil would only make their assimilation harder' suggest that this process began even before the *harkis* reached France.[31] In the camps and forest hamlets, as-similation efforts took a more systematic form, targeting specific sections of the *harki* population in different ways. Children were a key focus, lead-ing to the rapid creation of educational facilities. Even in the transit camp of Larzac within forty-eight hours, seven teachers, all military personnel, had taken charge of five hundred pupils.[32] Similarly, from 1963, Rivesaltes ran forty classes using fifty-one teachers, twenty-nine of them military personnel. Reports indicated that although a few children were already in possession of academic skills and qualifications, most had no previous education. Older children attended the Centre de promotion sociale et d'initiation professionnel where 600 of them learned to 'live like work-ers'.[33] Adult males were offered remedial educational classes, alongside 'initiation into the European way of life', where financial incentives were sometimes used to ensure regular attendance. The most pressing con-cern with regard to adult men, however, was employment since, as *Le Monde* reported with reference to Larzac, 'idleness is never a good idea'.[34] Various training programmes were provided within the camps. La Rye, in particular, became a destination for those considered fit for work, while employment in the forestry service was one of the principal selling points of the hamlets as far as the authorities were concerned.[35] Having a job was equally a priority for *harkis*, who were not only bored, but also humili-ated by their state of financial dependence. A 1965 report indicated some success in securing jobs for *harkis*, noting that 13,001 heads of families had been redirected into employment. Of these, 7053 had been found work in the industrial sector, 2189 in the forestry service, and 1634 in agriculture.[36]

When it came to women, the state also insisted that they be offered train-ing, not for the world of work, but rather for the home. Classes covered a variety of practical domestic skills such as sewing European-style clothes with a machine and French cooking. Language lessons were also provided as many women spoke little or no French. These initiatives closely paralleled ones directed at Algerian labourers and their families by social workers during the War of Independence which had sought to help them adapt to life in the metropole as a way to foster attachment to France and thus diminish support for Algerian independence.[37] This focus on Algerian women as conduits of modernity for the wider family unit was replicated with the *harki* community, as were many of the methods. The goals were also similar: even if the *harkis* did not need to be lured away from supporting Algerian independence, their ascription to French values and norms was deemed precarious, in need of constant monitoring and encouragement. Through educational and social initiatives, offered in the wider context of controlled living environments, the ethnic, cultural and religious differences that distinguished *harkis* from the majority French population were supposed to be, if not erased, then certainly confined to the private sphere.

Creating a narrative of progress

Access to the *harkis* during this period was strictly controlled. In the same way that the *harkis* needed permission to leave the camps, even for short periods of time, outsiders required authorisation to enter. The media, in particular, were kept at arms-length during the initial phase of the camps, allowed in only once it was felt that a suitable degree of order had been established. It was therefore not until March 1963 that journalists from the regional paper, *L'Indépendant*, were permitted onto the Rivesaltes site. The resultant four articles penned between 22 and 28 March by Claude Coueffec presented Rivesaltes as a smoothly functioning 'space of apprenticeship to citizenship and French culture' where *harkis* felt reassured by their treatment and by their new surroundings.[38] This was in keeping with previous press coverage of the Larzac camp in 1962, which had emphasised the 'humanity' with which the *harkis* had been treated.[39] Such reports noted an absence of 'bitterness' or 'acrimony' on the part of the grateful *harkis* who were presented as happy to put their trust in the army which had already saved their lives by bringing them to France.[40]

The narrative constructed for public consumption by the state and the media was therefore one of progress in which the *harkis* were shown to be gradually integrating by absorbing and then outwardly demonstrating French culture. This was true of *C'étaient les harkis*, a 15-minute broadcast within the *Cinq colonnes à la une* series that aired in June 1963. In this, the first piece to focus on the *harkis* since their arrival in France, and one of only a handful of programmes to feature the *harkis* prior to the 1990s, the state was depicted as proactively facilitating integration through a variety of endeavours. The extract opened with a shot of a *harki* passing before a judge, responding affirmatively when asked if he would like to retain his French nationality. This was followed by footage of various activities designed to hasten the assimilation process, including writing classes for men and lessons on housework where women apprehensively confronted a series of electrical appliances. The closing shots lingered on a *harki* family installed in a forest hamlet in a formerly abandoned village near Carcassone. Their children, named Gisèle and Jacques, were shown to be at ease conversing in French, implying that, for this family at least, the seeds of successful assimilation had been sown.[41]

'A brotherhood of misfortune'

C'étaient les harkis and other mainstream media portrayals did not ignore the difficulties faced by *harkis*. However, these were mostly cast as temporary obstacles that could and would be overcome through careful nurturing by the state. In contrast, recollections within the *harki* community, particularly among younger generations, painted a much more negative picture of these years. In addition to resentment at the controlling and quasi-colonial way in which they were treated, these sentiments were closely linked to the infrastructure of the camps, which were woefully inadequate for the demands being placed upon them. This was partly because the scale of the *harki* 'repatriation', as with that of the settlers, caught the authorities unprepared. Commenting on the large numbers housed under canvas rather than in permanent structures, a report by the Service d'accueil et de reclassement des Français d'Indochine et musulmans (SFIM) on Rivesaltes in October 1962 made it clear that families with young children 'absolutely cannot remain any longer in tents whose protection against the rain is illusory'.[42] Yet, conditions were little better in the barracks, into which the *harkis* were eventually moved by January 1963, with neither heat nor electricity. Even after the government unlocked funds for renovations in a bid to avoid negative publicity significant issues remained.[43] Overcrowding was a persistent problem with all the camps regularly exceeding their maximum capacity. At its mostly densely populated in the first week of December 1962, the 8885 inhabitants of the Rivesaltes camp considerably outnumbered the 6262 residents of the nearby town.[44] One of the principal consequences of overcrowding was ill health, caused by a combination of inadequate shelter, insanitary conditions and proximity, which ensured rapid transmission of diseases such as TB.[45] As the SFIM inspector at Rivesaltes highlighted, 'no social advancement activity can be effectively undertaken given the current living conditions of the *harkis*'.[46]

One result of the miserable situation in which the *harkis* found themselves was the formation of a collective bond. The *harki* 'community', like the *pied-noir* 'community', was not a natural phenomenon. During the war, 'harki' was an occupation, and quite a diverse one depending on whether you served in a GAD, as a *moghazni*, or as an actual *harki*. It was also often an activity that was undertaken for a limited period of time. Only in the post-1962 period did the term 'harki' come to signify a communally ascribed identity.[47] That *harkis* were recruited from a wide geographical area was reflected in the mixture of ethnicities, regions and dialects found within the artificial groupings created by the camps. Nonetheless, the shared experiences of loss, isolation and deprivation forged a powerful sense of unity and an awareness of the importance of mutual aid, particularly in the absence of external sources of support. Quotidian difficulties served further to erase distances between people, creating a sense of fraternity, even if as one *harki* descendant explained, it was a 'a brotherhood of misfortune'.[48] Community, in this case, was founded upon recent shared experiences, rather than on an innate sense of identification. This is not, however, to imply that the *harki* community so defined was either a homogenous, or an always harmonious, entity. As Tom Charbit reminds us, although there were commonalities among the *harkis*, there were also considerable differences – socio-economic, physical, personal – which affected the nature of their experience and treatment in France. The assessment by the authorities of a male *harkis'* aptitude for work, for example, shaped which institutional environment he and his family were placed in and the length of time they remained there, as did whether or not the *harki* had a family in the first place.[49] In examining the experiences of the *harkis*, it is therefore important to bear in mind the diversity of individuals within the collective.

Questions without responses: the silence of the *harkis*

Whereas bodies such as ANFANOMA rapidly mobilised European *rapatriés* in order to demand practical action from the state on their behalf, the *harki* community reacted differently. The most widely attested to characteristic of the *harkis* in the 1960s and 1970s was their silence, with respect both to their recent past and their current situation. Fatima Besnaci-Lancou explained how, once in France, her parents 'never again spoke of our past, as if our country of origin had never existed'.[50] In contrast to the *pieds-noirs*, there was no outpouring of memoirs, nor any national associations created to campaign for an improvement in their material conditions. In part, this was because *harkis* faced a range of linguistic, cultural and economic barriers that inhibited the transmission of memory. Those who arrived in France at the end of the war were overwhelmingly of rural origin, unskilled and illiterate, often with only a limited grasp of spoken French. Thrown into a completely alien world, simply adjusting to their new lives was a full-time occupation for most. Even those who possessed the advantage of being able to speak, read and write French discovered quickly that finding people willing to listen when you are part of a marginalised, socially disempowered minority was no easy task.

This situation was compounded by the physical isolation of the *harkis*, who were placed out of sight of the majority population. Many *harkis* furthermore spent time in several institutional locations before finally achieving permanent settlement. A typical trajectory was that of the Kerchouche family, who spent time in Bourg-Lastic, Rivesaltes, Bias and a forest hamlet in the Lozère department, before eventually moving into their own home in 1974, twelve years after they arrived in France.[51] This disruptive and often distressing process, which appeared to operate at random as far as the *harkis* were concerned, worked against the construction of social frameworks of memory, which usually require group and spatial stability.[52] Isolation was exacerbated by strictly controlled access to the *harkis*, which limited their interactions with autochthonous French people essentially to the staff overseeing them. Presented with few opportunities to engage even with those French people who lived in relative proximity to them, *harkis* were effectively segregated from mainstream society; a practice which undermined the government's claim to be helping the *harkis* with their 'apprenticeship' to France in a manner conducive to their eventual integration. Miller is emphatic about the ways in which the state's treatment of the *harkis* subjected them to an 'exilic existence' that 'socially excluded them from French society'. She also highlights how this initial isolation created a pattern that would be replicated over the longer term, ensuring that, even after moving into HLM apartments or their own homes, marginalisation, both physical and social, remained a significant part of the *harki* experience.[53] This is supported by *harki* daughter Sylvie T., who noted that had the state 'done its job' in terms of integration, being the child of a *harki* today would be nothing more than 'a detail' rather than a significant part of her identity.[54]

There was, additionally, a cultural component to silence linked to the importance of paternal deference, notions of honour and gender roles within Algerian families. In this context, men were required to provide for and preside over their families; they were not expected to be emotionally open or demonstrative. As one *harki* daughter explained, 'in our culture ... children don't ask questions of their parents. Especially not daughters of their fathers'. More persistently inquisitive children were rebuffed with the maxim 'the past is dead'.[55] According to the anthropologist Vincent Crapanzano, silence, particularly in the face of hardship, is a masculine virtue among Algerians, one which *harki* men refused to surrender.[56] The consequence for the woman quoted above was that she grew up 'with these questions without answers'.[57] Emotional distance was frequently compounded by the physical absence of fathers, who, if they were able to find employment, tended to work long hours and six days a week. However, the emasculated environment in which the majority of male *harkis* were forced to live undermined this authoritative ideal. Constrained by and dictated to by forces beyond their control, rendered passive and dependent outside their homes, many under- or unemployed and thus unable to support their families, or even to occupy themselves during the day, *harki* men suffered 'a veritable psychological earthquake' that inevitably affected their relationships within the family circle.[58]

A further obstacle to the organisation and transmission of memory was the lack of motivation among *harkis* to undertake such a task. One of the principal reasons for this was the fear that pervaded the community. The environments in which they lived exported the mentalities and power structures of colonial Algeria, while also rendering the *harkis* dependent upon the French authorities to meet their most basic needs.[59] In these circumstances, the potential for abuses of power by those in charge was considerable. Condemning the mentality that reigned in Bias, one doctor – assigned to the camp for three months at the age of twenty-five, but who ended up working with *harkis* for thirty years – accused the *pied-noir* staff of treating the *harkis* 'like natives': 'they belittled them, manipulated them, humiliated them. They were thrilled to have brought a morsel of colonial Algeria back with them'.[60]

Inside the self-enclosed worlds of the camps and forest hamlets with their vastly unequal power structures, the threat of punishment was potent and used regularly to keep the *harkis* 'in line'. Insults, arbitrary discipline and deprivations were predominantly suffered in silence by *harkis* because there was no other option, no external recourse. Sanctions ranged from being deprived of food, money, or privileges, to expulsion from the camp. Older children could be sent to one of three disciplinary youth centres in Pau, Moumar and Gelos (Pyrénées-Atlantiques). There are also accounts of adults, like Boussad Azni's father, being committed to Candélie, the *harki* psychiatric hospital, in retaliation for rule breaking or insubordination.[61] Being deported was, however, the ultimate threat. Upon discovering the living conditions at Rivesaltes, Dalila Kerchouche's parents dared not complain because they were 'terrified by the idea that the soldiers would send them back to Algeria'.[62] These fears followed the *harkis* far beyond the walls of the camps. Almost thirty years after leaving the camps, when Kerchouche told her mother of her intention to write a book tracing their family history, she was surprised by her reaction: '[My mother] said to me, fearfully: "And if they reproach us?" Me, outraged: "If anyone has reproaches to make, it's you, not them".' Only as Kerchouche learns about her parents' history does she begin to understand the source of their ongoing anxieties.[63]

These fears existed alongside the trauma of the exceptionally violent end of French Algeria, which left both physical and mental scars. The majority of *harkis* fled, fearing, with great justification, for their lives. Even though they were thankful to have survived, no *harki* emerged unscathed. Many had lost family members, or had witnessed scenes of atrocity, while others had themselves been the victims of violence, including torture. This was in addition to the trauma of having to leave their homes, belongings and, often, members of their family behind with little or no forewarning and frequently at great personal risk. The legacies of these experiences manifested themselves in a variety of ways, including in the bar of the Bias camp where the *harkis* 'hung out all day'. Here, according to Azni, 'They drank, played cards, argued, fought amongst themselves. All this violence in them was the echo of past violence they had suffered, but turned back against themselves. It was a kind of slow suicide'.[64] Among the reasons given for admitting sixty-nine *harkis* to the Candélie psychiatric hospital in 1969, one finds listed conditions including schizophrenia, manic depression, chronic delirium and alcoholism; domestic violence was also a noted phenomenon within the camps.[65] Even if not at this extreme end of the spectrum, many *harkis* were in a state of shock. Traumatic experiences tend to inhibit expression, making it unsurprising that any process of mourning or coming to terms with the past was carried out in silence during these years.[66] Speaking about the camps he grew up in, Azni described them as full of people 'imprisoned inside their thoughts more surely than behind the barbed wire'.[67]

These silences did not mean the *harkis* had forgotten, not least because many bore physical reminders of their ordeals. Instead, silence was used as a coping mechanism. A former teacher who worked with the *harki*s in Manosque (Alpes-de-Haut-Provence) felt that the past was simply 'too hard [for them] to bear and even to explain.'[68] This was particularly the case when, according to the dominant narratives of the time, the 'choice' the *harki*s had made cast them as either Algerian traitors or French patriots. Of course, the reality of the situation was infinitely more complex and the notion of 'choice' distinctly problematic. Yet whatever the nuances of individual histories, the years 1954–62 were, for the majority of *harki*s, a past that was difficult for them to understand and assume themselves, let alone communicate to others. Upon reaching the age of thirty, one man asked his *harki* father to tell him about what had happened in Algeria. His father replied: 'What do you want me to tell you? I don't know myself what happened and you want me to tell it to you?'[69]

The diverse reasons which underpinned engagement with the French and the fact that the decision was often not one over which the *harki* was master, left auxiliaries with the conundrum of how to criticise their treatment by the French state from the position of having served France sometimes as a last resort, sometimes against their will, and almost always with less patriotic fervour and commitment than the pro-*Algérie française* lobby claimed. On a more personal level, *harki*s faced the difficulty of conveying the context in which their 'choices' were made to children who were either too young at the time to appreciate such things, or who had been born after 1962. It was even harder to rationalise such decisions given the circumstances in which *harki*s now found themselves. Many were afraid to even attempt to justify themselves to their children who had to live with the consequences of their actions.

A further complication lay in the label of 'traitor' that was originally attached to the *harki*s by the Algerian government, but which quickly radiated outwards into public consciousness. An opinion poll, published in *Le Monde* on 27 February 1992, revealed that the FLN's struggle during the War of Independence was understood by the French to be analogous to the actions of the Resistance during the Second World War. In such a schema, the *harki*s were assimilated to 'collabos'.[70] Some *harki*s appear to have internalised these perceptions, coming to see themselves as the traitors other accused them of being, often with serious consequences. Although Fatima's husband ostensibly blamed his poor health in France on the climate, his wife believed that he was 'above all, sick from being judged badly in Algeria like in France'.[71] The potency of this stigmatisation led many fathers to attempt to protect their children from guilt by association, surrounding them instead with a 'halo of silence'.[72] As one *harki* told Crapanzano, 'I don't want my children to know what I cannot forget.'[73]

Official representations of the *harkis*: between silence and vilification

These factors came together in a range of different combinations for the *harkis*, but the collective end result was the same: a silence surrounding the past so complete that one *harki* daughter wondered 'if our parents hadn't lost their memory?'[74] Yet, even if there had been a willingness among the *harkis* to speak out about their past, or to advocate for action to remedy their present circumstances, they faced an absence of supportive frameworks into which to insert any potential discourses. On the Algerian side, the *harkis* were confronted by the official narrative of the FLN government, which legitimated itself by propagating the myth of an entire nation collectively rising up as part of a consciously nationalist struggle for independence. The logic of the revolutionary mantra 'one hero, the people' dictated the denial of internal divisions or any substantial pro-French element, relegating the *harkis* to the role of a minority of 'traitors'. There has been little evolution in the public stance towards the *harkis* since 1962. The term 'harki' was and still is used against those deemed to have betrayed the Revolution through their collaboration with the French, but also more broadly to designate internal 'enemies' against whom the nation is encouraged to unite. Still forbidden from returning to Algeria, even for visits, in 2000 the current president, Abdelaziz Bouteflika, made it clear during his state trip to France that 'the time has not yet come for visits from the *harkis,* it's exactly like if you asked a Frenchman of the Resistance to shake the hand of a *collabo*'.[75]

Of course, not all *harkis* left for France at the end of the war, many remained, unwilling or unable to abandon their lives in Algeria. The experiences of these men and their families are difficult to trace, but the fact that laws still exist which discriminate against former *harkis*, banning them from particular occupations and from holding public office, gives a sense of the stigma that remains. This cycle of discrimination is perpetuated by school textbooks, the gatekeepers of official history and, as such, tightly controlled by the government. Such texts portray the *harkis* in a deeply negative light, including describing them as 'those who sold their national conscience for money, positions and titles'.[76] When not being denigrated for political purposes by the regime, the most common reaction in Algeria with respect to the *harkis* is simply silence. This is particularly true of the *harkis* themselves, who, for obvious reasons, do not wish to draw attention to this element of their past.

On the opposite side of the Mediterranean, the *harkis* faced 'a complicit silence', as a Gaullist vision of decolonisation took root that presented the process as a historical inevitability that allowed France to relieve itself of the burdensome colonial commitments and focus on modernisation.[77] Turning the page on the past was made a priority and the *harkis* became one of the principal casualties of the resultant state-sponsored erasure. Beginning with de Gaulle, this attitude extended into the presidency of Valéry Giscard d'Estaing and, although things did begin to change under François Mitterrand, it was not until Jacques Chirac took power in 1995 that the prevailing orthodoxy was significantly challenged. The silence emanating from the French state was further compounded by the fact that many *harki* children who grew up in the camps in the 1960s and 1970s also received their education there rather than attending local schools. Those who did receive a mainstream education would still not have gleaned much about their family history, since the War of Independence was not introduced into the curriculum until 1980 for students in the *troisième* year of secondary school and 1983 for final-year *baccalauréat* students. Even then, textbooks either omitted the *harkis* altogether, or mentioned them only briefly, usually as an appendix to the *pied-noir* departure in 1962.[78]

Yet, this cultural absence coexisted with an extensive preoccupation with managing the practical situation of the *harkis* to the point that one *harki* descendant, M. K., felt being forgotten about would have been the preferable option. 'Me, I would have liked them to forget me, to forget my father, for France and Algeria to forget us' since '[a]t least then we could have been like the *pieds-noirs*', in the sense of being left alone to get on with integration in their own way.[79] Although the state was willing to provide limited physical space for the *harki* community, albeit within carefully delineated parameters, there was no comparable willingness to provide cultural or memorial space for them. This was not specific to the *harkis*. In this period, the state was not prepared to engage in public discussion or commemoration of the War of Independence with any group connected to the conflict. But, unlike the *pieds-noirs, harkis* lacked the necessary economic, political, social and cultural capital to make their voices heard independently. There was no comparable body to ANFANOMA to act as an emissary or a buffer between the *harkis* and the state. ANFANOMA's occasional pieces evoking the situation of the *harkis* and their rhetorical demands for a certain level of treatment were in no way comparable to the efforts they undertook on behalf of the European *rapatriés*.

The silence of the state was also replicated within the French media, which could potentially have functioned as an alternative vector of transmission. At the close of the Algerian War, the mainstream press evinced little interest in the *harkis*. Although major daily newspapers such as *Le Monde* and *Le Figaro* ran occasional pieces on the *harkis* in the summer of 1962, particularly relating to the camps, the national press were principally focused on the transition to power taking place in Algeria, the hunt for and subsequent capture of Raoul Salan plus other remnants of the OAS, and the influx of European *rapatriés*. Even at a local level, the *harkis* did not merit much coverage. The regional paper *L'Indépendant*, whose geographical remit included the Rivesaltes camp, ran a 'Rapatrié' section for a full year, yet never once mentioned the *harkis*.[80] Visual images were even rare than text. The *Cinq colonnes et la une* clip from April 1962 showing a young, bespectacled *harki* anxiously predicting that 'there will be scores to settle' for having served under the French flag, has become ubiquitous in evocations of the fate of the *harkis* largely because there is so little other footage available.[81] For Béatrice Fleury-Vilatte, the 'gap' in public memory when it comes to the *harkis* is primarily explicable by the fact that the vast majority departed either under the auspices of the army, who were anxious not to attract attention to what they were doing, or clandestinely. This stands in contrast to the extensively documented departure of the European *rapatriés*.[82]

Brothers through blood spilled

The lack of supportive *cadres sociaux*, plus the many obstacles – practical, cultural and psychological – to the articulation and transmission of the past confined the *harki* community to silence in the postwar years. In the absence of any vocal mobilisation from the *harkis*, a series of self-appointed spokespeople external to the community stepped forward to offer their own representations. In particular, the former Muslim elite of colonial Algeria, French veterans and *pied-noir* activists all took it upon themselves to speak for the *harkis*. By professing a connection to and sense of responsibility for the *harkis*, these three groups created mutually reinforcing and thus powerful discourses. Enjoying material and cultural advantages not available to the majority of former auxiliaries or their descendants, these actors were able to dominate the portrayal of the *harkis* in the years immediately following Algerian independence.

One of the most prominent champions of the *harki* cause in the immediate postwar years was the Bachaga Saïd Boualam.[83] Born in 1906, the Bachaga Boualam came from family of Muslim notables with a long history of co-operation with the French. In 1946, after a twenty-year career, the he left the French army in order to administer his family's estate in the Ouarsenis region, presiding over 33,000 hectares and approximately

15,000 people, predominantly of the Beni Boudouane tribe.[84] The Bachaga Boualam entered the National Assembly in 1958 as a deputy, rising to the position of vice-president, which he held until 1962. During the War of Independence he was an ardent supporter of the French cause and, in July 1956, was placed in charge of the *harka* for his region. At the end of the conflict, the French government evacuated the Bachaga Boualam and his immediate family, a sizable entourage of sixty-seven people, installing them in a village, Mas Thibert, in the Bouches-du-Rhône department of southern France.[85] Mas Thibert rapidly became a focal point for *harkis*, to the extent that local authorities were forced to intervene in order to manage the number of new arrivals. In 1964, they created the Mazet estate, an agglomeration of prefabricated buildings where approximately sixty families were able to rent houses for one symbolic franc for a period of fifteen years. As with other state-created environments for the *harkis*, facilities at Mazet left a lot to be desired, even after improvements, such as the addition of classrooms and a cafeteria, although, unlike the camps, the space was not enclosed by barbed wire.[86]

In spite of the physical shortcomings of this environment, proximity to the Bachaga Boualam offered the *harkis* a reassuring sense of continuity with their previous lives, including with the customs of respect and loyalty that had prompted many to enrol in his *harka* in the first place.[87] The authority, both administrative and spiritual, exercised by the Bachaga Boualam in Algeria was thus transported with him to France where he remained a venerated figure among *harkis* from his former fief for many years. As one of the most visible Algerian Muslims in France, the Bachaga Boualam was widely regarded as the figurehead of the *harki* community by officials and the media; a role he actively embraced. Charismatic, articulate and politically savvy, the Bachaga Boualam used his reputation and means to campaign on behalf of 'his' *harkis*. Whether denouncing the government's 'politics of abandonment' to the National Assembly, criticising conditions in the camps, forging alliances with veterans and the *pieds-noirs*, or penning three books in as many years setting out his interpretation of the service rendered by the *harkis* to France and the duty of care owed them as a result, the Bachaga Boualam was tireless in his advocacy until ill health forced him to retire in the mid-1970s.[88]

The Bachaga Boualam viewed the *harkis* as the logical continuation of a long tradition of French military service that had taken their fathers to Monte Cassino and their grandfathers to Verdun. Pointing to their chests full of medals as evidence of the 'courage' and 'worth' of the *harkis* as combatants, the Bachaga Boualam underlined the sacrifices his own family and others had historically been called upon to make. 'Boualams have laid down their lives in the four corners of the globe in order to defend France' he passionately declared, 'and after that they dare to say that we are not French?'[89] The right to be and to remain French had therefore been earned through 'blood spilled' on various battlefields. This included during the War of Independence when the combination of service and sacrifice created a 'debt', which, the Bachaga Boualam argued, the French authorities failed to honour in 1962 when the army did not intercede to protect its auxiliaries.[90]

Indigenous elites like the Bachaga Boualam often benefited from and thus supported the presence of the French in Algeria. Echoing *pied-noir* narratives, the Bachaga Boualam evoked a pre-1954 atmosphere of harmonious inter-ethnic co-existence, casting Algeria as a country that would have been nothing without French impetus, but which was collectively constructed amidst an atmosphere of fraternal co-operation for the benefit of all.[91] Some mistakes were acknowledged, particularly not integrating more Algerians into French administrative structures. Such errors were, however, attributed to out-of-touch politicians in Paris, conveniently exculpating the *pieds-noirs* and notables such as the Bachaga Boualam from blame for the discriminatory aspects of the colonial system.[92] Out of this perception came the argument that the people of Algeria did not want independence, merely more autonomy and equality within the framework of continued affiliation with France.

Given this history, enrolling on the French side when the War of Independence broke out was considered to be the natural course of action by the Bachaga Boualam, who presented the decision of the *harkis* as a freely made choice. This allowed the war to be cast as 'an uprising against cut-throats and thieves, and the total fraternisation of Muslims and Frenchmen against this explosion of hatred'.[93] The strength of this pro-French sentiment, combined with the vastly superior resources at France's disposal, meant that, for the Bachaga Boualam, the eventual loss of the war could only be explained by weak-willed government in Paris. This set up a convenient opposition between the treachery of France in its short-term political incarnation and *la France profonde* to which the *harkis* and the Muslim elite remained loyal. 'We do not confuse true France with the one that betrayed us', explained the Bachaga Boualam; a distinction that allowed him to decry the abandonment of the *harkis* without jeopardising his argument that they had been right to choose the French side and deserved to be compensated for their sacrifices.[94]

As part of an educated and privileged minority, the Bachaga Boualam was in no way representative of the mass of former auxiliaries on whose behalf he spoke. He was also something of an anomaly within his own milieu since early *harki*-orientated activism was characterised by a lack of elite participation. In 1975, Ahmed Kaberseli, president of one of the rare *harki*-led associations, the Mouvement d'assistance et de défense des rapatriés d'Afrique du Nord (MADRAN), sent 130 letters to prominent French Muslims asking if they would be willing to assist the *harki* population; he received only two affirmative replies.[95] This potential isolation was, however, offset by the links the Bachaga Boualam was able to forge with other groups who took an interest in the fate of the *harkis*, particularly veterans and the *pieds-noirs*, both of whom advanced complementary discourses.

Brothers in arms

French soldiers who had served in Algeria concerned themselves with the *harkis* on the basis of their status as 'brothers in arms'. Practical support and political lobbying were undertaken by bodies such as the Association des anciens des affaires algériennes, composed of former SAS officers. Another significant organisation was the Comité Parodi, which was created on the initiative of young officers who had served in Algeria and was headed by the vice-president of the Conseil d'État, Alexandre Parodi. Among other issues, such groups campaigned to ensure that *harkis* were officially recognised as veterans and thus given access to pensions and other associated benefits; something the government only conceded in 1974. At the individual level, devotion to the *harkis* was exemplified by men such as Yvan Durand, a SAS officer in the Palestro region who resigned his commission in 1962 in order to secure passage to France for the *harkis* of his unit without contravening the orders of his superiors. Through his contacts in France and Algeria, Durand was able to arrange for a select group of twenty-five *harki* families, 133 people in total, to be transported to France where, after a brief spell in Larzac, they were installed in a specially created forest hamlet in Ongles (Alpes-de-Haute-Provence). Mirroring the biographies of other individuals who remained involved with the *harkis* beyond 1962, Durand went on to serve as an inspector with the SFIM where he was involved in the creation of several other hamlets, as well as training centres for *harkis* in Ongles and Salérans.[96]

In the course of their activities, these groups and individuals advanced a particular historical reading that cast the *harkis* as loyal soldiers who chose to fight for France because they wished to remain French. Exemplifying this trend was Georges Jasseron's series of brief portraits published in 1965 under the title *Les Harkis en France, scènes et témoignages*, whose content was strongly reminiscent of descriptions offered by the Bachaga Boualam. It is interesting to note that many of the men featured by Jasseron were not *harkis* at all, but rather career soldiers such as 'simple and brave' Saïd, who had been with the army since 1942, or Yayi, perpetually 'courageous and solid' whether fighting in Indo-China or in Algeria.[97] Placing *harkis* within this continuum of combat ignored not only the particular factors behind the creation of *harka* units, but also the very different fates that hinged upon whether an individual's contract with the army in 1962 was as a regular soldier or as an auxiliary. Accounts by Jasseron and other French soldiers in this vein thus erased the historically specific capacities and contexts in which *harkis* had been enrolled, replacing them instead with a series of generic attributes supposedly common to all Algerians who had served. Typical of such portrayals was Abdallah who 'has served France and served her well. His citations, his numerous wounds testify to this ... This France, he loves her, reveres her even, and is ready to fight and to die for her.'[98] It was qualities such as these that made the 'abandonment' of the *harkis* by politicians in 1962 particularly galling for French soldiers, bringing dishonour upon both the army and themselves.

The desire to alleviate their sense of shame by emphasising a personal commitment to 'their' *harkis* underpinned the activism of many French soldiers, whether this entailed helping *harkis* escape to France or aiding them once there. This was the self-proclaimed impetus for a group of sol-diers brought to trial in 1962 on charges of inciting disobedience for their efforts to save *harkis* by bringing them to France. As one of the accused, Jacques Lethiec, explained in his deposition: 'these men, we abandoned them, often with a guilty conscience ... but, to lighten our conscience, we tried to come to their aid.'[99] Georges Fleury was one of several former sol-diers to pay tribute to the *harkis* while also publicising their present-day plight when he dedicated his book, *Le combat des harkis*, 'To all the Muslims who remained loyal to us ... in spite of everything!'[100] Returning the compliment and emphasising the close links between the two groups, the Bachaga Boualam argued that if the *harkis* were a valuable and reli-able force this was owing, in no small part, to 'exemplary officers who had a passionate love for their men and their families' and who lived along-side them in Algeria, 'sharing their joys and their sorrows'.[101]

Believing that the experience of fighting with the *harkis* had given them a privileged insight into the 'true' sentiments and motivation of the auxiliaries, French soldiers assumed responsibility for 'their' *harkis*; speaking on behalf of those they deemed incapable of speaking for them-selves. The paternalism that frequently characterised relations between

officers and *harkis* in the Algeria was thus transported back to the mainland, while the close involvement of officers like Durand in the postcolonial trajectory of the *harkis* perpetuated such connections and attendant
attitudes. But just as the *harkis* were only part of the French forces during the conflict, after the war they formed only a fraction of the agenda
of the main veterans' associations. Attention within bodies such as the
Union nationale des combattants en Afrique du Nord (UNC-AFN) and
their left-wing rival the Fédération nationale de anciens combattants en
Algérie, Maroc et Tunisie (FNACA) was directed towards the *harkis* only
sporadically, and then always as a distinct and separate category.[102] Even
the existence of specifically dedicated associations and the support of
high-profile figures such as General Maurice Faivre and Colonel Bernard
Moinet produced few tangible gains for the *harkis* in the decades immediately following the war.

Brothers in exile

In conjunction with the Bachaga Boualam and veterans, *pied-noir* activists focused attention on the *harkis*, whom they characterised as 'brave'
and 'faithful' soldiers who 'chose France'.[103] *Rapatrié* associations like
ANFANOMA furthermore emphasised what they perceived as the similarities between the experiences of *pieds-noirs* and *harkis*: both comprised
groups of proud citizens who had ardently supported the continuation of
French Algeria, but whose wishes were thwarted by the government of
the day, particularly by de Gaulle, whose deceit and subsequent abandonment of the two communities forced them to flee in fear of their lives.
Together these common experiences and a shared status as Frenchmen
underpinned *pied-noir* campaigns to ensure that the *harkis* were appro-
priately recognised and treated by the state. As associations turned to culturally orientated activism in the 1970s, concerns regarding the material
circumstances of the *harkis* were increasingly accompanied by calls make
known the history of the community. This was the ambition of the Cercle
algérianiste's Jo Sohet, who, in 1979, declared his intention to play his part
in 'breaking the silence' surrounding this past, so as to 'pay homage and,
above all, bring justice to the *harkis*, brothers and companions in arms
through free choice, soldiers of France'.[104]

In general, the passion of such declarations outstripped the actual
amount of attention paid to the *harkis*. Although *pied-noir* associations
were careful to mention the *harkis*, particularly on occasions such as
annual conferences, anniversaries or the dedication of monuments, in the
1960s and early 1970s the *harkis* were a relatively marginal concern. They

were also a strategically motivated concern. From exile to displacement, discrimination and deprivation, whatever the *pieds-noirs* had suffered, the experiences of the *harkis* had been, and continued to be, much worse. For *pied-noir* associations the situation of the *harkis* therefore functioned as 'an amplification of their own', underscoring their case for the terrible and unnecessary suffering produced by the end of French Algeria, as much as it was a cause to be pursued in its own right.[105] The *harkis* also provided an alibi against charges of racism and exploitation levelled at *pieds-noirs*. The decision of over 200,000 Muslims – a figure that appears to amalgamate the approximately 120,000 auxiliaries with the 60,000 Algerians conscripted into the army – to risk their lives in order to defend French Algeria was regularly invoked as proof of the fraternal nature of the colony. This fraternity furthermore crossed the Mediterranean with Jasseron describing a *pied-noir* café in Rouen where European *rapatriés* gathered to 'recreate the ambiance of lost Algeria'. *Harkis* were 'naturally' present on such occasions where shared contemporary hardships made the two communities 'feel even more like brothers than in the old days'.[106] The Bachaga Boualam was a particularly useful ally for the *pieds-noirs* when making such arguments; his pre-1962 status and influence used regularly to refute suggestions that indigenous Algerians were treated as second-class subjects, rather than as equal citizens. When the Bachaga Boualam died in 1982, one of the many *pied-noir* tributes at his funeral read as follows: 'You are in death, as in life, the symbol of the fraternity between the populations of Algeria.'[107]

The connections between Muslim elites, veterans and *pieds-noirs* were long-standing and permeated various spheres, further facilitating the circulation of their overlapping discourses. Although they enjoyed nothing like the power of the state in terms of disseminating their representations of the *harkis*, these were generally the people with whom the *harki* community had the most contact, especially within the camps and forest hamlets. Beyond these environments, military figures such as General Edmond Jouhaud and the Bachaga Boualam regularly attended *pied-noir* events and enjoyed honorary positions within associations such as ANFANOMA and the Crecle algérianiste. Mas Thibert furthermore frequently hosted events where *harkis* from the locality mingled with assorted *pied-noir* and military guests. Filming one such event in 1977, *Les dossiers de l'écran* captured a tense exchange between a *pied-noir* woman and a *harki*, amidst an otherwise convivial atmosphere. In response to claims by the woman that *harkis* and *pieds-noirs* faced the same problems, the man pointed out that their different 'faces' meant that she was judged as French, whereas he was judged as an 'Arab' – a fact that significantly affected their respective 'problems', particularly relating to integration.[108] Although strongly denied by the woman on camera, the evidence presented in this chapter supports precisely this contention, demonstrating the ways in which the perceived differences of the *harkis* shaped their treatment in France.

In the 1960s and 1970s, *rapatrié* associations and their members were preoccupied with their Frenchness and the ways in which this could be used, first to obtain practical support from the state to rebuild their lives and then, later, to carve out a unique identity and place within the nation that would transform individual *rapatriés* into a community of *pieds-noirs*. In contrast, for *harkis* the ability to debate and define their own identity was one of the many forms of autonomy denied to them. Retreating into silence enabled others to create discourses on their behalf that rhetorically claimed the former auxiliaries as French, even as their day-to-day experiences served as a constant reminder of their otherness. Whether internally or externally generated, the representations of both *pieds-noirs* and *harkis* constructed in this period offered a partial and politicised image in accordance with the priorities of the groups responsible for them. Subsequent chapters will explore how these discourses came to be codified and embedded by *pied-noir* associations, at the same time as descendants of the *harkis* sought to deconstruct, contest and, ultimately, reclaim the image and history of their own community.

Notes

1 'Ils avaient choisi la France', *France horizon*, 45 (May 1962), 1.

2 'Le Discours de clôture du Président', *France horizon*, 50 (December 1962), 3.

3 'Discours de clôture du Président National Pierre Battesti', *France horizon*, 60 (December 1963), 18.

4 Todd Shepard, 'La République face aux harkis: questions aux historiens', *Les Temps modernes*, 666 (November–December 2011), 57.

5 For further discussion of this, see Shepard, 'La République', 57; Yann Scioldo-Zürcher, 'Les Harkis sont-ils des rapatriés comme les autres?', *Les Temps modernes*, 666 (November–December 2011), 90–8.

6 Shepard, 'La République', 61.

7 Alain Peyrefitte, *C'était de Gaulle* (Paris, 2002), p. 209; Todd Shepard, 'Excluding the *Harkis* from Repatriate Status, Excluding Muslim Algerians from French Identity', in *Transnational Spaces and Identities in the Francophone World*, ed. by Hafid Gafaiti Patricia M. E. Lorcin and David G. Troyansky (Lincoln, NE, 2009), pp. 95–8.

8 François-Xavier Hautreux, *La Guerre d'Algérie des harkis, 1954–1962* (Paris, 2013), pp. 367–8; Shepard, 'Excluding the *Harkis*', p. 103.

9   Jeannette E. Miller, 'A Camp for Foreigners and "Aliens": The Harkis' Exile at the Rivesaltes Camp (1962–1964)', *French Politics, Culture and Society*, 31:3 (Winter 2013), 27.

10   Shepard, 'Excluding the *Harkis*', p. 101.

11   Hautreux, *La Guerre d'Algérie*, pp. 306–22; Chantal Morelle, 'Les Pouvoirs publics français et le rapatriement des harkis en 1961–1962', *Vingtième siècle*, 83 (July–September 2004), 113–19.

12   Hautreux, *La Guerre d'Algérie*, p. 321.

13   Shepard, 'Excluding the *Harkis*', p. 106.

14   Boussad Azni, *Harkis, crime d'état: généaolgie d'un abandon* (Paris, 2002), p. 52.

15   Between April 1959 and July 1962, more than 3000 FLN prisoners occupied this site simultaneously and more than 10,000 in total passed through it at some point. Marc Bernardot, 'Être interné au Larzac', *Politix*, 69 (2001), 40.

16   Bernardot, 'Être interne au Larzac', 40, 48.

17   Miller, 'A Camp for Foreigners and "Aliens"', 26.

18   Catherine Wihtol de Wenden, 'Harkis: le paradoxe identitaire', *Regards sur l'actualité*, 175 (November 1991), 36.

19   Miller, 'A Camp for Foreigners and "Aliens"', 37.

20   Abderahmen Moumen (ed.), *Ils arrivent demain ... Ongles, village d'accueil des familles d'anciens harkis* (Ongles, 2008), p. 33.

21   Maurice Faivre, *L'action sociale de l'armée en faveur des musulmans, 1830–2006* (Paris, 2007), p. 112; Miller, 'A Camp for Foreigners and "Aliens"', 37.

22   Wihtol de Wenden, 'Harkis', 37.

23   On the notion of *encadrement*, see Hautreux, *La Guerre d'Algérie*, p. 380; Miller, 'A Camp for Foreigners and "Aliens"', 31–2.

24   Tom Charbit, 'Un petit monde colonial en métropole: le camp de harkis de Saint-Maurice-l'Ardoise (1962–1976)', *Politix*, 76 (2006), 33.

25   Joël Mettay, *L'archipel du mépris: histoire du Camp de Rivesaltes de 1939 à nos jours* (Canet, 2008), p. 108.

26   Bernard Derrieu reports that this practice lasted from 1965 until 1973. *La Cité de tapis: une communauté de rapatriés d'Algérie* (Pézenas, 1997) p. 31. See also the testimony of Emmanuel B. in Julien Chapsal, *Harkis à vie?* (Trézélan, 2006), p. 35.

27   Saliha Abdellatif, 'Le Français musulman ou une entité préfabriqué', *Hommes et migrations*, 1135 (1990), 32.

28   Abdellatif, 'Le Français musulman', 32; Mettay, *L'archipel du mépris*, pp. 120–2.

29   Small amounts of money were made directly available to *harkis*, but this was at the discretion of the camp directors who could withhold these sums as punishment for a variety of infractions. Hautreux, *La guerre d'Algérie*, p. 377.

30   Charbit, 'Un petit monde colonial', 40.

31   Réné Pleiber, 'Le Drame des harkis réfugiés', *L'Aurore* (23–24 August 1962), p. 4.

32   Michel Legris, 'Harkis et Moghaznis au Larzac', *Le Monde* (10 July 1962), p. 3.

33   Mettay, *L'archipel du mépris*, p. 113.

34   Legris, 'Harkis et Moghaznis', p. 3.

35 Tom Charbit, 'Sociographie des familles de harkis de Saint-Maurice-l'Ardoise', *Migrations études*, 128 (September 2005), 4.

36 Abderahmen Moumen, 'Camp de Rivesaltes, Camp Saint-Maurice-l'Ardoise: l'accueil et le reclassement des harkis en France', *Les Temps modernes*, 666 (November–December 2011), 117. Tom Charbit, 'Saint-Maurice-l'Ardoise: socio-histoire d'un camp de harkis (1962–1976)', *Migrations études*, 130 (September 2005), 10.

37 Amelia H. Lyons, 'The Civilizing Mission in the Metropole: Algerian Immigrants in France and the Politics of Adaptation during Decolonization', *Geschichte und Gesellschaft*, 32 (October–December 2006), 491.

38 Mettay, *L'archipel du mépris*, p. 103.

39 Legris, 'Harkis et Moghaznis', p. 3; 'Le Camp de Larzac (Aveyron) transforme en mechta', *L'Aurore* (16–17 June 1962), p. 4.

40 Legris, 'Harkis et Moghaznis', p. 3.

41 'C'étaient les harkis', *Cinq colonnes à la une*, aired 7 June 1963 (Channel 1).

42 Cited in Moumen, 'Camp de Rivesaltes', 110.

43 Moumen, 'Camp de Rivesaltes', 112.

44 Miller, 'A Camp for Foreigners and "Aliens"', 23.

45 Miller, 'A Camp for Foreigners and "Aliens"', 30.

46 Moumen, 'Camp de Rivesaltes', 111.

47 Hautreux, *La Guerre d'Algérie*, p. 388.

48 Fatima Besnaci-Lancou, *Fille de harki*, with Marie-Christine Ray (Paris, 2003), p. 81.

49 Charbit, 'Saint-Maurice-l'Ardoise', pp. 1–12.

50 Besnaci-Lancou, *Fille de harki*, p. 109.

51 Dalila Kerchouche, *Mon père, ce harki* (Paris, 2003).

52 Marita Eastmond, 'Stories as Lived Experience: Narratives in Forced Migration Research', *Journal of Refugee Studies*, 20:2 (June 2007), 254. This observation has also been made of the Algerian immigrant population in France who suffered similarly precarious living conditions in *bidonvilles* and *foyers*. See Jim House and Neil MacMaster, *Paris 1961: Algerians, State Terror and Memory* (Oxford, 2006), p. 266.

53 Miller, 'A Camp for Foreigners and "Aliens"', 24–5.

54 Chapsal, *Harkis à vie?*, p. 47.

55 Quoted in Jean-Jacques Jordi and Mohand Hamoumou, *Les Harkis, une mémoire enfouie* (Paris, 1999), p. 121.

56 Vincent Crapanzano, *The Harkis: The Wound that Never Heals* (Chicago and London, 2011), p. 84.

57 Jordi and Hamoumou, *Les Harkis*, p. 121.

58 Abd-el-Aziz Méliani, *Le Drame des harkis* (Paris, 2001), p. 196.

59 Charbit, 'Un petit monde colonial', 45. Choukri Hmed notes a similar scenario among Algerian immigrants who lived in SONACOTRA foyers during the 1960s and 1970s. See ' "Tenir ses hommes": la gestion des étrangers "isolés" dans les foyers SONACOTRA après la guerre d'Algérie', *Politix*, 76 (2006), 11–30.

60 Cited in Kerchouche, *Mon père*, p. 148. Others, especially military person-
    nel, have collected testimony from former camp residents that contradict
    accounts like Kerchouche's. See, for example, Maurice Faivre, 'Introduction
    historique', in *Harkis: soldats abandonnés* (Paris, 2012), p. 32.
61 Anzi, *Harkis*, pp. 121–3.
62 Kerchouche, *Mon père*, p. 57.
63 Kerchouche, *Mon père*, p. 15.
64 Azni, *Harkis*, p. 119.
65 Faivre, *L'Action sociale*, p. 204.
66 Eastmond, 'Stories as Lived Experience', 258.
67 Azni, *Harkis*, p. 117.
68 Saïd Bouamama, *Héritiers involontaires de la guerre d'Algérie: jeunes
    Manosquins issus de l'immigration algérienne* (Manosque, 2003), p. 43.
69 Bouamama, *Héritiers involontaires*, p. 40.
70 Jean Michel Dumay, 'Un enseignement en sourdine', *Le Monde* (27 February,
    1992), p. 10.
71 Fatima Besnaci-Lancou, *Nos mères, paroles blessées* (Léchelle, 2006), p. 75.
72 Emmanuel Brillet, 'La Contingence et la geste: le harki, l'indicible du "mouve-
    ment de l'histoire"', in *L'époque de la disparition: politique et esthétique*, ed. by
    Alain Brossat and Jean-Louis Déotte (Paris, 2000), p. 144.
73 Crapanzano, *The Harkis*, p. 83.
74 Cited in Jordi and Hamoumou, *Les Harkis*, p. 123.
75 'Duplex à Bouteflika', *JA2 20 heures*, aired 16 June 2000 (FR2).
76 This particular example is from a textbook in the 1990s. For others, see Lydia
    Aït Saadi-Bouras, 'Les Harkis dans les manuels scolaires algériens', *Les Temps
    modernes*, 666 (November–December 2011), 206.
77 Maurice Faivre, 'Les Français musulmans dans la guerre d'Algérie: les repré-
    sailles et l'oubli de la France', *Guerres mondiales et conflits contemporains*, 180
    (October 1995), 164.
78 Jo McCormack, 'Memory in History, Nation Building and Identity: Teaching
    about the Algerian War in France', in *Algeria and France 1800–2000: Identity,
    Memory, Nostalgia*, ed. by Patricia M.E. Lorcin (New York, 2006), pp. 137–8.
79 Cited in Jordi and Hamoumou, *Les harkis*, p. 55.
80 Mettay, *L'archipel du mépris*. p. 96.
81 'Algérie: la fin de la guerre', *Cinq colonnes à la une*, aired 6 June 1962 (Channel 1).
82 Béatrice Fleury-Vilatte, *La Mémoire télévisuelle de la guerre d'Algérie 1962–1992*
    (Paris, 2000), p. 75.
83 Used by the Ottomans and continued by the French, the title 'bachaga' was
    given to high-ranking indigenous functionaries or regional leaders.
84 Guilia Fabbiano, 'Les Harkis du Bachaga Boualam. Des Beni-Boudouanes à
    Mas Thibert', in *Les Harkis dans la décolonisation*, p. 114.
85 The Bachaga Boualam and his immediate family were evacuated on 18 May
    1962. A further seventy-three members of his family were brought to France
    at the end of the month. By September 1962, 166 people were resident in Mas
    Thibert. Fabbiano, 'Les Harkis', p. 117.

86 Fabbiano, 'Les Harkis', p. 118.

87 Fabbiano, 'Les Harkis', p. 115.

88 Saïd Boualam, *Mon pays, la France* (Paris, 1962); Saïd Boualam, *Les Harkis au service de la France* (Paris, 1963); Saïd Boualam, *L'Algérie sans la France* (Paris, 1964).

89 Boualam, *Mon pays*, pp. 14, 47.

90 Boualam, *Mon pays*, p. 97.

91 For a fuller discussion of these *pied-noir* narratives, see Chapter 3.

92 Boualam, *Mon pays*, p. 34.

93 The Bachaga Boualam's interpretation of the conflcit was also informed by his virulent anti-communism. See *Mon pays*, pp. 31, 115.

94 Boualam, *Mon pays*, p. 92.

95 Mohand Hamoumou, *Et ils sont devenus harkis* (Paris, 1993), p. 39.

96 Moumen, *Ils arrivent demain ...*, p. 25.

97 Georges Jasseron, *Les Harkis en France, scènes et témoignages* (Paris, 1965), pp. 13, 17.

98 Jasseron, *Les Harkis en France*, p. 19.

99 'Livre blanc de notre honte et de la passion des harkis', *La Nation française*, supplement 317 (1962), 5. The authors of the supplement attributed the acquittal of the men to the testimonies they collected and reproduced.

100 Georges Fleury, *Le Combat des harkis* (Versailles, 1989).

101 Boualam, *Mon pays*, p. 224.

102 See their respective newspapers *La Voix du djebel flame* (UNC AFN) and *L'ancien d'Algérie* (FNACA).

103 'Ils avaient choisi la France', 1.

104 Jo Sohet, 'Les Harkis, ces oubliés de l'histoire 1962–1978', *L'Algérianiste*, 5 (15 March 1979), 27.

105 Joëlle Hureau, *La Mémoire des pieds-noirs de 1830 à nos jours* (Paris, 2001), p. 174.

106 Jasseron, *Les Harkis en France*, p. 109.

107 'Un grand Français nous a quitté', *Aux échos d'Alger*, 4 (May 1982), 10.

108 'Harki', *Les Dossiers de l'écran*, aired 17 May 1977 (A2).

Consolidation, 1975–91

3

Creating an identity

The silence of the *harkis* enabled *pied-noir* activists to construct their own narratives about that community. In a similar manner, so the continued silence of the French state with respect to the War of Independence during the 1970s and 1980s created space for an increasingly extensive and organised network of *rapatrié* associations to establish their version of these events. The genealogies of identity and memory that developed alongside this growth of associative life was then inscribed across a variety of spaces from the literary and visual to the social and the physical. As this chapter will show, the mutually affirmed collective lexicon of *pied-noir* identity that emerged during the late 1970s and 1980s presented the colonial era as one of progress and inter-ethnic harmony under the benevolent auspices of the French, with the pioneering settlers playing an instrumental role in the 'civilisation' of the land and its people. With the acknowledgement of few, if any, inequalities in French Algeria, the conflict of 1954 to 1962 was depicted as the result of the machinations of a handful of fanatics, rendering independence a tragic mistake forced upon the Algerian people against the wishes of the majority. This narrative cast the *pieds-noirs* as innocent victims of a politically motivated decolonisation, allowing them to dwell at length on the irreplaceable quality of the land they had left behind which contrasted sharply with the present state of Algeria under FLN rule. The creation and consolidation of what Clarisse Buono calls the *pied-noir* 'meta-memory'[1] was not confined to the pages of the association press, but possessed social and physical dimensions as well. The establishment of a set of dates and places where *pieds-noirs* could gather to commemorate the past afforded individuals a stable set of occasions through which to reaffirm their historical and cultural roots as well as their present-day existence as part of a collective. Although organised by specific associations or community leaders, these events attracted *pieds-noirs* in the thousands, even tens of thousands, from all across France. Complementing these endeavours were attempts to physically anchor the *rapatriés* in France by erecting physical markers symbolising the duality of their Franco-Algerian identity, including monuments and even a *pied-noir* town.

The ability of *pied-noir* narratives to invest these different spaces exposed the limits of state silence. In spite of the continued absence of any official commemorations, politicians found themselves increasingly compelled to engage with the former settlers and their demands. The election of Valéry Giscard d'Estaing to the presidency in 1974 was perceived as a watershed moment by *pieds-noirs*, bringing to an end more than fifteen years of Gaullist domination and fostering hopes that a more favourable political climate would now take hold. The centre-right liberal Giscard and his socialist successor, François Mitterrand, reached out to the *rapatrié* community in their presidential campaigns, creating expectations that electoral support would be rewarded. Once in office, both men therefore came under pressure from *pied-noir* activists to fulfil their promises by acknowledging the community and its demands, particularly by extending existing compensation measures. Assessing Giscard's seven years in power, one *pied-noir* commentator applauded the President's desire to make 'amends for past forgetting' by recognising the identity of the French from Algeria and by reasserting the value of their history. Nonetheless, the same author lamented the insufficiencies of the compensation law passed in 1978 and the President's failure to accept the actions of 'defenders of French Algeria', a reference to members of the OAS to whom Giscard refused to extend a full amnesty.[2] Instead, it would be Mitterrand (of whose sympathies many *pieds-noirs* were deeply suspicious, owing to his left-wing political credentials), who would satisfy this long-standing demand. The development of *pied-noir* activism in this period thus took place against a backdrop of ongoing commemorative silence at the national level on one hand but, on the other hand, a progressive extension of existing material support by the state and strategically motivated interaction with the community at the grassroots level by specific politicians.

Managing diversity

The pressure exerted on politicians came not just from established bodies like ANFANOMA, but from a host of new organisations, modelled after the increasingly successful Cercle Algérianiste, who were intent on defining and expressing what it meant to be a *pied-noir*, even if not all of them were comfortable with using that term. *Pied-noir* activism was able tap into the post-1968 landscape of expanding identity politics and the increasing prevalence of claims for recognition and belonging premised on culture.[3] In France itself, such demands were encouraged first by Giscard's regionalism initiatives and subsequently by Mitterrand's *droit à la différence* policies alongside Gaston Defferre's 1982 decentralisation laws, all of which created new spaces for minorities claiming particular regional, cultural and religious identities. Much of this thriving cultural activism was driven by *amicales*, a type of socially orientated, usually small-scale association, bringing together *rapatriés* on the basis of a shared former profession, place of birth, or similar facet of identity. Within *amicales* the emphasis was on recreating a sense of community through the preservation and valorisation of a collective past. 'We're here to rediscover our Sétif, our region ... purged of anything that could sadden us', explained the president of the newly formed Amicale des Sétifiens in 1970. 'Today we have revived a spirit, a union founded on friendship, loyalty, we have recreated an ambiance, a warmth that flourishes even more now perhaps than during the long years when it remained buried in a secret corner of our hearts sometimes weighing heavily upon us.'[4]

To facilitate such an atmosphere, *amicales* organised regular events where their members could come together and reminisce, while their magazines and newsletters created virtual communities through photographs, personal recollections and historical articles.[5] Although diverse, the topics and issues addressed by *amicales* and other types of associations were bound together by a discernible core of consistently highlighted themes that transcended their organisational boundaries. These themes frequently echoed those voiced by individual *pieds-noirs* in the many novels, memoirs and autobiographical histories published during this period.[6] In particular, the desire expressed by Francine Dessaigne to use her own story to provide 'consolation' to her fellow exiles and a 'lesson' in the true history of the community to the metropolitan French was writ large within the culturally orientated bodies that flourished from the mid-1970s onwards.[7] As *pied-noir* author and historian Camille Brière explained, 'each *pied-noir* has the urgent duty to preserve, like the most precious deposit, the values which contributed to the formation of his people and to transmit these values to his children along with an understanding of his past'.[8] While not denying that the experience of every *pied-noir* was unique, associations nonetheless sought to bring coherence

to otherwise fragmented accounts by grouping multiple, mutually reinforcing narratives under the umbrella of a single organisation or publication. With associations serving as a 'unifying link', the disparate lives
and recollections of individual settlers were thus amalgamated into a
collective vision of the *pied-noir* community and its past.[9] In 1978, five
years after it was originally written, the manifesto of the Cercle algérianiste was amended to reflect precisely this responsibility when it stated
that the movement 'must be the expression of the collective conscience
of our scorned, exiled and dispersed community in order to save from
oblivion and nothingness the little that remains of our magnificent and
cruel past'.[10]

This process of aggregation gave individual *pieds-noirs* a way of locat-
ing their personal experiences within larger narratives and trajectories
and, therefore, of identifying with a wider community as defined by
associations and activists. It also enabled associations to create a communal repository that was cohesive, consensual and thus resistant to
unsanctioned interpretations. The intention of associations was to reinforce through repetition, prioritising the substantiation of a familiar and
accepted set of narratives over novelty and nuance. As Jay Winter explains,
groups of people 'create scripts which omit, correct and occasionally lie
about the past. Repeated frequently enough these scripts become formu-
laic or iconic, which is to say they tell truths rather than the truth'.[11] In
the case of the *pieds-noirs,* these scripts were repeated within, but also
across associations, increasing their potency. Every decision about what
to commemorate involved a decision to simplify a story by leaving certain elements out, meaning that over time those aspects of the *rapatrié*
past that were unable to obtain wider recognition became the nuances
of personal experience lost in the translation from individual to collective representations. Although there were always exceptions, deviations
from the quickly established norm diminished over the life of *pied-noir*
associations as the central identity of the group and its members became
increasingly defined and rooted. Distance from the events of 1962 further facilitated the ability to mythologise and unify disparate narratives
resulting in a strong but narrow collective 'we' that spoke within carefully
established parameters.

Of course, individuality within *pied-noir* narratives was not completely erased by the existence of associations; personal expressions of
history and memory persisted alongside collective endeavours. In this
capacity, Joëlle Hureau speaks of identity 'freelancers' who played a
'not negligible' role, even if the specificities of their voices 'frequently
digress[ed] from the outlines traced by association programmes'.[12] One

of the arenas in which these 'freelancers' could most often be found was
on television. Although relatively small in number, programmes devoted
to the *pieds-noirs* in the late 1970s and 1980s tended to privilege personal
contributions from a combination of 'ordinary' and famous *pieds-noirs*
over and above statements from association representatives seeking to
speak for the wider community.[13] This was also the case in several collections of testimony published in the 1980s. These volumes were designed
primarily to showcase *pied-noir* success stories and to convey the various ways in which *rapatriés* had contributed to the postcolonial nation
at a time when many felt ignored, even denigrated, by the metropolitan French. Underlining the presence of *pieds-noirs* in all spheres of life,
celebrities such as the singer Enrico Macias and the comedian Robert
Castel featured alongside eminent doctors, academics, politicians and
businessmen, even the occasional woman. In addition to the twenty-five
figures profiled in the main text, Ysabel Saïah's 1987 book, *Pieds-noirs et
fiers de l'être* [*pieds-noirs* and proud of it], included an A-to-Z of successful *rapatriés* totalling forty pages.[14] Inevitably, such an array of individuals produced divergent, even conflicting, viewpoints. In particular, the
high proportion of Algerian Jews featured in such texts highlighted the
heterogeneity of the community, especially as these tended to be the contributors with the most problematic relationships to the term 'pied-noir'
and to the identity associated with it. As Jean-Luc Allouche forcefully
stated with respect to his fellow *rapatriés*:

> I like neither merguez [a spicy North African sausage], nor 'tchatche'
> [chatter], nor 'patouète' [a form of settler dialect], nor their paternalism
> towards 'our Arabs', nor their boastful blindness, nor their *petit blanc* nos-
> talgia … I don't like them, even though I am not so naïve as to not see how
> much I resemble them.[15]

In spite of such differences, the editors behind these collections were
nonetheless keen to stress the common threads that bound their contributors together as part of an identifiable wider community. Hence
Richard Koubi's insistence that, although they may have followed 'opposing paths', all eleven of the *pieds-noirs* featured in his collection of portraits remained 'conscious of belonging to the same family whose name
they carry and honour'.[16]

Recalling French Algeria

Associations equally sought to manage diversity, keeping it within accept-
able limits so as not to undermine the image of a cohesive community

they were seeking to embed for purposes such as lobbying. By collating and disseminating individual accounts, associations aimed to ensure that each *pied-noir* was able to serve as 'the roots of the others'.[17] The pages of association magazines, newsletters and bulletins consequently supplied a series of personal yet universally resonant experiences revolving around a common canon. The testimonies and articles that evoked these experiences were presented in parallel, rather than juxtaposed in ways that could pit them against each other.[18] Utilising a particular visual and rhetorical grammar, associations claimed to be demonstrating and defending the existence of a specific community structured around a set of shared ideas. Exploring the content of association publications during the late 1970s and 1980s when this shared lexicon was being consolidated reveals the strategic choices being made by activists concerning what they wished to emphasise or obscure to their readers and why. The vision of the past formulated by and through associations is, in turn, central to understanding the behaviour of the *pied-noir* community in the postcolonial period.

As the one experience common to all *rapatriés*, departure from Algeria became a foundational pillar of the collective identity constructed by associations. Signalling a moment of dramatic rupture, the summer of 1962 represented the clear demarcation between a happy, carefree life in Algeria and a difficult metropolitan trajectory marked by misery and suffering. Construed as a wholly negative experience from departure through to arrival, those few months would, as the historian Jean-Jacques Jordi noted, 'structure a memory and forge a collective mentality that persists to this day'.[19] Indeed, for Brière it was through these 'trials' that the *pied-noir* community 'became conscious of its difference [from the metropolitan French], of its unity and thus its identity'.[20]

Recollections conveyed through associations tend to focus on the 'final morning', with the decision to leave Algeria presented as a deeply reluctant but necessary one. The dilemma faced by the settlers was encapsulated in the phrase 'the suitcase or the coffin', which became shorthand for the lack of choice they felt they had in 1962. Deeply embedded in *pied-noir* mythology, this notion legitimated compensation claims made against the state, while also underpinning the *pied-noir* sense of themselves as victims of forces beyond their control.[21] In narrating departures, which were often hasty and improvised, *pieds-noirs* stressed the chaos of the roads, airports and ports; the queuing, often over several days, without food or water; the constant fear of FLN attacks; and the pitiful sight of families trying to carry entire lives in a suitcase. Accounts usually featured, and indeed often ended with, one last lingering look at Algeria and a contemplation of the magnitude of what was occurring. After being painfully wrenched from their homeland, the hope was for a sympathetic welcome in France but, as discussed in the first chapter, this did not come to pass: 'We searched for something', recalled one *pied-noir*, 'we found nothing'.[22] The coldness of the reception accorded to the *rapatriés* in 1962 rendered exile a double rupture, separating the community both from Algeria and from the metropolitan French.

Although geographically detached from Algeria, the land remained an integral part of the *pied-noir* identity, arguably more so now that it was no longer physically accessible. 'Like other *pieds-noirs*, I have lost Algeria', the author Louis Gardel explained. 'But it has not left me. It will never leave me. It is in me until I die. I am made of it.'[23] The irreplaceable qualities of a land where '[t]he natural setting was so magnificent, the colours so bright, the odours so sweet that we did not need much to be happy', rendered Algeria a veritable paradise lost.[24] So unique was the experience of living there that it could only be adequately understood by other *pieds-noirs*, creating an exclusive club with its own rites, rituals and language. In recounting her life story to the anthropologist Michèle Bausant, one *pied-noir* women stated: 'when we say "the land of Algeria" ... it means nothing to you, nothing at all, for me, it is this red earth, a little powdery; I have it in my hands, you see, I have it in my eyes, I smell it. How do you pass that on, it's impossible!'[25] Reliving the sights, sounds and smells of French Algeria took up a considerable portion of association publications. As a 1994 survey of *L'Algérianiste* readers revealed, the elements of most interest to members were history, testimonies and features on the towns and villages of French Algeria.[26] Often illustrated using sources from the personal archives of readers, these publications attest to a wealth of historical material possessed by *pieds-noirs*, which associations saw as their duty to preserve and share. In addition to lengthy and nostalgia-laden accounts of idyllic prewar lives, frequently anchored in the innocent years of childhood, the former colonial territory was brought back to life through evocations of food, language, art, humour, history and architecture.

Considerable emphasis was placed on the linguistic particularities of the settlers as a way to convey the richness of the community's identity and heritage. Alongside calls to take pride in the distinctive *Algérie française* accent, articles explaining or written in *pataouète*, a dialect combining French, Spanish, Italian and Arabic words, were also popular. Often these included reproductions of the colonial-era Cagayous cartoons penned by Augustin Robinet or modern equivalents such as *L'Algérianiste's pataouète* column written by Fulgence, a pseudonym for

Charles-André Massa.[27] Striking an equally light note were humorous cartoons such as the *Pieds-noirs magazine* series 'the Sebou gang', based around a mischievous trio of stereotyped children, consisting of Ernest, the blonde European ring leader, Driss, the Arab with an unbridled love of couscous and an aversion to soap, and Izaak from the Jewish community, whose friendship and exploits recalled the insouciance and of colonial life, while also reinforcing the message of inter-ethnic harmony propagated across the rest of the magazine.[28] The emphasis on childhood as a frame for recollections of the past more generally across association publications can be read, according to Renato Rosaldo, as a strategy for depoliticising the narratives being offered by turning 'the responsible colonial agent into an innocent bystander'.[29] An alternative interpretation is that representations anchored in childhood signal the way in which departure from Algeria was not simply a rupture with the past, but also a coming of age moment for certain *pieds-noirs*.

Establishing the contours of this shared cultural patrimony also involved highlighting the ways in which the specific environment of French Algeria shaped those who grew up in it. Possessing 'a warm temperament', the typical *pied-noir* was spontaneous, generous and open. Courageous and hard-working, they nonetheless knew how to take pleasure in life. Endlessly sociable and hospitable, *pieds-noirs* were devoted to family and deeply respectful of their ancestors, but could also be 'a bit of a show off, a bit of a fatalist'.[30] The communal attributes promoted by associations appear to have seeped into metropolitan consciousness as revealed by a 1987 poll published in the *Nouvel Observateur*, in which 75 per cent of respondents stated that they were familiar with the term *pied-noir*. The two principal characteristics those polled associated with the community were courage (30 per cent of respondents) and ambition (23 per cent), although only 24 per cent recognised the role played by the former settlers in the expansion of the French nation.[31]

The historian Yann Scioldo-Zürcher is not alone in noting that such representations reduced the diverse community that actually populated French Algeria to a stereotype comprising the most visible elements of their popular culture.[32] This was particularly problematic given that many of the badges of cultural distinction vaunted by associations in the post-1962 period, such as *pataouète*, were precisely the elements that many settlers sought to distance themselves from during the colonial era on account of their 'unFrench' nature. However, for associations and their activists, cataloguing the different elements of an idealised French Algeria and the community who lived there underlined the value of the patrimony they felt had been forced to abandon at the end of the war. Amidst ongoing battles to secure adequate financial compensation, emphasising their cultural heritage was also a way of demonstrating that the loss experienced by the *pieds-noirs* in 1962 was not something that could simply be measured in material terms, but also 'touched their soul'.[33]

Living in harmony

Recalling or recreating settler culture was not simply an end in itself. It also enabled associations to construct a series of arguments that justified their understanding of the events leading to the creation and then dissolution of French Algeria. One of the key elements within this historical schema was the image of colonial Algeria as a harmonious, multi-ethnic 'melting pot' where different races and religions were able to coexist under French rule. Classrooms were a regularly invoked symbol of the coming together of different populations, with schools providing 'the first contact with the other', but also 'the first friendships transcending differences'.[34] Class photos supplied by readers visually attested to this combination of diversity and fraternity, proving a popular way of rebutting evidence of the uneven and unequal access to education that actually prevailed in French Algeria. They also tapped into the well-established republican tradition in which schools functioned as privileged sites of integration and in the formation of a national consciousness.

The presence of different communities who lived distant yet cordial lives was the closest most *pied-noir* associations came to conceding inequality in French Algeria. The more common stance was to insist that 'the *pieds-noirs* lived in harmony with the Arabs'.[35] This was most aptly illustrated through the 'good Arab' that every *pied-noir* seemingly knew and who functioned as the exception to an unspoken general rule. Underlining the power relations that shaped life in French Algeria, it is noticeable that 'good Arabs' generally arose in the context of serving the *pieds-noirs*: selling items to them in the marketplace, working on their land, cooking and cleaning in their homes, looking after their children. Tellingly, Jacques Attali recalled how the only Arabic words he knew as a child were commands.[36] Examples of harmonious community interaction also tended to revolve around the relatively superficial 'charm of reciprocal exchanges, particularly traditional pastries on national holidays'.[37] In this way, the 'good Arab', with whom *pieds-noirs* recalled warm relations, served to exculpate them from charges of racism and iniquitous privileges. Alongside these instances of contact with individual, familiar Algerians existed a category of unknown and therefore threatening

'Arabs' or 'Muslims', who, although mentioned much less frequently, underlined the continuing need for a 'civilising' French presence and the challenges associated with that endeavour.[38]

That the settlers also lived in harmony with Algeria's Jewish population was rarely explicitly stated, but instead taken for granted as part of the 'melting pot' metaphor. Discussions of Jews usually took place in the context of highlighting particular religious customs and ceremonies to show how well versed the settlers were in the traditions of those they lived alongside as a way of implying closeness. The social and cultural separation created by colonial power structures, not to mention the virulent anti-Semitism that regularly reared its head in French Algeria, were omitted from association narratives.[39] On an individual basis, Algerian Jews sometimes contributed articles or testimonies to *pied-noir* publications that tended to express nostalgia for many of the same aspects of French Algeria as other *rapatriés*. But, there was no significant organised Jewish presence within the *pied-noir* associational milieu since, upon arrival in 1962, Algerian Jews largely chose to orientate themselves towards the French Jewish community. Instead, the most common way in which Algerian Jews were inserted into association narratives was through coverage of contemporary celebrities with Jewish ancestry, who were held up as exemplary members of the *rapatrié* community. During the 1980s, the most prominent *pied-noir* mascot in this regard was the singer Enrico Macias, who was regularly invited to perform at or participate in association events – including judging the annual Miss Pied-Noir contest – and whose burgeoning career was chronicled in detail by the *pied-noir* press through interviews, photographs and concert reviews. In the eyes of associations, Macias's Jewish origins reinforced his *pied-noir*-ness, enabling him to be cast as embodying the values activists wished to attach to the community as a whole, namely harmonious diversity, tolerance and success. The mainstream media equally treated the singer as a *pied-noir* spokesperson; a role that Macias appeared to willingly embrace.[40] After all, it was the popularity among *pieds-noirs* of *Adieu mon pays*, his lyrical eulogy for his lost homeland, that launched his musical career in the early 1960s. During the 1990s, Macias disappeared from public view. When he reappeared at the end of the decade, he placed a much greater emphasis on his Judeo-Arab cultural heritage as his identifying trait, particularly in terms of musical influence. Although this distanced him from the conventional *pied-noir* identity he had previously been aligned with, crowds at his recent concerts reveal that he nonetheless remains deeply popular amongst *rapatriés*.[41]

'From chaos to light'

Relations between the different communities of French Algeria were good, so *pied-noir* associations argued, because everyone recognised the effort the settlers had put into establishing themselves and their families in the land and appreciated the benefits their arrival had brought. Deeply ingrained in association literature, the myth of pioneering ancestors sought to overturn the stereotype of the wealthy and exploitative land-owner or *gros colon*, offering in its place a narrative of humble people fleeing poverty and persecution in search of a better future. People who arrived in Algeria with nothing but who, through hard work and tenacity, had succeeded in establishing modest yet happy lives. From this invest-ment in the land and the sacrifices made – the death toll for the early settlers was extremely high, owing to the inhospitable terrain and dis-eases such as cholera – stemmed a strong sense of roots and entitlement. As the president of RECOURS, Jacques Roseau explained: 'Over genera-tions, the sense of our permanence in this French land installed itself in the hearts and minds of all the French of Algeria. Our attachment to what could only be our homeland was obviously passionate.'[42] A debt of grati-tude was thus owed, and frequently acknowledged, to these ancestors who provided the present-day community with a positive material and moral heritage to take pride in. 'I have no regrets about being *pied-noir*', Jean-François Gonzales defiantly stated, 'no shame at all regarding the ancestors who developed this country, on the contrary, I am very proud.'[43] By bringing together individual stories of triumph over adversity, asso-ciations created a collective narrative of progress for the colony which was then anchored within the broader, but equally positive, history of the French empire.

Associations agreed that colonial Algeria was 'a totally French cre-ation.'[44] The lack of an innate sense of national identity on the part of the indigenous inhabitants, owing to centuries spent under foreign rule, was deemed to have rendered the country a blank canvas onto which the French could paint their own values and systems of government. Within this narrative, the landing of French troops in 1830 served as a founda-tional moment, signalling the beginning of a radical transformation ac-complished in co-operation with, rather than in opposition to, the wishes of the Algerian people. The details of the bloody conquest and lengthy 'pacification' process were largely ignored by associations who instead cast the invading soldiers as liberators who freed Algeria from the tyr-anny and backwardness of the Ottoman Empire. The nationalist revolt that broke out 124 years later was thus denied legitimacy by associations who argued that Algeria had no identity separate from France and that the country the FLN claimed as their own had, in fact, never existed. The establishment of Algeria as part of France's empire was simply accepted as a historical fact by associations; no discussion of the legitimacy of colonialism as a policy was ever undertaken. Instead, the French presence was justified with reference to the material benefits of their rule. From the moment they set foot on Algerian soil, the French were credited with vastly improving all aspects of life by building roads and railways, establishing successful commercial enterprises such as vineyards, and providing services like sanitation, health care, education and democratic government. As the Cercle algérianiste's Maurice Calmein boasted, 'it was not a question of occupying a country, but of making all the pieces'.[45] When recalling the scale of these achievements, articles adopted a highly empirical perspective, as if veracity was proportionate to the volume of statistics quoted. Through a 1988 article in *Aux échos d'Alger*, we thus learn that 'the gift' given to the FLN in 1962 was 'enormous', including 19,000 km of modern surfaced roads at a cost of 15.5 billion new francs, 4250 km of railways and five major airports valued at 20 billion new francs. So numerous were the contributions made by France that the list went on for twelve pages and continued into the next issue.[46]

The Algeria that emerged from the pages of association publications was thus an entirely French and a wholly positive creation. As Josseline Revel-Mouroz, director of the Centre d'études pied-noir (CEPN) made clear, even though this 'patrimony' had been cruelly 'amputated' in 1962, the duty to remember it and to defend its legacy remained.[47] It is furthermore worth noting that when the *rapatriés* first arrived in France their perceptions of colonialism were not significantly at odds with majority opinion. The fact that most metropolitans were pleased to see an end to the war in Algeria did not automatically mean they were anti-colonial in their wider views, simply that they were tired of a costly and disruptive conflict. However, by the time Revel-Mouroz had made her comments in 1996, *pied-noir* interpretations of empire were increasingly out of step with contemporary sensibilities. Nonetheless, *pied-noir* associations have remained deeply attached to the *grandeur* of empire, regarding themselves as the last surviving remnants of a valuable project to which their ancestors contributed greatly and from which the French nation benefited enormously. Always present to some degree, the defensive thrust of this position has become more pronounced as *pied-noir* and scholarly understandings of colonialism have grown further apart, particularly from the 1990s onwards. Hence the increasingly explicit references to the need to correct metropolitan misperceptions shaped by a supposed leftist intellectual hegemony that called on the French to 'obsess over' and 'feel guilty' with respect to the colonial past. Rather than buying into this false 'bad conscience', *pied-noir* associations were determined to dispel what they regarded as metropolitan ignorance, while simultaneously giving their descendants a vision of the past of which they could be proud. As the founding charter of the Amicale des Sétifiens proclaimed: 'We have a rich past that we are proud to be able to reclaim and about which we have nothing to deny, nothing to cut out.'[48]

The War of Independence

Concentrating on the harmonious and prosperous pre-1954 era heightened the tragedy of the ignominious end suffered by French Algeria, while simultaneously deflecting attention away from the specific context, causes and course of decolonisation.[49] The War of Independence was not, however, a subject that associations avoided entirely. Rather, the conflict was selectively invoked so as to produce an account focused on those events which had the greatest impact upon the settler community. In this schema, November 1954 to March 1962 tended to be skimmed over, although exceptions were made for particularly brutal FLN operations such as the ALN-orchestrated attacks in August 1955 on Philippeville and nearby towns which, over the course of three days, left seventy-one European civilians dead.[50] Attention was instead primarily directed at the post-ceasefire period, which encompassed the most traumatic moments of the war for *pieds-noirs,* including the escalation of violence, particularly kidnappings, in the final months, the fate of the *harkis,* and the 'exodus' itself.

Although the signing of the Evian Accords on 19 March 1962 represented a watershed moment in the war, it is a date many *pieds-noirs* would prefer to see erased rather than remembered. From their perspective, the ceasefire did not end the conflict, but rather marked an intensification of violence as demonstrated by the fact that more Europeans, and certainly more *harkis*, were killed after this date than in all the previous years of fighting. In the light of the casualties, commonly cited by associations as 150,000 *harkis* and up to 25,000 settlers, the commemoration of 19 March was considered to be not only disrespectful towards those killed after that point but also tantamount to 'celebrating' a defeat like Sedan in 1870. The long-running campaigns to secure official recognition for this date in the national commemorative calendar by the left-leaning veterans association FNACA, which consists primarily of former conscripts, have therefore been met with equally persistent resistance from *pied-noir* associations.

A central plank of *pied-noir* activism for the past fifty years, opposition to the commemoration of 19 March has acted as a catalyst for
co-operation between associations. Petitions were regularly circulated,
particularly in response to an increasing number of streets named after
this date by local municipalities; by September 2002, over 3000 *communes*
had a '19 mars' square, street, bridge or park, while Paris followed suit in
2004.[51] More militant *pieds-noirs* have repeatedly taken to the streets to
voice their opposition to any official recognition being accorded to this
date. In 1982, during the course of a live televised debate held outdoors
in Montpellier to mark the twentieth anniversary of the cessation of hostilities, a large crowd gathered holding aloft banners reading '19 March,
shame for France'; their protests becoming so vocal that the host threatened to terminate the broadcast. François Delmas, Montpellier's mayor
from 1959 until 1977, had been a staunch opponent of naming streets
after this date. Continuing this stance, his successor, the socialist Georges
Frêche, can be seen during the broadcast standing amidst the protesting
pieds-noirs.[52]

Campaigns intensified in the late 1990s as the government began
discussing which date should be selected to officially commemorate the
Algerian War. ANFANOMA kept a particularly close eye on these debates,
reprinting key parliamentary exchanges in *France horizon* and producing
lists of how deputies had voted on the issue. Those who voted against
assigning an official commemorative status to 19 March were praised for
having 'done their duty', while 'sanctions' were proposed for those who
had voted in favour.[53] In 2001, the *pied-noir* community appeared to have
achieved victory when 5 December, a date with no war-related meaning,
was adopted as France's official day of commemoration. But their success
was short-lived: in November 2012, the Senate definitively adopted a law
instituting 19 March as a national day to honour the memory of civilian and military victims of the Algerian War.[54] In spite of this decision,
campaigns against the commemoration of 19 March continue within
pied-noir associations reflecting their determination to prevent any positive significance being attributed to this date. This strategy is indicative
of the broader commitment of activists to inscribing their version of the
past into the public narrative of the war and to prevent different interpretations from gaining authority.

De Gaulle: the great decoloniser

Connected to the *pied-noir* rejection of the commemoration of 19 March is
the argument that Algeria was lost by France rather than won by the FLN.

In the discourse of *pied-noir* associations, the FLN were almost never recognised as combatants with a legitimate cause. Instead, they were painted
as a minority of fanatics subject to external pressures for whom violence
was the natural recourse. This stance served the dual purpose of highlighting the unrepresentative nature of the FLN's rebellion and their unsuit-
ability to rule in the post-independence period. Both these claims support
the idea that the continuation of French Algeria was what all settlers and
most Algerians actually wanted. *Pied-noir* resentments over the way the
war was handled by politicians in Paris are telescoped into the figure of
de Gaulle who, as president, introduced the idea of 'self-determination'
and resultant plebiscites on independence which are blamed for the end
of French rule. Arguments relating to the inevitable tide of history, or to
colonies as an increasing impediment to the modernisation of France, cut
no ice with the *pieds-noirs*, who see in de Gaulle only a 'politics of abandonment'.[55] This hatred is given a particularly sharp edge by the belief that
it was the settlers who, through mass demonstrations in May 1958, were
instrumental in bringing de Gaulle back to power; an act of support they
undertook on the understanding that he was as committed to keeping
Algeria French as they were. That de Gaulle initially nurtured this impression, not least through his 4 June 1958 address to an enormous and vocal
crowd of settlers in Algiers during which he infamously declared 'I have
understood you', only made his subsequent 'betrayal' the more egregious.
Indicative of the longevity of this animosity, when it was proposed to erect
a statue of de Gaulle in Nice in 2011, the Cercle algérianiste responded
by accusing the municipality, which they had always considered friendly
towards the *pieds-noirs,* of 'turning its back' on the community.[56]

   In attempting to comprehend the shift from de Gaulle's 'long live
French Algeria' proclamation in Mostaganem in June 1958, to his advocacy of 'self-determination' in January 1961, the only reasons *pied-noir*
associations can find are selfish ones pertaining to the General's insatia-
ble need to 'quench his thirst for greatness'.[57] Over a century of collective hard work spent developing Algeria was thus sacrificed in a single
phrase uttered by one man. The simplicity of this reading of the war is
facilitated by the wholly positive presentation of life in French Algeria
prior to 1954: refusing to engage with the complexities of colonisation,
particularly its negative aspects, removes the need to do so with respect
to the end of the empire. Decolonisation thus becomes the product of the
egoistical whim of an individual, rather than an intricate process with
multiple degrees and loci of responsibility. This exonerates the *pieds-noirs*
from accountability for their fate, making them appear instead as pawns
in a larger political game beyond their control.

Staying true to your word

As far as *pied-noir* associations are concerned, the actions of de Gaulle during the Algerian war eclipsed his status as the saviour of France during the Second World War. This is reflected in their attempts to downplay the role of the de Gaulle, emphasising instead the contributions of the Armée d'Afrique and military figures with a colonial pedigree such as General, later Marshall, Alphonse Juin, or General Henri Giraud. Yet, while minimising de Gaulle's historical significance between 1940 and 1945, associations simultaneously sought to use the principle he established of legitimate opposition to a government no longer acting in the best interests of the nation to justify illegal actions committed in the name of the *Algérie française* cause, particularly with respect to the OAS. Noting that de Gaulle had been condemned to death by the Vichy regime for treason, putsch and OAS leader Edmond Jouhaud went on to argue 'Our action, likewise, in April 1961, was perhaps illegal but legitimate in our eyes.'[58] According to this system of logic, the putsch was an understandable response to the betrayal represented by the notion of self-determination. The failure of the attempted coup was then used to justify the establishment of the OAS as the last hope of a community who had been abandoned by their own leaders and who wished only to safeguard their homeland.[59] There is a clear current within the *pied-noir* press that has prominently and consistently promoted the actions of the OAS and their leaders. These narratives also give the impression that the OAS enjoyed the full support of the settler community (a belief also common among the general public, especially in the early 1960s). Such conclusions have been challenged by numerous scholars, who argue that what support did exist was largely symbolic, a way for the settlers to express their opposition to the policies of the French government being enacted in Algeria. This support furthermore declined demonstrably as the group's actions became more violent and indiscriminate. It should also be borne in mind that there were only an estimated one thousand active members of the OAS in Algeria and two hundred in France.[60]

Downplaying the extreme nature of the OAS, associations made only vague references to the exact actions of the group and rarely mentioned attacks conducted against civilians in Algeria and France. Accusations that it was the OAS's scorched earth policy that made the continued presence of the settlers in Algeria after independence untenable were also vehemently refuted. On the contrary, the OAS were credited with protecting vulnerable citizens in the wake of the ceasefire; the actions of these 'soldiers of the shadows' demonstrating their sense of duty towards those abandoned by the state to the 'fury' of the FLN.[61] In contrast to de Gaulle, members of the OAS, particularly those who came from the French armed forces, were portrayed as understanding the importance of remaining 'true to your word'. Alongside notions of loyalty, the terms 'honour' and 'duty' featured regularly in conjunction with the putsch and the OAS, although the most frequent allusions were to the Resistance and to the OAS as its heir. Embodying all these values was Jean Bastien-Thiry, who was put to death by firing squad for his role in the August 1962 assassination attempt against de Gaulle at Petit Clamart. The stoicism of this young, handsome and devoted father during both his trial and execution earned him the veneration of many within *pied-noir* community.[62] This admiration was expressed in a variety of ways, including a monument in Béziers (Languedoc) to him and other OAS 'martyrs' paid for by Cercle algérianiste members and bearing the inscription 'Shot for having defended French Algeria. Never forget their sacrifice.'

The actions of the pro-*Algérie française* lobby were therefore not represented as extreme responses to unique circumstances, but rather as the continuation of political and moral traditions whose legitimacy was already established. Beyond descriptions in the pages of association publications, sectors of the *pied-noir* community enjoyed a close relationship with defenders of the *Algérie française* cause, including former members of the OAS. These connections date back to the earliest years of the *rapatrié* presence in France. Both the FNR and the Comité nationale des rapatriés et spoliés were created at the initiative of Jouhaud, who, along with Raoul Salan, was also a member of the Cercle algérianiste's 'committee of honour'. Both men regularly appeared at *pied-noir* gatherings, where they were warmly welcomed and widely fêted. This was in addition to the passionate campaigns waged by associations for amnesties, not just for prominent figures like the putsch generals, but for all those who remained imprisoned as a result of their wartime activities. Upon their deaths, in 1984 and 1995 respectively, Salan and Jouhaud were given lengthy eulogies by the majority of associations who praised them as patriotic and courageous men of honour.[63]

26 March and 5 July 1962

Regarding the war more generally, the two crucial dates from the perspective of the *pied-noir* community are 26 March 1962, when French troops fired on a crowd of settlers demonstrating on the rue d'Isly in Algiers, killing forty-six and injuring 150, and 5 July 1962, when between 500 and 1000 Europeans were kidnapped or killed following violence which broke out amidst independence celebrations in Oran.[64] Although there were also Algerian casualties, what makes this second date particularly notable for *pieds-noirs* was that the remaining French troops, garrisoned in Oran under the command of General Joseph Katz and obeying orders from Paris, did not immediately intervene to protect the settlers. The centrality of these two 'massacres' is indicated by the scale and regularity of the coverage afforded to them by associations, many of which also hold annual commemorations on one or both of these dates and have done since 1962.[65]

Both 26 March and 5 July were perceived as moments that definitively set the *pied-noir* community apart, indicative of the 'total rupture' with both Algeria and France that occurred in 1962.[66] The fact that it was French forces who either fired on or failed to protect French citizens constitutes the most shocking aspect for those who experienced these events. With respect to the rue d'Isly, Ludovic Berthe recalled the collective sense of astonishment when the settlers realised that the French army had opened fire on its own citizens: 'The unthinkable is true. Hatred invades the heart, but also an immense despair, the feeling that one hundred and thirty years of history have, in one block, collapsed around us. The wound remains open and will never heal completely.'[67] The sense of separation was reinforced by the belief that the rue d'Isly and Oran had both fallen victim to a 'conspiracy of silence' orchestrated on behalf of a deliberately falsified official history.[68] In the face of this silence, associations argued that it was imperative to make the truth about both events known and to guard their memory. This was the impetus behind Geneviève de Ternant's three-volume series, *L'agonie d'Oran, 5 juillet 1962*, which, over the course of a decade, compiled an extensive collection of photographs and eyewitness accounts.[69] De Ternant intended her book to serve as 'a cenotaph' for those missing or killed, claiming that, even if 'imperfect', the volumes would at least have the merit of 'shouting to the whole world what they [the state] wanted to hide, forget, deny'.[70]

As with other key moments in their history, deconstructing the narratives offered by *pied-noir* associations about these two dates reveals a basic formula consistently applied. Emphasising the tranquillity and fraternity that had previously characterised the rue d'Isly and Oran, associations extracted these locations from the context of an increasingly violent conflict nearing its eighth year, making the events instead seem anomalous. A similarly stark juxtaposition was created between victims and aggressors with each side clearly delineated. 'The people of Algiers going to support their brothers in Bab-el-Oued', who, for the past three days, had been 'prisoners of a more than menacing

French army', was how *Aux échos d'Alger* explained the context for the rue d'Isly shooting.[71] The reasons behind the French military block-ade remained ill-defined in these accounts, with no mention of the fact that the Bab-el-Oued neighbourhood had been cordoned off in an attempt to break the power of the OAS and the cycle of violence they had unleashed on the city since the Evian Accords. Stressed instead was the peaceful nature of a crowd in which 'No one [was] armed, except with bouquets of flowers and flags'.[72] Deleting the OAS from the equation simultaneously removed any shades of grey, leaving a clear line between innocent and guilty.

The situation in Oran was equally rendered in black and white, with Katz, by obeying orders to keep his men in their barracks dur-ing the riots, conveniently placed to act as the villain of the piece. No account is taken of the restrictions under which Katz was operating, namely that the French forces were, as of 5 July, a foreign army in an independent sovereign nation. Nor is any mention made of the fact that Oran was a noted OAS stronghold and, as a result, had witnessed some of the most intense violence in the post-ceasefire period; the omission of such context allowing blame to be fully focused on Katz. Indicative of this was the response from associations to the publication of Katz's memoirs in 1997, at a point when the War of Independence was returning to public attention. One particularly scathing editorial in *Pieds-noirs magazine* ran as follows: 'General Katz has reappeared like Dracula thirsting for the blood of our martyrs ...As this indi-vidual doesn't have the decency to keep quiet and to die forgotten by all, we must react'.[73]

Finally, there was the assertion that the rue d'Isly and Oran were pre-meditated by the ultimate source of all *pied-noir* suffering, de Gaulle. Schoolteacher and Algiers inhabitant Roger Braiser recalled how he was telephoned on the morning of 26 March 1962 by one of his former pupils, a 'Muslim', who warned him: 'Sir, watch out! De Gaulle's given orders. He needs four hundred dead in the streets of Algiers by tonight.' What came to pass that day convinced Braiser that 'as in Oran, there was no destiny but a conspiracy organised in order to assassinate inno-cents'.[74] This and other accounts reprised the trope of the 'good Arab' with various *pieds-noirs* citing individual Algerians who attempted to shelter and protect them.[75] In the hands of *pied-noir* associations, the rue d'Isly and Oran deaths were thus rendered as unprovoked tragedies that were subsequently covered up, placing a burden of truth upon those who lived through these events to ensure that the dates and their victims were not forgotten.

The social and physical dimensions of memory

Speaking on an episode of *Les Dossiers de l'écran* devoted to considering what 'remained' of the past for those from Algeria, the author Jeanine de la Hogue appealed to her fellow *pieds-noirs* to write about their lost homeland in order to recreate it 'stone by stone' and thus leave a legacy for future generations.[76] This is essentially what the narratives offered through association publications sought to do. But, as Joëlle Hureau reminds us, this process was 'not limited to words and images fixed on the page', but equally possessed spatial and social dimensions.[77] Sharing Hureau's conception of memory as a form of social space, *pied-noir* associations organised regular *rassemblements* (gatherings) in order to commemorate a set calendar of religious, patriotic and war-related dates including Ascension, Assumption, Easter, 8 May, 11 November and 26 March. This 'calendar' enabled the *pied-noir* community to maintain its coherence in the present by affording individuals a predictable set of occasions through which to interact and (re)affirm their existence as a collective. Owing to his foundational role in the Cercle algérianiste, Calmein is worth quoting at length on the importance of *rassemblements*:

> Whatever the origin of the gathering you find throughout the same atmosphere where the joy of reunions mixes with the tears of painful memories and where the pleasure of being together dominates … Plunging furtively into a suddenly present happy past, far from metropolitan incomprehension, warm, in the heart of the tribe, pleasure – fleeting but oh how intense – in one fell swoop making you forget material problems, the dispersion of families and the anguish of starting over.

Through such occasions, the 'gaping wound' that Calmein saw in the heart of every *pied-noir* as a result of being 'wrenched' from French Algeria could finally find 'the semblance of healing'.[78]

The absence of familiar geographical landmarks in France only heightened the poignancy of the places at which *pieds-noirs* gathered; hence the reason that such sites were often re-baptised for the day with names of towns and streets from Algeria. In the words of Andrea Smith, being able to come together and surround themselves with memories and artefacts from the past, particularly food and drink, helped *pieds-noirs* to 'reweave a social fabric' and thus to establish a sense of 'social continuity'.[79] Although some *pieds-noirs* have chosen to undertake trips, often labelled as 'pilgrimages', to Algeria to revisit their former homes and communities, most have not.[80] Consequently, *rassemblements* offer a powerful way for *pieds-noirs* who physically reside in France but continue to dwell emotionally in Algeria to reconcile temporarily these two facets of their lives. Attendance at these events therefore cannot be taken as proof of overt support for the agendas of the associations organising them. For individual *pieds-noirs*, they may simply have been a chance to reunite with friends and to maintain a sense of connection to the past by returning, at least in spirit, to Algeria. Yet, for associations it was strategically important to be able to attract large numbers to their gatherings, since this bolstered their claims concerning their abilities to represent and influence the wider *rapatrié* community.

Rassemblements have been a feature of *pied-noir* life since the early 1960s. After three years of occupying themselves with the practical necessities of re-establishing their lives, *Midi: le magazine pieds-noirs* was pleased to report that over Easter and Pentecost 1965, readers had been able to come together, 'finally releasing this sigh of relief, finally breathing, finding again the joys of our youth'. Illustrating the article were photographs of groups of *pieds-noirs* picnicking outdoors, playing games, dancing and generally having a good time, confirming for the author of the piece that, irrespective of the actual name or place, 'wherever we find ourselves will be a "pied-noir" corner for the whole day'.[81] The best known and largest *pied-noir* gathering is the annual Ascension Day 'pilgrimage' to the purpose-built cathedral of Notre Dame de Santa Cruz in Mas-de-Mingue, which began in 1966. On the outskirts of Nîmes, the site houses a statue of the Virgin Mary which, legend has it, saved the people of Oran from a cholera epidemic in 1849. The statue was transported from Oran to Mas-de-Mingue specifically in order to provide a focal point for the displaced Oranien community. Giving 'a physical existence to a lost past', the site was envisaged as protecting the community from contemporary 'plagues', such as exile, isolation and loss of faith.[82] Reflecting the importance of religion as a source of identity among the former settlers, crowds of 10,000 were reported from early on and by the 1980s, at the peak of *pied-noir* activism, numbers were reported to be nearing the 100,000 mark. Outside of Ascension, Baussant states that the site receives approximately 10,000 visitors a year, often as part of day trips organised by *pied-noir* associations. To accommodate these numbers, the site has undergone considerable expansion. In addition to the original chapel and grotto, it now boasts a gallery, a 'museum of memory', a reception room, a 2500m² esplanade, a fountain and gardens, plus a set of bells repatriated from Algeria. The vast majority of this work has been financed by donations from *pieds-noirs* themselves. Although the number of 'pilgrims' has fallen in recent years, Nîmes has retained its status as the best-attended *pied-noir* event, particularly in major anniversary years, like 2012, which saw crowds again reach tens of thousands.[83]

Major anniversary years inevitably heightened the significance of the opportunity to 'mix culture and conviviality' represented by *rassemblements*. This was reflected in a series of quinquennial national gatherings that began with the '25 years after' event held in June 1987, which saw an estimated 40,000 *pieds-noirs* descend on the town of Nice to reunite and reminisce on an unprecedented scale.[84] Those who came to Nice between 25 and 28 June 1987 were able to view exhibitions devoted to life in French Algeria; watch military parades and a reconstruction of the landing of French troops in 1830 at Sidi-Ferruch; attend film screenings and round tables with notable *pied-noir* experts such as Pierre Goinard; indulge in North African cuisine and worship at the specially convened open air Mass. Visitors could also browse stalls set up by associations of all types and sizes, many of which became venues for unexpected reunions between former friends, neighbours and colleagues, who had often had not seen each other since 1962. For the relatively small Amicale gardoise des enfants algérois (AGEA), having a stall in Nice was a significant financial undertaking that occasioned much debate in the pages of their newsletter. In spite of an overall loss of 5451 francs, President Francette Mendosa felt that the decision to attend had been the right one. This was not only because she remained confident that their losses would be recouped through new members, in addition to the seventy-nine signed up in Nice itself, but because of the unique experience of being among so many other *pieds-noirs*.[85]

Outside of the personal and emotional appeal of the event, associations were conscious that the Nice gathering offered an unparalleled opportunity for the *pied-noir* community to proclaim proudly its identity and to demonstrate its numerical strength, cohesion and vitality to the wider world.[86] The desire to convey what French Algeria had really been like to younger generations and to the wider French population also motivated many, including the event's main organiser Paul Mefret.[87] In this regard, the Cercle algérianiste left Nice highly satisfied with the results of their engagement with the general public, reporting that, through evidence and argument, their stall had succeeded in exposing 'a little known Algeria and a forgotten France', something that 'for many of our visitors was a revelation'.[88] However, Geneviève de Ternant, president of the Amicale des oraniennes du Côte d'Azur (AOCAZ), was less convinced of the value of the exercise. She claimed that there were very few non-*pieds-noirs* in attendance, despite the fact that the gathering, with its many different attractions, represented a great opportunity for a family day out. While agreeing with the Cercle algérianiste that those who did come along were warmly welcomed and pleasantly surprised by what they discovered about

French Algeria, overall she felt the event was 'a lost opportunity for fraternisation and integration' and that this was 'a shame'.[89]

The unprecedented size of the Nice gathering, coupled with the
quarter-century anniversary of 1962 and the new compensation law making its way through parliament resulted in the presence at the event of
several high-profile politicians including the then prime minister Jacques
Chirac and the FN leader Jean-Marie Le Pen. Indeed, the FN sponsored
giant billboards on the route to the *rassemblement* proffering the party's
fraternal greetings to the *pieds-noirs*. With the next round of presidential elections less than year away, Le Pen was keen to be seen supporting
the occasion as part of what one news anchor referred to as his electoral
'seduction operation' with respect to the *rapatriés*.[90] The occasion also
generated significant media interest with most national newspapers and
television channels featuring the *rassemblement* in some capacity. Media
coverage was generally positive, emphasising the *pieds-noirs'* successful
socio-economic integration and confirming their status as an established
and accepted minority within France.

Following the success of Nice, mass anniversary gatherings were subsequently held every five years in locations including Paris, Marseille,
and Nîmes. Yet although popular and prominently covered within the
pied-noir press, these occasions were never quite able to match the atmosphere and impact of Nice. This was partly because they lacked the
unique confluence of political and commemorative factors, which gave
a particular degree of national visibility to the *pieds-noirs* in 1987. Ahead
of that event, ANFANOMA had predicted that Nice would show that the
pieds-noirs represented 'a force that France will have to take account of
from now on'.[91] Indeed, by showcasing the vibrancy of the cultural side of
pied-noir identity, associations had sought to prove that there was much
more to the community than simply a quest for financial recompense.
Looking back several years later in the pages of *Pieds-noirs magazine*,
Michel Sanchez argued that Nice had opened up a new era in the history
of the *pied-noir* community. In addition to demonstrating the attachment
of the *rapatriés* to both France and Algeria, the fact that '[n]o community as scattered as this one would be able to bring together so many of
its members' had provided convincing evidence that the *pieds-noirs* were
not 'an endangered species'.[92]

Inscribing the past in stone

The problem with *rassemblements*, whatever their size, is that they are
only able to embody memory in social spaces for a fixed period of time;

the past fragments and ebbs away as the participants return to their individual lives. *Pied-noir* associations have therefore also sought ways of
inscribing the community more permanently in the national landscape,
particularly as their members had been forced to leave behind in Algeria
almost all physical traces of their previous lives. Cemeteries were one of
the most painful things to leave behind; the inability to visit the graves
of loved ones, particularly on occasions such as All Saints Day, serving
as a poignant reminder of the rupture represented by 1962. Creating
physical markers in metropolitan France represented an important way
for *pieds-noirs* to ensure that a trace of their community would be pre-
served, while simultaneously anchoring themselves in the soil of their
new homeland. Expressing an attachment to France and a desire for that
connection to be acknowledged, the physical reinscription of *pied-noir*
history was, as Andrea Smith has recently argued, more outward facing
and 'assimilatory in spirit' than scholars have hitherto acknowledged.[93]

In the 1980s and early 1990s, the *pied-noir* community were given official physical recognition through the approval and construction of six
Maisons des rapatriés. Subsidised by local authorities, these buildings,
located in Montpellier, Marseille, Cannes, Aix-en-Provence, Nice and
Grenoble, provided office space for associations and a rendezvous point
for local *rapatriés*. Although small, such gestures were symbolically significant according to Daniel Leconte because they enabled *pieds-noirs* to
'entertain the hope of being recognised one day by the national community'.[94] Most *pied-noir* activists were not content, however, to wait for the
state to act, preferring to take matters into their own hands. This was
evident in the series of statues, monuments and plaques to the French
presence in Algeria that have been designed, funded and erected since
the 1960s on the initiative of associations.[95] One of the earliest examples
was a memorial to the *rapatriés* in the Aix-en-Provence cemetery created
in October 1965. This was an apt location given that the memorial was
intended to symbolise the graves that the community had been forced to
abandon in 1962 and thus to serve as a site where *pieds-noirs* could 'pray
while thinking of their dead left on the other shore of the [Mediterranean]
sea'.[96] A noted absence from the inauguration ceremony was Roger Frey,
the minister of the interior with responsibility for *rapatriés*. Those present
included the Bachaga Boualem and the OAS lawyer and far-right presidential candidate Jean-Louis Tixier Vignancourt, who placed a wreath
and gave a speech expressing his 'solidarity' with the *rapatrié* community.[97] Many similar structures have been erected in the years since, with
varying degrees of support from the local authorities. Like the inscription
on Nice's Mémorial des rapatriés, inaugurated in 1973, these structures

are meant to remind the wider nation that 'there once was a prosperous French Algeria, happy and harmonious' so that they 'never forgot those who worked and died for it'.[98]

At a local level, particularly in areas of France with high concentrations of *pieds-noirs*, a certain version of the Franco-Algerian past was thus quickly inscribed upon the landscape through monuments, ceremonies and street names. Prior to the 1990s, opposition to this process surfaced only occasionally. One such occasion was 8 June 1980, when, a few days prior to its inauguration, a bomb destroyed a monument in Toulon to the 'martyrs' of French Algeria, including the OAS member Roger Degueldre. In spite of the destruction, the dedication ceremony went ahead, attended by Jouhaud, the Secretary of State for *rapatriés* and the Deputy Mayor of Toulon. The debris of the original structure was conserved and incorporated into the design of a replacement memorial on the same site. The return of the War of Independence to public consciousness during the 1990s brought the memorialising efforts of the *pied-noir* community under greater scrutiny generating increasingly levels of controversy. As subsequent chapters will show, in spite, or perhaps because of, rising levels of criticism and opposition, associations have remained committed to commemorating those on the extreme edges of the *Algérie française* cause, determined to secure a place within the nation's physical commemorative landscape for *all* their war dead, irrespective of the circumstances in which they died.[99]

'A town like no other'

Combining the social and the physical dimensions of *pied-noir* collective memory is the town of Carnoux-en-Provence (Bouches-du-Rhône). Described in 2000 by its deputy mayor, Melchior Calandra, as 'a town like no other', Carnoux is indeed a unique place.[100] Founded in the mid-1950s by *rapatriés* from the newly independent Morocco who envisaged creating 'a small lot' where they could enjoy a peaceful retirement, the nine original inhabitants quickly found themselves overwhelmed by an influx of *pieds-noirs* in 1962. That year, the number of residents climbed sharply to 242; by 1964, it had leapt even more dramatically to 2000.[101] Under the dominant influence of the *pieds-noirs,* Carnoux grew into a sizeable town, receiving official recognition from the local municipality in 1966. More importantly, it was transformed into a living museum dedicated to the preservation of the memory and culture of French Algeria. Nostalgia and selective remembering were given free rein in this physical and historical re-creation of an idealised Algeria that included a church named

after the famous Notre Dame d'Afrique basilica which contained a caril-
lon of four bells and a black Virgin Mary, both transported from the
former colonial territory. French Algeria lived on in the daily activities
of Carnusiens who, after a hard day's work, could wander down to their
local café to enjoy an *apéro* of anisette with a side of merguez, indulge in
some *tchatcha* with their neighbours, or simply share memories of their
former lives. As one resident proudly proclaimed in the early 1960s,
'we've kept our customs, we've kept the lifestyle', while three decades
later Carnoux was still being described as 'the continuation of our paradise lost'.[102]

The permanence of Carnoux enabled it to operate as a kind of continual *rassemblement* where residents could immerse themselves in the
ambiance of French Algeria simply by stepping out of their front door.
Offering a unique form of physical and social familiarity, Carnoux functioned as a sanctuary where *pieds-noirs* could take refuge from the chaos
and trauma of their recent history, as well as from a metropole they felt
had consistently failed to understand them.[103] In contrast to the 'space of
rejection' that confronted the settlers in 1962, Carnoux promoted itself
as somewhere *pieds-noirs* could relax knowing that they would be 'welcomed by friends and understood by people who had faced the same
difficulties'.[104] More than simply a refuge from the real world, Carnoux
also symbolised 'the *pieds-noirs'* act of faith in the future'. As one resident
proudly declared 'We've rebuilt a city, rebuilt a life with our memories',
even though the majority of Carnoux's buildings were, in fact, constructed
not by *pieds-noirs,* but by Algerian migrant labourers.[105] Marketed as a
space that owed nothing to France and the French, Carnoux stood as
proof of the *pied-noir* community's independence and self-sufficiency.
'Our history is not old', explained one Carnusien, 'but what pride to be
able to say: a town created by *rapatriés* for *rapatriés*. We did it; we built
it.'[106] Carnoux was therefore presented as the embodiment of success on
the *pieds-noirs'* own terms, without compromising or diluting the distinctiveness of their identity and culture.

Of course, Carnoux has never been an exclusively *pied-noir* preserve. The town was able to grow to its present-day size of approximately 7000 inhabitants primarily because of its success in attracting
non-*pieds-noirs* with the requisite skills and capital. Not all of the original residents approved of such developments, fearing they would dilute
the town's distinctive identity. Such sentiments, alongside evolutions in
the broader cultural and commemorative context, help to explain the
creation, in 1984 and 1999 respectively, of two *pied-noir* associations in
the town: Carnoux racines and Racine pieds-noirs. The use of the term

'racine' or 'root' in both their names underlines the importance of the stability and permanence offered by Carnoux. Together with the archival documents contained in the town's Médiathèque Albert Camus, these initiatives represented attempts to avoid commemorative complacency by fostering an active and engaged relationship with Carnoux's *pied-noir* heritage amongst both residents and the wider *rapatrié* community. The development of associations in Carnoux was therefore both a logical complement to, and a necessary evolution of, the historical and memorial functions served by the town. All were designed to ensure that having succeeded in re-creating a little slice of Algeria in France, the hard work of the *pieds-noirs* would not fall to ruins.[107]

Nostalgérie

The collective vision articulated by and through *pied-noir* associations on paper, in social spaces and physically is often labelled as *nostalgérie*, defined as a 'pathological nostalgia for Algeria'.[108] The word 'nostalgia' derives from the Greek *nostos* meaning homecoming and *algos* meaning pain. It arises typically in the context of cultural stress, severe identity dislocation and complex or rapid social change.[109] What makes nostalgia particularly applicable to the *pieds-noirs* is that it 'defines itself by its inability to approach its subject', in this case the 'lost' land of French Algeria, for 'There can be no nostalgia without the sense of irreversibility'.[110] In the context of empire, Patricia Lorcin has recently insisted on the difference between 'imperial nostalgia', which she regards as being associated with the loss of empire and with visions of past imperial grandeur, and 'colonial nostalgia', which pertains to the loss of socio-cultural standing, that is to say, the loss of the colonial lifestyle.[111] By generalising and exaggerating particular aspects of their lived experiences, the myths created and disseminated by *pieds-noirs* about French Algeria gravitate more towards colonial nostalgia. However, their bitterness over the end of French Algeria and the resultant loss of status, both their own and France's, belie fundamental elements of imperial nostalgia.

Exemplifying the critical stance of many historians, Christopher Lasch has highlighted how nostalgia suppresses the complexity of the past. He argues that its victim is 'worse than a reactionary; he is an incurable sentimentalist. Afraid of the future, he is also afraid to face the truth about the past'.[112] Viewed in this manner, nostalgia possesses a 'screen function' which, by idealising the past, inhibits mourning and thus prevents movement towards the future.[113] But others, notably Peter Fritzsche, have called for a conceptualisation of nostalgia that acknowledges its constructive

potential alongside its paralysing elements.[114] Speaking with reference
to the French Revolution, Fritzsche claims that the 'presence of absence'
inherent in nostalgia is worth paying attention to because it has the 'effect
of repeatedly scribbling up the clean slate of modern development and
raising unbidden questions about the origins of social identity, the given-
ness [sic] of the here and now, and the possibility of contrary movements
in the flow of history'.[115] In line with this perspective, the pieds-noirs constituted a visible reminder in 1962 of a past most were anxious to forget. They have retained this position primarily because of their refusal
to suppress their cultural identity in order to assimilate. Defending and
disseminating their own interpretations therefore constitutes a strategy
of 'self-preservation in an alien culture' that revolves around a sustained
effort by pied-noir activists not to allow others to write them out of history,
or impose external definitions upon them.[116] Nostalgérie in this context
can be read as a consciously formulated counter-history that, irrespective of its accuracy, poses questions about the dominant official narrative.
This was particularly significant during the 1970s and 1980s when there
was, in effect, no public discussion of the war, nor much engagement –
academic, political, or cultural – with France's colonial past.

There are, nonetheless, limits to this reading. Although association
narratives provide valuable insights into life in French Algeria and colonial mentalities, they also display many of the negative attributes associated with nostalgia. One example is the lack of self-awareness among
certain pieds-noirs, which renders them unwilling or unable to acknowledge the privileges they enjoyed and their complicity in the colonial system. Furthermore, in refusing to accept the validity of other perspectives,
pied-noir associations, like other identity-based groups, are often less
interested in engaging constructively with the past than in controlling its
narration. These elements make it difficult to subscribe to the argument
made by the association of Mémoire d'Afrique du Nord that pied-noir
nostalgia is simply a benign form of reminiscing. 'Why not tell us a
humorous or original anecdote' encouraged the association's magazine,
inviting readers to share 'a funny or touching recollection that allows us
to walk through the paths of memory with you'.[117] In reality, what associations offer are not random individual recollections, but a much more
conscious commemorative strategy based upon the reiteration of key
propositions relating to a mythologised past that underwrite particular
facets of the present-day identity of the community that activists want
to project.

In 2002, the French scholar Eric Savarèse published a book about the
'invention' of the pieds-noirs.[118] The term was apt, for although associations

claimed they were simply chronicling and preserving a pre-existing culture, in reality they were formulating a new set of discourses. In the same
way the *pied-noir* community has always been an artificial construct, so
too are the history and culture attached to it by associations. This is not
to suggest that the memories invoked are themselves false, rather what
is put forward as 'remembrance' is often 're-creation' or 're-presentation'
in the light of current circumstances and priorities.[119] During the 1970s
and 1980s, an array of associations and their activists worked to create
and maintain their own official history and identity in rhetorical, social
and physical terms. The process of establishing a 'meta-memory' for the
community was framed by the sense that recent history had treated the
pieds-noirs unfairly.[120] By recasting the past and seeking to refute the
many misperceptions they felt the metropolitan French held about them,
activists and associations endeavoured to build a collective vision that
would enable *pieds-noirs* to take pride in their history while simultaneously sharing in a contemporary communal identity.

One of the rationales behind the creation of this 'meta-memory' was
the claim that the state and official history had forgotten the *pieds-noirs*,
placing the 'duty of memory' entirely upon their shoulders. Yet, the reluctance of France to discuss its colonial past was of benefit to associations;
the fact that no one apart from the *pieds-noirs* was openly discussing
these subjects, in either popular or academic spheres, meant that there
were few dissenting voices or sources of empirical data with which associations needed to deal. The way was essentially left clear for activists to
construct their own, internally directed, version of events and to foster
their own collective myths. By the time contradictory interpretations and
competition from other memory carriers began to emerge on a significant scale in the 1990s, the *pied-noir* lexicon was firmly established and
its deployment sufficiently well-rehearsed that it was able to withstand
these challenges. Although the emphasis given to certain elements has
varied over the years, the central tenets of the vision of the past created by
pied-noir associations has changed little since the 1980s. Having successfully developed a broadly consensual and clearly defined set of narratives,
associations saw no need to modify their stance. On the contrary, many
associations now regard the consistent nature of their historical discourse
as proof of its veracity.

What did change was the context in which the *pied-noir* community was
operating as the war returned to public consciousness during the 1990s.
This altered commemorative landscape created potential new audiences,
but also rivals in the form of other groups seeking space and acceptance
for their understanding of the past. In some respects, this may have saved

pied-noir associations from ossification. For beneath their many activities and outward appearance of dynamism, there was a fear among some activists that the insularity of speaking primarily to other *pieds-noirs* was leading to a certain sterility. The re-emergence of the colonial past into the public arena brought with it new debates to participate in, new causes to champion, and a newly interested public and government to try to win over. This, in addition to other prominent topics during the 1990s on which the *pieds-noirs* possessed strong views, such as immigration, Islam, the wearing of the veil and the rise of the political far right, all created new opportunities and avenues for engagement. As the established vehicles through which this activism was channelled, associations were able to retain their prominence as 'the active bond' for the wider community.[121]

Only by understanding the logic behind the vision of the past that *pied-noir* associations felt under increasing pressure to defend in the 1990s is it possible to contextualise the ways in which these organisations responded to the evolving commemorative climate. That *pied-noir* activists developed a version of the past to justify their present position and validate their worldview is not in itself remarkable. All memory-carrying groups filter the past, indulging in what Savarèse calls 'a liberating amnesia', in order to produce a history that is 'deliberately embellished' and which 'erases shadowy zones'.[122] What is noteworthy about *pied-noir* associations is the speed with which they solidified a collective narrative, the extent of the consensus established and the stability of this 'meta-memory' over several decades. More broadly, the significance of *pied-noir* activism in this period lies in the ways in which and the extent to which it set the agenda for contemporary postcolonial politics. In essence, *pied-noir* associations provided a model of collective mobilisation and a way of framing questions about memory and history that, as subsequent chapters will show, other groups simultaneously borrowed from and reacted against as they sought to advance their own strategic readings of the colonial past. By getting there first, *pied-noir* associations were able to shape the terrain of postcolonial civil society. While the contours and positions established by *pied-noir* associations did not remain unchallenged, they were also not completely swept aside as new actors increasingly entered the arena. Just like the community itself, the historical narrative promoted by associations would prove highly durable.

Notes

1 Clarisse Buono, *Pieds-noirs de père en fils* (Paris, 2004), p. 100.
2 Pierre Maestre, 'Réflexions', *Les Français d'AFN et d'Outre Mer*, 42 (28 January 1983), 1.

3   E.F. Isin and P.K. Wood, *Citizenship and Identity* (London, 1999), p. 43.

4   'Notre charte', *Sétif de l'Hexagone*, 1 (October 1970), 2.

5   See *L'écho d'Oran* which, in 1966, became *L'écho de l'Oranie* produced by the Amicale des oraniennes du Côte d'Azur (AOCAZ); *Aux échos d'Alger* by the AGEA; and *Sétif de l'Hexagone* by the Amicale des Sétifiens.

6   For a critical discussion of these texts, see Jeanine de la Hogue, *Mémoire écrite de l'Algérie depuis 1950: les auteurs et leurs oeuvres* (Paris, 1992); Anne Roche, 'Deuil et mélancolie dans quelques autobiographies "nostalgériques" de l' "après 1962"', *Cahiers de sémiotique textuelle*, 4 (1985), 95–110; Amy L. Hubbell, 'The Wounds of Algeria in Pied-Noir Autobiography', *Dalhousie French Studies*, 81 (Winter 2007), 59–68.

7   Francine Dessiagne, *Déracinés!* (Paris, 1964), p. 4.

8   Camille Brière, *Ceux qu'on appelle les pieds noirs* (Paris, 1984), pp. 245, 281.

9   Jean-Jacques Jordi, *1962, l'arrivée des pieds-noirs* (Paris, 1995), p. 123.

10 Joëlle Hureau, *La Mémoire des pieds-noirs de 1830 à nos jours* (Paris, 2001), p. 254.

11 Jay Winter, 'Thinking about Silence', in *Shadows of War: A Social History of Silence in the Twentieth Century*, ed. by Efrat Ben Ze'ev, Ruth Ginio and Jay Winter (Cambridge, 2010), p. 23.

12 Hureau, *La Mémoire des pieds-noirs*, p. 256.

13 For illustrations of this, see 'Pour ceux d'Algérie, que reste-t-il du passé?', *Les Dossiers de l'écran*, aired 5 April 1983 (A2); 'Droit de réponse aux pieds-noirs', *Droit de réponse*, aired 8 November 1986 (TF1); 'Les pieds-noirs, ça va?', *Les Dossiers de l'écran*, aired 20 October 1987 (A2); 'Rapatriés: 25 ans de nostalgie', *Camera 2*, aired 22 June 1987 (A2).

14 Ysabel Saïah, *Pieds-noirs et fiers de l'être* (Paris, 1987), pp. 223–68.

15 Monique Ayoun and Jean-Pierre Stora (eds.), *Mon Algérie: 62 personnalités témoignent* (Paris, 1989), p. 45.

16 Richard M. Koubi, *Pieds-noirs belle pointure* (Paris, 1979), p. 10.

17 Francette Mendosa, 'Editorial', *L'écho de l'Oranie*, 190 (May–June 1987), 1.

18 Buono, *Pieds-noirs*, p. 75.

19 Jean-Jacques Jordi, 'The Creation of the Pieds-Noirs: Arrival and Settlement in Marseilles, 1962', in *Europe's Invisible Migrants*, ed. by Andrea L. Smith (Amsterdam, 2003), p. 63.

20 Brière, *Ceux qu'on appelle*, p. 240.

21 To question the 'suitcase or the coffin' thesis therefore provokes considerable hostility, as journalist Pierre Daum discovered when he began publishing interviews with Europeans who had remained in Algeria after independence. Even though Daum was clear that he was not claiming all settlers could have stayed in 1962, his research nonetheless raised the uncomfortable issue of why, if it was possible for some to remain and survive, so many *pieds-noirs* had rushed to leave their beloved homeland. Pierre Daum, *Ni valise ni cercueil: les pieds-noirs restés en Algérie après l'indépendance* (Arles, 2012), p. 27.

22 'L'Algérie dix ans après: les rapatriés', *Quatrième mardi*, aired 30 May 1972 (Channel 1).

23 Ayoun and Stora, *Mon Algérie,* p. 252.

24 Cited in Danielle Michel-Chich, *Déracinés: les pieds-noirs aujourd'hui* (Paris, 2000), p. 16.

25 Juliette in Michèle Baussant, *Pieds-noirs: mémoires d'exils* (Paris, 2002), p. 434.

26 'Les lecteurs répondent...', *L'Algérianiste* 68 (December 1994), 2–3.

27 See, for example, Fulgence, 'Ces barbares des plages', *L'Algérianiste,* 49 (March 1990), 91–5; Fulgence, 'Des mots', *L'Algérianiste* 52 (December 1990), 82–5.

28 The cartoons were penned by Achdé (Hervé Darmenton) as a favour for his *pied-noir* friends who ran the magazine. In correspondence with the author, Darmenton explained that the strips were done in the style of the famous Moroccan cartoon 'Zbib et Barnabé' and in fact drew for inspiration on a combination of family stories about life in Morocco in the 1920s (the Sebou is a river in Morocco), as well as his own memories of growing up in the south of France in the early 1960s, where, he stated, 'multi-racial' groups of friends were common. Although not directly set in Algeria, the tropes evoked in these strips were still very much in keeping with the ethos and message of *Pieds-noirs magazine.* Unfortunately, it was not possible to secure permission to reproduce any of the cartoons.

29 Renato Rosaldo, 'Imperialist Nostalgia', *Representations,* 26 (Spring 1989), 108.

30 Brière, *Ceux qu'on appelle,* p. 247; Anne Roche, 'Pieds-noirs: le "retour"', *Modern and Contemporary France,* 2:2 (1994), 160.

31 Poll conducted by SOFRES and published in the *Nouvel Observateur,* March 1987. Cited in Saïah, *Pieds-noirs,* p. 27.

32 Yann Scioldo-Zürcher, *Devenir métropolitain: politique d'intégration et parcours de rapatriés d'Algérie en métropole (1954–2005)* (Paris, 2010), p. 391.

33 Brière, *Ceux qu'on appelle,* p. 9.

34 Maurice Calmein, '10 sur 10 pour nos enseignants', *L'Algérianiste,* 14 (15 May 1981), 2.

35 Christian Gillet in Peter Batty, *La Guerre d'Algérie* (Paris, 1989), p. 18.

36 Koubi, *Pieds-noirs,* p. 15.

37 Pierre Goinard in Ayoun and Stora, *Mon Algérie,* p. 149.

38 When referring to the colonial period, associations generally use the terms 'Arab' and 'Muslim' interchangeably, unless they wish to make a specific point about Arabs in relation to Algeria's Berber population.

39 Among the growing scholarship on anti-Semitism and the position of Jews in French Algeria, see, in particular, Joshua Cole, 'Antisémitisme et situation coloniale pendant l'entre-deux guerres en Algérie: les émeutes antijuives de Constantine (août 1934)', *Vingtième siècle,* 108 (October–December 2010), 2–23; Samuel Kalman, *French Colonial Fascism: The Extreme Right in Algeria, 1919–1939* (New York, 2013).

40 See, for example, 'Les pied-noirs vingt ans après', *La Rage de lire,* aired 5 March 1980 (TF1); *Les Chevaux du soleil tribune,* aired 27 November 1980 (TF1); 'Les Pieds-noirs, ça va?', aired 20 October 1987.

41 Programmes documenting Macias's renewed relationship with his Judeo-Arab roots include 'Enrico l'Andalou', *Music planet,* aired 24 March 2001 (ARTE);

'Enrico Macias', *Ombres et lumière*, aired 14 March 2003 (FR3); 'Enrico Macias, le chant de la mémoire', *L'été des documents x3*, aired 10 August 2007 (FR5).

42 Batty, *La Guerre d'Algérie*, p. 22.

43 'Rapatriés: 25 ans de nostalgie', aired 22 June 1987.

44 Bernard Coll in 'Droit de réponse aux pieds-noirs', aired 8 November 1986.

45 Maurice Calmein, *Dis, c'était comment, l'Algérie française?* (Friedberg, Bayern, 2002), p. 14.

46 R. Finkbender, 'Quand l'Algérie était française', *Aux échos d'Alger*, 23 (September 1988), 3–15; 24.

47 Josseline Revel-Mouroz, 'Le Centre d'études pied-noir (CEPN)' in *Marseille et le choc des décolonisations*, ed. by Jean-Jacques Jordi and Emile Temime (Aix-en-Provence, 1996) pp. 195–6.

48 'Notre charte', 3.

49 Joëlle Hureau, 'Associations et souvenir chez les français rapatriés d'Algérie', in *La Guerre d'Algérie et les français*, ed. by Jean-Pierre Rioux (Paris, 1990), p. 525. This observation is also made in Buono, *Pieds-noirs*, p. 75.

50 Overall, 123 people were killed. In addition to European civilians, this number included thirty-one soldiers and police officers, and twenty-one Algerians. Some of the worst violence took place in the small mining town of El-Halia where thirty-seven Europeans were killed, including ten children, by Algerians they had worked alongside for many years. See Martin Evans, *Algeria: France's Undeclared War* (Oxford, 2012), pp. 134–5.

51 Jan C. Jansen, 'Politics of Remembrance, Colonialism and the Algerian War of Independence in France', in *A European Memory? Contested Histories and Politics of Remembrance*, ed. by Małgorzata Pakier and Bo Stråth (New York and Oxford, 2010), p. 279.

52 *Montpellier: 20 ans accords d'Evian*, aired 19 March 1982 (A2). See also Emile Chabal, 'Managing the Postcolony: Minority Politics in Montpellier, c. 1960 to c. 2010', *Contemporary European History*, 23:2 (2014), 249.

53 *France horizon*, 428–9 (January–February 2002), 12.

54 Patrick Roger, 'Le 19 mars, journée du souvenir pour les victimes de la guerre d'Algérie', *Le Monde* (1 December 2012), p. 12.

55 Two referendums were held. The first, on 8 January 1961, was in relation to self-determination, the second referendum, to approve the Evian Accords, was held on 8 April 1962.

56 'Nice tourne le dos aux pieds-noirs', *L'Algérianiste*, 134 supplement (June 2011), 1.

57 Gilbert Debono, 'Le Coup d'état du 13 mai 1958', *Midi: le magazine pieds-noirs*, 11 (May 1966), 7.

58 Cited in 'Les Quatre généraux les plus décorés de France', *La Lettre de Véritas*, 2 (April 1996), 1.

59 'La France et son histoire', *Pieds-noirs magazine*, 15 (May 1991), 4; Gevay, 'C'est la faute de l'OAS …', *L'écho de l'Oranie*, 159 (March–April 1982), 9.

60 For a recent example of this argument, see Emmanuelle Comtat, *Les Pieds-noirs et la politique quarante ans après le retour* (Paris, 2009), p. 78.

61 José Castano, 'L'OAS', *Les Français d'AFN et d'Outre Mer*, 72 (22 June 1984), 7.

62 Bernard Moinet, 'Bastien-Thiry s'est sacrifié pour la France', *Pieds-noirs d'hier et d'aujourd'hui*, 55 (March 1995), 25.

63 See, for example, Edmond Jouhaud, 'Hommage au général Salan', *L'Algérianiste*, 27 (15 September 1984), 2–3; 'La Mort du général Salan', *France horizon*, 254 (July–August 1984), 1; 'Souvenir- fidelité', *Les Français d'AFN*, 74 (28 September 1984), 3; Roger Brasier and Maurice Calmein, 'Le Général Jouhaud', *L'Algérianiste* 72 (December 1995), 2–4; 'Edmond Jouhaud: le général de l'Algérie mort', *France horizon*, 364–5 (September–October 1995), 12–13, 24.

64 Fiona Barclay, 'Reporting on 1962: the Evolution of *pied-noir* Identity across Fifty Years of Print Media', *Modern and Contemporary France* 23:2 (2015), 207.

65 See, for example, 'In memoriam', *France horizon*, 46 (June 1962), 3; Paule Mathieu, '5 juillet 1962. Le massacre des innocents', *L'écho d'Oran*, 12 (July 1965), 4.

66 'Rapatriés: 25 ans de nostalgie', aired 22 June 1987.

67 Ludovic Berthe, 'La Tragédie du 26 mars 1962 la rue d'Isly', *Pieds-noirs magazine*, 13 (March 1991), 26–7.

68 While it is true that these episodes are less well known than, say, the Battle of Algiers, both the rue d'Isly and Oran do feature in the majority of academic treatments of the War of Independence. There is also academic research on Oran, see Fouad Soufi, 'L'histoire face à la mémoire: Oran, le 5 juillet 1962', in *La Guerre d'Algérie dans la mémoire et l'imaginaire*, ed. by Anny Dayan Rosenman and Lucette Valensi (Saint-Denis, 2004), pp. 133–148; Fouad Soufi, 'Oran, 28 février 1962, 5 juillet 1962. Deux événements pour l'histoire, deux événements pour la mémoire', in *La Guerre d'Algérie au miroir des décolonisations françaises* (Paris, 2000), pp. 635–76.

69 Geneviève de Ternant *L'agonie d'Oran 5 juillet 1962*, 3 vols. (Calvisson, 1991–2000).

70 de Ternant *L'agonie d'Oran* (1991), p. 3. A similar project was undertaken for the rue d'Isly by Marie-Jeanne Rey and Francine Dessaigne, both of whom also penned popular memoirs focusing on this event. See *Un crime sans assassins: Alger 26 mars 1962* (Perros-Guirec, 1994).

71 Berthe, 'La tragédie', 26; 'Le 26 mars 1962 ... le 26 mars 1982', *Aux échos d'Alger*, 2 (May 1982), 3.

72 Berthe, 'La Tragédie', 26.

73 'Faut-il un nouveau miracle à Santa Cruz?', *Pieds-noirs d'hier et d'aujourd'hui* 79 (May 1997), 5. See also Joseph Katz, *L'honneur d'un général: Oran, 1962* (Paris, 1993); Joseph Katz, *Une destinée unique: mémoires 1907–1996* (Paris, 1997).

74 Roger Braiser, 'Le 26 mars 1962', *L'écho de l'Oranie*, 219 (March–April 1992), 19.

75 See, for example, M.J. 'Oran, ville martyre', *Pieds-noirs magazine*, 4 (May 1990), 19.

76 'Pour ceux d'Algérie', aired 5 April 1983.

77 Hureau, *La Mémoire*, p. 87.

78 Maurice Calmein in Ayoun and Stora, *Mon Algérie*, p. 126.
79 Andrea L. Smith, *Colonial Memory and Postcolonial Europe: Maltese Settlers in Algeria and France* (Bloomington, IN, 2006), p. 188.
80 For further discussion of this phenomenon, see Claire Eldridge, 'The *Pied-Noir* Community and the Complexity of "Coming Home" to Algeria', in *Coming Home? Conflict and Return Migration in Twentieth-Century Europe*, Vol. 2, ed. by Scott Soo and Sharif Gemie (Cambridge, 2013) pp. 12–32.
81 'Les Pieds-noirs fêtent la mouna', *Midi: le magazine pieds-noirs*, 2 (June 1965), 10–12; Smith, *Colonial Memory*, p. 191.
82 Baussant, *Pieds-noirs*, p. 21; Susan Slyomovics, 'Algeria Elsewhere: The Pilgrimage of the Virgin of Santa Cruz in Oran and in Nîmes, France', in *Folklore Interpreted*, ed. by Regina Bendix and Rosemary Lévy-Zumwalt (New York, 1995), p. 342.
83 Baussant, *Pieds-noirs*, pp. 25–37; 'Pèlerinage de pieds-noirs au sanctuaire de Santa Cruz', *Le Jour du Seigneur*, aired 10 June 2012 (FR2).
84 Valérie Esclangon-Morin, *Les Rapatriés d'Afrique du Nord de 1956 à nos jours* (Paris, 2007), p. 348. *Pied-noir* associations typically give much higher figures for this event ranging from 100,000 to 300,000 attendees.
85 '25 ans après', *Aux échos d'Alger*, 19 (September 1987), 12.
86 'Rapatriés: 25 ans de nostalgie', aired 22 June 1987.
87 Saïah, *Pieds-noirs*, p. 29.
88 Jo Sohet, 'Avec vous: vingt-cinq ans … et trois mois après', *L'Algérianiste*, 39 (September 1987), iv.
89 'Editorial', *L'écho de l'Oranie*, 191 (July–August 1987), 1.
90 'Rassemblement rapatriés', *JA2 20 heures*, aired 26 June 1987 (A2).
91 '25 anniversaire rassemblement', *France horizon*, 282 (May 1987), 14.
92 Michel Sanchez, 'Nice 1987', *Pieds-noirs magazine*, 16 (June 1991), 8–9.
93 Smith, 'Settler Sites of Memory', 72–6; Smith, *Colonial Memory*, p. 171.
94 Daniel Leconte, *Les Pieds-noirs: histoire et portrait d'une communauté* (Paris, 1980), p. 272. For an expanded discussion of the history of Montpellier's Maison de rapatriés, see Chabal, 'Managing the Postcolony', 248.
95 Edifices created specifically by and for *pied-noir* associations should be distinguished from the numerous monuments that were repatriated from Algeria to France at the end of the War of Independence, even though some of these have been re-appropriated as commemorative sites. For a detailed survey of these repatriated artefacts, see Alain Amato, *Monuments en exil* (Paris, 1979). For analysis of the postcolonial trajectory of one such monuments, the statue of the Duc d'Orléans, and its significance as a site of commemorative struggle, see Jennifer E. Sessions, 'Repatriating the Duc d'Orléans: The Entangled Politics of Postcolonial Commemoration', in *Algeria Revisited: History, Culture and Identity, 1830 to the Present*, ed. by Rabah Aissaoui and Claire Eldridge (London, forthcoming 2016).
96 'Le Mémorial des rapatriés a été inauguré à Aix-en-Provence', *L'écho d'Oran*, 16 (November 1965), 7.
97 'Le Mémorial', 7.

98   For analysis of the layers of memory and significance inscribed onto this structure, see William B. Cohen, 'Pied-Noir Memory, History and the Algerian War', in *Europe's Invisible Migrants*, p. 137; Raphaëlle Branche, *La Guerre d'Algérie: une histoire apaisée?* (Paris, 2005), p. 25.

99   For further discussion of this, see Chapter 8.

100   'La Cité des pieds-noirs', *La Cinquième rencontre*, aired 6 June 2000 (La cinquième).

101   Jordi, *1962, l'arrivée* p. 103; 'Naissance d'un village: Carnoux', *Cinq colonnes à la une*, aired 7 October 1966 (Channel 1).

102   Léo Palacio, *Les Pieds-noirs dans le monde* (Paris, 1968), p. 23; 'La cité des pieds-noirs', aired 6 June 2000.

103   Cited in Michel-Chich, *Déracinés*, p. 128.

104   Melchior Calandra, 'Être pied-noir trente ans après', *Français si vous parliez*, aired 1 February 1993 (FR3); Thérèse Rodolico, 'Carnoux-en-Provence. Cité nouvelle des rapatriés', *Bulletin de la Société de Géographie Marseille*, 76:5 (1966), 55.

105   Jean Chaland, 'Carnoux: l'acte de foi des pieds-noirs en l'avenir', *Pieds-noirs d'hier et d'aujourd'hui*, 92 (July–August 1998) 11; 'La cité des pieds-noirs', aired 6 June 2000.

106   Jordi, *1962, l'arrivée*, pp. 102–3; 'Naissance d'un village', aired 7 October 1966.

107   A more extended discussion of Carnoux and the *pied-noir* community can be found in Claire Eldridge, '"Le Symbole de l'Afrique perdue": Carnoux-en-Provence and the *Pied-Noir* Community', in *France's Lost Empires: Fragmentation, Loss and la fracture coloniale*, ed. by Kate Marsh and Nicola Frith (Lanham, MD, 2011), pp. 125–36.

108   Smith, 'Settler Sites', 65.

109   Peter Fritzsche, 'Spectres of History: On Nostalgia, Exile and Modernity', *American Historical Review*, 106:5 (December 2001), 1591.

110   Fritzsche, 'Spectres of History', 1595.

111   Patricia M. E. Lorcin, *Historicizing Colonial Nostalgia: European Women's Narratives of Algeria and Kenya 1900-Present* (New York and Basingstoke, 2012), p. 9.

112   Cited in David Lowenthal, 'Nostalgia Tells It Like It Wasn't', in *The Imagined Past: History and Nostalgia*, ed. by Christopher Shaw and Malcolm Chase (Manchester, 1989), p. 20.

113   Nancy Wood, *Vectors of Memory: Legacies of Trauma in Postwar Europe* (Oxford and New York, 1999), pp. 145–6.

114   Fritzsche, 'Spectres of History', 1592.

115   Fritzsche, 'Spectres of History', 1593.

116   Andreea Deciu Rítívoí, *Yesterday's Self: Nostalgia and the Immigrant Identity* (Lanham, MD, 2002), p. 32.

117   'Supplément', *Mémoire plurielle*, 9 (October 1996), 8.

118   Eric Savarèse, *L'invention des pieds-noirs* (Paris, 2002).

119 Lucette Valensi, 'From Sacred History to Historical Memory and Back', in *Between Memory and History*, ed. by Marie-Noëlle Bourget, Lucette Valensi and Nathan Watchel (Chur, Switzerland, 1990), p. 80.

120 Buono, *Pieds-noirs*, p. 100.

121 Maurice Calmein in Ayoun and Stora, *Mon Algérie*, p. 128.

122 Esclangon-Morin, *Les Rapatriés*, p. 329; Eric Savarèse, *Algérie, la guerre des mémoires* (Paris, 2007), p. 213.

4

Breaking the silence

During the summer of 1991, the south of France witnessed a series of
harki protests. Areas with high concentrations of *harkis* and their
families, such as the Cité des Oliviers in Narbonne (Aude), the town
of Saint-Laurent-des-Arbres (Gard) and the site of the Bias camp
(Lot-et-Garonne), featured regularly in local and national media, particularly when demonstrations turned to violence. In news reports, footage of night skies backlit by burning cars with silhouettes of young men
brandishing sticks and throwing rocks was interspersed with interviews,
conducted during daylight hours, in which these same youths gave verbal expression to their frustrations, holding placards or wearing T-shirts
demanding 'justice' for the *harkis*. This was not the first incidence of
unrest, but rather the culmination of a series of episodes attesting to
mounting levels of tension within the *harki* community.[1] The events of
1991 were regularly compared to the summer of 1975, the last time discontent had reached similar levels. Indeed, one of the main factors behind
the 1991 protests was the lack of progress towards integrating the *harki*
community made since 1975, in spite of government rhetoric and a range
of commissions and initiatives. Resentment at the ongoing physical and
socio-economic marginalisation was most keenly felt by the younger elements of the community, namely those born in France after 1962 who were
now young adults. Their anger crystallised around the issue of unemployment, which was reported to be approaching 80 per cent among those
aged from eighteen to twenty-five in the Rivesaltes area.[2] Being unable
to find or keep jobs, in spite of access to various government-sponsored
training schemes, was the most visible manifestation of the wider discrimination to which these men and women felt they were subjected.

Even the French public seemed to concur: a poll in 1989 revealed that 42 per cent of respondents considered the *harkis* a community 'apart' and on the margins of society, while only 34 per cent thought their integration had been a success.[3]

Confirming this lack of progress towards integration was the fact that the practical demands of the 1991 campaigners were essentially the same as those voiced during protests sixteen years previously. However, the activists who came to the fore in 1991 were also consciously trying to do something new in terms of strategy. Deliberately seeking to 'set a cat among the pigeons', this new generation of militants wanted to break with existing patterns of mobilisation to create a co-operative, federative and, crucially, independent network. They additionally wanted to reorientate *harki* activism so that it extended beyond demands for material support and into historical and commemorative arenas.[4] Both elements were underpinned by an insistence on the need for recognition of the community as French. For children of *harkis*, this revolved primarily around measures to ensure that their full socio-economic insertion was realised. For older generations, the *harkis* themselves and their spouses, it was framed in terms of gaining recognition for their history as a means to validate their contribution to the nation and thus revalorise their position within it. This latter combat involved a two-pronged strategy whereby the history of the *harkis* was to be drawn out of silence at the same time as control of the resultant narratives was to be wrested away from external commentators and placed in the hands of the community itself. To understand this drive for autonomy, both in terms of how *harki* activism was organised and the ends to which it was directed, it is necessary to examine the relationships between the community and other interested parties in the years leading up to 1991.

1975

The French public were first alerted to the plight of the *harki* community on a significant scale in 1975 when a spate of demonstrations captured national media attention.The months of May through to July saw members of the *harki* community engage in marches and strikes, block roads and occupy symbolic sites within camps, forest hamlets and local municipalities, beginning in the Bias camp but quickly spreading elsewhere. In June, the director of the Saint-Maurice-l'Ardoise camp and Colonel Deluc, the secretary general of the Comité national pour les musulmans français, more commonly known as the Comité Parodi, were taken hostage by youths armed with guns and dynamite. These initial acts were accompanied by calls for the closure of the camps, the amelioration of conditions in the forest hamlets, and concrete measures to facilitate integration. By August, events had taken a different turn as six Algerian workers were held hostage. This retaliatory act followed the detention of Borzani Kradaoui, the child of a *harki* who had gone to visit family in Algeria with his mother, but who had been prevented from returning to France by the Algerian authorities. The release of Borzani, along with two other *harki* children detained in Algeria around the same time, did not immediately calm the situation, as evidenced by the kidnapping of Djelloul Belfadel, secretary of the local branch of Amicale des Algériens en Europe (AAE) in Unieux (Loire) on 16 August. Targeting Algerians in this way was designed to highlight the issue of free circulation between France and Algeria,which was still denied to the *harkis* even as measures were coming into force that permitted family reunification for Algerians working in France. Viewed together, Régis Pierret argues that these two strands of the 1975 protests demonstrated the *harki* community reacting both to their banishment from Algeria and their rejection by France.[5]

For most of the 1975 protestors, however, it was their day-to-day living conditions that served as the greatest impetus to action. Conditions in the two remaining camps, Bias and Saint-Maurice-l'Ardoise, and in the various forest hamlets had deteriorated considerably as buildings, which had only ever been designed as temporary shelters, had now been in use for more than two decades. A sense of this can be gained from the 1972 annual report for Bias, which requested that showers be installed in the *harkis'* homes, in place of the communal showers that residents had to pay to use; that the buildings be disinfected; that streetlights be installed; that a bus into the nearby town of Villeneuve be organised; and that a new public telephone be provided, the last one having mysteriously been blown up several months previously.[6] Additionally, those born in these spaces were now reaching adulthood, bringing to the fore a range of issues that had not been apparent when these settings were first conceived.[7] Chief among these was the marginalisation fostered by these environments. Describing Saint-Maurice-l'Ardoise in 1975, *Le Monde* referred to it as 'a genuine ghetto' that 'physically and morally' isolated the *harkis* from the rest of the population, reinforcing the perception that the *harki* community were unlike the rest of the French population.[8] According to one former Bias resident, *harkis* in the camps were treated like 'pariahs': 'No one dared to approach us because they'd been told things about us: that we were savages. People didn't even dare to pass in front of the Bias camp, they were really afraid. They'd only do it in a car.'[9]

Such treatment undermined the claims of the state that the *harkis* were full French citizens, not only for the minority still living in the camps and forest hamlets by 1975, but with respect to the community as a whole. Yet, in some senses, the self-enclosed worlds of the camps and hamlets insulated the *harki* community from the racism gathering pace in France during the 1980s and which particularly targeted those of North African descent. It was often only upon leaving these environments that the children of *harkis* gained a true sense of how wider society viewed them and their parents. Descendants of *harkis*, particularly those born in France and who had never known Algeria, found the discrimination to which they were subjected deeply frustrating. One nineteen-year-old man related how he had telephoned a hotel restaurant advertising for waiting staff only to be told, upon giving his name, that the position had already been filled. When he called back a short while later and gave a 'French' name, he was invited for an interview.[10] Similar stories abound with respect to attempts to secure employment, accommodation, even entrance to cafés and nightclubs; hence the wider resonance of the refrain used by the four youths who took the Saint-Maurice-l'Ardoise director hostage: 'We want to be fully French and not half-French.'[11]

The failure of the state to fulfil its stated aim of integrating the *harkis* had been obvious long before 1975. It was starkly highlighted in 1970, for example, via a short televised documentary focusing on the *harki* community living in a purpose-built estate on the edge of the town of Saint-Valérien (Vendée). With one or two notable exceptions, such as the pharmacist, Madame Varres, the town's inhabitants did not regard the arrival of thirty-seven *harki* families as a positive event. 'I am not racist', one letter to the local paper ran, 'but I think we must show ourselves to be very vigilant towards these people.' Elected on an anti-*harki* platform, the local mayor defended his position in similar terms claiming that he was not against the presence of the *harkis* per se, simply that there was too high a 'concentration' of them and that they would have more chance of a successful integration if they were dispersed. The *harki* community was acutely aware of these negative perceptions, which manifested themselves in racist incidents, difficulties finding employment, or being paid less than 'French' workers for those able to secure jobs in nearby factories. This was a particularly cruel irony given that the presence of the *harkis* had provided considerable stimulus to the local economy, resulting in new shop fronts and other signs of prosperity for Saint-Valérien. The fact that the best pupil in recitation at the local school was the daughter of a *harki* did little to dispel the overall sense of mutual resentment and incomprehension that pervaded the programme.[12]

Similar themes would be reprised seven years later by *Les Dossiers de l'écran* in a sixty-minute documentary which reiterated the limited employment opportunities available to *harkis*, the ongoing challenges of adapting to life in France and the varying warmth of the 'welcome' they had been offered. However, the worst-case scenario of those who were left 'without work, without family, without accommodation … [with] no justice', was offset by success stories such as the young couple, both with *harki* fathers, whose jobs as a teacher and a butcher had enabled them to purchase a modern house in a 'French' community. Both emphasised the difficulties they had faced along the way, including suspicion from local residents when the husband first set up his business and the fact that he claimed he was charged a higher rate at the abattoir as a result of the colour of his skin.[13] Nonetheless, the tone of this broadcast was more optimistic, perhaps reflecting the momentum of events following 1975, which had witnessed apparently radical changes in the state's approach to the integration of the *harki* community.

A key demand of the 1975 protestors was the closure of the camps, the most prominent symbol of their marginalisation and 'non-French' status. Victory on this issue appeared to come on 6 August 1975, when the government announced that Saint-Maurice-l'Ardoise would cease operations by the end of 1976. Two days later, the first of the 744 people still living on the site departed. The last families were evacuated fourteen months later on 22 October 1976, before bulldozers moved in to raze the camp to the ground.[14] This reflected the government's new approach to the *harkis*: dispersal. Acknowledging that the camps and forest hamlets had acted as barriers to integration, the state now pledged to get rid of them. The rapid disappearance of Saint-Maurice-l'Ardoise served as a publicly visible example of this new policy. Yet, the actual changes implemented were less dramatic than they first appeared. The residents of Saint-Maurice-l'Ardoise, for example, were simply regrouped in nearby locations, such as Lodève (Hérault), usually in some form of state-allocated and monitored accommodation. In a similar fashion, the remaining inhabitants of the Bias camp found the land on which they lived sold to the municipality, re-baptised the 'Hameau d'Astor', and made into a social housing complex. Those who were not 'dispersed' by the state continued to live on the site into the 1980s, while those who were moved on remained in the immediate vicinity and on the margins of society.[15]

In addition to perpetuating geographical concentrations of *harki* families, the principle of official tutelage and oversight also remained largely intact, although responsibility, including financial, for the *harkis* was delegated from the centre to local municipalities as part of the Mitterrand regime's regional devolution policy. The impact of this process was, in many respects, detrimental. Although local authorities were keen to accept the money attached to *harki* families, they were less enthusiastic about taking on board the myriad associated responsibilities. Indeed, activists like Hacène Arfi regard 1975 as the point at which problems within the *harki* community really took hold; the removal of the safety net of centralised control and support leaving many unable to cope with life beyond the confines of the camps and forest hamlets.[16] Nor were the *harkis* themselves necessarily in favour of relocation. Behind the vocal agitation of younger members of the community stood an older generation who took comfort from the stability of their surroundings. For these men and women, familiarity and a sense of community established over many years outweighed the negatives of rapidly deteriorating physical conditions and segregation from mainstream society.[17] As the sociologist Saliha Abdellatif highlights, 'ghettos' offer a certain sort of protection whereby the material and psychological security that comes from living alongside people similar to you removes the risk of being judged 'undesirable', instead creating a space of 'recognition and mutual acceptance'.[18] Consequently, even though leaving the camps represented improved accommodation and a chance at a new life, for some, like the family of thirty-nine-year-old Akila, it was simply too difficult. Her family, she explained, simply did not have the strength to face a 'second uprooting'.[19]

Employment, which became a stated government priority in response to the demands of the 1975 protestors, provides another example of the appearance of change disguising continuity of practice. New initiatives were launched, including seventeen Bureaux d'information, d'aide administrative et de conseils (BIAC) in areas with sizeable *harki* populations. Their purpose was to provide assistance in matters of housing and employment to all members of the community, not just those in specific sites, thus indicating an expansion of state support. By 1981, however, the BIACs had been closed, criticised for being both ineffective and partisan in their distribution of funds. Lasting from 1984 until 1987, the Office national à l'action sociale educative et culturelle (ONASEC) had an equally short lifespan and was accused of an even greater misuse of state funds; the resultant scandal helped to fuel the dissatisfaction that underpinned the 1991 protests.[20] In addition, both BIAC and ONASEC essentially replicated the aims and approaches of the Comité Parodi, which dated back to the 1960s. This failure to innovate in terms of approaches to the *harki* community, in spite of several specially convened commissions of inquiry, was further visible in the ongoing cycle of training schemes offered and undertaken by children of *harkis* which failed to result in employment on any mean-ingful scale. Boussad Azni possessed six vocational qualifications or CAPs (Certificat d'aptitude professionnelle), but was unable to find work, while the closure of the forest hamlets removed job stability for many of the older generation.[21]

Elites and associations

Reflecting on the outcomes of 1975, *harki* daughter Dalila Kerchouche felt the most significant impact of the protests was that they shattered the image of the *harkis* as 'the eternal submissive auxiliary, docile and faith-ful'. For her, the symbol of this defiance was M'hamed Laradji, a char-ismatic orator who relished standing up to the authorities.[22] Emerging as the figurehead of the 1975 protests, Laradji was constantly present as an interlocutor between the authorities and the activists as the events of the summer unfolded. Key to legitimating Laradji's claims to repre-sent the *harki* community was his status as the founder and leader of the Confédération des Français musulmans rapatriés d'Algérie (CFMRAA). The CFMRAA was one of a range of '*harki*–led' associations that appeared in the 1970s and which cast themselves as a break with the previous pat-tern of allowing external voices to speak for the community. The first such association was MADRAN, which was founded in 1971 and presided over by Ahmed Kaberseli. This was soon joined by the Front national des Français rapatriés de confession islamique (FNRFCI), headed by Ahmed Djebbour with close involvement of Jean-Claude Khiari, as well as the Union nationale des anciens combattants français de confession islam-ique (UNACFCI) under the auspices of Captain Rabah Kheliff. Alongside Laradji's CMFRAA, these bodies appeared to represent a new dynamism and sense of autonomy within the *harki* community. Yet, as with the gov-ernment's response to 1975, appearances proved deceptive. Behind this burgeoning associational network lay a complex mixture of continuity and change with respect to the public representation of the *harkis* that helped shape the context from which the events of 1991 developed.

To begin with, none of these new *harki* representatives were, in fact, *harkis*. Some, notably Kheliff, had served in the French military, but this was as career soldiers not auxiliaries. For others, their backgrounds lay in political or administrative connections to the colonial authorities: Laradji was the nephew of the former Cherchell deputy Mohamed Laradji, while Djebbour had served as a deputy for Algiers. All were concerned with the *harkis*, but the gap between them and those they sought to represent was indicated by the dominance of the term 'français musulman' rather than 'harki' in the names of their associations, their public statements and their associational literature. For Mohand Hamoumou, this elitism was epitomised by *Le Rappel*, a bi-monthly magazine produced by Kamel Kabtane of the Conseil national des Français musulmans (CNFM), an attempt in the late 1970s to federate these new associations into a single body. *Le Rappel*, according to Hamoumou, lacked incisive content, serving instead as a vehicle for a new breed of 'younger, more cultivated' association leaders who 'tried to remind the political parties that "posh" [*bon chic, bon genre*] French Muslims exist'.[23] These new leaders were furthermore accused of participating in a 'resurgence of the neo-colonial caïdal system and of its "béni-oui-oui" [yes men]' through their 'electoral haggling' and their 'race for subsidies'.[24] These issues were compounded by the fact that financial assistance from the state was often used to further individual interests and political ambitions rather than to serve the *harki* cause, while competition for such funds precluded the creation of a single national body or spokesperson. Instead, subsidies kept associations divided, consigning initiatives such as the CNFM to failure.[25] As a result, the majority of associations operated at the local level, with only a handful able to claim a regional, let alone national, presence. The apparently robust numerical health of an associational movement that had witnessed the creation of approximately two hundred new organisations in the 1970s thus belied various weaknesses.[26]

These weaknesses were displayed to the nation at large in 1977 during a televised discussion that was broadcast in the wake of *Les Dossiers de l'écran*'s documentary about the *harkis* of Saint-Valérien.[27] Departing from the norm of inviting *pieds-noirs* or the military to speak on behalf of the *harkis*, the participants consisted primarily of spokespeople from the new associations, including Laradji, Kaberseli, Kheliff and Khiari. In this way, the programme reflected the increased profile and mobilisation of the *harkis* in the wake of the 1975 protests. Representing the state was Djellorel Bourakba of the permanent inter-ministerial commission for French Muslims and Jacques Dominati, the secretary of state for *rapatriés*. Completing the line-up was Colonel Deluc of the Comité Parodi, who had been taken hostage in the course of the 1975 protests. The assembled guests were able to agree on various issues, notably the long history of service by Algerians within the French army prior to the War of Independence, the many problems faced by the children of *harkis* in the present day and the importance of free circulation between France and Algeria. But, overall the discussion was heated with Laradji acting as the main point of tension. His vague and rambling answers repeatedly drew the ire of his fellow association representatives, who accused him of attempting to sabotage the broadcast and criticised him for presenting a highly negative 'spectacle' of the community to the viewing public. The voiceover that interjected at various points to relay telephone comments from the audience at home appeared to confirm this, noting that many callers were frustrated by the lack of clarity emerging from the discussion and were requesting that the guests answer directly the questions being put to them. In return, Laradji spent much of the ninety-minute broadcast complaining that he was not being allowed to speak in this 'masquerade' of a show. The mutual animosity on display reflected the wider competition between these men and their associations for control over the public presentation of the *harki* community. This competition had already seen Laradji, the government's privileged interlocutor in 1975, lose this coveted position to Khiari of the FNRFCI; the fact that the FNRFCI was itself a secessionist faction of the CMFRAA only adding insult to injury. The FNRFCI gained this favoured status partly as a result of the government's perception that its leader, Djebbour, had delivered votes from within the *rapatrié* community that helped Giscard secure the presidency in 1974. Dejbbour was thus regarded as more 'serious' than the volatile Laradji, who prided himself on his aggressive, action-orientated campaigning.[28]

In addition to Lardji's behaviour, divisions emerged over the use of the term 'harki', which Khiari felt denied the Frenchness of the former auxiliaries, and the extent to which these men and their families should be the focus of government attention. The position of Bourakba was that it was detrimental to remain overly preoccupied, as he felt the documentary preceding the discussion was, on those *harkis* who were still 'protected' and 'assisted' by the state. According to him, these individuals represented only a tiny minority of the overall 'French Muslim' community, but were obscuring the many examples of those who had successfully integrated into French society. Bourakba's assertion prompted Laradji to denounce him as simply the voice of the state, while, in more measured tones, Khiari, Kheliff and Kaberseli all argued for the need to remain concerned with the most vulnerable within the wider community. Kheliff, in particular, acknowledged that his and Bourakba's 'privileged' position as fully integrated citizens should not lead them to talk only about 'former civil servants', but also the 'disadvantaged'.[29]

These exchanges exposed the contrasting approaches between those who wanted to convince the state that 'French Muslims' were valuable allies who deserved to be taken seriously within the political process, versus those who sought state guarantees of action on behalf of the least favoured elements of the community, which they, as community representatives, would be closely involved in shaping and implementing. Also apparent was the importance of the state to both these positions. Dominati, in his capacity as the secretary of state, appeared highly receptive to arguments in favour of further assistance for the most deprived elements of the *harki* community in recognition of their status as French citizens. Indeed, his first contribution to the discussion paid homage to those who had engaged on the French side and stressed that, in terms of the assembled guests, 'we are among Frenchmen'.[30] In keeping with the flurry of activity in the wake of the 1975 protests, Dominati's presence and comments were designed to demonstrate the commitment of Giscard's government to improving the situation of the *harkis*. Equally, the various association representatives were careful to acknowledge what had been done for the *harkis* as a way of showcasing their willingness to work with those in power to achieve their aims. In spite of a few pointed exchanges, the cordiality between Dominati and the various *harki* representatives stood in sharp contrast to the open hostility displayed between these same men and Laradji.

'We are all *harkis*'

The *Dossiers de l'écran* debate represented something of a high watermark in terms of visibility for the new associational movement. Unable to cohere or to establish a substantial national base, activism dwindled and association membership declined noticeably during the 1980s. At the end of 1991, a handful of large associations existed with only seven of these receiving national subsidies, including the CFMRAA, FNRFCI and UNAFCI.[31] The UNACFCI continues to the present day, even surviving the death, in 2008, of Kheliff, its founder and long-standing president. However, most organisations suffered the same fate as the CFMRAA, which disintegrated following the death of Laradji. This decline was thrown into relief by the growth of the *pied-noir* associational movement during the same period. Although *pieds-noirs* were noticeable by their absence from the *Dossiers de l'écran* discussion, the same could not be said of the 1975 protests nor of the *harki* associational movement as a whole. Indeed, as Laradji was dominating the stage in 1975, behind him stood the shadowy figure of Monsieur Christophe, the CMFRAA's mysterious second in command who was rumoured to have links to the newly created FN. Monsieur Christophe was also close to Eugène Ibagnes of Union syndicale de défense des intérêts des Français repliés d'Algérie (USDIFRA), a hardline *pied-noir* association noted for their physical, often armed, defence of *rapatrié* rights, who appeared at various key moments during the summer of 1975.[32] For *harki* activists like Boussad Azni, it was people such as Monsieur Christophe and Ibagnes who helped ensure that the momentum of 1975 was co-opted for the ends of the *pied-noir* community, in the process turning the *harkis*, including Laradji, into their stooges.[33]

The sudden visibility of the *harkis* on the national radar offered *pied-noir* activists a new source of leverage in their ongoing quest to secure compensation measures. By allying themselves with the 1975 protestors, *pied-noir* associations were able to give the impression that they formed part of an even larger lobbying and voting bloc, thus increasing their negotiating power vis-à-vis the state. Supporting such a reading of events is the prominence of indemnities as an issue during the 1975 protests. Although compensation was a long cherished *pied-noir* objective, it was largely irrelevant to the *harkis* who generally possessed neither the material wealth in Algeria, nor the necessary documentation that would enable them to benefit from the kinds of schemes being proposed.[34] When new compensation measures for the *pieds-noirs* were introduced in 1978, no provision was made for the *harkis*. Furthermore, although the *harkis* never completely disappeared from the pages of the *pied-noir* associational press, there was a lull in coverage after the closure of the transit camps. In the wake of 1975, however, the prominence of the community once again rose. It was at this moment, for example, that ANFANOMA decided to create a commission to focus specifically on the *harkis*, while in 1978 the Cercle algérianiste launched a project to help promote the integration of the *harkis* as one of three main decisions taken at their annual congress.[35]

'We are all *harkis*' proclaimed the Cercle algérianiste, as the *pied-noir* community sought to frame their involvement in 1975 as the logical continuation of their long-standing support for their *rapatrié* 'brothers'.[36] This supportive relationship was acknowledged at the highest levels when, in the spring of 1977, Giscard attended a *méchoui* for *pieds-noirs* and *harkis* as a symbol of the government's commitment to the *rapatrié* community broadly defined. Speaking to the assembled guests, the President repeated assurances that the *harkis* were 'Frenchmen like any others', albeit Frenchmen who had experienced 'greater difficulties' which left them in need of 'yet more attention'. At the same time, he was careful to 'congratulate' the *pieds-noirs* present for the 'solidarity' they had shown towards the *harkis*.[37] In contrast to the French public, who were only just discovering the plight of the *harkis*, and political parties who, associations claimed, were only interested in the community as election fodder, *pied-noir* activists therefore positioned themselves as committed and faithful advocates of the *harki* cause, who had been there from the start.

The historical narratives accompanying such declarations was unchanged from the pre-1975 era, while demands made on behalf of the *harkis* mirrored those of the protestors themselves. Camps thus ceased to be useful spaces of protection and adaptation as the *pieds-noirs* had portrayed them in the 1960s. Now they were depicted as barriers to integration and denounced as part of a wider failure on the part of successive governments to treat the *harkis* as French citizens. Remedying this situation would involve financial aid, but also a rehabilitation of the image of the *harkis*. The lack of public knowledge about the community having, the Cercle algérianiste believed, created a situation whereby 'a symbol of courage, loyalty, dignity and patriotism' was being transformed into an entirely different symbol, that of 'dependent and occasionally violent vagrants'.[38] Reversing this scenario formed part of a broader need for the nation to re-evaluate its colonial past in Algeria. 'We cannot on the one hand, continually soil the memory of French Algeria, insulting the memory of those who fought for it and on the other hand want to render justice to the *harkis*', explained Maurice Calmein in the pages of *L'Algérianiste*. 'We owe to this community the clear affirmation that its choice in 1962 was just, legitimate, and honourable.'[39]

Pied-noir activists thus took the demands of the *harkis* and wove them into a larger project to reclaim the colonial past from those who would denigrate its value and importance. Making this argument required perpetuating the notion that *pieds-noirs* and *harkis* formed a single *rapatrié* community. This apparent unity was symbolised in the 1980s through the creation of Jeune pied-noir (JPN), an association led by Bernard Coll and his wife, Taouès Titraoui, who was also the daughter of a *harki*. Through initiatives like the 'Hommage aux harkis' campaign launched in 1987, and via close links with other *pied-noir* associations who regularly allocated Coll and Titraoui space and support, JPN proved adept at using a range of platforms to publicise the situation of the *harkis*, while simultaneously stressing the links that bound them to the *pied-noir* community.[40]

Titraoui was one of several figures within the *harki* community seemingly happy to ally themselves with the *pieds-noirs*. Another was Brahim Sadouni, a *harki* who gained notoriety after he undertook two lengthy marches across France in 1985 and 1987 to raise awareness the plight of his fellow auxiliaries. Addressing the studio audience of 'Les pieds-noirs, ça va?', he affirmed that 'the *pieds-noirs* in general are people who support us a lot'.[41] Sadouni's presence on a *pied-noir*-orientated discussion panel reflected a pattern at this time of affording *harkis* visibility as part of the wider *rapatrié* community. When no *harki* representative was included, *pied-noir* guests would always ensure that reference was made to the community. Often this task fell to Coll, who was a regular guest on the gradually expanding number of Algeria-related programmes broadcast during the 1980s.[42] Others, however, criticised the involvement of *pieds-noirs* in the *harki* cause and denounced the implications of this interference: 'They [the *pieds-noirs*] are always there … at the political level we have always been represented by *pieds-noirs*. Basically, when measures have been taken in our favour, it is the *pieds-noirs* who profit from them.'[43]

Exacerbating this trend was the power differential between the two communities which widened in the 1980s as *harki* activism was unable to maintain momentum following 1975. This created situations in which it was expedient for *harki* activists to cooperate with the *pied-noir* community as a way to enhance their own visibility and public presence, even though this often came at the expense of being in control of the narrative being told about them. The ongoing entanglement of the two communities and the unequal benefits that stemmed from this proved an increasing source of discontent as the years wore on, helping to explain the determination of 1991 activists to reclaim autonomy. So central was this notion to the events of 1991 that even *pied-noir* associations were forced to acknowledge it. As the Cercle algérianiste noted, by refusing any compromise of principles and any political amalgamation, even with *rapatrié* associations who 'have always defended their cause', this new generation of militants had showed their determination to protect their movement from 'drifting away' from its central goals.[44]

Allies, adversaries and Algerians

The emergence of *harki* activism also needs to be considered against a wider political backdrop that witnessed the rapid emergence of immigration as a national preoccupation. This was driven by a potent combination of socialist *droit à la différence* policies, the progressive encroachment of the FN on the political scene, particularly their insidious rhetoric concerning the 'problem' of immigration, a sharp rise in racist violence, and the high-profile mobilisation of the immigrant community and their descendants in response to these developments. The *harkis* could not help but be drawn into this maelstrom, their North African heritage enmeshing them in a complex and often volatile relationship with France's Algerian population.[45] At the same time, political leaders, from Giscard to Mitterrand via Le Pen, all sought to utilise the *harkis* in service of their broader ideological strategies and perceived electoral needs.

This resulted in policies that oscillated between distinguishing the *harkis* from Algerians in France on the basis of their service to the nation and resultant citizenship, and erasing the specificities of their postcolonial trajectories in order to amalgamate both into a single ethno-cultural community.[46] This political manoeuvring inevitably informed interactions between children of both *harkis* and Algerians as they grappled with the extent to which they wished to ally with or stand apart from the supposed historical 'enemies' of their parents.

On the surface, there were many similarities between the two groups that pointed to the utility of co-operation. Perhaps the most striking was their comparable socio-economic situations as both struggled to find work in a tough economic climate and in the face of racial discrimination. Like children of *harkis*, a significant proportion of descendants of Algerian immigrants possessed French nationality. Regardless of what it said on their identity card though, more often than not they found that 'for the French, an Arab is an Arab'.[47] Even the careful distinctions drawn by the political far right between *harkis*, depicted as loyal and patriotic soldiers of France, versus job stealing, benefit cheating Algerian immigrants, collapsed at the level of the street when the two became physically indistinguishable and were thus both vulnerable to harassment. In the context of expressing regret that the state had 'denied rifles to the first generation [of *harkis*] and denied brooms to the second', secretary of state for repatriates Raymond Courrière noted that being victims of unemployment and marginalisation was at least easing relations between the two communities.[48] These relations were further improved by the fact that children of *harkis* and Algerian immigrants tended to share the same physical spaces as both found themselves grouped together in high-rise estates on the edges of major cities. In contrast to initial efforts to keep the two communities apart, lest historical animosities lead to conflict, daily interaction at school or on the streets was now the norm. Although they were culturally orientated towards France (the nation in which most had grown up), these young men and women retained a strong sense of their common Algerian heritage. Islam proved a particularly important unifying cultural marker. Even those who were non-practising still tended to observe certain rituals and festivals, helping to instil a sense of community that stood outside of recent history. Islam could also serve as a source of refuge in the face of hostility from mainstream society.[49]

Although their respective histories were different, both groups existed as part of diaspora communities, cut off from a homeland dear to their parents but unknown to most of them. This was particularly the case given that children of Algerians faced similar levels of parental silence with respect to the past, including the circumstances that had brought them to France and that caused them to remain there.[50] The Algerian community equally faced externally imposed and politically motivated readings of the past. Through its French-based satellite, the AAE, the Algerian government propagated a univocal vision of the years 1954–62 as a period when the entire Algerian population, regardless of location, was united in a nationalist struggle for independence.[51] The AAE acted as guardians of the official history and memory of the Algerian community in France, denying legitimacy to recollections that did not fit with the state-sanctioned narrative, such as the significant numbers of Algerians in France who belonged to the rival nationalist organisation, the MNA during the war. As the successor to the Fédération de France du FLN, the AAE was able to draw upon a legacy of efficient organisational networks and extensive data on Algerians in France to aid them in this task.[52]

Many of the similarities between descendants of *harkis* and Algerians were therefore embedded in a sense of exclusion from French society and from their own history. This prompted both groups to mobilise in order to create an autonomous identity and place that would allow them to move beyond the idea that they were, as one activist put it, just 'the illegitimate children of two illegitimate histories'.[53] The best-known example of this strategy in action was the Marche pour l'égalité et contre le racisme, often referred to as the 'Marche des beurs'.[54] The brainchild of Toumi Djaïdja of the Minguettes *banlieue* in Lyon, the march was intended to promote equality and raise awareness of the problem of racism and its increasingly violent manifestations. '[Y]ou can die from racism in France today', explained the SOS-Racisme president, Harlem Désir in his memoir of the Marche pour l'égalité era.[55] This was something that both Toufik Ouanes and Habib Grimzi discovered to their cost. Ouanes was only nine years old when she was killed on 9 July 1983 by a bullet fired from the window of a house in an estate in La Courneuve, near Paris. The killer, René Algueperse, explained that the child was too noisy when playing outside. Nineteen-year-old Habib Grimizi was travelling between Bordeaux and Vintimille by train, while on a visit to France from his native Oran, when he attracted the attention of three legionnaires. The men harassed Grimizi repeatedly before finally throwing him from the moving train. This horrific act was subsequently dramatised in Roger Hanin's 1985 film, *Train d'enfer* [hell train], but behind well-publicised cases such as these lay thousands more incidents of racially motivated brutality. These included several perpetrated by the forces of law and order, who were accused of unjustly targeting the North African community and of frequently using excessive force. Djaïdja, in fact, came up with the idea for the 1983 march while recovering in hospital after being injured during an altercation with the police.

The march capitalised on a favourable political climate in which the PS's pursuit of a pluralist vision of the nation had translated into the right to form association for foreigners and a range of initiatives designed to affirm the value of different cultures and their compatibility with those of the Republic.[56] But it equally came in the wake of the FN's breakthrough in the March 1983 municipal elections after the mainstream right-wing Rassemblement pour la République (RPR) and centrist Union pour la démocratie française agreed to strategic alliances with Le Pen's party in certain towns. It was within this dualistic context that the thirty-two original marchers, who departed almost unnoticed from Marseille on 15 October 1983, arrived in Paris two months later to be greeted by a 100,000 strong crowd and an audience with President Mitterrand. Having begun as a protest against discrimination and racism, the march evolved into the positive affirmation of a new element of society.[57] To journalist Mouloud Mimoun, it represented 'the first claim of full citizenship'. 'For the first time there has emerged on the national scene a whole new category: young *beurs* from the *banlieues* who French society had never thought to look straight in the eye, or dared to.'[58] The sociologist Saïd Bouamama equally felt that French society had 'discovered another face of the *banlieue*. A face that spoke, animated, organised, debated, thought and proposed'.[59]

Among the key figures involved in the march were several children of *harkis*, including the hunger-striking activist Abdelkrim Klech, Bouzid Kara, who wrote a memoir of his participation, and Djaïdja himself.[60] This was not an identity Djaïdja publicised and his *harki* heritage did not emerge until after the conclusion of the march. Once revealed, it was seized upon as a sign of *rapprochement* between children of *harkis* and Algerians, leading to a range of commentaries in the burgeoning *beur* press written from a 'brothers in discrimination' perspective that drew historical parallels between the situations of the two communities.[61] Several associations were also founded which aimed to unite the descendants of the two populations. The most famous of these was undoubtedly France Plus, which sought to get ethnic minority candidates onto electoral lists. Other examples included Mixture, a group founded in Villeneuve-sur-Lot in 1984, whose 'outstretched hand' philosophy sought to foster a dialogue between children of *harkis* and Algerians, as did Radio Figue.[62] Collectively, such developments suggested the ability of the common denominator of discrimination to transcend traditional historical divisions. This was certainly the case for *harki* descendant and march participant Mohamed Haddouche who felt that '[t]he struggle against racism and for integration has nothing to do with being the child of a *harki* or an immigrant. We're all in the same boat. At least in this regard, we have to try to go in the same direction.'[63]

Grassroots cooperation was facilitated by the a-historicity of the *beur* movement under whose auspices most of these initiatives fell. The majority of organisations and projects shared a practical, contemporary orientation revolving around issues of racism and citizenship. They also shared a common perception of themselves as a conscious reaction against the passivity of their parents' generation in the face of injustice and discrimination. Thus, for Abdel Aïssou, the first *beur* sub-prefect elected in Nice, the 1983 march was the moment when 'we became aware that our generation had a different history to that of our parents'.[64] This was, of course, an oversimplification of their parents' lives, which ignored the numerous examples of historical activism going back as far as the Étoile nord-africaine (ENA) in the 1920s and 1930s, encompassing membership of the MNA or FLN in the 1950s and 1960s, up to the Mouvement des travailleurs arabes, which was founded in 1973. It was, however, a representation that found an echo in the media which emphasised the novelty of these mobilisations, rarely providing any historical context.[65]

There was also a practical rationale behind such a-historicity. Lacking proper access their North African cultural heritage, yet simultaneously unable to fully situate themselves within French society, which stigmatised and rejected them, for many the logical response was to create a new identity that broke with cultural and historical genealogies.[66] This helps to explain the predominantly local character and preoccupations of associations and of activists whose identities were rooted in their immediate environments. 'We live with the only culture that is really ours', one activist reported, 'that of the *quartiers*. We call ourselves "Farid from Les Minguettes", "Omar from Chatenay".'[67] In a similar manner to the *harki* camps, *quartiers* were simultaneously symbols of exclusion and familiar safe havens where identities could be expressed with greater freedom. As one self-identified *beur* put it: 'Neither Algerian like my father, nor French like on my identity card, I am an Arab citizen of Vaulx-en-Velin [a suburb of Lyon] … I've never set foot in the *bled* and I think in *verlan*. My community is that of the Arab faces of my *quartier*. The rest, it's not my story!'[68]

A-historicity, embodied in the notion of 'the rest' not being their 'story', furthermore offered a way to avoid engendering divisions in the new movement given the diversity of its participants. This idea is supported by Bouzid's observations of relations between those on the march.

The fact that they included 'Arabs of all nationalities – Algerian, Tunisian, Moroccan, French' was not an issue, he said. People 'couldn't care less about the nationality of others' because of the recognition that 'they were all equal in the face of rejection'. This stood in sharp contrast to his previous experience of discussions among his friends in Aix-en-Provence which, he noted, frequently ended in a 'battle' between those who were 'French Muslims' and those who had retained their 'nationality of origin' leading him to conclude that 'the effects of the Algerian War had not finished making themselves felt'.[69]

The triumphal arrival of the marchers into Paris in December 1983 was both the beginning and the pinnacle of an anti-racist mobilisation that rapidly fragmented after that point.[70] Subsequent *rassemblements,* such as Convergence '84, held the following year, failed to attract anywhere near the same numbers as participants from a broad range of involved communities ebbed away. High-profile offspring initiatives, such as SOS-Racisme and France Plus, quickly became mired in rivalry and accusations of complicity with the PS, while many grassroots activists felt that the 'beur' label had been co-opted by the media and politicians who emptied it of its original meaning. Finally, and perhaps most significantly, little changed in the daily lives of those on whose behalf the march had been undertaken.

The Marche pour l'égalité therefore appears to have represented a unique moment in the sense of providing an inclusive forum for children of *harkis* to join with descendants of Algerian immigrants under the banner of fighting discrimination that was common to them both. However, outside of this specific event it is difficult to find evidence of shared spaces of activism and mobilisation in any sustained capacity. Interviewing children of *harkis* and Algerians in in the town of Manosque (Alpes-de-Hautes-Provence) several years later, Bouamama was struck by the 'live animosity' that continued to exist between the two communities with one of his interviewees stating: 'We need to organise … We need to do something, to fight together, but in Manosque it's not possible, we are too divided'.[71]

The source of such divisions often lay precisely in the socio-economic commonalities that had brought children of *harkis* and Algerian immigrants together for the Marche pour l'égalité. Being in the same situation could bring about recognition of the utility of cooperation and collective action, but it could also bring awareness that both groups were essentially competing for the same scarce resources. The latter scenario, which was the everyday reality for most children of *harkis* and Algerians, produced a heightened sensitivity to any perceived special treatment being given to one community over the other. It also fostered a determination to play whatever cards could potentially give an advantage. For descendants of *harkis*, this had traditionally been the French citizenship of their parents and themselves, which distinguished them from the Algerian immigrant community. In fact, this privileged position was gradually being eroded by alterations to the Nationality Code designed to facilitate access to citizenship for increasing numbers of children of foreign-born parents in the 1980s.[72] Nonetheless, *harki* descendants continued to emphasise the unique context in which their nationality had been acquired, arguing that the loyalty and sacrifices of their parents should be rewarded in subsequent generations by ensuring complete and equal access to the various facets of this hard-won citizenship, hence the prominent and recurring demand to be treated as fully French. This was also an argument made by the FN who, as part of their 'national preference' platform, used comparisons between the *harkis* and those they labelled 'immigrants' from North Africa to accuse the government of failing to provide adequately for its own citizens. It found a further echo in the *pied-noir* community with ANFANOMA's Marcel Crozatier asking the following, in relation to the *harkis*: 'Why deliberately forget them in the distribution of rewards, reserved too often for those who did not have the courage to be or to make themselves French when that profession brought with it no advantages?'[73]

To have the history of their parents ignored and to find themselves amalgamated with 'immigrants' on the basis of their name or appearance were galling for children of *harkis*. This was especially the case when those who had fought against France between 1954 and 1962 were seen to be benefiting from state support in ways that the *harki* community felt they had not. Children of *harkis* would no longer accept their status as 'victims of the ingratitude of the nation' warned Sadouni in 1991, prior to the new round of *harki* protests. Since they had chosen to remain French in 1962, 'we need to give them the possibility of equality with the rest of the nation', Sadouni argued, rather than continuing to bracket them alongside Algerian immigrants.[74] Such feelings were compounded by the perception among many children of *harkis* of being rejected by the Algerian community in France. Attesting to this are accounts of being subjected to 'son of a traitor' taunts and of having to hide their *harki* family background at school or when socialising. This was the case for Abderahmen who described how, at university in the late 1980s, 'when I was with Maghrebins, I was ill at ease. I said that I was the son of an immigrant. I was ashamed of my parents who had fought against their country.'[75] Whereas, Azni felt left in a sort of identity limbo by the the fact that 'My ancestors weren't Gauls. But Algerian immigrants don't recognise me as one of theirs.'[76] These examples underline Guilia Fabbiano's point that similarities in their physical environments and quotidian experiences did not alter the fact that the Algerian War was a past that continued to have a very different significance for the two communities.[77]

The sense of competition felt by some children of *harkis* was enhanced by the Mitterrand regime's positive stance towards the incorporation of immigrants and their descendants into the national community, as well as by the prominence accorded by the media and the government to the *beur* movement. One of the most tangible achievements of the march, for example, was the granting of ten-year combined work and residency permits for immigrants. No specific measures on behalf of the *harki* were advanced, in spite of several high-profile marchers being part of that community. This led to feelings of resentment such as those expressed by Sadouni in the aftermath of the Marche pour l'égalité: 'We spilled our blood for this country ... we lost our homes, we were cut off from our families, and ultimately we remain outcasts. No one is bothered about us at all.'[78] His solution was to organise two marches of his own in 1985 and 1987 to show that the children of Algerians were not the only youths with problems deserving of national attention.[79] Explaining the rationale behind his first trek, Sadouni stated: 'The *beurs* marched from Marseille to Paris and they were heard. Ok then, I'll march from Dunkerque to Marseille!'[80] Sadouni's plan was, however, frequently hampered by the insistence of his hosts in various towns on conflating his march with the causes espoused by the *beur* movement. The socialist mayor of Vitrolles, for example, joined Sadouni for the final stage of his march wearing a SOS-Racisme 'Touche pas à mon pote' [hands off my mate] badge which had become an iconic symbol of the anti-racist movement. This, on top of the Mayor's welcome speech the previous night, during which he had spoken repeatedly of the racism that foreigners, particularly immigrant labourers, faced in France without mentioning the *harkis,* left Sadouni decidedly irritated. So much so that he asked the Mayor to remove the badge because it risked distracting people from the true focus of his march.[81]

The example of Sadouni's march captures in microcosm the issues faced by *harki* activists as they attempted to carve out a space for their own campaigns. This was a complex process involving a series of choices about when and how to disentangle themselves from external vested interests versus when it was prudent, even desirable, to make common cause with others, or at least to borrow their tactics. These decisions did not take place in a vacuum, but rather were made in response to France's changing political and socio-economic climate during the late 1970s and 1980s. In addition to negotiating what autonomy would look like in a practical sense, the children of *harkis* also had to grapple with the question of what or whose story they wanted to tell through their activism, a process that illuminated the difficulties inherent in their quest for control over their own history and trajectory.

Reclaiming the narrative

In 1991, when large-scale unrest once again broke out within the *harki* community, one of the distinguishing features in comparison to 1975 was the conscious reclamation of 'harki' as an identifying label. In her description of the road blocks set up as part of the 1991 protests, one militant, Dalia, explained how when she and others stopped cars in order to educate drivers about the *harki* community they were able to 'say out loud that we were *harkis*'.[82] The roots of this reclamation are often identified in the failure of the 1983 march and of the *beur* movement more generally to secure the 'right to indifference' and thus the right to be seen as just like any other French person, indicated by the ongoing discrimination and marginalisation faced by the children of *harkis*.[83] If being fully French was therefore not an option, the activists of 1991 at least wanted to be able to define the terms on which they stood apart. It was in this context that the journalist Philippe Bernard noted a 'sudden thirst' for the 'hidden history' of their own community among the 1991 protestors.[84] Re-appropriating the past was seen as a way for *harki* children to obtain retrospective historical justice by rewriting the narrative of their parents' past, but also as a way of enabling them to situate more clearly their own identity in the present. 'In order to be different from my parents, I had to feel the same as them', wrote Saliha Telali. 'To continue my path in life, I needed to know their lives.'[85] Such endeavours were regarded as a way of overcoming the 'crisis of identity' that sociologists and anthropologists were increasingly interested in documenting among children of *harkis* who felt themselves to be neither French nor Algerian, but rather lost in a no-man's land somewhere in between.[86]

Unfortunately, the practical resources available from which to construct such a historical narrative were limited. Parental silence was still the norm, although this was not an absolute phenomenon. In spite of protestations that 'the past, our parents didn't speak of it', those who have spent time interviewing children of *harkis* note a surprising amount of factual and anecdotal knowledge about the past.[87] In seeking to explain this apparent paradox, Laurent Muller suggests that *harki* family histories are 'over-determined by a kind of secret that no one speaks of but that everyone knows'.[88] In this context, fragments of the past trickled down to children in ways analogous to how familial memories are transmitted more broadly – not necessarily through explicit and specific modes of communication, but rather in the course of daily interactions.[89] Anecdotes related by mothers to their children concerning life in Algeria, outbursts of paternal anger or emotion following Algeria-related news items, parental conversations overheard and relayed by the oldest sibling, especially at family gatherings or occasions where other *harkis* were present – all these scenarios suggest ways in which morsels of the past could have been received by children of *harkis* while growing up.[90] In some cases, these quotidian scraps could be supplemented by the memories of older children who had made the journey from Algeria to France in the 1960s. The problem was that there was no external framework into which to insert these internally received memories. Thus for Telali, 'These hints could only be frightening for me, in as much as they had no echo in society, in the media, in school.'[91]

One of the only external resources available to children of *harkis* were the discourses constructed about their community by French Muslim elites, veterans and the *pieds-noirs*. Adopting ideas found within these groups, activists also employed the notion of the *harkis* as 'French through blood spilled', a particularly prominent slogan during the 1991 protests. Similarly, a long history of military engagement on behalf of the French, combined with the loyal service of the *harkis* during the Algerian War, were used to underline the 'debt' that France owed to its auxiliaries. There was also a clear rebuttal of the notion that the *harkis* had been traitors; the accent instead was placed on the community's status as victims of forces beyond their control. The *harki* association MADRAN's campaigns were particularly focused on what Benjamin Stora calls the 'martyrology' of the community, with the association arguing consistently that the *harkis* were 'loyal Muslims' who had been 'abandoned defenceless' in 'the most ignominious conditions'; a situation of neglect that was then perpetuated by the French authorities after 1962.[92] One of the components most strongly internalised by *harki* descendants was a sense of collective suffering and injustice, a feeling only heightened, in the opinion of Stéphanie Abrial, by parental silence which was often construed as covering unimaginable trauma and grief.[93]

Sociologist Emmanuel Brillet argues that the absence of an internally generated collective memory exposed children of *harkis* to a 'loss of inherited identity' which, in turn, made them vulnerable to externally imposed definitions.[94] But looking at the kinds of narratives *harki* activists borrowed from others there was clearly a process of selection at work whereby the discourses adopted had a strategic value or corresponded to something that resonated with their own experiences. At no point, for example, did activists reproduce the defence of colonialism that the *pied-noir* community and the Bachaga Boualam had attempted to extract from the service of the *harkis*. The issue of the 'choice' made by the *harkis*, an ideologically loaded concept in the narratives of others, was also avoided. This may have been because the reasons for enrolment were and remain one of the least known facets of the *harki* experience. It may have also been because the actual reasons for enrolment, many of them involving a lack of volition, if not outright coercion, threatened to compromise the claims being advanced by activists against the state for recognition and recompense that were predicated on the faithful service rendered by the *harkis* to France.

The fragmentary nature of the knowledge possessed by *harki* activists often resulted in a tendency to legitimate the narratives being offered with reference to the collective *harki* experience. As Azni put it, 'we have all, more or less, lived the same heartbreaks, the same stupefactions, the same deceptions'.[95] Universalising the limited information available in order to strengthen the case being made was a logical response to the situation faced by activists in the 1970s and 1980s. One of the consequences of this was to essentialise the *harki* experience, a trend that was visible from early on. The most obvious example was the way in which the camps were established as a touchstone within *harki* activism, in spite of the fact that not all *harkis* and their families passed through these spaces, while those who remained for any significant length of time represented only a fraction of the overall community. As Jeannette Miller argues, it was the discourse surrounding the 1975 protests that helped to create the 'incorrect notion of a homogenous *harki* experience' that centred on the camps as 'the lasting symbol of the entire *harki* population's failed integration and marginalisation'. This notion would go on to shape how officials understood and treated the community.[96]

It is true that protest rhetoric, in both 1975 and 1991, essentialised the histories of the *harkis*, a trend that once begun proved difficult to reverse. Nonetheless, the choice of the camps as a symbol for the wider *harki* experience was effective given what *harki* activists were seeking to achieve. Although only a minority spent long periods of time in the camps, approximately half of the *harki* community did pass through one of these spaces. The camps consequently became a point of commonality for a range of individuals as well as a point of continuity across generations. The violence, both symbolic and actual, directed at the community in these spaces came to stand for the broader suffering experienced by the *harki*s. The camps also proved a potent way to communicate the uniqueness of the *harki* community's position and history, hence their totemic status in narratives and campaigns.

The version of the past that *harki* activists were able to articulate in 1991 and in the years following was thus a patchy, composite entity that was much less cohesive and codified than that of the *pied-noir* community. Aside from the 'hot' summers of 1975 and 1991 and their immediate aftermaths, the *harki* community remained largely on the margins of popular awareness and government agendas, hence mounting frustrations within the community as material conditions failed to significantly improve. Yet, in spite of limited practical achievements, the years between 1975 and 1991 were, nonetheless, crucial for the *harki*s. They signalled a progressive awakening within the community regarding the need to take action and to direct that action themselves, even though the struggle to disentangle their cause from the vested interests of others continues to the present day. Beyond 1991, the most significant change was the channels and forms through which the *harki* community articulated its sense of self and history, including a revival of associations, albeit on a very different basis to those of the 1970s. In this period, the narratives surrounding the *harki*s both solidified and diversified as they were carried forward by different representatives from within the community to a variety of audiences. Finally, just as the political and socio-economic landscape of the 1980s proved crucial to the evolution of *harki* activism, so too would the wider context of the 1990s. As much as 1991 was a turning point for the mobilisation of descendants of the *harki*s, it was also a key year for the portrayal of the War of Independence in France, as the 'silence' perceived as shrouding the conflict began to breakdown. As the public became more engaged with this past, in turn forcing the state to take a more active interest and role, this naturally had implications for the evolution of the activism of the children of the *harki*s and that of the *pied-noir* community, as well as the relationship between the two.

Notes

1 These included hunger strikes in 1984 and 1987 in the Évreux cathedral in Normandy and the Madeleine church in Paris, as well as several demonstrations and marches to draw attention to the situation of the *harki*s.

2 Laurent Muller, *Le Silence des Harkis* (Paris, 1999), p. 8.

3 Carried out by SOFRES on behalf of the Délégation aux rapatriés, 1000 adults were surveyed between 6 and 8 April 1989. Cited in Stéphanie Abrial, *Les Enfants de Harkis: de la révolte à la intégration* (Paris, 2002), p. 54.

4   Quote attributed to Hacène Arfi, cited in Mohand Hamoumou and Jean-Jacques Jordi, 'Harkis et pieds-noirs: le souvenir et la douleur', *Guerre d'Algérie magazine*, 4 (July-August 2002), 41.
5   Régis Pierret, *Les Filles et fils de harkis: entre double rejet et triple appartenance* (Paris, 2008), p. 63.
6   Patrick Jammes, *Médécin des harkis au camp de Bias, 1970–2000* (Paris, 2012), p. 17.
7   Of the estimated 200,000 members of the *harki* community in 1975, two thirds were under twenty years old. See Anne Heinis cited in Michel Roux, *Les Harkis ou les oubliés de l'histoire* (Paris, 1991), pp. 324–5.
8   R.B., 'Des Français qu'on dit à part entière', *Le Monde* (3 June 1975), p. 37.
9   Pierret, *Les Filles et fils de harkis*, p. 57.
10 R.B. 'Des Français', p. 37.
11 'Encore des harkis en colère', *L'Aurore* (20 June 1975), p. 16.
12 'Les Harkis de Saint-Valérien', *Panorama*, aired 17 April 1970 (Channel 1).
13 'Harki', *Les Dossiers de l'écran*, aired 17 May 1977 (A2).
14 Roux, *Les Harkis*, pp. 356–7.
15 Roux, *Les Harkis*, pp. 352–6.
16 Muller, *Le Silence*, p. 129.
17 The physical dilapidation of institutional environments became an apt illustration of the paradoxes of the government's attitude towards the *harkis*. Prior to 1975, the state was reluctant to commission improvements to the camps and forest hamlets because this would contradict its rhetoric that such spaces were only required temporarily while the *harkis* effected their state-sponsored apprenticeship to France. After 1975, when the emphasis shifted to dispersal as the best means to facilitate integration, the state and, later, local authorities who assumed responsibility for these sites, resisted calls for improvements on the grounds that this would encourage the *harki* community to remain in environments that inhibited their assimilation. The collective result was decades of neglect of structures that were in any case unfit for purpose from the outset. See Roux, *Les harkis*, p. 361.
18 Saliha Abdellatif, 'Les Français-musulmans ou le poids de l'histoire à travers la communauté Picarde', *Les Temps modernes*, 452–4 (March–April–May 1984), 1831.
19 Akila, cited in Stéphan Gladieu and Dalila Kerchouche, *Destins de harkis: aux racines d'un exil* (Paris, 2003), p. 93.
20 Catherine Wihtol de Wenden, 'La vie associative des harkis', *Migrations société*, 1:5–6 (October–December 1989), 15.
21 'Dossier: Harki', *Pieds-noirs magazine*, 18 (September 1991), 20.
22 Dalila Kerchouche, *Mon père, ce harki* (Paris, 2003), p. 181.
23 Mohand Hamoumou, *Et ils sont devenus harkis* (Paris, 1993), p. 308.
24 Régis Pierret, 'Les Enfants de harkis, une jeunesse dans les camps', *Pensée plurielle*, 14 (2007), 40–1.
25 Muller, *Le Silence*, p. 77.

26 Abderahmen Moumen, 'De l'absence aux nouveaux porte-parole: évolution du mouvement associatif harki (1962–2011)', *Les Temps modernes*, 666 (November–December 2011), 162.

27 'Harkis', aired 17 May 1977; 'Et pourtant ils sont Français', *Les Dossiers de l'écran*, aired 17 May 1977 (Channel 2).

28 Sung Choi, 'From Colonial Settler to Postcolonial Repatriate: The Integration of the French from Algeria, 1962 to the Present', unpublished doctoral dissertation, UCLA, 2007, p. 233; Hamoumou, *Et ils sont devenus harkis*, p. 300; Abderahmen Moumen, *Les Français musulmans en Vaucluse 1962–1991* (Paris, 2003), p. 151.

29 'Et pourtant ils sont Français', aired 17 May 1977.

30 'Et pourtant ils sont Français', aired 17 May 1977.

31 Moumen, 'De l'absence', 165.

32 The tactics of USDIFRA and their relationship to the wider *pied-noir* community will be discussed in Chapter 5.

33 Boussad Azni, *Harkis, crime d'état: généaolgie d'un abandon* (Paris, 2002), p. 129.

34 Wihtol de Wenden, 'La Vie associative', 20.

35 Maurice Calmein, 'Un dynamisme efficace', *L'Algérianiste*, 5:4 (December 1978), 2.

36 Calmein, 'Un dynamisme', 2. This was a striking choice of phrase given that the revival of activism within the Jewish community during the 1970s would prove a crucial point of reference for later *harki* mobilisation.

37 'Allocution du Président de la République', *France horizon*, 184 (May 1977), 21.

38 Maurice Calmein, 'Editorial: riches de nos différences', *L'Algérianiste*, 6:5 (15 March 1979), 4.

39 Maurice Calmein, 'Editorial: les fils de la colère', *L'Algérianiste*, 55 (September 1991), 2.

40 For further details on the 'Hommage aux harkis' campaign, see Taouès Titraoui and Bernard Coll, *Le Livre des harkis* (Bièvres, 1991), pp. 252–4.

41 'Les Pieds-noirs, ça va?', *Les Dossiers de l'écran*, aired 20 October 1987 (A2).

42 Examples of Coll's interventions on behalf of the *harkis* include 'Pour ceux d'Algérie, que reste-t-il du passé?', *Les Dossiers de l'écran*, aired 5 April 1983 (A2); 'Droit de réponse aux pieds-noirs', *Droit de réponse*, aired 8 November 1986 (TF1); 'Arlette Laguiller', *Ciel, mon mardi!*, aired 4 June 1991 (FR3).

43 An anonymous son of *harki* cited in Jacques Delarue, 'La Malédiction des enfants de harkis', *Matériaux pour l'histoire de notre temps*, 26 (January–March 1992), 36.

44 Calmein, 'Editorial: les fils de la colère', 2.

45 The distinction between *harkis* and Algerians does not in any way deny the Algerian origins and attachments of the *harkis*; it is used simply for clarity when discussing the two communities.

46 For an overview of these political machinations, see Sung Choi, 'The Muslim Veteran in Postcolonial France: The Politics of the Integration of Harkis after 1962', *French Politics, Culture and Society*, 29:1 (Spring 2011), 24–45.

47 'Peut-on échapper à la haine ordinaire?', *Ça se discute*, aired 28 May 1997 (A2).

48 The reference to brooms refers to the inability of the state to provide employment for the children of *harkis*, even in low-paid jobs like street sweeping.
Choi, 'The Muslim Veteran', 37.

49 For further discussion of the role of Islam within the *harki* community, see
Marwan Abi Samra, 'Fidèles à la France et à l'islam: les harkis', *Quo Vadis*
(Autumn–Winter 1993), 103–06; Pierret, *Les Filles et fils de harkis*, pp. 127–34.

50 For further discussion of silence within the Algerian community, see Jim
House and Neil MacMaster, *Paris 1961: Algerians, State Terror and Memory*
(Oxford, 2006), pp. 265–75. The connections between *harkis* and Algerians
in France, as opposed to between their children, will be explored further in
Chapter 6.

51 Amicale des Algériens en Europe, *Réfléxions sur l'émigration algérienne*
(Paris: Amicale des Algériens en Europe, 1978), p. 2.

52 For further discussion of the AAE and its relationship with the immigrant
community, see House and MacMaster, *Paris 1961*, pp. 276–9, 304–6; and the
AAE's own publication, known respectively as *L'Algérien en Europe* (1962–82);
La Semaine de l'émigration (1982–85); and *L'actualité de l'émigration* (1985–91).

53 Salem Kacet, cited in Yvan Gastaut, 'Le Racisme anti-maghrébin et les
séquelles de la guerre d'Algérie', *Hommes et migrations*, 1174 (March 1994), 41.

54 'Beur', is a slang term for Arab that rose to prominence during the 1980s,
although it was actually coined in the 1970s. For discussion of its use and
problematic status, see Alec G. Hargreaves, *Multi-Ethnic France* (New York
and London, 2007), pp. 90–2.

55 Harlem Désir, *SOS Désirs* (Paris, 1987), pp. 175–6.

56 For an overview of this policy, see Henri Giordan, *Démocratie culturelle et
droit à la différence* (Paris, 1982).

57 Saïd Bouamama, *Contribution à la mémoire des banlieues* (Paris, 1994), p. 20.

58 Cited in Nora Barsali, François-Xavier Freland and Anne-Marie Vincent,
Générations beurs: français à part entière (Paris, 2008), pp. 97–8.

59 Saïd Bouamama, *Contribution*, p. 20.

60 Bouzid, *La Marche: traversée de la France profonde* (Paris, 1984).

61 See Nacer Kettane, *Droit de réponse à la démocratie française* (Paris, 1986),
p. 96; Laurent Muller, 'Enfants d'immigrés, enfants de harkis', *Confluences
Méditerranée*, 34 (Summer 2000), 141; Wihtol de Wenden, 'La vie associative',
20. For examples of articles within the *beur* press, see *Sans Frontière* whose
archives are available digitally at www.odysseo.generiques.org [28 July 2014].

62 For further information on these associations and the relationships they were
able to foster, see Wihtol de Wenden, 'La vie associatif', 20–1.

63 Cited in Rosella Spina, *Enfants de harkis et enfants d'émigrés: parcours croisés,
identités à recoudre* (Paris, 2012), p. 218.

64 Barsali et al., *Générations beurs*, p. 25.

65 See Daniel A. Gordon, *Immigrants and Intellectuals: May '68 and the Rise of
Anti-Racism in France* (Pontypool, 2012) p. 216.

66 This phenomenon is referred to as the 'double absence' after Abdelmalek Sayad, *La Double absence: des illusions de l'émigré aux souffrances de l'immigré* (Paris, 1999).

67 Farida Belghoul, cited in Gordon, *Immigrants and Intellectuals*, p. 202.

68 Farouk B., cited in Ahmed Boubeker, 'La Prochaine fois le feu: les trois âges de la rupture des banlieues', *Contemporary French Civilization*, 31:1 (Winter-Spring 2007), 181.

69 Bouzid, *La Marche*, pp. 41–2.

70 For further evaluation of 1983, the *beur* movement and its significance, see Louisa Zanoun (ed.), '1983. La Marche pour l'égalité et contre le racisme', Special issue, *Migrance*, 41 (2013), 1–233; Christian Delorme, 'Le "Mouvement beur" a une histoire', *Les Cahiers de la nouvelle génération*, 1 (1984), 18–46; Ahmed Boubeker and Mogniss H. Abdallah, 'Douce France: la saga du mouvement beur', *IM'média* (Autumn–Winter 1993), 1–108; Saïd Bouamama, *Dix ans de marche des beurs: chronique d'un mouvement avorté* (Paris, 1994).

71 Saïd Bouamama, *Héritiers involontaires de la guerre d'Algérie: jeunes Manosquins issus de l'immigration algérienne* (Manosque, 2003), pp. 111, 153.

72 For an explanation of changes to the Nationality Code in this period and their implications, see Hargreaves, *Multi-Ethnic France*, pp. 152–65.

73 Marcel Crozatier, 'Les Droits de l'homme et la civisme aux "beurs"', *France horizon*, 263–4 (June–July 1985), 7.

74 Brahim Sadouni, 'Harki: la mattraque est elle la solution de nos problèmes?', *Pieds-noirs magazine*, 11 (January 1991), 26.

75 Cited in Pierret, *Les Filles et fils de harkis*, p. 179.

76 Azni, *Harkis*. p. 127.

77 Giulia Fabbiano, 'Mémoires postalgériennes: la guerre d'Algérie entre héritage et emprunts', in *La Concurrence mémorielle*, ed. by Geoffrey Grandjean and Jérôme Jamin (Paris, 2011), p. 140.

78 Sadouni's activism prior to this point had consisted of a brief spell in the PCF and a more sustained involvement as vice-president of M'Hamed Laradji's CMFRAA. Brahim Sadouni, *Destin de harki*, with Alexandre Grigarigntz (Paris, 2001), p. 170.

79 Sadouni's first march was organised around the idea of exposing the hollowness of de Gaulle's famous claim that France's territory extended from Dunkerque to Tamanrrasset in southern Algeria. Unable to get to Tamanrrasset because of his status as a former *harki*, Sadouni settled for a route that began in Dunkerque and ended in Marseille. His second march in 1987, which paid hommage to 'forgotten' French Muslim 'heros', commenced in Rouen and finished in Monte Cassino where Sadouni's own father had been wounded while fighting for France in the Second World War. Sadouni, *Destin de harki*, p. 171.

80 Sadouni, *Destin de harki*, pp. 170–1.

81 Sadouni, *Destin de harki*, p. 181.

82 Giulia Fabbiano, 'Devenir-harki: les modes d'énonciation identitaire des descendants des anciens supplétifs de la guerre d'Algérie', *Migrations société*, 20:120 (November–December 2008), 164.

83 Scholars who have made this argument include Moumen, 'De l'absence', 164; Fabbiano, 'Devenir-harki', 165.

84 Philippe Bernard, 'Harkis: au nom des pères les enfants des anciens supplétifs dénoncent l'injustice dont ils sont victimes', *Le Monde* (10 July 1991), p. 1.

85 Saliha Telali, *Les Enfants des Harkis: entre silence et assimilation subie* (Paris, 2009), p. 15.

86 See, in particular, Hamoumou, *Et ils sont devenus harkis*; Nordine Boulhaïs, *Histoire des harkis du nord de la France* (Paris, 2005); Muller, *Le silence*; Abrial, *Les enfants de harkis*.

87 Derrieu, *La Cité de tapis*, p. 36.

88 Muller, *Le Silence*, p. 95.

89 David Lepoutre with Isabelle Cannoodt, *Souvenirs de familles immigres* (Paris, 2005), p. 290.

90 For further discussion of this, see Muller, *Le Silence*, pp. 95–111.

91 Telali, *Les Enfants*, p. 13.

92 Ahmed Kaberseli, *Le Chagrin sans la pitié* (Paris, 1988), pp. 44, 94; Benjamin Stora, *La Gangrène et l'oubli: la mémoire de la guerre d'Algérie* (Paris, 1991), p. 208.

93 Abrial, *Les Enfants*, p. 201.

94 Emmanuel Brillet, 'A Remarkable Heritage: The "Daily Round" of the Children of the Harkis, between Merger and Vilification', *Immigrants and Minorities*, 22:2–3 (July–November 2003), 340.

95 Azni, *Harkis*, p. 100.

96 Jeannette E. Miller, 'A Camp for Foreigners and "Aliens": The Harkis' Exile at the Rivesaltes Camp (1962–1964)', *French Politics, Culture and Society*, 31:3 (Winter 2013), 17–18.

PART II

The 'Return' of the War of
Independence, 1991–2012

Acceleration, 1991–2005

5

Hardening attitudes

During the 1970s and 1980s, *pied-noir* associations focused their attention on creating a rich, communal store of consensual discourses about the past designed to reflect particular attributes related to the contemporary identity of the community. The key strengths of this 'meta-memory' were its malleability, which enabled it to be deployed in a variety of guises, and its resonance among individual *rapatriés*, binding them together within a fluid but robust collective narrative. Beyond the realm of culture, however, the cohesiveness of the *pieds-noirs* proved fragile. This became increasingly apparent during the 1990s when the evolving context surrounding the Algerian War brought new pressures to bear upon the community. Amidst these altered circumstances, it became harder for *pied-noir* activists to conceal from a newly attentive public gaze, but also from their own members, the many fractures that had marked the community from its inception. Although unity was trumpeted as the community's most valuable attribute, dissent and division were never far from the surface in what would prove to be a pivotal but also tumultuous decade.

Prior to the 1990s, successive governments resisted mounting grass-roots pressure from increasingly mobilised activists for official commemorative gestures on a national scale. Specific material concessions, ranging from financial aid in the form of new compensation laws for the *pieds-noirs* to the closure of the camps and the creation of the BIAC and ONASEC schemes for the *harki* community, were promised and implemented by both the right and the left when it proved politically expedient. But during their terms as president, neither Pompidou, Giscard or Mitterrand was prepared to engage in any substantive public discussion of the Algerian War, fearing, with good reason, that state involvement in this complex area would serve only to revive divisions within society. The commemorative terrain was thus left to the groups concerned, who operated primarily in relation to their own constituencies. In the 1990s, however, the French state was overtaken by developments, both domestic and international, which cumulatively pushed politicians to consciously address the Algerian War and its place within the history and memory of the nation. The impact of these evolutions was twofold. First, while public interest in this facet of France's past had always existed, as attested to by the sustained market for publications dealing with the war, it now reached new peaks.[1] What had largely been a private and individualised interest now became a national phenomenon as debates over different aspects of the conflict raged across various media, provoked in no small part by the broadcasting of the widely viewed documentary series *La Guerre d'Algérie* and *Les Années algériennes* at the beginning of the decade.[2] This revived national interest enabled a variety of memory-carrying groups to occupy increasingly prominent positions within the public realm. Something that, in turn, prompted the state to take its first 'tentative steps' towards officialising a national memory of the war as it sought to control and shape these memorial discourses.[3]

The 'return' of the war

The 'conditions of possibility' that facilitated these developments were multiple.[4] Several occurred beyond France's borders as seismic shifts in the international system brought about new relationships between nation-states and their inhabitants, as well as between notions of past, present and future.[5] Events in the Arab world ranging from the first Palestinian Intifada to the first Gulf War via the violence that wracked Algeria during the 1990s as the military-backed state sought to defeat Islamist insurgents, focused French attention on these regions, espe-cially given the Hexagon's growing Muslim population. This changing social composition also meant that issues of immigration and integration remained prominent. The concerns of the *beur* generation and the debates surrounding the *droit à la différence* that marked the 1980s evolved into anxiety about the ability of French national identity to withstand the effects of the 'social fracture' and the related 'colonial fracture', against a backdrop of progressive electoral gains by the FN.[6] The renewed repub-lican consensus that emerged as one response to these issues squared off against a nascent postcolonial critique championed by bodies such as the Association pour la connaissance de l'histoire de l'Afrique contemporaine (ACHAC), which questioned the Republic's universalist pretensions as part of a rediscovery of colonial history within French academia.[7]

Of further academic relevance was the boom in memory studies in which France played a prominent role courtesy of Pierre Nora's work on 'realms of memory'.[8] One of the more concrete manifestations of this turn to memory was the renewed attention devoted to the Vichy period. Building on the revival of Jewish memories that had begun in the 1970s, the 'Vichy syndrome', as chronicled by Henry Rousso, reached its peak in the 1990s.[9] Sensitising the general population to questions of memory and silences with respect to traumatic pasts, as well as underlining the nation's capacity for iniquity, the public processing of the Vichy years proved an important catalyst in reviving popular interest in the War of Independence. This was particularly true of the prosecutions of a series of key figures connected to the Occupation that riveted the nation, none more so than the 1997–98 trial and conviction of the prominent Gaullist politician Maurice Papon for crimes against humanity stemming from his role in the deportation of 1690 Jews, including 233 children, when he was prefect of the Bordeaux region during the Second World War. Also highlighted in the course of this heavily mediatised court case was Papon's tenure as Paris Chief of Police during the demonstrations of 17 October 1961, which saw peaceful Algerian protestors violently suppressed by the forces of law and order resulting in the deaths of up to 200 people. The involvement of Papon in these two 'dark' episodes of French history helped fix the idea of some kind of continuity between the Vichy and the Algerian War in the minds of many.[10] This was in spite of Rousso's own insistence that while there were certain similarities, including the central role played by the concepts of a 'duty of memory' and 'victimhood' and the shared difficulty of creating a consensual form of national commemoration, the two conflicts remained distinct, as did their commemorative afterlives.[11]

At the political level, the 1990s witnessed the coincidence in power of President Jacques Chirac, who had served in Algeria, and Prime Minister Lionel Jospin, who cut his political teeth opposing the conflict. Their cohabitation, from 1997 until 2002, further fuelled public awareness of Algeria as both men sought, in different ways, to tackle certain legacies of the conflict. Jospin's administration broke the government's silence surrounding 17 October 1961, acknowledging for the first time that the actual death toll for that night was far higher than the long-cited official figure of two. Jospin also oversaw measures to increase access to the archives for historians wishing to investigate certain aspects of the Algerian War, again particularly relating to 17 October 1961.[12] Chirac already had a track record of intervention in favour of the *pied-noir* and *harki* communities prior to the start of his presidential term in 1995, including shepherding

the 1987 compensation law through parliament when he was prime minister under Mitterrand. As a result, he was perceived by many *pieds-noirs*
as a sympathetic figure within government, in spite of his Gaullist roots.
It was under Chirac that steps were taken to incorporate the legacy of
the Algerian War into French commemorative culture with the inauguration, in November 1996, of the first state monument to the conflict in the
Square de la Butte du Chapeau-Rouge in Paris. However, the obscure location of the monument, combined with the fact that it was dedicated not to
the Algerian War specifically, but rather to those soldiers killed in North
Africa between 1952 and 1962, showed the limits of the state's commemorative policy.[13] More significant and community-specific commemorative
acts would come towards the end of Chirac's tenure when he oversaw the
creation of a national memorial to French soldiers and *harkis* killed in
Algeria on the Quai Branly in 2002, instituted a national day of homage
for the *harki* community in September 2001, and authorised a further
round of financial compensation for *pieds-noirs* and *harkis,* in addition to
official acts of recognition for both groups, via the 23 February 2005 law.

By demonstrating a new willingness on the part of the state to engage
with the war and its legacies, Chirac helped to legitimate the campaigns of
pieds-noirs and other activists, creating 'institutional relays' and 'frameworks of memory' that gave the narratives being championed by such
groups points of anchorage at the national level.[14] When inaugurating the
1996 memorial, Chirac was careful to specify: 'I do not want to return to
the causes of these often fratricidal conflicts, nor to the tragedies these
battles produced.' Instead, he stated, the purpose of the monument was
to honour those who had given their lives for France, including civilians 'who died on soil enriched for one hundred and thirty years by their
parents' work'.[15] Yet, although Chirac ultimately hoped to find a way for
diverse memories to coexist as part of the national patrimony, as subsequent chapters will demonstrate, in fact his actions incentivised activists
to compete against each other for the favour of the state. This exacerbated
the very divisions he was hoping to quell, particularly given the imbalance in the resources possessed by different groups and their consequent
abilities to make themselves heard in the national arena.[16]

Multiple voices

Although competition came to characterise memories in the public
sphere as the 1990s wore on, at the beginning of the decade there was
considerable optimism that the reflections prompted by the thirtieth anniversary of the end of the Algerian War signalled a new, more

open era of discussion. 'It took thirty years, a generation, for the film *Le Chagrin et la pitié* to persuade the French to accept a less mythical history [of the Second World War]', opined the historian Benjamin Stora. 'In the same way, on the eve of the thirtieth anniversary of the Evian Accords, it is time to take on, in all its aspects, the history of this war.'[17] This was certainly Stora's raison d'être, as evidenced by two of his major historical projects: the monograph *La Gangrène et l'oubli* and the documentary series, *Les Années algériennes*. Appearing simultaneously in 1991, both were informed by Stora's interest in the way traces of the past persist in the present and by his personal history as a 'repatriated' Algerian Jew from Constantine. *Les Années algériennes*, in particular, was conceived of as a conscious reaction against the 'official history' embodied in other recent documentaries by Yves Courrière, Denis Chegaray and Peter Batty.[18] In contrast, Stora's intention was not to recount the history of the war but rather to 'understand' it through the different memories of those involved. For this reason, he deliberately sought out anonymous witnesses, representing a spectrum of viewpoints, and brought them together in a single space; not so as to establish any grand narrative, but rather to highlight 'an infinitely more complex reality'.[19] *La Gangrene et l'oubli* was animated by a similar intention to 'do history in a different way' by using memory as an object of study.[20] The book was criticised by scholars who were as yet unconvinced by memory as an academic tool through which to access the past, whereas *Les Années algériennes* generated a storm of discussion because of its conscious juxtaposition of divergent perspectives. Defending his documentary, Stora argued that only by accepting the polyvalent nature of the conflict could French society begin to process this complicated but integral part of their national past.[21] Yet, in spite of considerable hostility from certain communities, notably the *pieds-noirs*, Stora was optimistic about the possibilities in the early 1990s for 'bridges', 'convergences' and 'dialogue'.[22]

This positivity was reflected in the name and in the ethos of Coup de soleil [a bit of sunshine], one of several associations in the 1990s dedicated to fostering communication and overcoming a Manichean image of the various communities that had comprised French Algeria. Referring to such associations as 'Mediterranean', Valérie Esclangon-Morin argues that their inclusivity, particularly with respect to younger generations, was indicative of a commitment to building a community not on something that had ceased to exist (i.e. French Algeria), but rather on a continuing sense of fraternity born of common geographical and cultural roots.[23] Coup de soleil, which Stora was closely involved with, was one of the most prominent of these bridge-building organisations largely due to the stature of its founder, Georges Morin. A *pied-vert*, Morin was a settler who initially remained in Algeria after independence. He came to France in 1966 in order to prepare for the entrance exam to the prestigious Institut d'études politiques in Grenoble.[24] After narrowly missing out on selection two years running, Morin opted instead to take up an administrative post at the University of Grenoble, using his new role to establish a link between his institution and the University of Constantine. Forging connections across the Mediterranean would become his trademark as he went on to pursue a political career with the PS serving as advisor to various Ministers, particularly under the Mitterrand regime, where he was dubbed 'Monsieur Maghreb'.[25]

Founded in 1984, Coup de soleil complemented these activities. Its initial impetus was to 'bring something to the anti-racist struggle', but this soon evolved into a broader desire to bring together '*Beurs*, French Muslim *rapatriés*, Jews of the Maghreb, Maghrebins of France or *pieds-noirs*' in order to 'show, study, understand and explain' the affairs of their shared region of origin. The association's eponymously titled magazine covered a range of topics including the Gulf War, rising civil unrest in Algeria, the 1991 *harki* protests, commemorations of the thirtieth anniversary of 17 October 1961, the place of Berbers in Algeria, as well as developments in other Mediterranean countries such as Spain and Portugal. Aware that there was much which historically separated these communities, Morin nonetheless remained confident that when it came to evoking memories or presenting their vision for the future, they would be able to find common ground. In particular, he argued that all these groups had successfully overcome the challenges of integrating into a new society and should now come together to help children of 'Maghrebins' in France do the same.[26]

Morin was conscious that Coup de soleil represented a different approach and perspective to what he referred to as the 'innumerable' *pied-noir* associations who 'express themselves always more loudly than the others and whose opinions, taken up by numerous media, slip into *nostalgérie* for French Algeria'. By speaking out, Morin sought to correct this biased picture, expressing the views held by 'half the *pieds-noirs*. Except we never hear them!'[27] With 5000 'sympathisers' by 1990, Coup de soleil was by no means a small operation, although Morin's political connections ensured that it enjoyed a higher profile that it perhaps otherwise would have done.[28] Its intellectual and left-leaning political focus, indicated by contributors such as Leïla Sebbar and Rachid Mimouni, meant that it was addressing itself to a rather different audience than the Cercle algérianiste and ANFANOMA. Coup de soleil, but also organisations like

Pieds-noirs pour l'Algérie, which saw itself as a 'natural intermediary' between the populations north and south of the Mediterranean, thus testify to the existence of an alternative side to *pied-noir* activism that is frequently overlooked.[29]

A harder edge

Morin was correct when he noted that organisations like Coup de soleil tended to be drowned out by other *pied-noir* voices. This was particularly true in the 1990s, which witnessed the birth of a more radical breed of *pied-noir* association, whose intemperate and combative rhetoric would come to occupy a disproportionate amount of space within the emerging commemorative climate. This new environment compelled *pied-noir* activists to project their historical understanding outwards to a greater extent, leading Raphaëlle Branche to compare the situation to that of a disorganised orchestra in which each instrument played its part of the score without worrying about the neighbouring instruments, except in the sense of ensuring that it could be heard above them.[30] In applying this metaphor to the *pieds-noirs*, although they carried on playing the same tune, during the 1990s their audience expanded considerably as the War of Independence grew in public prominence. Yet, the orchestra simultaneously grew as more memory carriers began 'playing'. Because these new sections were not necessarily in harmony with the *pieds-noirs*, activists felt that they had to play louder, more insistently, and in a more diverse array of settings in order to ensure that their interpretation was the one conveyed to the listeners.

This evolution can clearly be seen through the life of the publication *Les Français d'AFN*, which took its name from a long-running column by René Attard dedicated to the *pieds-noirs*, which was published in *L'Aurore*, a mainstream newspaper sympathetic to the *Algérie française* cause.[31] When *L'Aurore* decided to bring Attard's column to an end in 1980, he launched *Les Français d'AFN* as an independent endeavour, envisaging it as a forum where *pied-noir* associations could come together.[32] In its early years, this was precisely how the publication functioned. Its 'associational life' section reported on the activities of a variety of bodies, including regional branches of the Cercle algérianiste and ANFANOMA, while other content echoed the concerns and narratives of the wider activist community in the 1980s by commemorating 26 March and 5 July, reporting on the annual pilgrimage to Nîmes, profiling successful *pieds-noirs* and immersing readers in nostalgic recollections of happy childhoods in Algeria. In 1984, however, Attard endorsed a newly formed alliance of twelve existing associations, the Fédération pour l'unité des rapatriés, réfugiés et de leurs amis (FURR) as the best chance to forge unity among the *rapatrié* community.[33] FURR was the brainchild of Joseph Ortiz, a diehard *Algérie française* supporter who had been sentenced to death and forced into hiding following his role in settler-led insurrection known as the week of barricades in January 1960.[34] He was given amnesty in 1968 and returned to France, settling in Toulon where he was active in both *pied-noir* and far-right circles. As the voice of FURR became increasingly dominant within *Les Français d'AFN*, so the ideology of the magazine shifted considerably to the right, while the space afforded to other *pied-noir* associations diminished. By the late 1980s, FURR was firmly in control of *Les Français d'AFN*, with Ortiz's 'straight talking' editorial column setting the tone for what had become a radical publication that openly endorsed voting for the FN.

The magazine folded shortly before Ortiz's death in February 1995, but its spirit, and several of its contributors, would live on in the association Véritas, created in March 1996 by former Mayor of Algiers, Joseph Hattab Pacha. The association's monthly publication, *La Lettre de Véritas*, was edited by Hattab Pacha's sister, Anne Cazal, who had previously served on the editorial board of *Les Français d'AFN* and who wrote the preface to Ortiz's republished autobiography in 1999. With a self-proclaimed circulation of 2,500, *La Lettre de Véritas* distinguished itself through it stark views, aggressive polemic, often with religious overtones, and hyperbolic historical comparisons.[35] Although the gamut of topics covered was similar to other *pied-noir* publications, the level of invective and the overt ideological positioning set *La Lettre de Véritas* apart. Discussions of de Gaulle and the OAS, demonised and lionised respectively to an extreme degree, provide some of the best illustrations of this. The General was regularly castigated by Véritas as 'totalitarian dictator' who unleashed 'a true genocide' on the French of Algeria, including the *harkis*, all in service of his 'pride and personal ambition'.[36] This all stood in sharp contrast to the actions of the OAS, who were neither 'terrorists' nor 'fascists', but rather a 'great movement of patriotic resistance' who deserved to be rehabilitated.[37] Véritas also employed graphic images to illustrate their articles, presenting readers with front cover photographs of dead bodies lying on steps of the rue d'Isly post office on 26 March 1962; close ups of individuals allegedly tortured by the FLN, including *harkis* whose noses or genitals had been cut off; and images of children killed or mutilated as a result of FLN bombs.[38]

It would be easy to dismiss groups such as FURR and Véritas as simply the radical fringe of the *pied-noir* community were it not for the fact that other associations regularly gave them column inches and were prepared to join with them in collective initiatives implying endorsement of their opinions and tactics among portions of the wider community. The most welcoming publication has been *Pieds-noirs magazine*, another 1990s arrival on the activist scene, but many other groups from the Groupement national pour l'indemnisation des biens spoliés ou perdus outre-mer (GNPI) to *amicales* like the AOCAZ have also featured Véritas. And although absent from the pages of *France horizon* and *L'Algérianiste*, both ANFANOMA and the Cercle algérianiste have officially collaborated with Véritas as part of various campaigns, including against the commemoration of 19 March.

The quest for unity

In addition to feeling compelled to compete with other memory carriers for the attention of a newly sensitised French public, *pied-noir* associations were also competing against each other for the loyalty of their own community. Whereas Rosemary Averell Manes argues that each association 'operates as a largely autonomous entity', evidence indicates that while each organisation may have its own particular constituency, they do not operate in isolation.[39] Instead, over the years they have formed a dense network whose relations, so their spokespeople claim, are characterised by principles of mutual assistance and support that replicate the close communal ties of French Algeria. Advertising space has always been devoted to the activities of other groups, while joint ventures such as *rassemblements*, inaugurations, commemorations and petitions were common. Cross-fertilisation was further indicated in publications by the tendency to quote from the same canon of Algerian writers and their works, particularly figures from the 1930s 'Algerianist' literary movement such as Robert Randau and Jean Brune. Prominent contemporary activists like Jo Sohet, Pierre Goinard, Geneviève de Ternant and Anne Cazal were regularly featured by a range of association, with the same texts often reproduced simultaneously in multiple publications. Television programmes relating to the *pieds-noirs* furthermore revealed a cast of recurring association representatives, notably Jacques Roseau of RECOURS and Bernard Coll of JPN. Finally, there has always been considerable movement between associations with activists gaining experience in one organisation before launching their own. Maurice Calmein's time as a militant in the FNR in the 1960s, for example, serving him well when he came to found the Cercle algérianiste in 1973.[40]

Interconnectedness is something that has been actively promoted by associations from the outset. In 1965, *L'écho d'Oran* emphasised the importance of 'solidarity' and 'friendship', reminding its readers of the proverb:

Defeated, divided, a country dies.
Defeated, united, a country lives again.[41]

The first edition of *L'Algérianiste* opened with a similar intent, declaring: 'We wish to maintain our identity, living as we want to, proud of our past and strong because of our fraternal links'.[42] Constant vigilance was deemed necessary, as there were plenty of people, particularly politicians, who would seek to sow disunity among the *rapatriés* for their own gains. Given that divisions served only to 'blunt the possibilities for defence', *pieds-noirs* were encouraged to put minor disagreements aside for the greater good of the community.[43] This was presented as the only way to guarantee survival as a collective entity and the best chance of obtaining satisfaction in their campaigns for recognition and recompense.

When faced with a perceived external enemy, *pieds-noirs* seemed naturally to adhere to this precept, banding together to protect themselves and their patrimony. In spite of the tensions between their associations and styles of activism, Roseau and Coll joined forces to defend Roland Di Constanzo of USDIFRA, a group towards which neither man was well disposed, after he embarked upon an aggressive and embarrassing denunciation of other *pied-noir* associations during an episode of the television programme *Ciel, mon mardi!*[44] Even as he verbally attacked them both live on air, Roseau and Coll sought to justify Di Constanzo's behaviour as an inevitable consequence of the lack of opportunities afforded to *pieds-noirs* by the media to present their case. This was followed by a double-page autopsy of the programme conducted by *Pieds-noirs magazine*, in which Roseau and Coll reiterated their support for 'our friend' Roland, whose 'moving and forceful intervention' had enabled the *pied-noir* community 'to give a stronger, more united and even more powerful image of itself'.[45] Alongside solidarity, irreproachability was similarly valued within the community. 'Our behaviour must be as dignified as it is firm', stressed Calmein, 'and prove that, for us, moral values such as a sense of honour, of fraternity remain essential'.[46] This became increasingly important in the 1990s as the attention of the nation turned towards groups connected to the Algerian War. Acknowledging that no community was perfect, strategies were proposed for dealing with the occasional 'black sheep' whose behaviour risked 'harming' the rest of the community.[47] Self-policing was thus advocated to bring any rogue elements back into line before they could tarnish the collective image projected to the outside world.

Associations have always recognised that they would be more powerful if they combined forces. But in spite of much rhetoric, unity in a
practical sense has proven elusive. 'It has been a long time' complained
Calmein, 'since the too numerous captains of our countless ships ceased
to have any influence over what would have been a powerful Armada'.[48]
The principal problem, as deduced by Calmein, was that competition
among the 'too numerous captains' for control over the image and voice
of the community made rivalry and division endemic among associations. As early as November 1956, the Union des Français d'outre-mer
fused with the Association des Français d'Afrique du Nord et d'outre-mer
to form ANFANOM, with a final 'A', standing for 'et leurs amis' (and their
friends), added in 1958 to create ANFANOMA. Yet at the association's annual conference in February 1957, disagreements were so severe that a faction broke away to form the Fédération nationale des Français d'Afrique
du Nord et d'outre-mer (FNFANOM). This was on top of a long-standing
rivalry between ANFANOMA and RANFRAN.[49] These early years established a pattern that continues to the present day, whereby jealousies and
infighting have progressively fractured the community into ever-smaller
groups.[50]

In counterpoint to this bewildering array of fusions and splits, there
have been a series of attempts to federate *pied-noir* associations into larger
blocks, none of which have endured. One of the more successful was
the FNR, which debuted in 1965, promising to pursue 'energetically' the
material and moral goals of the community. In 1969, following his release
from prison and amnesty, General Jouhaud was elected as president of the
FNR, which included representatives from all the key associations of the
day. The existence of the FNR demonstrated an acknowledgement that
forming a single lobby was the most effective way of making politicians
take note of *rapatrié* demands. But such realisations have not proven sufficient to transcend rivalries between member associations and to hold
the FNR, or the various federative bodies that succeeded it, together in
the long term. Further complicating matters was the rapid growth in the
number of *pied-noir* associations. When the FNR was formed there were
only three associations able to claim a national profile – L'Algérienne,
RANFRAN and ANFANOMA – whereas by the mid-1980s there were
twenty, in addition to hundreds of local organisations and *amicales*.[51]

For many years, the French public were unaware of the tensions sim-
mering beneath the apparently calm and unified surface of the *pied-noir*
community. This all changed, however, on the night of 5 March 1993
when the RECOURS leader, Jacques Roseau, was shot and killed by
three *pied-noirs* in their sixties – Gérard Huntz, Jean Claude Lozano and

Marcel Navarro – who were all members of USDIFRA. When initially questioned by police, Huntz proudly situated his actions as the logical continuation of his former adherence to the OAS. In describing the attack, he emphasised how '[a]t the top of the driver's window, I fired three rapid shots. That had a meaning: three shots like the three letters OAS. I aimed for the head.'[52] The media seized upon these words, presenting them as proof that, more than thirty years on, the Algerian War had still not ended for some people. In exposing the *pied-noir* community to an unprecedented level of national scrutiny, the murder investigation and subsequent trial publicly highlighted the deep-seated rivalries embedded in the associational movement. It seems no coincidence that these tensions showed most visibly when the spotlight was shining with unaccustomed intensity upon the community in general and the stakes, in terms of claiming part of the newly opened up commemorative public space, were so high. The assassination of Roseau, arguably the ultimate sign of a hardening of attitudes, thus serves as a useful prism through which to explore the impact of the 1990s on the internal dynamics of *pied-noir* activism.

The ultimate recourse

Roseau began his activist career during the War of Independence mobilising students in defence of French Algeria. Following brief stints in both the army and the OAS, he came to Montpellier in 1962 where he continued to combine studying law with militancy, now on behalf of the newly exiled settlers as president of the Association des fils de rapatriés et de leurs amis.[53] In 1976, after more than a decade with few tangible gains to show for his efforts, Roseau came to the conclusion that the only way to make real progress was to form a pressure group to lobby at the highest political levels. He therefore created RECOURS, later RECOURS-France, which sought to mobilise *pieds-noirs* to vote tactically in areas where they were numerically significant in order to pressure politicians and governments into acceding to their demands.[54]

This concept was first put into practice in the 1977 municipal elections, where it produced several shock results. RECOURS' most high-profile scalp was Montpellier's incumbent mayor, François Delmas, who had been in post since 1959. Delmas was unseated by the socialist candidate, Georges Frêche, in large part because of the latter's close alliance with Roseau, which helped him 'steal' the *rapatrié* vote, as the press described it.[55] Known as the 'elastic line', this practice, which could be used either to support or sanction, depending on the situation, was followed by RECOURS for the next decade in local and national contests, and at both ends of the political spectrum. RECOURS' call for the *pieds-noirs* to switch their allegiance from Giscard to Mitterrand in the 1981 presidential election was an example of a sanction vote after the former was deemed not to have delivered on the promises he had made to the *pieds-noirs* in 1974. The socialists were then subjected to the same treatment in the 1983 municipal elections when it was felt that Mitterrand had been too slow in 'rewarding' the *rapatriés* for their electoral support two years previously. By the 1986 legislative elections RECOURS had lined up behind Chirac as leader of the right-leaning RPR. Following Chirac's appointment as prime minister, *pieds-noirs* were rewarded with a range of favourable measures which, in addition to the 1987 compensation law, included a new secretary of state for repatriates, André Santini, the cancellation of outstanding but frozen *rapatrié* debts, five hundred million francs worth of aid for the *harkis,* and the creation of a national committee for a (never realised) memorial in Marseille dedicated to the 'civilising work' of the French overseas.[56]

The potential of block voting had long been recognised with elections providing, in the words of Emmanuelle Comtat, an 'opportune moment to jog the memory of the political class'.[57] In the 1965 presidential election, the *rapatrié* vote was believed to have produced strong results for the, ultimately unsuccessful, far-right candidate, Jean-Louis Tixier-Vignancourt in certain departments, notably the Bouches-du-Rhône, the Var and the Alpes Maritimes. Support for Tixier-Vignancourt, a lawyer who had acted on behalf of members of the OAS, was presented as a way for *pieds-noirs* to punish de Gaulle for his Algerian policies. When Tixier-Vignancourt failed to make it into the second round, he encouraged his supporters to transfer their votes to Mitterrand, de Gaulle's socialist challenger, in order to continue the quest to 'politically eliminate' those whom they considered 'responsible' for the loss of French Algeria.[58]

Associations like ANFANOMA, while claiming to be apolitical, also sought to direct their members towards certain candidates. The common stance of being 'apolitical' was understood as not being in the pocket of any one party or individual, but retaining the independence to decide whom to support based on what incentives were being offered.[59] ANFANOMA thus regularly invited those standing in municipal, legislative, and presidential elections to address their members through the pages of *France horizon* to explain how their candidature would benefit the community. The association also developed strong relationships with local politicians who proved themselves sympathetic to the *rapatriés* such as Jean and Jacques Médecin, a father and son who served consecutively as mayors of Nice from 1947 until 1990. Both men regularly attended or sent messages of support to gatherings and commemorations organised by ANFANOMA. In return, the Médecins received column inches, particularly in the run up to elections, in which they could outline their support for and actions on behalf of the *pieds-noirs*. Replicating the networks of patronage and paternalism that had characterised politics in French Algeria, most of the relationships cultivated through associations were with politicians of the right and far-right. It is therefore unsurprising that in national elections the community gave their votes predominantly to right-wing candidates. At the local level, however, *pieds-noirs* were willing to vote for the left and even the far-left if the candidate in question was deemed sympathetic or had a track record of concrete measures in favour of the community. It was for this reason that, addition to backing the socialist Frêche in Montpellier over several decades, *pieds-noirs* also lent their support to Georges Kioulou, the long-standing communist mayor of Échirolles (Isère) and, under the direction of RECOURS, helped to install the communist Paul Balmigère as mayor of Béziers in 1977.[60]

Voting was an important way in which the *rapatriés* could exercise their rights as French citizens, thus underlining their place within the national community. By engaging with the political process in this way, groups like ANFANOMA were furthermore attempting to mobilise the nascent *pied-noir* community so as to pressure politicians to pay attention to their demands. This was especially the case in the early years following repatriation when major policies and financial measures were still being debated and introduced, meaning there was much to play for. However, it was only with RECOURS in the mid-1970s that this lobbying potential was brought successfully and consistently to bear. Headline grabbing early successes, such as Frêche's triumph in Montpellier, raised the profile of RECOURS, while media coverage, combined with Roseau's political acumen and carefully cultivated connections, enabled the association to rapidly gain institutional legitimacy. Dubbed the 'voice of the *pieds-noirs*' by the press, Roseau managed to make his organisation but, more specifically, himself the key point of reference as far as those in power were concerned.[61] As journalist Jacques Molénat quipped, 'whoever says "pied-noir" says "Roseau".[62] In the wake of his assassination, tributes paid across the political spectrum, from the former liberal president Giscard to the head of the PCF, testified to the contacts and influence Roseau had enjoyed at the highest levels. Roseau's close relationship with Chirac was reflected in the 'great emotion' felt by the prime minister at the death of 'this generous personality, profoundly devoted to the *pied-noir* and *harki* cause', who had 'contributed much to their integration within our national community'.[63] In this sense, Roseau underscored the value to the *pied-noir* community of being publicly represented by authoritative figures who enjoyed high social status, considerable cultural capital and excellent contacts among the elites, a pattern that dated back to the 1960s when ANFANOMA president Colonel Pierre Battesti was able to exploit both his military status and his parliamentary connects as deputy for the Seine-et-Marne region on behalf of his fellow *rapatriés*.

At first, many within the *pied-noir* community welcomed Roseau's organisation, particularly following their early achievements. 'I remain convinced', wrote activist Marcel Bellier, 'and I am not the only one, if I am to believe the letters I receive, that we owe to RECOURS the little piece of justice brought by the indemnification law [of 1987]'.[64] But this early enthusiasm soon gave way to criticism, much of which centred on the perception, fuelled by media coverage, that Roseau represented the entire *pied-noir* community. In an open letter to Roseau, Michel Pittard, one of the original founders of RECOURS, complained:

> You present RECOURS as the most important *rapatrié* association ... You claim, on the other hand, that RECOURS is the voice of the *rapatrié* community. This is a breach of trust! It is your absolute right to speak in the name of your association and your members, but you have no authority to speak in the name of all *rapatriés*.[65]

The overtly political focus of RECOURS also represented a clear break with existing styles of activism, thus challenging the authority of established organisations. ANFANOMA, in particular, denounced the obsession with 'unity at any price' and the media hype surrounding the new association. In the summer of 1977, this led to a sustained spat that pitted the AOCAZ, who supported RECOURS, against ANFANOMA and RANFRAN, who did not. Conducted through the pages of their respective publications, *France horizon* and *L'écho de l'Oranie*, the altercation saw ANFANOMA's president claim that rather than fostering unity, Roseau's organisation was destroying 'the excellent spirit of agreement' his association had spent decades developing.[66]

Tied to these criticisms were often accusations that RECOURS was elitist and out of touch, simply a 'personal tribune' for Roseau.[67] Claims that association leaders were using their positions to further their own careers rather than the interests of the wider *pied-noir* community were not uncommon, but Roseau's high-profile political relationships gave such allegations a particular edge. In essence, by demonstrating that it was possible for the *pieds-noirs* to speak with a single, influential voice and by channelling that voice through his association, Roseau attained a status that many other groups coveted and resented anyone else possessing. Even *harki* activists became entangled in these power struggles with Hachemi Bounini of the FNRFCI denouncing Ahmed Kaberseli for serving as head of RECOURS' co-ordinating committee for *française musulmans;* a committee, Bounini claimed, that consisted only of one man and which undermined the steps 'French Muslims' had taken to prove that the paternalistic era of *l'Algérie de papa* was over.[68]

'Chirac's towel rail'

It was not only RECOURS' status that aroused anger, but also their policies. One of the association's most contentious measures was supporting Chirac given his past Gaullist allegiances. When *Pieds-noirs magazine* grilled Roseau on this political position he defended it on pragmatic grounds, arguing: 'I am not at all Gaullist. I am fundamentally anti-Gaullist ... we [RECOURS] support candidate with the label "friends of the *rapatriés*" and the most able to help *rapatriés* at the parliamentary or local level ... It was a call for a tactical vote.'[69] Yet, for many this was an unacceptable ideological compromise and a betrayal of the past, irrespective of the material benefits that supporting Chirac brought. Denounced for similar reasons was Roseau's advocacy of co-operation between the *pied-noir* community and the Algerian government in order to aid development and combat the rise of Islamic fundamentalism. For Roseau, defending the interests of the displaced settlers did not entail renouncing his attachment to the land from which they had been exiled, nor his desire to see an independent Algeria prosper; as he told one interviewer, 'Love always prevails over hate.'[70] Such opinions were not widely shared among other *pieds-noirs,* many of whom indicted Roseau as a 'pro-Arab traitor.'[71] This was a particular issue for Roseau's killers, with Lozano stating that 'We reproached Roseau for his rapprochement with Algeria and the FLN government, when I say "we" I mean 85 per cent of *rapatriés.*' Huntz similarly accused Roseau of betraying the *pieds-noirs* by 'forgetting' the past too quickly, telling police: 'He wanted to erase Algerian history [meaning the history of the settlers in Algeria]. I couldn't accept it.'[72] Much of this resentment crystallised around the rumour that, during the televised debate following the final episode of *Les Années algériennes,* Roseau had shaken hands with Yacef Saadi, leader of the FLN in Algiers. This act is mentioned in multiple criticisms of Roseau, including the testimonies of all three of his assassins who described it variously as 'unacceptable', 'intolerable' and 'disgusting'. Navarro later expanded on this point: 'I simply said that he was a bastard to do that, given all we had suffered in Algeria.' However, as a specially arranged screening during the trial revealed, the rumour was false; Roseau walked past Saadi in order to shake the hand of the host, but did not greet Saadi himself.[73] In the aftermath of this dramatic revelation, the lawyer for the Roseau family suggested that these negative stories had been deliberately disseminated as part of a concerted effort to discredit Roseau.[74]

Roseau's most implacable critic was Eugène Ibagnes of USDIFRA, an association noted for its radical views, strong-arm tactics, and murky connections to the far-right. USDIFRA was founded in 1965 by Roger Peigts, whose brother, Claude, was executed by the state for assassinating the Algiers police commissioner, Roger Gavoury. The association prides itself on being the most ardent defender of the *rapatrié* community in France. Particularly focused on those with an agricultural connection, USDIFRA's activities have included using armed militias to prevent seizures of land by the state when *pied-noir* farmers went into debt. There was furthermore evidence that Ibagnes – once memorably described as a '*pied-noir* Rambo' – was behind the short-lived 'Justice pied-noir' bombing campaign in the mid-1970s.[75]

RECOURS were equally hostile towards Ibagnes, with Roseau frequently denouncing the extremism he believed organisations like USDIFRA were engendering amongst the *pieds-noirs*. Pre-dating the founding of RECOURS, their rivalry went back to October 1975 when twelve heads of associations, including Roseau, then president of the Association des fils de rapatriés et de leurs amis, and Ibagnes, met in Paris to explore the possibility creating a united front. Unfortunately, competition among those present over who would get to speak for the *pied-noir* community on a forthcoming episode of *Les Dossiers de l'écran* derailed the discussions. Following the selection of Guy Forzy of the Union des comités de défense des agriculteurs rapatriés by popular vote, Ibagnes walked out causing the attempted union to collapse. It was shortly after this episode that Forzy and Roseau announced the creation of RECOURS with themselves in the roles of president and spokesperson respectively.[76] Hostility between Roseau and Ibagnes intensified following the public début of the Conseil national supérieur des rapatriés in July 1991. Headed by Ibagnes, this new attempt to unify *pied-noir* associations was dismissed by Roseau as inconsequential, to which Ibagnes responded that Roseau was simply 'Chirac's towel rail'.[77] Nor was their animosity confined to words. On 7 November 1991, a group of men beat and tried to strangle Roseau as he left a conference venue in Nice. A few months earlier, Roseau had been the victim of a failed kidnapping attempt in Paris. USDIFRA was implicated in both attacks and in other threats made against Roseau. In the wake of these incidents, Roseau requested protection from the government, briefly employed a personal bodyguard and was rumoured to carry a gun at all times.[78]

In the light of this acrimonious history, members of RECOURS were quick to point the finger for Roseau's murder at USDIFRA, citing, in particular, Ibagnes' openly stated ambition to become spokesperson for the *pied-noir* community. But beyond the membership of the three assassins, no concrete link was ever proven between USDIFRA and Roseau's death. The connection between USDIFRA and the political far right proved equally difficult to pin down, although Ibagnes did welcome Jean-Marie Le Pen onto his property for a *méchoui* in support of the three incarcerated suspects on 23 November 1993. The relationship between the *pied-noir* community and the far right has been much debated. That Le Pen resigned his seat as a parliamentary deputy in order to enrol in the parachute regiment and fight to keep Algeria French is deemed to have won him the support of many *pieds-noirs*, while as leader of the FN, Le Pen has consistently and explicitly courted *rapatrié* voters. However, the percentage of *pieds-noirs* that have and do vote for the far right is much harder to establish. And, as is the case with the electoral support the FN receives from the wider French population, any such votes are likely to be due to more factors than simply the Algerian War.[79] Yet for many commentators in 1993, both USDIFRA and the FN had Roseau's blood on their hands. The coincidence of timing between the FN's first electoral successes in the south and the launch of USDIFRA's offensive against Roseau being too striking to ignore.

Roseau's consistent public opposition to the FN made him a thorn in Le Pen's side with one journalist describing him as 'the number one obstacle to the FN's strategy vis-à-vis the *pieds-noirs*'.[80] According to former USDIFRA lawyer, René Blanchot, when the FN was weak the *pieds-noirs* largely ignored Le Pen, preferring to give their votes to more powerful and established parties. Only as the FN grew in strength did they appear increasingly attractive to the *pieds-noirs*.[81] In fighting for the attention of the *rapatriés*, Le Pen considered Roseau to be his enemy. Upon hearing of his death, Le Pen remarked 'a crime is a crime and must be punished, but I had no regard for Jacques Roseau'.[82] Equally, the growing influence of the FN threatened to undermine RECOURS' claim to represent the *rapatrié* community. In the ensuing battles for the loyalty of the *pieds-noirs,* the past increasingly encroached upon the present, reigniting the embers of bitterness that had continued to smoulder within certain segments of the community since 1962. For journalist Philippe Bernard, it was with the rise of the FN 'that the ghosts of the OAS and of its "lost soldiers" truly made a re-appearance in the life of Jacques Roseau'.[83]

The last victim of the Algerian War?

Does this then make Roseau, as the press were quick to claim, 'the last victim of the Algerian War'?[84] Much of the commentary in this vein stemmed from Huntz's initial confession, which concluded with the following defiant assertion: 'I want to say that this is a political act. I want the OAS to continue to live so as to create an effective barrier to the fundamentalism that menaces France and its children. Long live France and the OAS.'[85] Such statements led many to ask why, thirty years on, 'the Algerian War continues in the minds of certain *pieds-noirs*, nourishing a hatred capable of killing a man'?[86]

Certain commentators sought the answer in the shock and trauma that accompanied the end of French Algeria, arguing that many *rapatriés*, including the three accused, had never recovered from these experiences. Others ascribed more personal motivations to the assassins, suggesting that they were seeking to become, in the eyes of their community, the heroes they had failed to be when members of the OAS.[87] A further factor was the socio-economic disparity between Roseau and his killers. Navarro met his co-conspirators when he joined USDIFRA. He came to the association because his house was in danger of being repossessed and he hoped USDIFRA could help him as it had helped other *pieds-noirs*, including Lozano and Huntz, when they had experienced similar financial difficulties. All three men had records for petty crimes, had failed to hold down steady jobs and were living on benefits at the time of the assassination. In contrast, Roseau earned over two million francs in the year preceding his death.[88] Testifying to the fact that not all *rapatriés* had succeeded in rebuilding their lives after 1962, this lack of success in the present seems to have greatly heightened the importance of the past to the three killers as all that they had to hold on to; their memories of, and attachment to, French Algeria growing in intensity as their contemporary situations deteriorated.[89] Haunted and obsessed by the past, the lives of Huntz, Lozano and Navarro had effectively stopped in 1962. Huntz's daughter described her father as a man imbued to the point of paralysis with nostalgia, stating that conversations 'always came back to [Algeria]. He experienced repatriation as a betrayal, the loss of an identity'. While Lozano told the police, 'we have lost everything, our land, the sea, the sun, our homeland, that's why there will be no forgetting'.[90]

By the time the court case opened in December 1996, it was there-fore being hyped as the 'the last trial of French Algeria'. In line with wider trends relating to the judicialisation of the past, people were keen to see this not as a simple murder trial, but rather as an opportu-nity to render judgement on the history of the War of Independence in much the same vein as was hoped for with the concurrently unfold-ing Papon prosecution. Indeed, after Papon's trial, the Roseau case was the most closely followed in France that year. It was always optimis-tic to think that seventy-six hours of courtroom debate could put to rest thirty-four years of bitterness, nearly eight years of war, and one hundred and thirty two years of colonisation. Yet trial observers were to be further disappointed by the fact that the accused proved com-pletely unequal to the task of historically redeeming the *Algérie fran-çaise* cause.[91] The three men who entered the dock at the end of 1996 were a far cry from the defiant orators of April 1993. Their infirmities were underlined by a particularly sharp-tongued journalist, who wrote the following of Lozano, Huntz, and Navarro respectively: 'The first is half blind, the second crippled by arthritis, and the third does not have many brains. It is the trial of three grandfathers who mistook themselves for Zorro.'[92] Retracting their initial confessions, all three men were now arguing that far from a deliberate political statement on behalf of an ever-vigilant OAS, the assassination had been an 'an accidental blunder'.[93]

Instead of the grand historical justifications they were expecting, the public were greeted with virtually silent defendants whose 'ideology', it quickly became apparent, was limited to the rote repetition of a formula of second-hand accusations, causing *Le Point* to write that Roseau had done more to defend the three men in the course of his activism than they did for themselves in court.[94] Huntz, Lozano and Navarro were thus transformed from fanatical combatants in an unfinished war into three old men blinded by petty jealousies and frustration at their own failures in life; men who had submerged themselves in bitter nostalgia to the point of committing an absurd crime. Rather than the last vic-tim of the Algerian War, it is therefore perhaps more accurate to see Roseau as the first victim of the memory of the conflict. He was killed because his ideas were increasingly at odds with the views and priori-ties of other associations and their activists, something that, amidst the heightened commemorative climate of the 1990s, became increasingly unacceptable.[95]

Criticisms from USDIFRA and others centred on the idea that by putting his own ambitions ahead of the principles of the community he claimed to represent, Roseau was guilty of 'forgetting' the past and its present-day stakes. Yet, in reality, Roseau was strongly committed to campaigning on behalf of his *rapatrié* compatriots. He always used the public platforms he was given to highlight issues close to *pied-noir* hearts by refuting the stereotype of the *gros colon*, stressing the fraternal nature of colonial Algeria, and criticising the lack of governmental attention paid to the community, including the *harkis*.[96] Articulate, well connected and charismatic, Roseau was the ideal representative for the *pied-noir* community: upon being asked what he would like to drink during an interview, he requested mineral water, wryly adding 'Not Evian!'[97] The problem was that Roseau sought to combine his activism with a desire to move on and look to the future. In contrast to his killers' obsession with the past, Roseau, in one of the last interviews he gave, stated: 'You need to know how to turn the page without tearing it.' He went on to speak of his 'bitterness' over the conclusion of the war, but also his determination to 'not live in eternal anger'.[98] In seeking to preserve the past without becoming trapped by it, Roseau had, by this point, developed a historical sensibility that enabled him to acknowledge the achievements, but also the flaws, of French Algeria. He was furthermore willing to engage in dialogue with those traditionally classed as *pied-noir* 'enemies' and, as the consummate politician, knew when principles should give way to pragmatism. This was epitomised by his recognition that it was counterproductive to refuse to co-operate with Chirac's administration on the basis of a historical grudge against Gaullism when there were real gains to be made.

For certain *pied-noir* associations and their adherents, however, Roseau's words and deeds violated sacred historical principles, while his personal prominence and the influence this afforded him rubbed further salt into the community's unhealed wounds. Even before his assassination, the community had begun to respond to these perceived betrayals by turning its back on Roseau. This is evident from the frequency with which criticisms were voiced in *pied-noir* publications, particularly around the thirtieth anniversary of the end of French Algeria in 1992. In September that year, *Pieds-noirs magazine,* considered by many as USDIFRA's mouthpiece, ran a series of articles encouraging their readers to speak out against Roseau, whom they presented as a source of division rather than unity.[99] Around the same time, *France horizon* ran a piece criticising Roseau for 'claiming still to represent a community that he has disowned in its entirety'.[100] Branded as a 'black sheep' and a traitor to the values and history of the *pieds-noirs*, Roseau was therefore reprimanded, first of all in print and then, finally, physically.[101]

The desert

At the conclusion of their trial on 18 December 1996, Huntz and Lozano were condemned to twenty years in prison; Navarro received a slightly reduced sentence of fifteen years. Huntz died in prison in 2001, Navarro was released the same year and Lozano was freed in 2003 with both men disappearing into obscurity. In contrast, on 5 March 1994, the first anniversary of his death, a 300-strong crowd gathered to witness the inauguration of a memorial to Roseau in Montpellier.[102] In terms of his wider legacy, what the Roseau episode illustrates is the way in which fidelity to commonly understood precepts of history and memory came to be perceived as vital for legitimating claims to incarnate the image and values of the *pied-noir* community. This trend exacerbated tensions between associations as each sought to exploit the past in order to gain adherents and discredit rivals, hoping ultimately to secure the mantle of *pied-noir* spokesperson. Yet, in spite the stakes and the ambitions of the actors involved, Roseau's position has remained vacant since his death, confirming that, rather than the divisive figure many sought to paint him as, Roseau was in fact a rare 'source of reference in a community plagued by endless "squabbles"'. As his cousin and fellow RECOURS activist Gilbert confessed, 'behind Roseau, let's be honest, it's a desert'.[103]

The heterogeneous nature of the *pied-noir* population, combined with a long history of acrimonious rivalry among associations, meant that unity, or rather the outward appearance of unity, was always going to be difficult to attain and then maintain. In the absence of an illusionist of Roseau's skill, the community has remained fractured; ANFANOMA spokesperson, Jacques Martin, conceding that with Roseau's death 'the community has truly lost its voice, its beacon, its best defender'.[104] USDIFRA remains confined to the margins of the *pied-noir* community, while the circulation figures for *Pieds-noirs magazine*, dropped so low that they were forced to suspend publication between September 2000 and November 2003. Even RECOURS has struggled without Roseau, their membership figures down from a peak of 60,000 in the 1980s to less than 10,000 in the mid-1990s.[105] Yet the association remains active and individual members have gone on to forge successful political careers suggesting that RECOURS was able to maintain its connections to the institutional elite in the aftermath of Roseau's death. In 1997, for example, Gilbert Roseau, with support from Frêche, was elected as the PS deputy for Montpellier. Two years previously, the co-founder of RECOURS, Guy Forzy, was made a *rapatrié* representative within Alain Juppé's government, although in typical *pied-noir* style, this decision caused considerable friction within the association, particularly between Gilbert Roseau and Roland Dessy.[106] Roseau's political legacy can also be seen in the campaigns of the Parti pied-noir (PPN), founded in 1999 by Christian Schembré, which aims to gain electoral representation for *pieds-noirs* at the local and European levels. As with RECOURS, the rationale for the creation of the PPN was the lack of progress made in terms of fulfilling *pied-noir* demands through conventional processes of association mobilisation, although Schembré has been far less successful in his politicking than Roseau.[107]

Rivalries within the *pied-noir* community pre-date the competitive commemorative climate of the 1990s. The existence of bodies such as RECOURS, which straddle the supposed divide between the eras of silence and cacophony, furthermore testify to the previously under-appreciated continuities in memory activism. Nonetheless, the 'return' of the war to public attention accelerated and radicalised this existing activism with the Roseau case representing an extreme instance of a broader process of hardening with respect to history and memory. In many ways, this process strengthened the consensus regarding the cultural identity of the *pieds-noirs* established by associations in the preceding to decades. Overall, however, the 1990s witnessed a decline in *pied-noir* mobilisation as many older members of the community made their peace with history, while the bonds formed by younger generations with this past were not as strong. Reflecting on their successes and on the 60,000 members that RECOURS had been able to claim in the 1980s, Gilbert Roseau remarked that 'it was another era'.[108] Yet, although fewer in number, those associations who remain active, as well as new arrivals on the scene such as Véritas, have evinced an increasingly uncompromising attitude.[109] A similar pattern was also evident more generally with respect to the War of Independence in French society. In spite of his optimism at the beginning of the decade that a new era of dialogue about the war was beginning, by 1995 Stora found himself living in exile in Vietnam following death threats against him and his family. In his autobiography, he noted: 'Feverish history, memory to the point of obsession, the search for hidden truths: writing about Algeria, its bloody and passionate relations with France, remains a perilous exercise.'[110]

This feverish obsession with the Algerian War intensified throughout the 1990s and into the new millennium, although the focus of the debates it engendered shifted as issues such as torture and the place of postcolonial minorities in France came increasingly to dominate the agenda. *Pied-noir* activists have plenty to say on these subjects, but so too do many other groups with a connection to the war. As a result, although rivalries within the community and the competitions for control over the way in which the past is represented have not ceased, it is now harder to find traces of these within the public realm. Instead, the perception of a unified, albeit diminishing, community has been recreated and reinforced by the fact that *pied-noir* associations have largely been visible in the context of vigorously contesting discourses related to external events and groups: defending the military in the wake of the 2000 *Le Monde* torture controversy; protesting against the 2001 decision by Mayor of Paris Bertrand Delanoë to commemorate the 17 October 1961; or campaigning to protect Article 4 of the 23 February 2005 law.

Such efforts have prompted renewed attempts to establish a unified front of associations, including the Coordination nationale des Français d'Algérie (CNFA), created in the wake of the abrogation of Article 4. Supported by the Cercle algérianiste and *Pieds-noirs d'hier et d'aujourd'hui* (formerly *Pieds-noirs magazine*) amongst others, its stated objective was 'the pooling of our respective resources so as to provide suitable responses to our detractors, of all kinds, with all the rigour of which our community is capable if it organises itself and gathers together'.[111] A few years earlier, amidst the *Le Monde* torture controversy, the Comité de liaison des associations nationales de rapatriés (CLAN-R) initiative was launched. Based on a collection of associations including ANFANOMA, RANFRAN and the GNPI who had been loosely co-operating since 1971, the decision to formalise these links was taken in 2000, at which point Véritas and USDIFRA were added to the roll call.[112] Neither the CNFA nor CLAN-R has attained the same level of influence as Roseau enjoyed. Indeed, Véritas withdrew from CLAN-R in 2010 shortly after announcing the creation of their own federative body, the Rassemblement national des Français d'Algérie et leurs amis (RNFAA). Indicative of its highly uncompromising stance was the group's original title: the Organisme autonomie de sauvegarde or OAS.[113] None of the major *pied-noir* associations rallied to RNFAA, in spite of heavy promotion through the pages of *Pieds-noirs d'hier et d'aujourd'hui*. Even the leaders of RNFAA were forced to acknowledge the sense fatigue among the wider community regarding yet another initiative promising to overcome internal divisions. 'A majority of our fellow citizens have taken refuge in doubt and then, finally, in devastating scepticism', a RNFAA spokesperson wrote. 'We understand their hesitations'.[114] Professions of 'good faith' and reassurance of the strength of the RNFAA's collegiality apparently failed to convince as the following year the group bemoaned the fact that 'the first and not the least problem is the refusal or the silence of Associations when it comes to joining our Rassemblement'.[115] These examples demonstrate that as histories and memories of the Algerian War and of French colonialism in the public arena have become increasingly plural, *pied-noir* associations have continued to invest in unifying initiatives as the best way to battle against this expanding array of perspectives, despite the fact that these efforts have rarely proven effective. This underlines an ongoing commitment to their own precepts concerning the importance of projecting unity, even if such endeavours are, ultimately, only temporary masks behind which a messier and more antagonistic reality persists.

Notes

1 Approximately 2000 titles had been published across a range of genres by the beginning of the 1990s; at the end of the decade estimates stood at 3000. Raphaëlle Branche, *La Guerre d'Algérie: une histoire apaisée?* (Paris, 2005), pp. 18–23.

2 *La Guerre d'Algérie* (five episodes), dir. Peter Batty, aired 12, 19 and 26 August, 2 and 9 September 1990 (FR3); *Les Années algériennes* (four episodes), prod. Benjamin Stora, aired 23 and 30 September, 7 and 8 October 1991 (A2).

3 Jan C. Jansen, 'Politics of Remembrance, Colonialism and the Algerian War of Independence in France', in *A European Memory? Contested Histories and Politics of Remembrance*, ed. by Małgorzata Pakier and Bo Stråth (New York and Oxford, 2010), p. 276.

4 Jim House and Neil MacMaster, *Paris 1961: Algerians, State Terror and Memory* (Oxford, 2006), p. 299.

5 House and MacMaster, *Paris 1961*, p. 299; Andreas Huyssen, *Twilight Memories: Marking Time in a Culture of Amnesia* (New York and London, 1995), p. 5.

6 For discussion of the 'colonial fracture', see Pascal Blanchard, Nicolas Bancel and Sandrine Lemaire, *La Fracture coloniale: la société française au prisme de l'héritage colonial* (Paris, 2005).

7 For discussion of these issues, see Emile Chabal, 'La République postcoloniale? Making the Nation in Late Twentieth Century France', in *France's Lost Empires: Fragmentation, Nostalgia and la fracture coloniale*, ed. by Kate Marsh and Nicola Frith (Lanham, MD, 2010) pp. 137–52. More information on ACHAC can be found at www.achac.com [21 October 2014].

8 Pierre Nora (ed.), *Realms of Memory*, 3 vols. (New York, 1996–8).

9 Henry Rousso, *The Vichy Syndrome*, trans. Arthur Goldhammer (Boston, MA, 1994).

10 The Vichy trials, including Papon's, and their impact will be discussed further in Chapter 8.

11 Henry Rousso, 'Les Raisins verts de la guerre d'Algérie', in *La Guerre d'Algérie (1954–1962)*, ed. by Yves Michaud (Paris, 2004), pp. 141–3. For scholars claiming the existence of a comparable 'Algerian Syndrome', see Anne Donadey,

"Une certaine idée de la France": The Algerian Syndrome and Struggles Over French Identity', in *Identity Papers: Contested Nationhood in Twentieth Century France*, ed. by Steven Unger and Tom Conley (Minneapolis, MN, 1996), pp. 215–33; David Schalk, 'Of Memories and Monuments: Paris and Algeria, Fréjus and Indochina', *Historical Reflections/Réflexions historiques*, 28:2 (2002), 241–54.

12 Joshua Cole, 'Entering History: The Memory of Police Violence in Paris, October 1961', in *Algeria and France 1800–2000: Identity, Memory, Nostalgia*, ed. by Patricia M.E. Lorcin (New York, 2006), p. 121.

13 Jansen, 'Politics of Remembrance', p. 281; Schalk, 'Of Memories and Monuments', 245.

14 House and MacMaster, *Paris 1961*, p. 309. Although House and MacMaster are referring specifically to memories of 17 October 1961, their points are applicable to other memories of the War of Independence.

15 Full text available at www.lesdiscours.vie-publique.fr/pdf/967017000.pdf [21 October 2013]. Also cited in Jansen, 'Politics of Remembrance', p. 281.

16 On the differing abilities of groups to make themselves heard in this new climate, see House and MacMaster, *Paris 1961*, p. 303.

17 Benjamin Stora, *La Gangrène et l'oubli: la mémoire de la guerre d'Algérie* (Paris, 1991), p. 9.

18 'Guerre d'Algérie. Mémoire enfouie d'une génération', *Moeurs en direct* (three episodes), dir. Denis Chegaray, aired 7, 14 and 21 November 1982 (A2); *Guerre d'Algérie*, dir. Yves Courrière, aired 21 October 1982 (FR3) although the documentary was originally made in 1970; *La Guerre d'Algérie*, aired 12, 19 and 26 August, 2 and 9 September 1990 (FR3).

19 Benjamin Stora, *Les Guerres sans fin: un historien, la France et l'Algérie* (Paris, 2008), pp. 96–7.

20 Stora, *Les Guerres sans fins*, pp. 72–4.

21 The varied and passionate reactions to *Les Années algériennes* are encapsulated in the animated studio debate held after the broadcasting of the final part of the documentary. See 'Spécial guerre d'Algérie', *Mardi soir*, aired 8 October 1991 (A2).

22 Stora, *Les Guerres sans fins*, p. 148.

23 Valérie Esclangon-Morin, *Les Rapatriés d'Afrique du Nord de 1956 à nos jours* (Paris, 2007), p. 355.

24 Approximately 200,000 settlers remained in Algeria after independence. When Houari Boumediene overthrew President Ahmed Ben Bella in 1965, this number halved. By the end of the 1960s, 50,000 were still present, although most of these would leave during the violence of the 1990s. Only a few hundred remain today, including a handful of Algerian Jews. Pierre Daum, *Ni valise, ni cerceuil: les pieds-noirs restés en Algérie après indépendance* (Arles, 2012), pp. 24, 44. There is little scholarship on the *pieds-verts*, but there are a growing number of collections of testimony and documentaries, including Jean-Jacques Viala, *Pieds-Noirs en Algérie après indépendance: une expérience socialiste* (Paris, 2001); Assiya Hamza, *Mémoires d'enracinés: mes rencontres*

avec ces pieds-noirs qui ont choisi de rester en Algérie (Paris, 2011); *Rester là-bas,* dir. Dominique Cabrera, aired 13 December 1992 (ARTE); 'D'une rive à l'autre', *La Case de l'oncle Doc,* dir. Marie Colonna, aired 6 March 2000 (FR3).

25 Daum, *Ni valise,* pp. 130–2.

26 *Coup de soleil,* 6 (October–November 1990), insert.

27 Morin quoted in Daum, *Ni valise,* p. 122.

28 Georges Morin, 'Editorial', *Coup de soleil,* 6 (October–November 1990), 1. Today the association can be found at: www.coupdesoleil.net [22 October 2013].

29 Founded in Montpellier in 1983, the association later became Pieds-noirs de la deuxième génération. Valérie Esclangon-Morin, 'La Mémoire déchirée des pieds-noirs', *Hommes et migrations,* 251 (September–October 2004), 108.

30 Branche, *La Guerre d'Algérie,* p. 7.

31 AFN stands for French North Africa.

32 Edmond Jouhaud, 'Un périodique qui sera nôtre voit le jour', *Les Français d'AFN,* 1 (November 1980), 2.

33 René Attard, 'Une priorité: l'unité des rapatriés dans une opposition unié', *Les Français d'AFN,* 79–80 (28 December 1984), 1, 4. The creation of FURR was covered in 'Un front commun pour la défense de nos intérêts', *Les Français d'AFN,* 67 (6 April 1984), 3.

34 For a summary of these events in his own words, see Jo Ortiz, *Mon combat pour l'Algérie française* (Helette 1964; reprinted 1999).

35 This figure comes from deposit slips completed by the association and left inside copies of their publication in the Bibilothèque nationale de France (BnF). These slips declared a circulation of 2000–2500 copies of *La Lettre de Véritas* in 2000, rising to 2800 in 2001.

36 'La Chronique d'Anne Cazal: message reçu Colonel', *La Lettre de Véritas,* 12 (April 1997), 3; 'Entretien avec Madame Bastien-Thiry', *La Lettre de Véritas,* 12 (April 1997), 12; Joseph Hattab Pacha, 'Le Mot du Président', *La Lettre de Véritas,* 8 (December 1996), 2.

37 'Les Faussaires de l'histoire', *La Lettre de Véritas,* 22 (April 1998), 5. The piece was in response to an article in *Le Point* concerning the OAS. See also *La Lettre de Véritas* front covers for issues 10 (February 1997) and 22 (April 1998).

38 No details are given regarding the provenance of these photographs. Some, such as shots of decapitated heads with genitals inserted into their mouths, are established forgeries. Other images, including photographs from the March 1962 rue d'Isly shootings are genuine historical artefacts. In general, unless the photograph is particularly well known, it is impossible to verify the context in which the images were taken and thus the accuracy of the captions attached by Véritas.

39 Rosemary Averell Manes, *The Pieds-Noirs 1960–2000: A Case Study in the Persistence of Subcultural Distinctiveness* (Bethesda, MD, 2005), p. 111.

40 Maurice Calmein, 'L'Algérianisme: une radio libre!', *L'Algérianiste,* 20 (15 December 1982), 3.

41 'Editorial', *L'écho d'Oran,* 10 (May 1965), 1.

42 Maurice Calmein, 'L'Algérianisme an V', L'Algérianiste, 1 (15 December 1977), 3.

43 Attard, 'Une priorité', 1.

44 'Arlette Laguiller', Ciel, mon mardi!, 4 June 1991 (FR3).

45 'Les pieds-noirs, Dechavanne sur TF1', Pieds-noirs magazine, 17 (July–August 1991), 46. For further discussion of unity and division within the pied-noir community, particularly with respect to this broadcast, see Claire Eldridge, 'Unity above all? Relationships and Rivalries within the Pied-Noir Community', in Vertriebene and Pieds-Noirs in Postwar Germany and France: Comparative Perspectives ed. by Manuel Borutta and Jan C. Jansen (Basingstoke, 2016), pp. 133–50.

46 Maurice Calmein, 'L'union avant tout', L'Algérianiste, 12 (15 December 1980), 5.

47 Calmein, 'L'union', 3.

48 Maurice Calmein, 'La Trêve de mars', L'Algérianiste, 41 (March 1988), 2.

49 Jean-Jacques Jordi, 'Archéologie et structure du réseau de sociabilité rapatrié et pied-noir', Provence Historique, 47 (1997), 180.

50 Maurice Calmein, 'L'unité…oui, mais! Oui, mais … quoi?', L'Algérianiste, 27 (September 1984), 4.

51 Attard, 'Une priorité', 1.

52 Transcript of Huntz's confession, cited in Emilien Jubineau, L'énigme Roseau: la parole pied-noir assassinée (St Georges d'Orques, 1997), pp. 127–30.

53 Montpellier was a popular choice with many rapatriés due to the city's location combined with its strong pro-Algérie française stance during the war. Also active within the pied-noir and student communities in Montpellier at this time were Cercle Algérianiste founders Maurice Calmein and Jacques Villard. Esclangon-Morin, Les Rapatriés, p. 217; Sung Choi, 'From Colonial Settler to Postcolonial Repatriate: The Integration of the French from Algeria, 1962 to the Present', unpublished doctoral dissertation, UCLA, 2007, p. 261.

54 'Interview: J. Roseau L'enfant terrible de la communauté', Pieds-noirs magazine, 16 (June 1991), 40.

55 Emile Chabal, 'Managing the Postcolony: Minority Politics in Montpellier, c.1960 to 2010', Contemporary European History, 23:2 (2014), 244–5.

56 Esclangon-Morin, Les Rapatriés, pp. 294–302.

57 Emmanuelle Comtat, Les Pieds-noirs et la politique quarante ans après le retour (Paris, 2009), pp. 280–2.

58 Due to France's three-year residency requirement, 1965 was the first election in which most rapatriés were eligible to vote. Comtat, Les Pied-noirs, pp. 281–2.

59 Le Réfugié pied-noir, 'Apolitisme', France horizon, 1:2 (July–August 1957), 1–2.

60 Comtat, Les Pieds-noirs, p. 171; Valérie Esclangon-Morin et al., 'Les Origines et la genèse d'une loi scélérate', in La Colonisation, la loi et l'histoire, ed. by Claude Liauzu and Gilles Manceron (Paris, 2006), p. 25. Frêche held power from 1977 until 2004, while Kioulou was in office from May 1945 until 1981, although obviously he would only have benefitted from pied-noir support after 1962. Balmigère had the shortest term, serving as mayor for only five years between 1977 and 1983.

61 Alain Rollat, 'La Préparation des élections législatives', *Le Monde* (12 February 1993), p. 8.

62 Jacques Molénat, *Le Marigot des pouvoirs: systèmes, réseaux, communautés, notables et francs-maçons en Languedoc-Roussillon* (Castelnau-le-Lez, 2004), p. 223.

63 In 1993, Roseau turned down an offer to stand as RPR candidate for the Hérault region on the grounds that he preferred to maintain his autonomy. At the time of his death, there were rumours that if Chirac won the forthcoming legislative elections that spring Roseau would be given a junior post within his government. 'Assassinat Roseau', *JT 20 heures*, aired 5 March 1993 (TF1).

64 Marcel Bellier, 'Deux mois après', *Lécho de l'Oranie*, 136 (May 1978), 1.

65 Michel Pittard, 'Lettre ouverte à M. Jacques Roseau', *Lécho de l'Oranie*, 205 (November–December 1989), 4; Attard, 'Une priorité', 1.

66 'Encore le RECOURS', *Lécho de l'Oranie*, 128 (June 1977), 1; 'Réponse du RANFRAN et de son président', *Lécho de l'Oranie*, 129 (July 1977), 1; 'Réponse de l'ANFANOMA et de son président', *Lécho de l'Oranie*, 131 (October 1977), 1.

67 René Blanchot, 'CNSR: l'après Roseau', *Pieds-noirs d'hier et d'aujourd'hui*, 36 (June–July 1993), 43; Louis Pelloux in Ysabel Saïah (ed.), *Pieds-noirs et fiers de l'être* (Paris, 1987), p. 153.

68 Hachemi Bounini, 'Attaque du FNRFCI contre une association et un journal', *Les Français d'AFN*, 27 February 1981), 4; 'Le CNRC répond au FNRFCI', *Les Français d'AFN*, 8 (13 March 1981), 2.

69 'Interview: J. Roseau', 40.

70 Maurice Peyrot, 'Trois anciens de l'OAS comparaissent devant la cour d'assises de l'Hérault pour le meurtre de Jacques Roseau', *Le Monde* (10 December 1996), p. 10.

71 Benjamin Stora, 'Guerre d'Algérie: 1999–2003, les accélérations de la mémoire', *Hommes et migrations*, 1244 (July–August 2003), 84.

72 Jubineau, *Lénigme Roseau*, pp. 127, 142.

73 'Spécial guerre d'Algérie', aired 8 October 1991.

74 Jubineau, *Lénigme Roseau*, pp. 171, 177, 184, 209.

75 Jubineau, *Lénigme Roseau*, pp. 27, 88; Molénat, *Le Marigot*, p. 221.

76 Roger Seguin, 'Encore la télévision', *Les Français d'AFN*, 42 (January 1983), 8; Molénat, *Le marigot*, p. 22.

77 This exchange was recalled by Ibagnes in the course of his police interview following the assassination, cited in Jubineau, *Lénigme Roseau*, p. 89.

78 Molénat, *Le Marigot*, p. 226; Jubineau, *Lénigme Roseau*, pp. 24, 32, 50.

79 For further discussion of this topic, see Comtat, *Les Pieds-noirs*, pp. 248–66; Eric Savarèse, 'Un regard compréhensif sur le "traumatisme historique". A propos de vote Front national chez les pieds-noirs', *Pôle Sud*, 34:1 (2011), 91–104; John Veugelers, 'After Colonialism: Local Politics and Far Right Affinities in a City of Southern France', in *Mapping the Extreme Right in Contemporary Europe*, ed. by Andrea Mammone, Emmanuel Godin and Brian Jenkins (London and New York, 2012), pp. 33–47.

80 Alain Rollat in Jubineau, *Lénigme Roseau*, p. 301.

81 Jubineau, *L'énigme Roseau*, p. 227.

82 'Factuel Roseau', *JT 13 heures*, aired 6 March 1993 (TF1).

83 Philippe Bernard, 'Jacques Roseau, de l'OAS à l'OAS', *Le Monde* (9 April 1993), p. 1.

84 This was the headline in *Le Figaro* the day after the announcement that the Roseau case would go to trial.

85 Jubineau, *L'énigme Roseau*, p. 130.

86 Bernard, 'Jacques Roseau', p. 1.

87 Jubineau, *L'énigme Roseau*, pp. 235, 318.

88 The police investigation revealed the exact figure to have been 2,302,036 francs for the year 1992. This sum came in part from several lucrative consulting contracts with large companies such as Carrefour. Jubineau, *L'énigme Roseau*, p. 84; Molénat, *Le Marigot*, p. 223.

89 The survey 'Pieds-noirs 2002' revealed that 39 per cent of the sample considered that their current situation was better than what they had in Algeria, 36 per cent felt this had remained the same, while 22 per cent felt their standard of living had deteriorated since coming to France. Research also indicated that those who suffered most as a result of the end of French Algeria were more likely to be attracted to extreme groups. Comtat, *Les Pieds-noirs*, p. 154; Savarèse, 'Un regard compréhensif', 93–5.

90 Jubineau, *L'énigme Roseau*, pp. 281, 184.

91 Jubineau, *L'énigme Roseau*, p. 345.

92 Jacqueline Remy, 'Le Dernier procès de l'Algérie française', *L'Express* (5 December 1996), p. 47.

93 Trial transcripts for Huntz cited in Jubineau, *L'énigme Roseau*, p. 174.

94 'Le Procès de l'absurde', *Le Point* (21 December 1996), p. 21.

95 For further discussion, see Esclangon-Morin, *Les Rapatriés*, p. 364.

96 For examples of Roseau's public defence of the *pieds*-noirs, see his interventions during 'Droit de réponse aux pieds-noirs', *Droit de réponse*, 8 November 1986 (TF1); 'Spécial guerre d'Algérie', aired 8 October 1991; 'Algérie: mémoires d'une guerre', *Caractères*, aired 22 November 1991 (FR3).

97 Philippe Bernard, 'Après la mort du porte-parole du RECOURS-France', *Le Monde* (9 March 1993), p. 15.

98 Bernard, 'Après la mort', p. 15.

99 'Jacques Roseau trahir plutôt qu'unir', *Pieds-noirs magazine*, 28 (September 1992), 10–11.

100 Yves Sainsot, 'Gardons-nous des panurge ...', *France horizon*, 336 (November 1992), 24.

101 Roseau's death received little commentary from *pied-noir* associations with the exception of *Pieds-noirs magazine* which, under its new moniker of *Pieds-noirs d'hier et d'aujourd'hui*, continued to posthumously reprimand Roseau. See Jean-Marc Lopez, 'Le Recours-France vient de perdre son porte-parole', *Pieds-noirs d'hier et d'aujourd'hui*, 35 (April 1993), 13.

102 Philippe Bernard and Jacques Monin, 'Le 5 mars 1993: trois pieds-noirs sous influence pour un crime mal éclairci', *Le Monde* (8 March 1994), p. 11; Molénat, *Le marigot*, p. 228.

103 Rollat, 'Jacques Roseau', p. 8; Gilbert Roseau cited in Jubineau, *L'énigme Roseau*. p. 19.

104 Alain Leauthier, 'L'inexorable reflux de la cause rapatriée', *Libération* (9 December 1996). Available at www.liberation.fr/france/1996/12/09/l-inexorable-reflux-de-la-cause-rapatrieel-integration-des-pieds-noirs-est-presque-achevee-roseau-mo_191534 [27 July 2015].

105 Leauthier, 'L'inexorable reflux'. In the same piece, USDIFRA's boast of 10,000 members was greeted with considerable scepticism.

106 Leauthier, 'L'inexorable reflux'; Chabal, 'Managing the Postcolony', 249.

107 For further discussion of the PPN, see Marie Muyl, 'Le Parti pied-noir: une opportunité européenne', *Pôle Sud*, 24 (2006), 59–73.

108 Leauthier, 'L'inexorable reflux'.

109 This has also been the case in Germany among associations formed by *Vertriebenen* or 'expellees' who were displaced at the end of the Second World War. For further discussion of this, see Pertti Ahonen, 'The German Expellee Organizations: Unity, Division and Function', in Borutta and Jansen (eds.), Vertribene and Pieds-Noirs (Basingstoke, 2016), pp. 115–131.

110 Stora, *Les Guerres sans fin*, p. 11.

111 Jean-Marc Lopez, '11 février une date à retenir', *Pieds-noirs d'hier et d'aujourd'hui*, 138 (February 2006), 5.

112 William Bénéjean, 'Enfin unis!', *France horizon*, 416–7 (November–December 2000), 24.

113 Following Hattab Pacha's death in autumn 2009 and the installation of Jean-Marie Avelin as the new president of Véritas, the name was changed to the less provocative RNFAA, although there was little moderation in terms of the collective's rhetoric and demands.

114 'Rassemblement', *Pieds-noirs d'hier et d'aujourd'hui*, 176 (July–August 2009), 10.

115 'Communiqué du RNFAA', *Pieds-noirs d'hier et d'aujourd'hui*, 191 (December 2010), 18.

6

Speaking out

In contrast to the embattled nature of *pied-noir* activism in the 1990s, the attention being devoted to the *harkis* by an increasingly aware state, media and general public began to move the community from the margins into the mainstream. This was reflected in a series of gestures from the state that built upon the principle, established by Giscard d'Estaing in 1974, that 'French Muslims' were entitled to 'national recognition'.[1] On 11 June 1994, this sentiment was translated into a unanimously adopted law acknowledging the moral debt owed by the Republic to its former auxiliaries.[2] Further gestures followed in line with the growing visibility of the Algerian War, including a government position for Hamaloui Mekachera, the president of the CNFM; the explicit inclusion, in 1996 and in 2002, of *harkis* in monuments to civilians and soldiers killed in North Africa; and ongoing financial aid that totalled 6.8 billion francs by 1999.[3] The new millennium witnessed the inaugural Journée nationale d'hommage aux harkis on 25 September 2001 when Chirac not only reiterated the gratitude of previous presidents towards the *harkis,* but also expressed regret for the massacres of 1962.[4] Finally, the passing of the 23 February 2005 law combined recognition of the sacrifices and suffering endured by the *harkis,* who were classified as part of the wider *rapatrié* community, with additional monetary compensation; the law also made it a crime to insult or slander *harkis.*

Many of these official measures came in response to rising levels of mobilisation among descendants of *harkis.* Consolidating the activist path they had begun to forge in previous decades, a new raft of grass-roots associations emerged alongside a series of prominent community spokespeople. At the same time, the history of the *harkis* began garnering greater media coverage. Together these developments raised the public profile of the community while simultaneously replacing ideologically driven interpretations that cast the *harkis* as either Algerian traitors of French patriots with a more nuanced historical picture. Creating new spaces for experiences that fell outside of previously narrow explanatory frameworks helped foster a greater willingness among *harkis* and their spouses to speak publicly about their past. This trend was further nurtured by concerted efforts from both activists and academics, many of whom were descendants of *harkis*, to collect and disseminate these voices. However, these evolutions also brought forth a range of issues, many of which paralleled those faced by *pied-noir* associations; namely a lack of unity among associations, the balance between individuality and cohesion within collective narratives, and the question of who possessed the legitimacy to speak on behalf of the wider community. In addressing these issues, this chapter explores the ways in which representations, both personal and collective, of the *harkis* were constructed and transmitted from the 1990s onwards.

The quest for grassroots unity in the 1990s

'As soon as a *harki* knows how to read and write, he creates an association', so the president of one such association told the *Libération* reporter Nicolas Beau.[5] Indeed, by the year 2000, approximately 540 *harki* associations existed; many of them led by younger members of the community whose formative activist experiences had come via the protests of 1975 and 1991.[6] In principle, forming associations was an effective strategy for the *harkis*, as for other minority groups, enabling them to combine forces in order to make their voices heard, while also confronting and surmounting common difficulties in a spirit of solidarity.[7] Yet, in practice, assessments of these associations have been highly negative. Criticised for their 'political immaturity and inefficiency', amongst other things, *harki* associations in the 1990s lacked many of the features of the more established *pied-noir* activist community, including inter-associational networks, a stable calendar of events and demonstrable lobbying potential.[8] Journalist Alain Rollat was particularly forthright when he wrote of *harki* militancy: 'Its sad history, since 1962, is dotted with hunger strikes, protest marches, various forgotten facts, a thousand individual revolts whose impact has always been limited.'[9] A crucial factor behind this was the ongoing material difficulties experienced by certain *harkis*. These tended to generate associations whose primary goal was to offer practical support to those in need in their immediate vicinity. Such focused concerns often did not lend themselves to establishing wider relationships between groups – a tendency further exacerbated by government subsidies. Described by Laurent Muller as a way of 'organising their disorganisation', financial aid from the state encouraged a proliferation of small groups and worked against the emergence of a single, powerful representative body.[10] The continued use of violence as a tactic with the recurrence, in 1993 and 1994, of the extreme style of protests characteristic of the 'hot' summers of 1975 and 1991, further divided the *harki* community. Some argued that these outbreaks were qualitatively different to the regular outbursts of unrest in the *banlieues* because *harki* protests were anchored in the defence of a precise historical cause and that they were furthermore justified given the discrimination endured by the community since 1962. Others, however, felt that the recourse to violence did more harm than good, undermining the legitimacy of the demands for reform presented.[11]

Arguably the principal obstacle for associations was the heterogeneity of the *harkis*. A 'community of destiny' rather than an organic entity, any unity that existed was largely a result of the shared trauma of exile from Algeria and marginalisation in France. Beneath this experiential commonality lay various intersecting and overlapping divisions, many of which, such as tribe, region, ethnicity and language, had deep historical roots.[12] Further fissures emerged after 1962, including a socio-economic generation gap with those born later, often outside the camps, tending to be better educated and better off. For the sociologist Stéphanie Abrial, the difficulties faced by *harkis* and their descendants in finding their place in French society in tandem with their sentiment of being caught between cultures and identities not only delayed the creation of associations, but resulted in a movement characterised by a destabilising combination of influences.[13] Beyond differences in origin, age and agenda, the *harki* community has also had to contend with diverse political allegiances. Some descendants eschewed *harki*-orientated activism in favour of 'beur' organisations such as SOS Racisme and Sans frontière, where they downplayed or even concealed their historical identity. A minority even turned to the FN including *harki* daughter Zohra T., who grew up in the Bias camp and stood successfully as the far-right candidate in Boé (Lot-et-Garonne) the 1998 regional elections.[14]

During the 1990s, *harki* associations therefore struggled to find common platforms and a cohesive voice. At the height of the 1991 protests, the delegation of *harki* representatives invited to talks with the government was riven by factionalism to the point that a joint appeal for calm had to be made by Mekachera and Hacène Arfi.[15] Consequently, the numerical proliferation of associations was not accompanied by depth or durability; of the 500 plus associations registered in 2000, less than 10 per cent were believed to be active.[16] Attempts to create federative bodies, such as the 'estates general' of 24–25 March 1990 that sought to unite 350 *harki* associations, also proved unsuccessful.[17] This produced a pattern whereby frustrations would build up within the most marginalised sections of the community, boiling over into protests ranging from hunger strikes to riots. But the momentum and visibility of these attention-grabbing events could not be sustained long enough for significant gains to be made because there was no strong and united grassroots base. Instead, as Mohand Hamoumou argues, following these manifestations of *harki* anger, silence would fall again, each time more heavily.[18]

What the *harki* community also lacked was a single representative capable of creating at least the outward appearance of unity and someone who could act as a privileged interlocutor with the state and the media as Jacques Roseau had done for the *pieds-noirs*. Such a figure was particularly necessary given the growing media profile of the community. As treatments of the Algerian War became more common, the *harkis* benefited from a greater number of broadcasts devoted solely to them, as well as from more sustained consideration as part of programmes with broader scopes.[19] Yet, rather than a continuation of previous trends which saw external commentators assume the role of *harki* ambassador, a succession of *harki* descendants were cast by the media as spokespeople for their community and thrust into the public spotlight. From the practical, grassroots militancy of Arfi and Abdelkrim Klech, to the media-savvy advocacy of Dalila Kerchouche and Fatima Besnaci-Lancou, to the academic-activist bridge formed by Mohand Hamoumou, this cohort was novel in many respects, not least because it included *filles* (daughters) as well as *fils* (sons) of *harkis*. Each fulfilled a different role in terms of representing the *harkis*: Arfi and Klech succeeded in attracting attention to the plight of the *harkis*, Kerchouche and Besnaci-Lancou helped to generate public empathy and humanise the population through their personal narratives, while Hamoumou was able to use his intellectual credentials to enhance awareness of the community in the political sphere. The public prominence of these men and women can be attributed to the fact that something in their approach resonated with the wider national mood concerning the War of Independence. Exploring the different facets of their activism therefore helps to illuminate the changing commemorative contexts surrounding the *harki* community since 1991.

The practical face of *harki* activism: Hacène Arfi and Abdelkrim Klech

The first of this cohort to obtain public notoriety were *fils de harkis*, Arfi and Klech. Gaining their formative protest experiences in the summer of 1991, both men remained within this action-orientated, grassroots tradition. Born in 1957 and 1953 respectively, Arfi and Klech were old enough to remember life in Algeria, the war and their migration to France. Emerging during the early stages of media interest in the *harkis*, their 'celebrity' was an unexpected by-product of their activism. Despite not seeking personal notoriety, both men were quick to appreciate its benefits in terms of raising the profile of their cause. They thus accepted the mantle of *harki* spokesperson and have proven tireless advocates for their parents and their contemporaries.[20]

Arfi's family fled Algeria in 1962 after his father was attacked by the FLN.[21] They passed briefly through Rivesaltes before ending up in Saint-Maurice-l'Ardoise, which Arfi described as a 'concentration camp' where he witnessed 'atrocious' scenes, including the *harki* who, one day, turned the rifle he always carried upon himself, his wife and their five children.[22] Arfi's own experiences of camp life prompted him, aged eleven, to slip under the barbed wire and run away for three days. 'When I returned', he told *L'Express* in 1997, 'I believed I'd been to Belgium. In fact, I'd slept a hundred metres from the camp.'[23] Like many of his generation, Arfi grew into a bored and frustrated adolescent who, unable to find work, would 'drink and fight in bars from morning to night'.[24] It was only upon finding employment in the forestry service at the age of twenty-two that his sense of injustice regarding the fate of the *harkis* was ignited. Initially, he tried channelling his anger into a book about his family's trajectory, but found that the more he wrote, the more he was opening old wounds. He therefore abandoned the project in favour of taking practical action, including occupying the Marseille prefecture armed with three fake grenades upon learning that the army planned to sell the land on which Saint-Maurice-l'Ardoise had stood to the French government for a single symbolic franc.[25]

It was his role during the 1991 protests that really catapulted Arfi into the national media spotlight, however, as he was broadcast nightly across the French news, leading bands of youths as they vented their frustrations following decades of neglect and broken promises. Arfi quickly became a person of note, as evidenced by his invitation to join the delegation assembled by the government to discuss measures to address the plight of the *harkis*. Yet, unlike Larradji in 1975, he also continued to enjoy widespread support from within his own community, becoming, in the opinion of Muller, 'one of the rare spokespeople truly recognised and appreciated by a great number of *harkis* of the first and the second generation'.[26] This is possibly because Arfi was not a *Français musulman*, nor did his 'fame' alter his material conditions; he currently works for the local municipality and continues to live close to the former site of Saint-Maurice-l'Ardoise in Saint-Laurent-des-Arbres alongside many other *harki* families from the camp. Although his activism has mellowed over time, Arfi remains firmly committed to the *harki* cause, speaking regularly on behalf of the community. He has also co-ordinated various commemorative events, including a ceremony in 1992 that paid homage to the *harkis* with the unveiling of a plaque at the Saint-Maurice-l'Ardoise site. The plaque reads 'Remember these men. They were not a myth', evoking a duty of memory that Arfi clearly feels compelled to ensure is honoured in his own lifetime, as well as by future generations.

Arfi shares this desire with Klech, who has said of his activism: 'I will make sure that the memory remains, that my children know'.[27] Klech's ultimate goal is to obtain justice, both material and moral, for the *harki* community. For him, this quest involves gaining official recognition that men like his father were not 'collabos', but simply people who 'fought alongside France in order to defend their homes'.[28] Klech's family trajectory parallels that of Afri's in many ways, except that upon arrival in France Klech was hospitalised due to his asthma, which meant that he did not experience life in the camps. By the time he was discharged, his family had moved to the Cité des Oliviers estate in Narbonne.[29] For Klech, the humiliation and suffering associated with belonging to the *harki* community crystallised around witnessing his father beaten and insulted as a 'traitor' in the street at the age of eleven: 'It was the first time I saw my father cry'.[30] Determined to restore the dignity of men like his father, Klech went on to combine sporadic employment with protest, including blockading the Marignane airport over the sacking of two *harki* employees in 1981 and spending two months obstructing the A96 as part of the 1991 protests.[31] However, it is his multiple hunger strikes that have brought him the most attention. Although a long-standing tactic among *harki* activists, Klech has taken this form of protest to new heights owing to the longevity, frequency and high profile of his campaigns, which has led many within the community to regard him as an 'icon'.[32] In 1997, for example, he and several other children of *harkis* camped outside the Hôtel des Invalides in Paris, the site that houses the national military museum. As he told the assembled journalists: 'We are here to cry: "Help, we will die from your indifference and from your contempt".

We want France to give our parents their dignity back before they are no longer of this world.' In response to his actions, the minister for solidarity and employment, Martine Aubry, issued a circular promising funds to assist descendants of *harkis* in finding employment.[33] Klech has gone on to protest several more times, including in 2006 in response to Georges Frêche's description of the *harkis* as 'sub-humans' [*sous hommes*].[34] His commitment to his cause has resulted in his hospitalisation on numerous occasions, but he has vowed that he will carry on 'to the end', insisting: 'I am ready to die so that the problem is definitively resolved.'[35]

Building bridges: Dalila Kerchouche, Fatima Besnaci-Lancou and the cultural diffusion of the *harki* narrative

The campaigns of Arfi and Klech proved effective in focusing media attention on the *harki* community, highlighting the plight of the most marginalised. In the early 2000s, new community representatives appeared who would forge a different kind of relationship with the French media and public. The year 2003 was particularly notable, witnessing the simultaneous publication of memoirs and autobiographical novels from four *filles de harkis:* Dalila Kerchouche, Fatima Besnaci-Lancou, Zahia Rahmani and Hadjila Kemoum.[36] These texts and their success paved the way for subsequent publications in a similar vein,[37] but also for filmic depictions of the *harki* past, including documentaries by *fils de harkis* Rabah Zanoun and Farid Haroud.[38] Highly educated and socio-economically successful, this new cohort of elite memory carriers have chosen to operate within the realm of cultural and media-based advocacy rather than practical action. A driving force behind of a broader reorientation within *harki* activism during the late 1990s and early 2000s, these 'memory entrepreneurs', have been able to utilise their own cultural capital in conjunction with the growing interest in the War of Independence to disseminate and embed new discourses concerning the *harkis* within the public space and imagination.[39] The advanced levels of education possessed by these descendants is particularly important given that they are telling the stories of parents who are often illiterate and whose first language is not French.

Driven by a desire to break the silence surrounding their family history, these men and women have used a range of genres to create ways for their fathers and their mothers to speak. Their depictions challenge externally generated visions of the community and its history, replacing them with more nuanced and diverse portraits. Although some works do contain creative and stylistic experimentations, namely Rahmani's *Moze*, this is usually not art for its own sake, but rather what Géraldine Enjelvin describes as 'writing as righting'.[40] Exposing the historical injustices to which their parents were subjected, these works also explore the authors' own relationship to the *harki* past and the ways in which it has shaped their lives. While not wishing to go as far as Vincent Crapanzano's contention that *harki* children have vicariously assumed the 'wounds' of their parents, their cultural output must nonetheless be read in part as a reaction to this past.[41] Evoking the impact of spending all day cooped up in an HLM apartment with her traumatised and grief-stricken mother between the ages of five and six, Saliha Telali writes: 'As a child, I cried with [my mother] over a history I did not understand. Her tears became mine, her fears followed me in my nightmares … The past took up all the space and haunted the present'.[42] Besnaci-Lancou similarly described the unspoken history with which she lived as a 'monster' that permanently inhabited her body. In common with other *harki* descendants, only by reconstructing this past through writing was she able, in effect, to reconstruct herself.[43] Learning more about their parents' pasts is therefore a way for these authors to take control of the *harki* narrative, while simultaneously using it to reflect upon their own identities and relationships to France.

Within this cohort, Besnaci-Lancou and Kerchouche have emerged as two of the best-known representatives, appearing regularly across a range of media to comment on the *harki* community while continuing to publish their own texts on the subject. In choosing dialogue over demonstration, they have taken the awareness established by Arfi and Klech and used this to build bridges connecting the *harki* community and the French public. Their style of activism suits the highly mediatised climate in which the War of Independence is now discussed, something that has helped render their message about the *harkis* accessible to the audiences they were seeking to connect with and inform.

Kerchouche, the younger of the two women, was born in 1973 in the Bias camp, although her family were to live there for only one more year before moving into their own house, twelve years after first arriving in France. Benefiting from a more integrated childhood, including a mainstream education, Kerchouche became a journalist for *L'Express* where she was tasked with covering the *harki* community. However, it was with the publication of her 2003 memoir-cum-history, *Mon père, ce harki*, that she achieved greatest prominence. Kerchouche envisaged her book as a way to understand and thus reconnect with her father, a man she has worshipped as a child but who had become a virtual stranger to her as an adult. This quest was also framed as a personal journey to discover and accept her own identity. As she learns more about her family history over the course of the book she is able to move from defining herself as 'a daughter of *harkis* ... with a small "h" like *honte* [shame]', to the point where she is able to lay claim to the identity of 'a daughter of *Harkis*, with a capital "H", like Honour'.[44]

Born in 1954, Besnaci-Lancou falls within the same age and experience bracket as Arfi and Klech, being just old enough to remember the war and her family's flight from Algeria. Once in France, Besnaci-Lancou spent her childhood in various camps, including Rivesaltes, but nonetheless attained a high level of education and went on to establish her own small publishing house. Unlike Arfi and Klech, who have always strongly identified themselves with the preceding generation, Besnaci-Lancou deliberately chose not to allow her parents' past to define her identity. 'Until now, I interested myself only occasionally with my community of misfortune', she wrote in her memoir, *Fille de harki*. 'I did not want to remain trapped in a cloistered identity', she continued. 'Being a *harki*, it is not hereditary ... I do not want my children to be "grandchildren of *harkis*" with all the despair that attaches to that.'[45] This all changed on 16 June 2000 when, during his state visit to France, the Algerian president, Abdelaziz Bouteflika, compared the *harkis* to 'collabos' in the Second World War. His remarks so offended Besnaci-Lancou that she sat down and, 'almost in a single burst', wrote her family story, conceiving of it as a way to 'erase the shame and create a barrier to the hatred', which was epitomised by Bouteflika's comments, particularly for her children.[46] While acknowledging the necessity of hunger strikes, demonstrations and even lawsuits, Besnaci-Lancou went on to specify that this was 'not my approach'.[47] Instead, like Kerchouche, she has chosen to operate primarily through the medium of the written and spoken word, following *Fille de harki* with a series of collections of testimony, conferences and historical volumes in collaboration with scholars such as Gilles Manceron.[48]

Exemplary narratives

'At first, I thought I was writing an individual history', Kerchouche confesses, only to realise that her story 'resembles the journey of thousands of anonymous people'.[49] Conscious of a similar imperative in her own work, Besnaci-Lancou has spoken of the dual function of her narrative as both a personal story and a vehicle for the collective memories of the broader *harki* community. Nina Sutherland describes *Fille de harki* and other similar works as 'collecto-biographies', conveying the sense in which they 'focus on the lives of the collective', whether the family unit or the wider *harki* population.[50] Although Kerchouche and Besnaci-Lancou are not themselves representative, particularly in a socio-economic sense, *harkis* and their descendants can nonetheless identify with elements of the stories they tell about their own and their families' experiences.[51] For Géraldine Enjelvin and Nada Kovac-Kakabadse, the ability of these texts to represent facets of the collective *harki* experience renders them a form of what Tzvetan Todorov terms 'exemplary memory', which, 'allows passing from particular to general, from event to pattern'. The content of their texts, but also the status accorded to their work and to them by the media have thus allowed Kerchouche and Besnaci-Lancou's writing to function as a 'catalyst, enabling previously unknown collective memories to become visible and legitimate'.[52] This is enhanced, particularly in Kerchouche's case, by the inclusion of archival documents and photographs that embed her personal account within a larger historical context.

Part of what gives Kerchouche's text its wider resonance is the shades of grey picture she paints of her father's wartime actions which, it is revealed, involved aiding the FLN while simultaneously serving as a *harki*. In rendering him 'neither a great hero nor a notorious traitor', Kerchouche continues a pattern of detaching the history of the *harkis* from the ideologically driven narratives of others. Her evolving relationship with her father, which forms the narrative core of *Mon père*, echoes the efforts of other *harki* offspring to learn about, comprehend and thus come to terms with the decisions made by their fathers. This ' "Harkeological" quest' is, in almost all cases, a conscious reaction against silence, undertaken in the knowledge that 'death and oblivion' are what await the *harkis*, 'if we, the children, do not bear witness'.[53]

These are not endeavours that have been confined to either women or to the written word. In his moving documentary, *Le Mouchoir de mon père*, Farid Haroud evokes the trajectory of his father Khélifa, who was incarcerated in eight different prisons in Algeria between 1962 and 1967. The film centres around a *mouchoir*, or handkerchief, on which the illiterate Khélifa secretly embroidered pictures to record his experiences and feelings during his captivity. Using military archives and interviews with family members and friends, Haroud sought to piece together a past of which his father had never spoken. In creating the documentary, Haroud stated that he hoped to leave a record of a man who had left so few historical traces of his own.[54] In a similar vein, Rabah Zanoun used his film, *Le Choix de mon père*, to give a voice to his previously silent father, Mohammed, filming him as he retraced the steps that led him to

the fateful 'choice' to become a *harki*. Working in France when the War
of Independence broke out, Mohammed followed his friends and joined
the FLN. But, when tasked with assassinating a member of the rival
MNA, he refused; an act that placed his life in jeopardy and forced him
to seek refuge with the French forces by enrolling as a *harki*.[55] In addition to foregrounding the bitter battle between the FLN and the MNA
for control of the Algerian population in France, the distinctiveness of
Zanoun's documentary lies in his determination to capture his father's
recollections in his own words, rather than relying on the testimony of
others. Reconstructing the trajectories of these men restores a sense of
agency, while also according them a status and individual identity, even
as their experiences stand for those of the wider community. Although
by no means devoid of ambiguity and conflicting emotions, the journeys
traced by these sons and daughters are characterised by their increasing
acceptance of their fathers and the varied motivations for their actions.

In addition to restoring the voices of their fathers, Kerchouche and
Besnaci-Lancou have both consciously created space for the wives
and widows of *harkis* to speak. Besnaci-Lancou, in her 2006 book *Nos
mères, paroles blessés*, collected the 'wounded words' of twenty *harki*
spouses, including her own mother. The project was prompted by the
reaction to her first book after which many women came up to her to
say: 'if I knew how to write, a thousand pages would not be enough
to recount all the miseries I've suffered since the Algerian War until
now'.[56] In spite of the book's title, *Mon père,* Kerchouche's mother plays
an equally central role in that narrative. Her follow-up project, *Destins
de harkis,* gave Kerchouche a further opportunity to collate accounts
from women within the community. This was her way of responding
to the fact that 'If the tragedy of the *harkis* is starting to emerge from
the shadow these last few years, the tragedy of their wives is a matter of
indifference. If the men have been scorned, their wives have been even
more so'.[57] Both women have therefore used their insider positions to
access testimony that has eluded other researchers. By presenting these
stories to the general public they hope not to only raise awareness of
the complexity of the *harki* experience, but to help 'other women coming out of "wars" or "exile" to one day lay down their burden'.[58] It is,
moreover, as Sutherland notes, a way of 'paying tribute' to the strength
of these women who held their families together in the face of trauma,
exile and loss.[59]

As a result of the efforts of Kerchouche, Besnaci-Lancou and others,
a growing body of collected testimony has emerged in parallel to more
autobiographically motivated texts. In contrast to the small number

of accounts written by former auxiliaries, such as Saïd Ferdi, Brahim Sadouni, Ahmed Kaberseli and Eric Taleb, that appeared in the 1970s and 1980s, today *harki* voices are primarily solicited and presented by the descendants of such men.[60] Besnaci-Lancou, a particularly prolific publisher of *harki* testimonies, combines multiple voices in a single publication, whereas others, such as Mehdi Chami, have opted to reproduce a single life story in depth.[61] These are often commemorative artefacts, densely illustrated with images, both historical and contemporary, of *harkis*, their families and their wider lives. This reminds readers of the individual humanity of the *harkis* and of their similarity to the rest of French society. As *harki* daughter and granddaughter Aïcha Kerfah told Rosella Spina, 'this history is not written in the archives, it is a memory transmitted through words', hence the importance of capturing these stories while those who carry them are still living.[62] By preserving and making public such accounts, children of *harkis* are seeking to ensure that future generations do not suffer from the same 'unspoken' and 'taboo' subjects they grew up with, making these projects that encompass and connect multiple generations.[63]

The context into which these testimonies are emerging is very different to that of the 1980s. In addition to the activism of *harki* descendants, whether individual or collective, and the evolutions in French commemorative culture outlined in this and the previous chapter, events in Algeria have also had an impact. Particularly significant was the army's hard-line repression of youth demonstrations during 'Black October' in 1988 which, by discrediting the ruling regime, helped to retrospectively legitimate the actions of the *harkis* who were presented as having opposed the violence associated with the FLN from its inception. Some have gone as far as to draw parallels between the violence of October 1988 and that of 1962, arguing that the *harkis* should be seen as the first victims of the FLN's armed brutality.[64] Developments on both shores of the Mediterranean have therefore created newly supportive frameworks for the memories that are now appearing. As Zoukhila, a *harki* spouse, told Besnaci-Lancou: 'Today, I am very proud that our children are fighting for the honour of their fathers. I am also happy to testify so as to leave a trace for our great-great grandchildren of our great adventure'.[65] The multiplication of information and testimonies concerning the *harki* community has given previously silent individuals an increasingly legitimated collective framework in which to anchor their personal experiences. By consciously soliciting testimony, *harki* descendants have reinforced the notion that what their parents have to say is valuable and important. This was the case for Djida, the wife of a *harki*, who told her interviewer: 'I've never spoken about what happened to us ... but now, it's different.'[66] With the passing of time, it has furthermore become easier on a practical level for the *harkis* to articulate their experiences, not least because after five decades living in France, the level of linguistic, cultural and socio-economic integration among the *harkis* has improved. Finally, entering the later stages of the lives appears to have prompted greater reflection on the past among many *harkis* and enhanced their desire to leave a trace for future generations.

Combining activism and academia: Mohand Hamoumou

Combining the trends of practical activism and cultural advocacy is Mohand Hamoumou, a successful academic and, since 2008, Mayor of Volvic (Puy-de-Dôme). Born in 1956 in Sétif into a family which, like many at the time, contained both *harkis* and FLN militants, Hamoumou's *harki* father was killed that same year. 'Repatriated' with the remainder of his family to France, Hamoumou grew up in various camps, later quipping: 'When I was little, I knew the joys of camping in the Larzac.'[67] One of several *fils de harkis* to have become academic analysts of their own communities, Hamoumou was awarded a doctorate from the EHESS in 1989 for his thesis which was later published as *Et ils sont devenus harkis*.[68] He went on, in 1998, to spearhead the federation of three pre-existing *harki* groups to create the Association justice, information et réparation pour les harkis (AJIR) whose name embodies the three core aims of the organisation.[69] Bolstering his credentials as an activist, Hamoumou's academic background created opportunities to extend the representation of the *harki* community into new spheres. In particular, he was able to establish himself as a privileged interlocutor between the *harkis* and the French state. Reminiscent of the attributes accorded to Roseau, in 2005 *Le Progrès* wrote: 'Media-savvy, charismatic, Mohand Hamoumou appears as the man for the job to take the struggle [of the *harkis*] to the political authorities.'[70]

Much of Hamoumou's influence has been channelled through AJIR, which, unlike associations of the early 1990s, has succeeded in establishing a national profile, possessing multiple regional branches across France.[71] One of the distinct features of AJIR is that the president is elected annually and no one individual may serve more than two consecutive terms. In the opinion of Régis Pierret, this has helped prevent the build-up of personal power bases that fatally weakened bodies such as M'hamed Laradji's CFMRAA, which was unable to outlast the departure of its founder.[72] AJIR pursues its agenda through a variety of initiatives, from providing practical assistance to *harki* families trying to navigate official bureaucracy in order to claim government assistance to events informing younger members about the community's history. Extending the parallels with RECOURS, AJIR also engages in lobbying, inviting politicians to their *rassemblements* to hear the demands and opinions of the *harki* community, mobilising the population in response to specific events and issues, as well as advocating support for particular candidates in elections. AJIR was closely involved with the discussions preceding both the Journée nationale d'hommage aux harkis in 2001 and the 23 February 2005 law, even though several of the association's suggestions did not make it into the final version of the legislation.[73]

Hamoumou is not alone among this new cohort of *harki* spokespeople in choosing to place his activism under the auspices of an association. Indeed, the formation of the Collectif national de justice pour les harkis et leur familles by Klech in 1997 following his hunger strike at the Hôtel des Invalides, is credited with providing the impetus for AJIR. Other examples include Coordination harka, which is run by Arfi; Kemoum's association, La Kahéna, which campaigns on behalf of *harki* wives and daughters; and Harkis et droits de l'Homme which, under the stewardship of Besnaci-Lancou has forged a close and beneficial working relationship with the LDH.[74] The high profiles of AJIR and Harkis et droits de l'Homme in particular suggest the potential for associations cast in a different mould to those of the early 1990s to serve as effective vehicles for the demands of the community. However, even though AJIR represents a departure from traditional patterns in some respects, it remains closely identified with Hamoumou, even though he is no longer the president. Scholars have furthermore noted that the prominence accorded to this new raft of organisations is, in large part, a reflection of the profiles of their founders, which were first attained outside of associational structures. Behind the energetic efforts of these emblematic leaders, actual engagement from within the *harki* community remains limited.[75] This raises questions regarding the legitimacy of such bodies to speak and act on behalf of the wider *harki* population, particularly in the light of the status and influence they have often been accorded by politicians and the media.

The *harki* experience

What is not in question is that the efforts of activists and cultural elites in combination with social and commemorative evolutions in France have led to a heterogeneous re-appropriation of the *harki* past. Diversity is a key attribute and, in many senses, the driving force behind this corpus of information, but there are equally a certain number of recurrent moments or themes around which narratives gravitate. The accounts of individuals thus exist within a particular collective framework whose primary thematic axes – enrolment, 'repatriation', conditions of reception and installation, relationships to France and Algeria – create a degree of overarching coherence. Central to these emerging narratives is the question of the circumstances surrounding enrolment with the French. Yet, this has also remained one of the least vocalised facets of the *harki* experience, with even spouses like Fatima stating 'my husband became a *harki* for reasons that, to this day, I don't know'.[76] The accounts that do touch on this subject are characterised by an attempt to detach the decision to become a *harki* from any ideological connotations, a point underscored by Besnaci-Lancou's assertion that the *harkis* 'were engaged *with* France and not for France'.[77] Thus, although many within the military and *pied-noir* communities maintain that the auxiliaries made a purposeful choice to side with the French, the testimonies of the *harkis* themselves reveal a messier reality.

Key to challenging the notion of politicised motivations is the point that at the time, working with the French was not perceived to be the betrayal that it later came to be portrayed as. The French had been in Algeria for more than a century and, during that time, had fought numerous wars with the assistance of colonial troops. This meant that many *harki*s had fathers and grandfathers who had served in the French army. The French had also been a dominant fact of life for so long that for most Algerians it was inconceivable that they would be vanquished, especially given their track record of subduing colonial rebellions. To men like Ali Tayeb France seemed 'invincible' and, consequently, 'we could not have imagined a different future'.[78] This is linked to the broader question of the extent to which nationalist sentiments had penetrated beyond a politicised minority and to the Algerian masses by the 1950s. The majority of *harki*s were from rural areas and knew little of what was happening outside of their immediate environs, especially given the high rates of illiteracy. 'History, we suffered it', argued one former auxiliary, casting himself and his fellow *harki*s as pawns in a game whose wider context they were almost entirely ignorant about.[79] These comments are echoed in Kerchouche's description of her father's enrolment: 'At the moment when he puts a cross, instead of a signature, at the bottom of his contract, he does not know that he is becoming a *harki*, a traitor to a cause that he is not familiar with and which passes him by'.[80] This adds great poignancy to his later statement: 'Me, I never chose France, I always considered myself Algerian'.[81]

Feeling oneself to be Algerian did not, however, automatically equate to enrolling in the FLN, not least because joining was no easy matter. The nature of the guerrilla war being waged forced the FLN to operate restrictive selection procedures; whereas on a practical level, the FLN were simply not able to equip, arm, and feed a large force, especially in the early stages of the conflict. Ancestral and personal rivalries further limited intake, while in the later stages of the war many within the FLN became anxious about potentially having to share their spoils with a slew of last-minute recruits.[82] Not only was a positive choice to side with the FLN problematic, many Algerians were repulsed by the conduct of the nationalists, in particular their brutality, which was often indiscriminate. Chafing under demands for food and money, alongside a set of rigorously enforced rules including the ban on smoking, the fact that many FLN soldiers 'did not conduct themselves honourably' was the last straw.[83] 'We would have been proud to help our brothers', testified one *harki* spouse, 'if they hadn't been so violent and authoritarian.'[84] Moreover, the general atmosphere of suspicion that reigned during the war meant that many *harkis* had family members killed by the FLN in the course of collective reprisals, cases of mistaken identity, because they were rumoured to harbour pro-French sympathies, or as part of pre-existing feuds. Acts such as these pushed some, if not directly into the arms of the French, then certainly away from the militant cause. Of course, the same was true of the French whose behaviour and tactics undoubtedly influenced many Algerians to side with the nationalists.

In all of this, protection was paramount. Whereas most *harkis* desired nothing more than to stay out of the conflict, the first FLN tract of the war clearly stated that neutrality was not an option. Algerians may have had little in terms of material possessions, but what they did have was very precious to them and they sought, above all, to protect it and their families as best they could. Subjected to intimidation and exaction by both the FLN and the French, often the choice of side came down to the simple fact of who was the more willing to provide a rifle. However, the French were able to offer other, equally powerful, incentives, principally money. The war destroyed rural economies, forcing men to enrol as *harkis* because they could see no other way to provide for their families. It was also not uncommon for one man to become a *harki* and use his wages to support the rest of the family, while his other male relatives fought for the less financially remunerative FLN. This was the 'complicated' situation in Yamina's family, in which her husband served as a *harki*, while his father fought with the FLN. Besnaci-Lancou's mother equally had one brother engage with the French, while the remainder of her siblings joined the FLN.[85] Given that these were practical rather than ideological arrangements, such divisions do not appear to have engendered great animosity at the time. Yet, in other cases, the allegiances of family members were crucial in determining on which side individuals found themselves. Ahmed Tabaali did not want to become involved in the conflict at all, but after a French SAS unit recruited his brother he felt compelled to follow him.[86] In contrast, rumours that Abdelkader Chami's brother had joined the FLN placed the family under suspicion from the French causing Chami to conclude that enrolling in the army represented 'the least bad solution'.[87]

These testimonies present becoming a *harki* as a practical necessity or a last resort, an assessment that chimes with Homer Sutton's description of the auxiliaries as 'neither heroes nor traitors', but rather 'exemplary victims of a colonial system which confiscated their choices'.[88] What comes across most strongly is that there was no grand patriotic narrative, or indeed any overarching rationale, simply a collection of individuals forced to respond to the situations in which they found themselves. Nor are the many reasons for enrolment cited mutually exclusive; they often coexisted. What unites these accounts is the hardships endured by Algerians during the war as a result of being caught between opposing forces. 'The Algerians were the first victims of the war', remarked Chami. 'Whatever they said, whatever they did, they were in the front line, caught between a rock and a hard place.'[89]

In all cases, the decision to engage with the French forces had dramatic and largely unforeseen consequences for those concerned. When asked about her husband's 'choice' for France, Seghira replied: 'France, I didn't choose it … Who chooses to leave their country? Who chooses to leave their family?'[90] Several *harkis* report being kept in the dark by French officers with regard to how the war was unfolding, particularly during the closing stages. Speaking in 2012, Brahim Sadouni noted that although other *harkis* in his unit began deserting in February 1962, it did not cross his mind to follow them: 'I didn't see the necessity because I knew nothing, no one explained anything to me.'[91] This professed ignorance of the bigger historical picture reinforces the notion of the *harkis* as victims of forces beyond their control, while also underlining the sense of shock and betrayal when they were suddenly disarmed and demobilised in the final months of the conflict.

Regarding the violence followed the signature of the Evian Accords, the *harkis* remain largely silent. When massacres are mentioned it is often in general terms to evoke the climate of terror that reigned at the time, or to describe the specific event that made them realise they had to leave

Algeria in order to save their own lives. In August 2001, France 3's nightly news programme featured testimony from Mohand Hamra who had spent four years in an FLN prison. Hamra recounted how the FLN took his fellow captives 'like animals to the slaughter', including one individual who had his limbs severed at the shoulders and hips before being 'planted like a fig tree'. Concluding with the assertion 'No one talks about it, they say these are lies, but I swear it is the truth', Hamra's testimony suggests that, in addition to being a legacy of trauma, continued silence may result from a fear of not being believed, so extreme were the acts witnessed.[92]

As more testimony appears, a greater sense of the different routes by which *harkis* and their families made their way to France has emerged. Although some accounts do revolve around organised military trans-fers, the images of French soldiers shepherding 'their' *harkis* across the Mediterranean in defiance of official orders that dominate narratives from outside the community are largely absent. Instead, the impro-vised, uncertain and mostly self-driven nature of the migratory process is emphasised. This is particularly true for those *harkis* who spent time in captivity in Algeria after the war. Once passage to France had been se-cured, emotions appear that range from relief to regret, sadness, anxiety and numbness. Several accounts testify to the tears of the woman as the boats pulled out of the port. In spite of thanking God that 'my husband was alive, my children were there', Khélifa Haroud's wife nonetheless found it 'hard' to leave Algeria and cried as she did so.[93] Others may have kept their grief to themselves, but they felt the loss of their homeland just as acutely. For Ali, there was a sharp contrast between the happiness of the returning French conscripts on board and the despair of auxiliaries such as himself as they watched Algeria recede into the distance.[94]

Arrival in France

The next points of anchorage for the memories of the harkis were the camps. Even though not all *harkis* passed through these spaces, they have become a focal point for the collective narrative of the commu-nity. In contrast to the brevity of accounts of departure from Algeria, more testimony is available concerning this phase of their lives. There is also a shift away from the predominantly masculine narratives through which histories of the war are related. In recollections of the camps and other institutionalised environments where the domestic and the pri-vate spheres assumed greater importance, the voices of women are more present. A common element within these accounts is the sense of shock upon arrival. Hoping for 'houses with a minimum of comfort', Chami

found the sight of a sea of khaki tents at Bourg Lastic particularly dispir-
iting: 'I couldn't believe my eyes, my morale was at rock bottom.'[95] The
fact that these men and woman arrived in France often with literally just
the clothes on their backs at the beginning of what was to become the
coldest winter on record only worsened the situation, helping to explain
why Achoura's principal recollections of Rivesaltes revolve around the
'cold' and 'isolation' she experienced there.[96] Poor physical conditions,
overcrowding, the lack of freedoms and enforced separation form the
metropolitan French prompting *harkis* to ask: 'Why have they put us in
prison? What crime have we committed?'[97]

One response to these environments was to cleave to customary habits
as a source of comfort. Several accounts describe how mothers sought to
recreate a little piece of Algeria in France in the sense of living close to
neighbours, continuing to speak their own languages, eating traditionally prepared food, where possible, and maintaining customary styles of
dress.[98] For Besnaci-Lancou, such actions were a product of the trauma
the *harkis* had suffered in 1962. 'Many, overtaken by the considerable
changes, took refuge in traditions. They remained frozen in the Algeria
of 1962. It was their way of being faithful to their roots.'[99] Links to the
past were also maintained through stories about Algeria. There may have
been little or no discussion of the war, but many children of *harkis* recall
being told anecdotes about ordinary life in Algeria, primarily by their
mothers. In such accounts, it was less the material conditions that were
missed, given the considerable poverty many had faced on a daily basis,
but rather the freedom to live as they wished surrounded by their friends
and loved ones. Families also intently followed events in Algeria, particularly via television. Kerchouche's family would 'religiously go quiet' as
soon as the news anchor said the word 'Algeria', while others used television as a way to visit their homeland virtually, as in the case of Azzedine,
who found himself 'filled with emotion' whenever Algerian landscapes
were shown.[100]

In keeping with the generally depoliticised tone of the testimonies, little explicit comment is offered on the postcolonial situation in
Algeria. Rather, most discussion revolves around the theme of nostalgia,
a phenomenon given a particular acuity by the fact that, unlike Algerian
immigrants, *harkis* are not officially permitted to return to Algeria. For
some, such as Ahmed Taabali, the nature of their experiences at the end
of the war irreparably damaged their relationship to their homeland leaving them with no desire to go back: 'Algeria, for me, is finished.'[101] But for
most, the inability to visit family and the graves of loved ones served as
a painful reminder of all that they had lost. As part of *Le Choix de mon*

père, Rabah Zanoun travelled with his father, Mohammed, to Algeria in 2007. While Rabah was able to enter the country, his father was stopped at customs and forced to take the first flight back to France. Although he says nothing, the devastating impact of this decision is clearly visible on Mohammed face.[102] Some, however, have been able to get around the official prohibition and make successful return voyages, especially wives of *harkis*. In spite of initial trepidation regarding the reception that would await them, the experiences of those who have gone back have been largely positive, although this has depended to a certain extent on the situation in Algeria at the time. Certainly, for Aïcha Baziz, who returned with her husband in 1985, 'the welcome was familial, friendly, everyone was pleased to see us'.[103] Yet, ultimately, these short trips do not change the reality of a permanent geographical separation and the overwhelming impression from the available testimony is of an abiding nostalgia for Algeria. 'I decided to leave in order to forget', explained Ali Tebib. 'But, obviously, the opposite happened.'[104] Such sentiments appear to be deepening with age, with Lakhdar telling Besnaci-Lancou how, 'Now that I am very old, I think about my country every day, I miss everything.'[105]

'A little anger against France'?

'I am Algerian before being French, that, no one can erase', Tebib stated defiantly when explaining his refusal to give his children French names.[106] His words reflect the stronger sense of an Algerian identity that emerges from personal testimonies than is often found in the pronouncements of the associations and spokespeople that constitute the community's public face. This is probably owing to the combination of the leadership of these organisations resting in the hands of children of *harkis*, for whom France is the country they grew up in, even if they nonetheless retain a strong sense of their Algerian heritage, and the practical necessity of stressing the ties that bind the *harkis* to France as part of demands put to the state. The majority of *harkis* furthermore possess French nationality having (re)claimed it in the early 1960s, adding legal confirmation to an identity long assumed for the community by veterans, *pieds-noirs* and even certain Algerians. But behind this status lies a more complicated relationship to France. As Kerchouche sarcastically notes, becoming French for a second time in December 1962 did nothing to improve her parents' situation: 'The identity card does not warm them up, does not feed their children and changes nothing about their living conditions.'[107] Given all that she learns of their treatment at the hands of the French, Kerchouche finds it difficult to understand why her parents do not display even 'a little anger' towards France. To which her mother responds: 'No ... France saved our life. You want us to ask for more?'[108] Such stoicism stands in contrast to the anger present among many of Kerchouche's generation. In explaining the motivation of his activism, Jacques Alim, president of AJIR from 2009 until 2013, stated: 'This injustice, this abandonment that my parents and all the *harkis* experienced, I wanted to shout about it loudly and clearly, trying to make it known to the state.'[109]

In an evolution of the notion of a 'blood debt' prominent in discourses about the *harkis* prior to the 1990s, a recurrent contemporary theme is the idea that France entered into a contract with its auxiliaries that the nation then failed to honour at the end of the war. 'If I did not really "choose" to defend the *tricolore*', Malek argued, 'I became a loyal soldier and I was one until the end. I fulfilled my part of the contact with the French state.'[110] The fact that they honoured their obligations, irrespective of whether they did so willingly, indifferently or under duress, forms a central plank of *harki* demands for recognition and recompense from the French authorities. Related to this is the view that France used the *harkis* and then cast them aside, disarming and demobilising them at the earliest opportunity before leaving them to their fates. This sense of having been deceived and then abandoned leads logically to the question of regret. Whereas *Français musulman* association representatives in the mid-1970s were united in their firm rejection of any such notion, opinions among *harkis* today are more divided.[111] Sadouni's uncle claimed to see regret etched on the faces of all the *harkis* he encountered, attesting to an emotion that was more often internalised than articulated.[112] Those who do express regret tend to present this as a result of their treatment at the hands of the French at the end of the war. 'With age', *harki* spouse Douya B. reflected, 'I realise that we made a mistake. In the eyes of the French, an Arab remains an Arab. If I could do it again, I would not fight for France.'[113] It is, however, only hindsight that affords the luxury of evaluating decisions in this manner. In the moment itself, *harkis* maintain they had no real choice; they simply did what they had to do.

Assuming the past in its entirety

Concluding the volume of testimony *Treize chibanis harkis*, Amar Assas of Harkis et droits de l'Homme called for the past to be assumed in its entirety: 'For us, it is not a question of glorifying this history, or, indeed mystifying it, or, in certain extreme cases, suppressing it.'[114] Yet, although there is now a growing body of testimony in the public domain, several aspects of the history of the *harkis* remain in the shadows. The most obvious missing element is what the *harkis* actually did during the war. By emphasising enrolment and abandonment, existing accounts reinforces a collective representation of the *harkis* as victims responding as best they could to circumstances beyond their control. There is therefore a marked reluctance to discuss elements of their past that implicate the *harkis* in acts that could contradict this image. Consequently, when referring to their duties as auxiliaries, these are almost always placed under the remit of safeguarding civilians. In part, these accounts reflect the fact that not all those labelled today as 'harkis' were part of military units, many were engaged in a civilian capacity to police and protect their local communities. But even those who admit to participating in active combat rarely provide specific details about their actions. In an interview with the *harki* B. F., Francis Mauro asked him the following question: 'Do you have memories of battles against the *fellaghas*?' After reflecting for a moment, B. F. replied: 'I could tell you about it for hours! But it isn't of huge importance!' The two anecdotes he eventually shares are about succeeding in situations in which his unit was on the defensive and greatly outnumbered.[115] The rare accounts in which *harkis* admit to killing someone are neither detailed nor dwelt upon, framed simply as an inevitable, if deeply unpleasant, part of warfare. While serving with the Force de police auxiliaire (FPA) in Paris, Tabaali's unit came under attack from the FLN in the Goutte d'Or neighbourhood. 'I fired on a man, he fell to the ground', Tabaali recounted. 'I thought he was an Algerian, like me, but war is war. He defended himself and I defended myself, I didn't have a choice.'[116]

In addition to referencing active combat, Tabaali's account is unusual because he was employed as part of the 'Paris *harkis*' of the FPA,[117] a role that is largely absent from recent testimonies, as well as from academic works outside of those dealing with the repression conducted against the Algerian community of Paris on 17 October 1961. One of the only television programmes to dwell at length on the role of the FPA was the two-part documentary 'Les harkis', aired in 1993. Yet testimony concerning the 'quite spectacular' record of the FPA *harkis* in breaking FLN cells came not from the *harkis* themselves, but from their former commander, Pierre de Roujoux.[118] The silence of the *harkis* can be partly attributed to the fact that those who served in the FPA were already in France at the end of the war and therefore better placed to avoid the camps, dispersing instead into the general population. As with *harkis* who served in Algeria, supportive *cadres sociaux* that might have facilitated the articulation of their experiences were absent in the years initially following 1962. No such frameworks have subsequently emerged. Instead, with the increasing amount of attention devoted to 17 October 1961 from the perspective of exposing the scale and wider context in which this act of repression was committed and then covered up, the conditions in which *harkis* of the FPA might be encouraged to speak out are arguably deteriorating. Finally, the specialised nature of the FPA's work leaves little room for the ambiguity that features in other accounts of *harki* duties. This is particularly true given the detailed accounts produced by both the *Algérie française* lobby, who sought to use the FPA as further proof of the terroristic and unrepresentative nature of the FLN, and by left-wing activists and commentators who denounced the FPA as instruments of colonial repression.[119]

In other respects, advances in knowledge about the war have produced more acceptance of the complexity of those years. The growing perception that this was a conflict from which no one emerged with clean hands appears to be fostering a greater willingness to examine uncomfortable and controversial aspects of the *harki* past. For example, although the practice of torture within the French army has been discussed by *harkis* since Ferdi's powerful testimony in *Les Années algériennes,* today these acts are being given a much more specific historical grounding – a development not unconnected to the re-emergence of torture as major topic of public debate. Some of the most in-depth testimony came from Rachid Abdelli in Patrick Rotman's 2002 documentary *L'ennemi intime.* Abdelli worked as an interpreter for the French and, as such, was present during multiple 'interrogations' of prisoners. He recalled how he had tried to advise those captured to speak quickly so as to minimise their suffering, but that most did not trust him. He also spoke of how he coped with this period stating: 'Everything was more or less unreal, we took it as a game, with a certain detachment, you transform reality into something that you can accept'; although after the fact he suffered from nightmares.[120] When pressed by Rotman about why he did not speak up at the time, Abdelli asked what he could have done, since 'everyone closed their eyes'.[121] Here, and in other accounts referring to torture, the *harkis* depict themselves as observers not participants, stressing that they were powerless to intervene. Such accounts also often include a reference to the violence to which the witnesses were themselves subjected, as if to imply some kind of balance or equivalence. Abdelli, for example was captured and tortured by the FLN, while in *Treize chibanis harkis* the contrition of Tayeb, who 'was present for all sorts of horrors', is juxtaposed against Malek who shows off his teeth, which are all false on account of a 'very sadistic man' who 'amused himself' by breaking them.[122]

Also conspicuous by their absence are the voices of those *harkis* who remained in Algeria after 1962. In many senses, the patriot/traitor dichotomy has today been replaced with the equally problematic binary of 'massacred in Algeria or saved in France'. Questioning the current focus on *harki* as an all-encompassing identity, in 2008 Sylvie Thénault called for greater attention to be paid to the fluidity of the wartime situation, especially the temporary nature of most auxiliary contracts, which meant that enrolment often constituted one of many episodes in their lives, rather than a defining moment.[123] Seven years later, the journalist Pierre Daum published a book on the 'last taboo' of *harkis* who remained in Algeria after independence which includes 300 pages of excerpts from the sixty interviews he conducted over two years in Algeria with former auxiliaries, former soldiers of the regular French army and other 'pro-French' Algerians.[124] Although challenging in terms of tracing such individuals in Algeria, who understandably do not publicise this aspect of their wartime activities, Daum's book represents a welcome intervention that further extends the diversity already introduced into histories of the *harkis* in recent years.

Whose voice?

In his 2011 study of the *harkis*, Crapanzano expressed frustration at his inability to break through the essentialised collective narrative of the *harki* experience he thought his interviewees felt a 'responsibility' to tell, to the individual stories he was seeking.[125] Through the repetition of a litany revolving around betrayal, abandonment and failed integration, Crapanzano argues that the *harki* community have become 'trapped' in 'the politically vested identity they have taken up – that they have been forced to take up'. This has the effect of fixing their identity and denying them the possibility of change or evolution.[126] As already noted, there are certain recurrent themes and motifs around which the currently available narratives gravitate. But in denouncing these for inhibiting access to some kind of unmediated individual account, Crapanzano is aiming at the wrong target. It is impossible to divorce the memories now emerging from the wider social, political and cultural context – in particular, from a heightened commemorative climate that includes a collective vision of history being put forward by the activist segment of the *harki* community, upon which rests a series of demands that they want the state to satisfy in line with similar gestures it has made towards other groups in France. Principal among these is the demand that the state acknowledge responsibility for the abandonment of the *harkis*, in 1962 and beyond, and take actions to rectify the consequences of this.

As Jim House has written with respect to the campaigns surrounding 17 October 1961, 'Memory here is not just about how present and past

are articulated: it also concerns how groups and individuals strategically invoke the past to bring about social change via collective action.'[127]
Emphasising certain elements while occluding others represents a process of choosing the most useful symbols or themes from a particular,
often limited, repertoire. This helps to explain why the camps loom
large in narratives from the *harkis*. Despite that fact that not all passed
through them, and that most of those who did spent only a limited time
there, the camps offer a particularly effective *lieu de mémoire* that encap-
sulates the notion that the *harkis* were 'abandoned' by the French state.
As such, the camps have come to stand for the suffering experienced
by the community in general. Thus although their dominance within
the narrative is a historical distortion, there are clear reason why this
is the case.[128] Furthermore, although Crapanzano dislikes the slippage
between 'I' and 'we' that he encountered among his interviewees, there is
a certain safety that resides in the collective that perhaps enables *harkis*
to articulate difficult facets of their own experiences under the guise of
a shared narrative. Given that we have access to only a fraction of the
potentially available testimony, these limited narratives have to substitute for a wider body of experience that will never be made public. It
is also the case that in order to render these accounts legible, a certain
coherence needs to be imposed on what are often partial and fragmentary recollections.

It is therefore unremarkable that, in spite of the diversity within the
available testimony – concerning, for example, reasons for enrolment –
this nonetheless exists within certain overarching collective frameworks
complete with omissions and distortions. Rather than criticising the
existence of these potentially essentialising structures, it is more productive to analyse the process by which they were formed and their implications. In terms of the *harkis* and their spouses, they are being asked to
recall events that happened several decades ago. In so doing, they are
also being asked to make statements that will reflect upon them and their
families in the present and that will be read in the light of existing representations of their history and community. It is not an issue of the veracity of their testimonies, but rather of giving consideration to the potential
influences of other narratives and contexts on the memories being offered
for public consumption. This is a particularly pertinent issue given that
so much of this new material has been made available through the efforts
of children of *harkis* who have collected and disseminated it. This reflects
an inverted process of inter-generational memory transfer also present
within the Algerian community in France, as catalogued by House and
Neil MacMaster with respect to 17 October 1961.[129]

Testimony gives us invaluable access to the intimate thoughts and emotions of individuals. But there is nonetheless a need to devote critical attention to the agendas of those producing these collections and how this might affect the narratives being offered. As primarily non-academic studies, there is virtually no discussion in these texts of the process by which accounts were obtained from *harkis*, even though what is presented is rarely simply direct testimony but also encompasses paraphrasing, translation into French, as well as descriptive and contextual scene setting details.[130] Besnaci-Lancou goes some way to acknowledging the mediation process in the introduction to *Des vies: 62 enfants de harkis racontent* when she states that it was not possible to include entire interviews. Instead, she selected excerpts, mostly to highlight different facets of the experiences of children of *harkis* and to avoid repetition. As with *pied-noir* edited collections of the 1980s, the resultant 'mosaic of viewpoints' was nonetheless intended to reveal certain common themes including 'the unswerving loyalty of the father ... painful memories of the camps ... [and] the request that the French state recognise its responsibility in the abandonment [of the *harkis*] in 1962'.[131] The demonstrable overlap between the issue raised by Besnaci-Lancou's interviewees and the motifs of her own activism, in this and her other collections of testimony, chimes with House's observation that subsequent generations reinvest events with new symbolic meanings that relate to their own concerns and priorities.[132]

In some cases, descendants of *harkis* have assumed the histories of their parents and used these to define their own identities. Abrial labels as 'protestors' those who 'still live with the memories of a past that does not belong to them but which they have re-appropriated'.[133] A classic example would be the *harki* daughter who, in the wake of the 1991 protests, participated in the delegation invited to discuss the community's situation with the Prime Minister. Emerging from this audience, she stood on the steps of the Hôtel Matignon and declared to the assembled press: 'We've had enough. We've been waiting for thirty years ...'; she was twenty-five and had been born in France.[134] One explanation for this kind of slippage is that many children remain unable to access their own parents' history and so compensate for this by assuming the collective *harki* narrative.[135] Furthermore, as *harki* activism has come to focus more on commemorative agendas, so the importance of the experiences of the *harkis* as a source of legitimation for the demands being advanced has grown. The phenomenon of 'borrowed memory', coined by Maurice Halbwachs and defined by House as 'a memory that we obtain from elsewhere – acquired or transmitted, in any case second-hand – when we have not experienced an event ourselves', has consequently played a significant role in the representations of *harkis* now circulating in the public domain. Yet, as House goes on to specify, these memories 'speak differently' and with a varying intensity to those who adopt them.[136]

A certain blurring of the boundaries between generations is also a result of experiential continuities born of the fact that the consequences of being an auxiliary did not end with the *harkis* themselves but shaped the lives of their children and grandchildren. As Klech explained, 'young people also feel hurt ... they are the ones paying to clean up the mess, they are the ones who are now paying for everything.'[137] Indeed, this is partly why the term 'harki' has become an all-encompassing one that, in its broadest iteration, also includes subsequent generations. As Arfi told the programme *Contre courant*, 'my identity, it's *harki*', while his daughters, who are also activists, define themselves in similar terms.'[138] The frequent entanglement of testimony with activism, the conflation of multiple agendas and generations, and the relationship between individual and collective narratives, all merit further academic attention as the body of available material pertaining to the *harkis* continues to expand across a range of genres.

Notes

1 Raymond Courrière, *Vaincre l'oubli* (Carcassone, 1984), p. 4.
2 Laurent Muller, *Le Silence des harkis* (Paris, 1999) p. 226.
3 For details of these financial measures, see William B. Cohen, 'The *Harkis*: History and Memory', in *Algeria and France 1800–2000: Identity, Memory, Nostalgia*, ed. by Patricia M.E. Lorcin (New York, 2006), p. 176.
4 Further discussion of the Journée nationale d'hommage aux harkis can be found in Chapter 8. For Chirac's speech, see: www.jacqueschirac-asso.fr/fr/les-grands-discours-de-jacques-chirac?post_id=2336 [17 April 2014].
5 Michel Roux, *Les Harkis: les oublis de l'histoire* (Paris, 1991), p. 377.
6 Mohand Hamoumou with Abderahmen Moumen, 'L'histoire des harkis et Français musulmans: la fin d'un tabou?', in *La Guerre d'Algérie: 1954–2004, la fin de l' amnésie*, ed. by Mohammed Harbi and Benjamin Stora (Paris, 2004), pp. 341–2. In 1999, Laurent Muller estimated that almost a third of associations were led by members of this generation. Muller, *Le Silence*, p. 20.
7 Nordine Boulhaïs, *Histoire des harkis du nord de la France* (Paris, 2005), p. 213.
8 Abderahmen Moumen, 'Les Associations harkis: de la revendication sociale au combat pour la reconnaissance', *Guerre d'Algérie magazine*, 4 (July–August 2002), 40.
9 Cited in Patrick Eveno and Jean Planchais (eds.), *La Guerre d'Algérie: dossiers et témoignages* (Paris, 1989), p. 366.
10 Muller, *Le Silence*, p. 77.

11   Stéphanie Abrial, *Les Enfants de harkis de la révolte à l'intégration* (Paris, 2002), pp. 178–84.

12   In his study of *harkis* in the north of France, Nordine Boulhaïs noted that one of the reasons the Association des Français musulmans rapatriés de l'Avesnois had proved so successful was that the majority of its members originated from the Chaoui tribe. In his eyes, this fact noticeably reduced 'the excess of individualism' found in other associations. Boulhaïs, *Histoire des harkis*, p. 222.

13   Abrial, *Les Enfants*, p. 23.

14   Patrick Jammes, *Médecin des harkis au Camp de Bias, 1970–2000* (Paris, 2012), p. 97; Rosella Spina, *Enfants de harkis et enfants d'émigrés: parcours croisés, identités à recoudre* (Paris, 2012), p. 240.

15   *Le Monde* (6 August 1991), p. 6.

16   Jean-Jacques Jordi and Mohand Hamoumou, *Les Harkis, une mémoire enfouie* (Paris, 1999), p. 41.

17   In contrast to trends in the south of France, the north saw a decline in the overall number of *harki* associations in the late 1990s and into the 2000s. Boulhaïs attributes this partly to an increasing number of federations among smaller associations. *Histoire des harkis*, pp. 235, 213–16.

18   Mohand Hamoumou, *Et ils sont devenus harkis* (Paris, 1993), p. 40.

19   For a flavour of the evolving coverage of the *harkis*, see 'Les Harkis', *Planète chaude*, aired 12 and 19 December 1993 (FR3); 'Les Harkis: les fils de l'oubli', *Les cinq continents*, aired 8 November 1994 (FR3); 'Amère patrie', *Documents*, aired 13 October 2006 (FR5); 'Harkis: des Français entièrement à part?', *Contre courant*, aired 25 April 2003 (FR2); 'La Blessure: la tragédie des harkis', *Hors série*, dir. Isabelle Clarke and Daniel Costelle, aired 20 September 2010 (FR3).

20   Both men have featured on various television programmes. Arfi's appearances include 'Les Harkis', aired 12 and 19 December 1993; 'Les Harkis: les fils de l'oubli', aired 8 November 1994; 'Harkis', aired 25 April 2003 (FR2). In addition to news coverage of his hunger strikes, Klech featured in *Harki: un traître mot*, aired 29 April 2002 (FR5) and 'Massacres pieds-noirs et harkis en 1962', *Mots croisés*, aired 3 November 2003 (FR2). The two men appeared together on 'La Situation des harkis', *7 et demi: sous dossier*, aired 13 November 1997 (ARTE).

21   For Arfi's account of his family's journey from Algeria to France, see Vincent Crapanzano, *The Harkis: The Wound that Never Heals* (Chicago, IL and London, 2011), pp. 110–12.

22   Muller, *Le Silence*, p. 53; Fatima Besnaci-Lancou, *Des vies: 62 enfants de harkis racontent* (Ivry-sur-Seine, 2010), p. 78.

23   Dalila Kerchouche, 'Hacène Arfi, fils de harki blessé à vie', *L'Express* (15 May 1997), p. 136.

24   Kerchouche, 'Hacène Arfi', p. 136.

25   There is some debate about the status of the grenades and the root cause of the occupation. Laurent Muller records that the grenades were genuine

ones left over from the Second World War that Arfi discovered accidentally, whereas in 2010 Arfi told Fatima Besnaci-Lancou that the grenades were fake. In contrast to Dalila Kerchouche's account for *L'Express* cited above, both Muller and Besnaci-Lancou report that it was being called up for jury service in Aix, which prompted Arfi's actions in Marseille because he felt that the French nation should be the ones on trial for their treatment of the *harkis*. Kerchouche, 'Hacène Arfi', p. 136; Muller, *Le Silence*, p. 54; Besnaci-Lancou, *Des vies*, p. 78.

26 Muller, *Le Silence*, p. 50.

27 Muller, *Le Silence*, p. 92.

28 Klech's relationship with his father is complicated. Although acknowledging that his father was not opposed to independence and stating that he 'approved' of his decision to become a *harki*, Klech went on to say that he personally would have fought with the FLN, albeit in a 'clean' manner. *Harki: un traître mot*, aired 29 April 2002.

29 Muller, *Le silence*, p. 56.

30 *Harki: un traître mot*, aired 29 April 2002.

31 Cédric Alviani, 'Harki solitaire face au dôme des Invalides', *Libération* (1 January 1998), p. 18.

32 See, for example, Fatima Besnaci-Lancou, *Treize chibanis harkis* (Paris, 2006), p. 85.

33 R. Maach, 'L'intransigeance amère des fils de harkis', *Libération* (6 October 1997), p. 17; Emmanuel Brillet, 'La Contingence et la geste: le harki, l'indicible du "mouvement de l'histoire"', in *L'époque de la disparition: politique et esthétique*, ed. by Alain Brossat and Jean-Louis Déotte (Paris, 2000), p. 152; Régis Pierret, *Les Filles et fils de harkis: entre double rejet et triple appartenance* (Paris, 2008), pp. 156–8.

34 Besnaci-Lancou, *Treize chibanis*, p. 85.

35 Sylvia Zappi, 'Grève de faim de deux fils de harkis pour que la France reconnaisse "ses fautes"', *Le Monde* (10 April 2000), p. 10.

36 Dalila Kerchouche, *Mon père, ce harki* (Paris, 2003); Fatima Besnaci-Lancou, *Fille de harki*, with Marie-Christine Ray (Paris, 2003); Zahia Rahmani, *Moze* (Paris, 2003); Hadjila Kemoum, *Mohand le harki* (Paris, 2003). There have been some attempts to claim that this represents the beginnings of 'harki literature' along the same lines as 'beur literature' of previous decades. However, most scholars feel that the corpus is currently too small to justify this description.

37 For later examples by *harki* offspring, see Saliha Telali, *Les Enfants des harkis: entre silence et assimilation subie* (Paris, 2009); Malika Meddah, *Une famille de harkis: des oliviers de Kabylie aux camps français de forestage* (Paris, 2012). In terms of works produced by those outside the *harki* community, see Mehdi Charef, *Le Harki de Meriem* (Paris, 1989); Yasmina Khadra, *La Part du mort* (Paris, 2004); Daniel Blancou, *Retour à Saint Laurent des Arabes* (Paris, 2012).

38 See 'Le Choix de mon père', *La Case de l'oncle Doc*, dir. Rabah Zanoun, aired 27 September 2008 (FR3); 'Le Mouchoir de mon père', *La Case de l'oncle Doc*, dir. Farid Haroud, aired 21 September 2002 (FR3).

39 The phrase is taken from Sylvie Durmelat, 'Transmission and Mourning in *Mémoires d'immigrés: l'héritage maghrébin*: Yamina Benguigui as "Memory Entrepreneuse"', in *Women, Immigration and Identities in France*, ed. by Jane Freedman and Carrie Tarr (Oxford, 2000), p. 173.

40 Géraldine Enjelvin, 'A Harki's Daughter's Offline and Online "parole cicatrisante"', *Australian Journal of French Studies*, 45:2 (2008), 136.

41 Crapanzano, *The Harkis*, pp. 10, 18.

42 Telali, *Les Enfants de harkis*, p. 52.

43 Enjelvin, 'A Harki's Daughter's', 137.

44 Kerchouche, *Mon père*, pp. 13, 195, 257. Kerchouche's subsequent projects have included a book of photographs with Stéphan Gladieu and a novel, *Leïla*, based on her sister's experience of growing up in various camps, which was also used as the screenplay for Alain Tasma's 2006 television film *Harkis*. The film received considerable publicity in advance of its 9pm prime-time airing on France 2, and some of its footage was also used alongside archival material and testimony in the documentary *Amère patrie*. See Dalila Kerchouche and Stéphan Gladieu, *Destins de harkis: aux racines d'un exil* (Paris, 2003); Dalila Kerchouche, *Leïla: avoir dix-sept ans dan un camp de harkis* (Paris, 2006); *Harkis*, dir. Alain Tasma, aired 10 October 2006 (FR2); 'Amère patrie', aired 13 October 2006.

45 Besnaci-Lancou, *Fille de harki*, p. 17.

46 Besnaci-Lancou, *Fille de harki* p. 83.

47 Besnaci-Lancou, *Fille de harki*, p. 119.

48 See Besnaci-Lancou, *Treize chibanis harkis*; Fatima Besnaci-Lancou *Nos mères, paroles blessées* (Léchelle, 2006); Fatima Besnaci-Lancou with Gilles Manceron, *Les Harkis dans la colonisation et ses suites* (Ivry-sur-Seine, 2008); Besnaci-Lancou *Des vies*; Fatima Besnaci-Lancou with Benoit Falaize and Gilles Manceron, *Les Harkis: histoire, mémoire et transmission* (Ivry-sur-Seine, 2010); Fatima Besnaci Lancou, *Des harkis envoyés à la mort: le sort des prisonniers de l'Algérie indépendante (1962–1969)* (Ivry-sur-Seine, 2014).

49 Kerchouche, *Mon père*, p. 173.

50 Nina Sutherland, 'Harki Autobiographies or Collecto-Biographies? Mothers Speak through their Daughters', *Romance Studies*, 24:3 (November 2006), 196.

51 Enjelvin, 'A Harki's Daughter's', 139.

52 Tzvetan Todorov, 'The Abuses of Memory', *Common Knowledge*, 5:1 (Spring 1996), 14; Géraldine Enjelvin and Nada Kovac-Kakabadse, 'France and the Memories of "Others": The Case of the *Harkis*', *History and Memory*, 24:1 (Spring/Summer 2012), 159, 164.

53 The context for these comments was the death of Kerchouche's grandfather as she was writing her first chapter. Kerchouche, *Mon père*, p. 53.

54 'Le Mouchoir de mon père', aired 21 September 2002.

55 'Le Choix de mon père', aired 27 September 2008.

56 Besnaci-Lancou, *Nos mères*, p. 19.

57 Gladieu and Kerchouche, *Destins de harkis*, p. 91.

58 Besnaci-Lancou, *Nos mères*, p. 20.

59 Sutherland, 'Harki Autobiographies', 198.

60 Saïd Ferdi, *Un enfant dans la guerre* (Paris, 1981); Ahmed Kaberseli, *Le Chagrin sans pitié* (Paris, 1988); Brahim Sadouni, *Le Drapeau: écrit d'un harki* (Paris, 1990); Brahim Sadouni, *Français sans patrie: la reconnaissance* (Rouen, 1985); Eric Taleb, *La Fin des harkis* (Paris, 1972).

61 Abdelkader Chami, Mehdi Chami and Geoffroy Sale, *Les Habits de mariage: itinéraire d'un harki* (Orléans, 2012).

62 Spina, *Enfants de harkis*, p. 209.

63 Dalila, the daughter of a *harki*, in Pierret, *Les Filles et fils de harkis*, p. 179.

64 Martin Evans, 'The Harkis: The Experience and Memory of France's Muslim Auxiliaries', in *The Algerian War and the French Army 1954–1962: Experiences, Images, Testimonies*, ed. by Martin S. Alexander, Martin Evans, J. F. V. Keiger (Basingstoke, 2002), p. 130.

65 Besnaci-Lancou, *Nos mères*, p. 112.

66 Jean-Jacques Jordi, 'Khélifa Haroud: harki, 1957–1967', in *Des hommes et des femmes en guerre d'Algérie*, ed. by Jean-Charles Jauffret (Paris, 2003), p. 370.

67 Cited in Céline Guiral, 'Une mémoire à fleur de peau', *Le Progrès* (24 June 2005), p. 21.

68 Hamoumou, *Et ils sont devenus harkis*. Other notable *harki* descendants who have become academics include Nordine Boulhaïs and Saliha Abdellatif. See Boulhaïs, *Histoire des harkis*; Saliha Abdellatif, 'Les Français-musulmans ou le poids de l'histoire à travers la communauté picarde', *Les Temps modernes*, 452:4 (1984), 1812–38.

69 www.harkis.com [15 April 2014].

70 Guiral, 'Une mémoire', p. 21.

71 For a sense of the type of activities AJIR undertakes and its profile, see the association's website: www.harkis.com [11 November 2013].

72 Pierret, *Les Filles et fils de harkis*, p. 196.

73 Pierret, *Les Filles et fils de harkis*, pp. 196–204.

74 For the full scope of the activities of Harkis et droits de l'Homme, see www. harki.net [11 November 2013]. Coordination harka and La Kahéna do not have dedicated websites. An additional association closely linked to a prominent activist was Boussad Azni's Comité national de liaison des harkis, which will be discussed in Chapter 8.

75 Abderahmen Moumen, 'De l'absence aux nouveaux porte-parole: évolution du mouvement associatif harki (1962–2011)', *Les Temps modernes*, 666 (November–December 2011), 166; Pierret, *Les Filles et fils de harkis*, p. 205.

76 Fatima in Besnaci-Lancou, *Nos mères*, p. 75.

77 Emphasis in the original. Besnaci-Lancou, *Fille de harki*, p. 71.

78 Besnaci-Lancou, *Treize chibanis*, p. 60.

79 Besnaci-Lancou, *Fille de harki*, p. 57.

80 Kerchouche, *Mon père*, p. 228.

81 Kerchouche, *Mon père*, p. 254.

82 Mohand Hamoumou, 'Comment pouvait-on être harki?', *Migrations études*, 23 (December 1991), 2.

83 Sabrina Kassa, *Nos ancêtres les chibanis! Portrait d'Algériens arrivés en France pendant les Trente Glorieuses* (Paris, 2006), p. 116.

84 Besnaci-Lancou, *Fille de harki*, p. 43.

85 Besnaci-Lancou, *Nos mères*, p. 23; Besnaci-Lancou, *Fille de harki*, p. 54.

86 Ahmed Tabaali in *Harkis: soldats abandonnés* (Paris, 2012), p. 145.

87 Chami, *Les Habits de mariage*, pp. 40–1.

88 Homer B. Sutton, 'Postcolonial Voices: Vindicating the *Harkis*', *Contemporary French Civilization*, 20:2 (1996), 238.

89 Chami, *Les Habits de mariage*, p. 74.

90 Besnaci-Lancou, *Nos mères*, p. 56.

91 Brahim Sadouni in *Harkis: soldats abandonnés*, p. 128.

92 'La mémoire des harkis', *Edition nationale*, aired 30 August 2001 (FR3).

93 Jordi, 'Khélifa Haroud', p. 365.

94 Besnaci-Lancou, *Treize chibanis*, p. 54.

95 Chami, *Les Habits de mariage*, p. 121.

96 Besnaci-Lancou, *Nos mères*, p. 105.

97 Kerchouche, *Mon père*, p. 56.

98 Régis Pierret argues that while life in the camps represented a loss of status for male *harkis*, their wives were able to re-establish traditional patterns of life and thus preserve a sense of continuity which mitigated the effects of their migration. Pierret, *Les Filles et fils de harkis*, p. 54.

99 Besnaci-Lancou, *Fille de harki*, p. 79.

100 Kerchouche, *Mon père*, p. 29; Azzedine in Besnaci-Lancou, *Treize chibanis*, p. 26.

101 Ahmed Taabali in *Harkis: soldats abandonnés*, p. 156.

102 'Le Choix de mon père', aired 27 September 2008.

103 Aïcha Baziz in *Harkis: soldats abandonnés*, p. 99. For further reflections on *harki* return visits, see Giulia Fabbiano, 'Être là. Les voyages au pays d'origine des familles harkies entre expérience mémorielle et situations d'apprentissage', in *Apprentissages en situation touristique*, ed. by Gilles Brougère and Giulia Fabbiano (Villeneuve d'Ascq, 2014), pp. 143–54.

104 Ali Tebib in Kassa, *Nos ancêtres*, p. 117.

105 Besnaci-Lancou, *Treize chibanis*, p. 13.

106 Ali Tebib in Kassa, *Nos ancêtres*, p. 120.

107 Kerchouche, *Mon père*, p. 62.

108 Besnaci-Lancou, *Treize chibanis*, p. 16.

109 Jacques Alim in *Harkis: soldats abandonnés*, p. 194.

110 Besnaci-Lancou, *Treize chibanis*, p. 17.

111 'Et pourtant ils sont Français', *Les Dossiers de l'écran*, aired 17 May 1977 (A2). It is still possible to find *harkis* who echo such sentiments as indicated by

contributions to the programme *Harkis: le crime,* aired 12 February 2002 (ARTE).

112   Sadouni, *Français sans patrie,* p. 7.

113   Julien Chapsal, *Harkis à vie?* (Trézélan, 2006), p. 26.

114   Besnaci-Lancou, *Treize chibanis,* p. 85.

115   Francis Mauro and Bathoche Mahious, *Compiègne, terre d'accueil pour les Harkis* (Agincourt, 2004), pp. 57–9.

116   Taabali in *Harkis: soldats abandonnés,* p. 150.

117   François-Xavier Hautreux objects to this label, arguing that the FPA were not *harkis* and that designating them as such was one of the main reasons why the metropolitan French held negative perceptions of auxiliaries who arrived in France after the war. *La Guerre d'Algérie des harkis, 1954–1962* (Paris, 2013), p. 379.

118   'Les Harkis', aired 12 and 19 December 1993.

119   See Saïd Boualam, *Les Harkis au service de la France* (Paris, 1963), p. 220; Georges Fleury, *Le Combat des harkis* (Versailles, 1989), p. 120; as compared to Paulette Péju, *Les Harkis à Paris* (Paris, 1961).

120   'Engrenages', *L'ennemi intime,* aired 5 March 2002 (FR3); Patrick Rotman (ed.), *L'ennemi intime* (Paris, 2002), p. 251.

121   'Engrenages', aired 5 March 2002.

122   Besnaci-Lancou, *Treize chibanis,* pp. 61, 18.

123   Sylvie Thénault, 'Massacre des harkis ou massacre de harkis? Qu'en sait-on?' in *Les harkis dans la colonisation,* pp. 90–1.

124   Pierre Daum, *Le Dernier tabou: les harkis restés en Algérie après l'indépendance* (Arles, 2015).

125   Crapanzano, *The Harkis,* pp. 10, 129, 178.

126   Crapanzano, *The Harkis,* pp. 175–80.

127   Jim House and Neil MacMaster, *Paris 1961: Algerians, State Terror and Memory* (Oxford, 2006), pp. 190, 291.

128   See also Géraldine Enjelvin, 'The Harki Identity: A Product of Marginalisation and Resistance to Symbolic Violence?', *National Identities,* 8:2 (June 2006), 117; Crapanzano, *The Harkis,* p. 175.

129   See House and MacMaster, *Paris 1961,* p. 324.

130   A notable exception to this is Mehdi Chami's account of his father Abdelkader's history, in which he discusses the difficulties Abdelkader had in speaking, not only because of the nature of what he was being asked to recall, but also because French was not his native language. It was therefore important for Mehdi to render his father's story in his own words and 'imperative' that Abdelkader recognised himself in his own narrative. But when recording, Mehdi also highlighted to his father contradictions or inconsistencies, while in the final text he used footnotes to clarify and expand upon points raised in the main body. These included editorial asides to indicate when Abdelkader's own memories differed from those of other *harkis.* Chami, *Les Habits de mariage,* pp. 5–7, 123–4, 144.

131   Besnaci-Lancou, *Des vies,* p. 10.

132 House and MacMaster, *Paris 1961*, p. 19.

133 Abrial contrasts 'protestors' to 'spokespeople' who possess a greater emotional and intellectual distance. This enables them to critique the behaviour of France towards their community while maintaining an awareness of the difference between the suffering of the *harkis* themselves and the challenges faced by their descendants. Such an attitude is made possible by the greater levels of integration often displayed by 'spokespeople' compared to 'protestors'. Kerchouche, Besnaci-Lancou and Hamoumou would all be examples of 'spokespeople'. Abrial, *Les Enfants de harkis*, pp. 213–16.

134 Mohand Khellil, 'Les Français musulmans rapatriés: d'ambiguïtés en malentendus', in *Les Rapatriés d'Algérie en Languedoc-Roussillon 1962–1992*, ed. by Mohand Khellil and Jules Maurin (Montpellier, 1992), p. 221.

135 Crapanzano, *The Harkis*, p. 85.

136 House and MacMaster, *Paris 1961*, p. 190.

137 Cited in Muller, *Le Silence*, p. 130.

138 'Harkis', aired 25 April 2003; Besnaci-Lancou, *Des vies*, p. 78.

Memory wars, 1999–2012

7

Friends and enemies

As France moved into the new millennium, the nation, according to Henry Rousso, also moved into a phase of 'hyper-memory' as the War of Independence became 'a continual and almost obsessive presence in the contemporary public space'.[1] The outward signs of this national preoccupation were multiple and frequently contentious since the more narratives entered the public domain, the greater the potential became for contradictions and conflicts between them.[2] It is the combative character of these developments that has attracted most attention, as both scholars and the general public deliberated over whether the nation had become mired in a 'war of memories'. This increasingly commonplace phrase conveys the sense that the divisive nature of the Algerian War is being replayed as different memory-carrying groups 'fight' to see their version of the past enshrined in official rituals and monuments under the patronage of a newly interested and invested state. The multiplication of gestures from the state towards specific communities, the frequent instances of high-profile controversy, particularly amidst a revival of passionate debates over France's colonial past more generally, combined with sustained and often sensationalised media interest lend credence to the idea that the current period is qualitatively distinct, in tone and intensity, even from the rapid developments of the 1990s.

For Benjamin Stora, the 'memory wars' phenomenon was intimately connected to the previous absence of the conflict from the public realm. 'Amnesia can work like a fragmentation bomb', he wrote. 'If hatreds and bitterness remain confined for too long in private space, they risk exploding in public space several dozen years later. Having not taken on the past in all its complexity, it explodes in the present in an anachronistic, disordered, out of control way'.[3] Less theatrically, Pascal Blanchard and Isabelle Veyrat-Masson asked whether the present situation was not 'the simple entrance into visibility of that which before played out in the ante-chamber of public debate among the silent frustrations of the "victims of history"?'[4] Critics of the 'memory wars' label argue that it creates a self-fulfilling prophecy, exacerbating differences of opinion and heightening tensions through dramatic, conflict-based vocabulary. As a result, groups and individuals are encouraged to view themselves as engaged in a perpetual 'battle' to ensure that their version of the past prevails over all others as part of a zero-sum game. Illustrative of this was Georges Dillinger's warning to Véritas members amidst the controversy surrounding Article 4 of the 23 February 2005 law. At a time when 'fabrications and manipulations' of the past had become 'formidable weapons in a battle that aims to deceive people in order to enslave them, and finally to make them disappear', Dillinger was clear that to refuse to engage in order to counter such falsifications would not only be 'a veritable desertion' but also 'suicidal' for the *pieds-noirs*.[5]

In a war, one is obliged to choose a side. This leads groups to view each other as 'allies' to be courted or 'enemies' to be defeated, creating 'a campaigning logic that, most often, refuses to take into account the suffering of others'.[6] As this chapter will argue, this climate has led *pied-noir* and *harki* activists to re-evaluate and sometimes reformulate their relationships with each other and with prominent groups connected to the war including veterans and Algerians in France. The present environment has also influenced the ways in which these two communities interact with key vectors of transmission such as the media and academia. Tracing evolutions in the nature of these relationships provides an insight into the identity struggles and power dynamics that have underpinned the surface manifestations of the 'memory wars' phenomenon over the past decade.

Continuity and change: the evolving relationship between *pieds-noirs, harkis* and veterans

Had *pieds-noirs* and veterans united, Antoine Prost argued, they could have been more successful in creating a 'community of victims' and in finding ways to collectively commemorate their experiences of the Algerian War.[7] Yet, although hostility persists between the former settlers and members of the left-leaning veterans' group FNACA, composed primarily of former conscript soldiers, especially with regard to 19

March 1962, there are multiple examples of career soldiers and the upper echelons of the armed forces who have maintained long-standing and productive alliances with *pied-noir* activists. As discussions of the War of Independence have increasingly focused attention on aspects of the conflict that both *pieds-noirs* and veterans would prefer not to highlight, the bond between the two has grown as they have worked together in a bid to dispute and discredit these new discourses and their proponents.

On 20 June 2000, *Le Monde* published an interview in which former FLN militant Louisette Ighilahriz discussed her capture and subsequent torture by General Jacques Massu's paratroopers during the Battle of Algiers.[8] The use of torture by the French army was not a new revelation and in fact had been the subject of much discussion during the war itself.[9] But in the heightened atmosphere of the early 2000s, and a mere two days after President Bouteflika's state visit to France had concluded, Ighilahriz's interview created a media frenzy. This was further fuelled by the diverse reactions to the revelations by key military figures. Colonel Marcel Bigeard simply dismissed Ighilahriz's claims as a pack of lies. In contrast, Massu, aged ninety-four and in poor health, distanced himself from the position he had taken in his 1971 autobiography that torture in the Battle of Algiers had been necessary, now confessing that it could not be justified and expressing regret for his actions.[10] Most sensationally of all, General Paul Aussaresses not only admitted to various illegal acts, including responsibility for the death of Larbi Ben M'Hidi, head of the FLN's operations in Algiers, who died while in the custody of the army in 1957, but vigorously defended his actions claiming that they been effective and that he would do the same again.[11] The controversy rumbled on for several years as Aussaresses found himself in court accused of war crimes by human rights groups. He was ultimately convicted and fined not for the acts themselves, which were covered by the postwar amnesties, but for justifying torture; he was also stripped of his Légion d'Honneur.

Both *pied-noir* associations and military figures had always vehemently refuted allegations of misconduct by the French army in Algeria. Yet, by 2000, although it was still possible to deny any personal knowledge or involvement, sweeping claims that the army had never tortured had ceased to be a plausible recourse. At the height of the debates generated by the piece in *Le Monde*, some *pied-noir* organisations, such as the Cercle algérianiste and the magazine *Pieds-noirs d'hier et d'aujourd'hui*, simply ignored what was happening, aside from oblique references to this being a difficult year in which the community found itself under attack. Those associations that chose to engage with the controversy did so in close collaboration with military figures, with all, as Stora noted at the time, adhering to the same script. This script essentially repeated Massu's original position that torture was used only in very specific circumstances, essentially confined to the Battle of Algiers, and that it was a necessary evil, which, by extracting information rapidly from FLN suspects, saved innocent lives.[12] Another tactic was to acknowledge certain excesses by the French forces, but to claim that these were outweighed by the brutality of the combat waged by the FLN. 'This lady [Ighilahriz] complains that she was tortured' began one particularly angry reader's letter in *France horizon*. 'Do you know what the FLN did to those who fell into their hands? They slit their throats from ear to ear, it was what they called the Kabyle smile, and with men they often cut off their genitals and put them in their mouths.'[13] Not only were FLN methods more barbaric, the magnitude of their violence was deemed greater, as indicated by the often-repeated statement that the FLN killed a higher number Algerians between 1954 and 1962 than the French did. Particularly effective in underlining the violence of the FLN was the fate of the *harkis;* the commonly cited figure of 150,000 deaths being a powerful statistic to wield, alongside graphic images supplied by Véritas of 'men, women and children, chopped into pieces, butchered, skinned alive, scalded, beyond the limits of savagery'.[14]

The use of the *harkis* in this manner highlighted the continuing phenomenon of externally generated, mutually reinforcing discourses about the former auxiliaries offered by veterans and *pied-noir* activists. Given that *harkis* have been all but absent from both the publications and commemorations of the two major veterans' associations, the FNACA and the UNC-AFN, save for a token mention in annual reports or during high-profile events such as the 2001 Journée nationale d'hommage aux harkis, the bulk of this ongoing commentary on the military side has been provided by individuals who commanded *harki* units.[15] Particularly notable in this respect are Colonels Bernard Moinet and Abdelaziz Méliani, and Generals Maurice Faivre and François Meyer.[16] In addition to leading auxiliary units during the war all, apart from Moinet, personally arranged transport to France for 'their' *harkis* at the end of the conflict and have remained in close contact with these families ever since.[17] As part of their multifaceted activism, all four men have penned memoirs to publicise the history of the community.[18] They have also all been regular fixtures at *pied-noir* events and within association publications, with Faivre enjoying a particularly high profile. Collaborating with *pied-noir* associations provided these and other military figures with an established platform from which to disseminate their message and the guarantee of a positive reception from a sizeable and like-minded audience. In return, associations benefited from having their perspectives on the *harkis* validated by respected members of the armed forces who could lay claim to an intimate knowledge of the auxiliaries and their experiences.

This mutually beneficial relationship is underpinned by a consensual interpretation of the *harkis* and their service to France. As in previous decades, the accounts put forward by military personnel emphasise the value and valour of the *harkis,* their skills and achievements in combat forming a much larger part of military narratives than within the auxiliaries' own testimonies. Recounting his time in the infamous Commando Georges, Lieutenant Colonel Armand Bénésis de Rotrou recalled how his unit was sent all over in order to 'eliminate' FLN units. He added that although some reproached the Commando for not always following orders, he felt their record in the field spoke for itself: while other units killed no 'fells' (*fellaghas*), Commando Georges killed fifty at a time.[19] In this context, the close bond between officers and 'their' *harkis* is usually attributed to the conscientious and compassionate leadership they received. 'I gave them dignity,' explained one such officer, Maurice de Kervénoaël, 'I respected them, I found that they fought marvellously and they sensed my admiration.'[20]

In contrast to the growing body of *harki* testimonies that emphasise the array of circumstances behind enrolment, *pieds-noirs* and former soldiers continue to present the *harkis* as men who were engaged 'firmly for France' and who were 'convinced they'd made the right choice.'[21] Introducing the 2012 collection of testimony, *Harkis: soldats abandonnés,* Faivre cited opposition to the tactics of the FLN, pro-French patriotism and the financial benefits of fighting with the French as the key factors underpinning service as an auxiliary. Yet, this assertion was contradicted in the book itself by contributors such as Aïcha Baziz, who said of her husband's enrolment: 'He did it out of fear, to protect himself. I don't know if it was a choice, if it was not rather a "non choice".'[22] What enables these two different interpretations to coexist is the point of commonality provided by the theme of abandonment. This has become the principal trope through which both veterans and *pied-noir* activists seek to connect their experiences with those of the *harkis,* claiming that all three groups were, in some way, betrayed by the French state.

The notion of a single *rapatrié* community, comprising both settlers and *harkis,* united by the shared experiences of terror at the hands of the FLN, a traumatic exile in 1962, and an ignominious welcome in France followed by years of marginalisation and silence, remains a staple of *pied-noir* association discourse. In the midst of Abdelkrim Klech's 1997

hunger strike, Yves Sainsot of ANFANOMA wrote: 'This community
[the *harkis*] is also ours. Who better than us to understand the pain, the
despair of our brothers in combat? They have known all the difficulties
that we ourselves have been through, even beyond the incomprehension,
the racism of the metropolitan French.'[23]

    Even as the amount of attention paid by *pied-noir* associations to the
harkis has risen in tandem with the public profile of the community, this
coverage remains wedded to the idea of the former auxiliaries as 'the forgotten of history'. On the eve of the first Journée nationale d'hommage
aux harkis in 2001, the Cercle algérianiste could be found arguing 'it is
high time that the silence concerning the abandonment and the massacre of those who served France with loyalty is broken and that our
country acknowledges the black stain on its history'.[24] A statement virtually identical in tone and vocabulary to Jo Sohet's 1979 article for the same
association which spoke of the need to 'break the silence' surrounding
the *harkis*.[25] This static view of the *harkis* represents a strategic choice
that has enabled *pied-noir* activists to perpetuate a wider discourse centred on unresolved injustice which, in turn, legitimates their continuing
campaigns on behalf of both themselves and the *harkis*.

    These campaigns rarely acknowledged the existence of an increasingly
organised and mobilised *harki* community. Instead, *pied-noir* associations regularly claim the credit when national attention is devoted to the
harkis. Sociologist Clarisse Buono found that even the Journée nationale
d'hommage aux harkis was framed by her *pied-noir* interviewees as the
result of *their* indefatigable campaigning, with no mention made of activism by *harkis* descendants.[26] Within *pied-noir* publications the norm is
still for articles pertaining to the *harkis* to be written by those who commanded them during the war, as indicated by the regularity with which
Faivre's by-line appears. Slights against the *harkis* continue to arouse
strong reactions from both veterans and *pieds-noirs* on the grounds
that if they do not stand up for the community then no one else will,
including the *harkis* themselves. 'It always falls to me to react vigorously
in order to defend their unjustly soiled memory', stated Meyer when he
sued journalist Marcel Péju for defamation after Péju made comments
in 2001 about the *harkis* similar to Bouteflika's 'collabo' remark.[27] More
recently, in 2006, *pied-noir* associations mobilised in consternation over
George Fréche's 'sub-humans' remark, in spite of a prominent and widely
supported series of protests undertaken independently by *harki* activists,
including a hunger strike by Klech.[28]

    As the *harki* community have become increasingly autonomous
in their activism they have begun to advance narratives that challenge

central tenets of the version of events propounded by *pieds-noirs* and veterans. Such instances have produced swift and often scathing rebuttals from within these two groups, with Dalilia Kerchouche emerging as a particular target. Kerchouche's characterisation of the military chief of the forest hamlet as a cruel and sadistic bully in her screenplay for the television film *Harkis* was denounced by Faivre in the pages of *L'Algérianiste* as wholly inaccurate on the basis that 'no forestry site was run by an officer; the boss of the site was generally a retired NCO'.[29] By focusing on this minor point of fact, Faivre avoided dealing with the substance of Kerchouche's claim regarding the treatment meted out to the *harkis* by those placed in charge of them, irrespective of their military rank. *Véritas* also dismissed Kerchouche's portrayal using the dubious logic that because it was courtesy of the actions of *some* French officers that certain *harkis* were able to escape from Algeria, *no* officer could then have treated them badly once they were in France.[30] Kerchouche's comments touched a nerve because they referred directly to the behaviour of *pieds-noirs* and soldiers towards *harkis,* undermining the image of concern, compassion and benevolent assistance that both groups have assiduously promoted since the 1960s. They also raised the thorny issue of the perpetuation of colonial-style relationships of control and domination into the postcolonial era. (Although *Véritas* preferred to attribute Kerchouche's 'errors' to ideological bias accusing her of 'the faithful recitation of the universal anti-*pied-noir* catechism'.)[31] The opposition of the associations run by Klech and Fatima Besnaci-Lancou to the 23 February 2005 law brought forth similarly politicised objections with the two activists accused of standing 'alongside communists, Trotskyists and notorious anti-colonialists'.[32] More than just ideological differences, such condemnations are also about trying to control narratives about the past, something that military representatives and the *pieds-noirs* are increasingly less able to do as the position of the *harkis* within postcolonial memory politics has strengthened.

Although figures like Kerchouche and Besnaci-Lancou have firmly kept their distance from *pied-noir* and veterans groups, Mohand Hamoumou, primarily through AJIR, has made common cause with the *pieds-noirs* when this served the interests of either the association or the wider community. Hamoumou has thus appeared at various *pied-noir* events, sharing platforms with the likes of *Véritas's* Anne Cazal. AJIR is an established contributor to *Pieds-noirs d'hier et d'aujourd'hui* and the association has also written articles for *Véritas*. One of these, authored by Hamoumou, called explicitly for *pieds-noirs* to provide practical proof of their rhetorical commitment to the *harkis* by supporting the 2001 relaunch of their

'Justice for the *harkis*' campaign. 'You often speak of solidarity towards the *harkis*', Hamoumou wrote. 'Here's a concrete occasion to prove it. Do you dare?'³³ In return, AJIR's website promotes past and present *pied-noir* lawsuits and includes a section in which the association pays homage to supportive figures like Meyer, who also possesses a standing invite to the association's annual conference. When seeking to mobilise opposition to the proposed 'Treaty of Friendship' between France and Algeria in 2005, AJIR went so far as to argue that *harkis* and *pieds-noirs* formed a single 'community of tragic destiny', who paid the price in 1962 for their 'double attachment to France and to the land of Algeria'.³⁴

In recognising that to ignore the *pied-noir* community would be akin to cutting off their nose to spite their face, Hamoumou and other *harki* activists have opted instead for calculated alliances that allow them to benefit from the resources of the well-established *pied-noir* associational network to further their own cause. These instances of cooperation have been facilitated by a resolute focus on postcolonial connections created by a shared sense of betrayal and abandonment directed against the French state. Entirely absent from these exchanges is any mention of the pre-1954 era. As will be discussed in the next chapter, this is in conformity with broader commemorative strategies, particularly those emanating from the state, that have stripped the history of the *harkis* of its colonial dimensions, presenting them instead simply as soldiers of France. Thus while strategically useful, such relationships reinforce a limited and historically problematic conception of the *harki* community.

Between envy and invective: *pied-noir* portrayals of Algerians

In sharp contrast to their consciously cultivated relationship with the *harki* community stand *pied-noir* representations of Algerians. The general absence of Algerians from *pied-noir* depictions of the colonial era, except when being used to make points about French Algeria as a harmonious multi-ethnic melting pot, differs markedly from their preoccupation with the Algerian community as it exists in postcolonial France. Colonial Algeria is furthermore clearly distinguished from present-day Algeria, which *pieds-noirs* regard as an entirely different and immeasurably poorer country for being separated from France. Indeed, one of the most prominent themes in accounts from *pieds-noirs* who have returned to Algeria for visits is the physical degradation of the country, which functions as a metaphor for a broader process of deterioration under the

FLN.[35] The problems experienced by Algeria since 1962 have consistently been used by *pieds-noirs* to justify their claims that decolonisation was a terrible mistake. The nation's descent into violence in the 1990s as the state and Islamic extremists locked horns proved particularly effective fodder for such arguments.[36] 'It is with sadness and bitterness that we see foundering this country that remains so dear and to which we are still profoundly attached', claimed ANFANOMA's Pierre Reveillaud in 1993. Yet, associations also evinced a certain grim satisfaction at 'The horror of these acts of brutality' which 'we have, unfortunately, known too well'.[37] Using contemporary events as proof of long-standing beliefs about Algeria and Algerians, associations attributed the violence of the 1990s not only to the 'implacable and dictatorial yoke' of the FLN, but to the violent nature of Islam itself, as evidenced throughout history from the Arab conquest of North Africa and the use of Christians as slaves to the 'tyranny' of the Ottoman Empire.[38] In a similar vein, the assassination of seven French monks from the monastery of Notre-Dame de l'Atlas in Tibhirine in March 1996 was deemed symptomatic of religious intolerance inaugurated by the FLN and frequently directed against the French.[39]

Given its magnitude and longevity, the conflict in Algeria received remarkably little coverage overall from *pied-noir* associations. Even bodies such as ANFANOMA, who devoted more space than most to the topic, did not include any comment on the situation prior to 1993. They were also erratic in terms of what they chose to comment on, failing, for example, to make any mention of the massacre of 200 civilians in the town of Bentalha in September 1997, one of the most horrific and widely reported incidents of the entire decade. This pattern reflects the weakness of transnational ties between *pieds-noirs* and their former homeland. While there is plenty of nostalgia within associations for the lost paradise was colonial Algeria, there is no meaningful engagement with the present-day nation.[40] As a result, although developments in Algeria were highlighted when relevant to wider arguments associations wished to make, on the whole *pied-noir* activists have preferred to focus their attention on the presence and behaviour of Algerians in France.

This presence has, according to Eric Savarèse, often been read through the prism of *pied-noir* experiences during the War of Independence, leading many to regard the contemporary Algerian community in the metropole as a threat to France in the same way that the FLN menaced colonial Algeria.[41] Such discourses have been given additional visibility and traction in a post-9/11 world, where Muslims are routinely painted as a terroristic threat to the West. In the wake of the attack on the Twin Towers, Véritas was only one of several *pied-noir* associations to remark that America was now experiencing the same fundamentalist-driven violence that they had been subjected to four decades previously in Algeria.[42] While the suggestion that anti-Arab racism was imported with the *pieds-noirs* in 1962 is flawed, not least because it ignores France's long history of discrimination, decolonisation has certainly shaped the character of these debates. Within *pied-noir* discourses, one way in which bitterness over the outcome of the Algerian War manifests itself is through hostility towards North Africans in France. What particularly rankles for *pieds-noirs* is their feeling that Algerians have been welcomed onto French soil while they can no longer live in Algeria and *harkis* cannot return even for visits.

Employing assimilationist rhetoric, associations often state that their objections are not to the presence of Algerians in France per se, but rather to their refusal to adopt French customs. According to *Pieds-noirs d'hier et d'aujourd'hui*, 'It is up to guests to make the effort to respect their hosts', rather than forcing their own cultural and religious traditions upon the nation.[43] Some associations go so far as to claim that the change in migratory patterns, from temporary stints completed by single men on a rotational basis to permanent family-based settlement, represents 'colonisation in reverse'; a deliberate attempt to culturally overwhelm France in revenge for the past.[44] Véritas has regularly argued that the continued arrival of Algerians represents an 'invasion' by 'a harmful immigration which believes that everything is owed to it'.[45] The emergence of hard-line groups like Véritas in the late 1990s, combined with ongoing public debates about immigration, headscarves and national identity has ensured that such discourses remain prominent within certain sections the *pied-noir* community.

As part of such rhetoric, the supposedly accommodating stance of the French government towards 'parasitic' migrants from North Africa and their descendants is juxtaposed with the hard work and self-sufficiency *pieds-noirs* were required to display in order to re-establish themselves when they arrived in 1962.[46] As Francette Mendosa indignantly protested to her readers:

Have we had charitable associations to carry us? No.
Have we created underground markets to survive? No
Have we burned cars? No
Have we attacked the police? NO.
We have rolled up our sleeves with the goal of sorting ourselves out, in the face of hostility towards us from parts of the [metropolitan] population.[47]

More than preferential treatment in a practical sense, in recent years *pied-noir* resentment towards Algerians in France has focused on what they see as the government's privileging of this history over theirs. Such arguments have always existed, but they have become more prevalent amidst the increasingly competitive commemorative climate. When the Cité nationale de l'histoire de l'immigration opened in 2007, the Cercle algérianiste noted 'without surprise' the speed at which the state had supported this project. This was viewed as especially galling when compared to the lack of progress on the long promised national memorial to 'overseas France' in Marseille, first mooted in the late 1980s, which, the association felt, had 'foundered in the shifting sands of political correctness'.[48]

The bulk of *pied-noir* commemorative resentment towards Algerians centres on 17 October 1961. Official silence in the wake of this night, combined with an acceleration of violence in France as the War of Independence drew to a close, including the death of nine Communists during an anti-OAS protest at the Charonne metro station on 8 February 1962, meant that 17 October 1961 was effectively 'forgotten' for many decades. It was brought back to public attention during the 1990s primarily through the activism of individuals with a personal connection to the event, such as Farid Aïchoune, and by the work of groups such as Au nom de la mémoire.[49] Today, a commemorative touchstone for the Algerian community in France, the night has attracted significant media and academic interest. It has also been the subject of a range of official gestures from the French state, most notably a plaque dedicated to those who died, which was unveiled on the Pont Saint Michel to mark the fortieth anniversary in 2001. Prominent left-wing politicians regularly attend the annual commemorations, including François Hollande as both presidential candidate in 2011 and then as president in 2012.

For *pied-noir* associations such attention is indicative of a wider commemorative imbalance whereby the French government falls over itself to recognise the loss of life of subversive militants, while deliberately ignoring the deaths of thousands of patriotic Frenchmen and women in Algeria, including the *harkis*. Groups such as Véritas argue that those who marched into the centre of Paris on 17 October were not peaceful civilians, but rather armed and dangerous enemies of the state. Therefore, not only was the actual loss of life far below what Jean Luc Einaudi claimed in his 'Marxist book', but any such deaths were justified as part of a necessary law and order exercise against the FLN, a 'small terrorist group at war with France'.[50] Victim status is thus denied to the Algerians and transferred instead to the *harkis* of the FPA who, it is claimed, were fired upon first and who only at that point responded by bravely defending the nation's capital, which was indeed their own nation's capital, as they

had done in the preceding weeks and months. Rallying against the practice of celebrating 'terrorists', a counter-demonstration was organised by
pied-noir associations to coincide with the unveiling of the Pont Saint
Michel memorial. Singing 'C'est nous les Africains' and shouting slogans
such as 'FLN assassins' and 'Where are our missing?', *pied-noir* protestors
demanded recognition for FLN victims in France. To this end they proposed an alternative plaque:

> To the memory of French victims of the FLN
> From 1956 to 1962 in the metropole
> 112 European civilians killed
> 597 European civilians injured
> 50 policemen and soldiers killed
> 393 policemen and soldiers injured.[51]

There are, in fact, certain similarities between 17 October 1961 and events
of 26 March 1962 on the rue d'Isly: a peaceful, unarmed crowd protesting against the imposition of harsh restrictions on their movements is
greeted with a disproportionate show of force by the French state and, as
a result, innocent civilians lose their lives. The event then disappears from
mainstream narratives of the war, creating a 'duty of memory' incumbent
upon witnesses to make the truth about what happened known. Yet, as
far as *pied-noir* associations are concerned, the different status of the victims imbues the two occasions with entirely opposite meanings.

Between empathy and envy: relationships between *harkis* and Algerians

Whereas *pied-noir* associations frequently used Algerians as a point of
contrast to the *harkis*, actual relationships between *harkis*, Algerians, and
their descendants are more complex. Although highly critical of the FLN
regime, both for its actions in 1962 and for its ongoing attitude towards
harkis, Besnaci-Lancou nonetheless asserted early in her autobiography
that 'My heart has always beaten to the rhythm of Algeria.' She went on to
conclude the book with the following statement: 'My dearest dream would
be a reconciliation with Algeria.'[52] Pursuing this objective, in September
2004 she met with former FLN militant Betoul Fekkar Lambiote in the
context of the annual Journée nationale d'hommage aux harkis. Engaged
in a conciliatory and hopeful dialogue, the two women agreed that
while adults undoubtedly retained strong emotions about the war, these
should not be passed onto subsequent generations.[53] Prior to the meeting, Besnaci-Lancou's association, Harkis et droits de l'Homme, issued a

manifesto in cooperation with the *pied-noir* associations RECOURS and Coup de soleil calling for the 're-appropriation of confiscated memories':

> Our parents, by choice, chance or force found themselves in different camps during the Algerian War. On both sides of the Mediterranean, the participants in this war have been classified according to a simplistic duality: the good guys on one side and the bad guys on the other. This simplification of history has taken root and has generated parallel paths, without words, between *harkis* and immigrants when everything [in their postcolonial situation] united them.[54]

Seeking to bring together these parallel itineraries, a few weeks later Besnaci-Lancou participated the annual commemoration of 17 October 1961 in the hope that both Algerians and *harkis* could 'accept their heritage with dignity and in fraternity'. Although many commended her actions, Besnaci-Lancou's stance was not universally appreciated with one 1961 demonstrator, Mohamed Barka, telling reporters 'The *harkis* have no place here. If I were the child of a *harki* I would be ashamed to come here'.[55] Equally controversial was the fact that Besnaci-Lancou agreed with Lambiote's suggestion that Algerians should not judge children of *harkis* for the actions of their parents, but rather pardon them. This position drew considerable ire from military figures such as Faivre, from the *pied-noir* community, and also from other *harki* activists. Mohamed Haddouche, then president of AJIR, used the pages of *La Lettre de Véritas* to claim that 'Asking for pardon from the FLN, it's liking asking the victim of cruelty to request forgiveness from their torturer!'[56] Such reactions indicate the ongoing tensions between the two communities and the challenges faced by those, like Besnaci-Lancou, who wish to foster a dialogue.[57]

One reason for the persistence of such obstacles is that vested social, economic and political interests keep both sides fixed in particular stances. The higher commemorative stakes of the current era, combined with the longevity of the issues involved, reduces the incentives for activists to risk moving away from their established positions.[58] But behind the proclamations of community and association representatives there is evidence that the reality is one of increasingly normalised interaction between descendants of *harkis* and Algerians in France. The renewed national preoccupation with the War of Independence has resulted in more information in the public domain about the conflict and those who participated in it, leading to greater levels of understanding concerning the experiences of *harkis* among children of Algerians in France. With this comes the ability to empathise with the situation of the *harkis* and

appreciate the similarities between the communities, while simultaneously acknowledging the ways in which the differences between their
parents have shaped their respective trajectories. As Farida, the daughter
of Algerians, put it:

> I think that *harki* families have been very badly welcomed, not only ma-
> terially but without any recognition of their political and military engage-
> ment … In comparison [with the Algerian immigrant population] the
> *harkis* experienced the same material difficulties but combined, in add-
> ition, with the rejection of the community from which they originated.

When asked how relations between the two communities could be improved, Farida emphasised the need for each side to 'respect without
judging' the choices and the 'non choices' of the other.[59] Haddouche, in
his capacity as AJIR president, similarly called for both sides to 'fully
accept the history of a common past in order to construct a future together'.[60] Although his critical response to Besnaci-Lancou's meeting
with Fekkar Lambiote cited above suggests that this is perhaps something
that is easier to profess than to realise in practice.

Anthropologist Giulia Fabbiano has coined the term 'post-Algerian'
to denote the space in which progressive links at the level of children and,
particularly, grandchildren of *harkis* and Algerians have been forged.
This is evidenced, among other things, by the growth of so-called 'mixed'
marriages and the increasing acceptance of this phenomenon by older
generations.[61] In this post-Algerian space, a shared understanding of the
past exists that differs in emphasis from that of previous generations and
which, due to the amount of time that has now elapsed, is less emotionally charged.[62] Nonetheless, points of tension remain, including the persistence of the taunt 'son of a traitor' levelled at children of *harkis*. Even
if, as Fabbiano argues, this phrase has lost some of its potency and is used
more as a convenient insult in disputes about other matters, it remains a
symbol of the sense of continuing exclusion from the Algerian community felt by some *harki* descendants.[63]

What has also persisted is sense of competition between the two
groups and a consequent sensitivity when preferential treatment is seen
as being accorded to one over the other. Whereas in the 1980s antago-
nism revolved primarily around material assistance, today symbolic support is equally relevant amidst recent high-profile government gestures
made towards both communities. Envy and resentment stemming from
perceived favouritism is often framed in terms of the different 'loyalties'
displayed by the two groups during the War of Independence. 'Me, I distinguish between the son of an immigrant and me', *fils de harki* Rachid

angrily told Régis Pierret. Expanding on this point, in language reminiscent of much *pied-noir* association discourse, he went on to argue:

> Immigrants, most of them fought against the French flag, they are here, they say that they are French... Me, what bothers me, it's for our parents, they cannot even go back [to Algeria] to see their dead. In contrast, they [immigrants], they come here, they go back there, they do what they want. They come here, they take advantage of everything, they insult us, what's that about?[64]

Thus, while there are descendants seeking reconciliation and ways to construct co-operative relationships, there remain others for whom the war and its legacies represent a fundamental and unbridgeable divide.

The anger that exists among certain *harki* descendants towards Algerians is not mirrored in the testimonies of their parents. Indeed, although they nostalgically evoke Algeria, there are almost no references made by *harkis* and their spouses to the present-day Algerian community, on either side of the Mediterranean. While for Algerians who spent the war in France and then remained, the nature of their experiences combined with the memorial dominance of 17 October 1961 means that the *harkis* of the FPA feature more prominently in their recollections than auxiliaries who served in Algeria. There is no denying that the Paris-based *harkis* were both hated and feared as a result of the harassment and brutality to which they subjected their fellow Algerians. 'Collaborators, henchmen, little chiefs [*petits caïds*], bastards' was how one Algerian referred to them, while another described the FPA as 'terror repatriated from Algeria'.[65] Yet, attitudes are not universally hostile. For former *harki* Ali Tebib, although contact between the two groups was 'impossible' in the 1960s, gradually 'relations with my Algerian cousins have improved'.[66] This improvement has entailed both recognition of the difficult situation faced by those who became *harkis* and a certain degree of empathy. Having witnessed the humiliating poverty inflicted upon Algerians by French colonialism, former FLN militant Saad Abssi stated that he was able to understand why people enrolled with the French, even if he also confessed that 'I do not know how I would react if I were actually faced with a *harki*.'[67]

The struggle for power between the FLN and the MNA, characterised by Algerians as a political war being waged above their heads that they were unable to avoid getting caught up in, seems also to have enhanced their ability to empathise with the *harkis*. In the same way that it was possible to have relatives fighting for the FLN and for the French, it was equally possibly for families to contain members of both nationalist factions. This was the case for Arezki Amazouz, whose mother's relatives joined the FLN, while his father, who was living in France at the time, allied himself with the MNA.[68] In a further demonstration of the fluidity of allegiances during the conflict, the decimation of the MNA by the FLN led some Algerians to become *harkis* as a way to protect themselves and their families from reprisals. This is not to deny that some Algerians did make conscious, politically motivated choices, particularly when it came to fighting for the nationalist cause. But it is noticeable that outside of official histories produced by and for the FLN, this aspect is generally not emphasised. Overall, testimony from Algerians, like that from *harkis,* acknowledges that people's actions during the war were dictated by a range of factors linked to the exigencies of an all-encompassing conflict that were often beyond the control of individuals.

The postcolonial trajectories of *harkis* and Algerians evince further commonalities, particularly concerning the manner in which their memories have entered the public domain. Like the *harkis,* silence was the dominant characteristic of the Algerian community for decades until activism by their descendants in the 1990s, much of it centred around commemorating 17 October 1961, brought forth the voices of those who had lived through these events. Underpinning this initial silence were a list of factors shared by both *harkis* and Algerians, including the absence of supportive *cadres sociaux*; economic, cultural and linguistic barriers; psychological inhibitions stemming from fear and trauma; and the difficulty of explaining a choice taken in very specific and complex circumstance to those with no first-hand knowledge of those conditions. Growing up amidst silence from within their own communities while being simultaneously defined and stigmatised by externally imposed interpretations pushed descendants of Algerians to embark upon endeavours similar to those of Kerchouche, Besnaci-Lancou and Hamoumou to retrieve and rehabilitate their parents' histories. Two prominent examples are Yamina Benguigui, who created the critically acclaimed documentary *Mémoires d'immigrés: l'héritage maghrébin* which captured the testimony of fathers, mothers and children from within the North African community in France, and the author Mehdi Lallaoui, who is also one of the animating forces behind the collective Au nom de la mémoire, which has done much to promote awareness of 17 October 1961.[69] Through their endeavours, figures like Benguigui and Lallaoui have sought to obtain a better understanding of their own identities and place within the French nation with the resultant narratives, like those from the *harki* community, combining the voices and agendas of multiple generations.

In terms of Algerian accounts now in the public domain, although there are obvious differences to the experiences of the *harkis,* there are also similarities. These include physical concentration in specific, often marginal, locales; the discrimination and exclusion to which they and their children have been subjected; the de-emphasising of ideological components in narratives of their wartime activities; and a complex postcolonial relationship to Algeria and France. These connections suggest the utility of moving away from histories that consider the *harkis* as wholly apart from the wider Algerian community in France.[70] Although singular in many respects, the history of the *harki* community can and should be related to the trajectories of their fellow countrymen. Such a move would furthermore contribute to the fulfilment of Sylvia Thénault's call for a research agenda that better acknowledges the fluidity of positions taken during the War of Independence and the complexities of its consequences.

The media

The rise in public attention devoted to the War of Independence has been both driven by and reflected in a greater representation of this history within the French media. As discussed in the previous chapter, *harki* descendants sought to capitalise on the increasing interest shown by this important vector of transmission in order to broaden public understanding of their community and its history. A more visible *harki* presence began with *Les Années algériennes,* which drew heavily on interviews with Saïd Ferdi, and continued in 1993 with the two-part documentary *Les harkis* devoted exclusively to the community. Aired in the wake of another summer of protests, to some extent *Les harkis* replicated pre-existing patterns by inviting military figures to speak on behalf of the *auxiliaries.* But the programme also attempted to break new ground by emphasising the different roles that fell under the generic harki label and by not shying away from evoking the violent nature of the auxiliaries' experiences, whether as victims or perpetrators.[71] Coverage accelerated in the new millennium, fuelled by high-profile events such as Bouteflika's state visit and the establishment of the Journée nationale d'hommage aux harkis. While the old guard of spokespeople from the *pied-noir,* military and *français musulman* milieux remained present and continued to reiterate their version of *harki* history, the balance tipped noticeably in favour of testimony from within the *harki* community itself, especially from younger generations.[72] There have also been conscious efforts to overturn various stereotypes about the *harkis,* including *La blessure: la tragédie des harkis,* which aired in September 2010. The documentary eschewed the usual scenario of interviewing elderly, slightly dishevelled *harkis* in the now derelict camps, their thick accents and broken French necessitating subtitles, thus underlining their ongoing marginality within the nation. Instead, viewers were presented with smartly dressed, articulate men sitting in mainstream spaces such as libraries. Focusing on *harkis* rather than their descendants, producers Isabelle Clarke and Daniel Costelle deliberately sought to challenge the still-dominant media portrayal of the community as unable to integrate successfully.[73]

In contrast to broadly sympathetic portrayals of the *harkis,* the relationship between *pieds-noirs* and the French media has been more fraught, primarily because of what activists see as the consistently biased and inaccurate portrait of the community diffused in the press, on television and over the radio. According to Pierre Dimech, the Cercle algérianiste's resident expert on the subject, this 'misinformation', which has multiple format and sources, entered a particularly virulent phase during the 1990s, having lain more or less dormant for the preceding three decades.[74] For example, although 'apparently plural', the written press was, according to *pied-noir* associations in reality, controlled by groups with the 'same source of inspiration', while television was under the sway of a forceful 'one directional wind' emanating from the 'anti-France political-media lobby'.[75] *Pied-noir* associations have thus mobilised against what they regard as a politically motivated conspiracy to distort history. The Cercle algérianiste has a well-established 'Committee of Vigilance and Riposte' alongside close ties to the Editions de l'Atlanthrope publishing house. Created in the 1970s by the Cercle's co-founder, Jacques Villard, the Editions de l'Atlanthrope is dedicated to disseminating texts by and for the wider *pied-noir* community. Countering 'misinformation' was an equally potent rationale behind the appearance of more hard-line *pied-noir* organisations in the 1990s. Véritas, whose full title is the 'Committee for the re-establishment of the historical truth about French Algeria', fervently pursued this mission through their regular 'Falsifiers of History' column, which responded to any negative coverage of the *pieds-noirs* across a broad range of media. The founding of *Pieds-noirs magazine* in 1990 was similarly deemed necessary by its editor Jean-Marc Lopez so that the truth could be disseminated by 'our own media' instead of having to rely on others, who 'always distort everything'.[76]

Framed as a David and Goliath style struggle, the combat against 'misinformation' is one that activists have committed to fighting with 'our bare hands. Until our last breath. And even beyond'.[77] One of the most common tactics employed is to sign petitions or write letters of complaint to various bodies and individuals highlighting inaccuracies in their presentation of the *pieds-noirs*. Here, the 'misinformation' itself matters less than the opportunity correcting it provides to publicly reiterate the central tenets of the collective lexicon. In the past two decades such activities have become more common with no one, from the president of the Republic down, deemed either too great or too small to spill ink over. With a greater range of competing historical narratives now in the public domain, it is no longer sufficient for association members to passively read and reminisce about past glories, this history now has to be actively defended by each and every *pied-noir* against increasingly visible alternative interpretations. Signifying the growth of more active forms of association participation befitting the increasingly dynamic commemorative context, letter writing offers a way to perpetuate a sense of communal belonging and engagement after the last page of the association's magazine or *newspaper* is turned. It requires effort, demonstrates investment and will, hopefully, galvanise others. As an aging population, the majority of whom are now retired, the *pied-noir* community are furthermore ideally placed to exercise the necessary vigilance against 'misinformation'.

Although very little escapes the notice of activists, there is a proportionate relationship between the profile of the media representation in question and the ensuing reaction. The broadcasting in the early 1990s of the documentary series' *La Guerre d'Algérie* and *Les Années algériennes* were therefore exceptional, not only in terms of the comprehensiveness of their treatments of the War of Independence, but for the level of commentary they provoked within the *pied-noir* community. Labelled 'the most violent media aggression' directed at the community since the exodus of 1962, Batty's *La Guerre d'Algérie* was deemed so objectionable that the Cercle algérianiste established a specific committee of opposition which they called 'Forbidden to dogs and *pieds-noirs*' in reference to the assertion by one documentary interviewee that neither Arabs nor dogs were allowed onto certain beaches during French rule.[78] Such criticism paled, however, in comparison to the opprobrium directed at the 'very subversive' *Les Années algériennes*, with Stora's Algerian origins adding an extra edge to the accusations levelled by *pied-noir* associations.[79] *L'Algérianiste* subjected the documentary to a twenty-three-page autopsy before concluding that rather than a historical endeavour, it represented 'an uncontrolled subjectivity' anchored in the most crass stereotypes of the settlers.[80]

Pied-noir objections to both documentaries, and to 'misinformation' more generally, stem from what they regard as an unbalanced content that favours the FLN and their supporters, while ignoring their suffering.

Such criticisms are also indicative of changes in media representations of the War of Independence, particularly on television. Documentaries such as *La Guerre d'Algérie* and *Les Années algériennes* aimed to provide broad-based coverage of the entire war, rather than simply focusing on the final few months as *pied-noir* associations were wont to do. They, and the programmes which followed, also purposefully highlighted aspects of the war that most *pied-noir* associations preferred to omit or downplay: the inequalities of the colonial system, the practice of torture by the French army, the violence of the OAS, and 17 October 1961. *Les années algériennes* furthermore ushered in a new era in terms of the way in which the conflict was discussed on camera. Host Daniel Bilalian heralded the studio debate following the final instalment of the series as the first time protagonists from all sides of the conflict had been assembled together on French television.[81] The diverse perspectives of figures including Bernard Tricot, one of the negotiators of the Evian Accords, Henri Martinez, a former OAS commando, *harki* Rachid Mimouni and former FLN militants Yacef Saadi and Mohammed Harbi ensured a lively programme.[82] In addition to providing compelling viewing, the passionate debates that arose from this and other similar programmes reinforced the idea that guests and the communities they represented were engaged in a fight against other actors and other versions of events. The hope of host Norbert Balit that participants would be able to 'speak dispassionately' in the programme following the final instalment of *La Guerre d'Algérie* has therefore never been realised.[83] On this and subsequent occasions, bringing together protagonists from different side of the conflict has rarely resulted in constructive or even informative dialogue. Instead, representative reiterate their own or their community's existing stance, while seeking to refute, as forcefully as possible, the propositions advanced by others. The considerable public exposure afforded by television only heightens the stakes of such exchanges and thus the intransigence of the views expressed.[84]

Prior to the 1990s, debates and documentaries on the war were less frequent and dealt largely with a single subject, event or group. Within this restricted offering, the *pieds-noirs* and their views were generally well represented with at least one community spokesperson present, often Jacques Roseau. There were also several occasions when *pieds-noirs* constituted the majority of participants, or were the sole focus of programmes.[85] Yet, the right to express their opinions is not something that *pied-noir* associations believe the French media has ever properly accorded them. Even when invited to participate in televised debates, as they continue to be to the present day, *pied-noir* activists still feel that they are not given the opportunity to speak freely. Michel Lagrot told *L'Algérianiste* that he felt unable to comment openly during an episode of *Ça se discute* in 2000 devoted to the question of what remained of *pied-noir* culture due to the fact that 'intellectual terrorism is sometimes obliged to resort to physical terrorism' and he was 'not completely sure of assistance' should such circumstances arise.[86]

Although there are certainly some activists who relish the opportunity to combatively debate the past, others prefer programmes produced by members of their own community, such as *Exergue* by Catherine Jeannin. Broadcast in the summer of 1992, it warmed the heart of AOCAZ president Geneviève de Ternant by enabling her to retrieve 'the true face of our fraternal and dynamic Algeria'. This 'true face' included all the key elements of the historical lexicon from the humble and hard-working settler, through the multicultural harmony of colonial Algeria, to the creation of the modern-day *pied-noir* 'without a land but not without culture'. Particularly revealing was de Ternant's concluding remark: 'For once a voice was given neither to the *porteurs de valises* nor to the FLN.'[87] Fifteen years later, Gilles Perez's three-part documentary, *Pieds-noirs, histoires d'une blessure* was given a similarly positive reception, the filmmaker's own *pied-noir* lineage deemed instrumental in creating sympathetic portrayal in line with wider collective discourses.[88]

'We are the witnesses'

Another important vector of transmission with which *pied-noir* associations and activists have a difficult relationship is the academic community. Scholars who advance supportive readings of the *pied-noir* past have been favourably received. Figures such as Faivre, Jean-Jacques Jordi, Jeanine de la Hogue and Jeanine Verdès-Leroux have all collaborated with associations, while the latter three also served as historical consultants on *Pieds-noirs, histoires d'une blessure*. The reverse is equally true: academics who have adopted more critical stances regularly have both their work and themselves denounced. This treatment has been meted out to an illustrious roster of names including Einaudi, Charles Robert Ageron, Raphaëlle Branche, Sylvie Thénault, Claude Liauzu and Claire Mauss-Copeaux, whose book on conscript soldiers during the Algerian War *Véritas* judged had 'probably come straight out of a false but fertile imagination'.[89] One individual, however, stands out in terms of the level of *pied-noir* opprobrium he attracts: Stora. His Algerian roots, left-wing political leanings and prominent media profile make him an obvious target for *pied-noir* associations who have variously described him as a 'Trotskyiste specialist of misinformation' and a 'pseudo-intellectual who distorts historical truth at his pleasure through the prism of his bad faith'.[90] But more than this, objections to Stora reflect a conflict between history and memory that lies at the heart of association discourses and discussions of the Franco-Algerian past more generally.

For Stora, a historian should be someone who, in seeking to explain the past, 'situates themselves within a rational logic' and who adopts a 'critical distance'.[91] Aware that the historian 'is not above the melee' and having never denied his own *engagé* status, Stora nonetheless understands his role as participating in research and dialogue in order to restore the past in its full intricacy. Although acknowledging the ways in which memory informs history and vice versa has been the crux of much of his own work, Stora still views the two phenomena as distinct.[92] In contrast, many *pied-noir* activists find it difficult to distinguish between history and memory. Rather than rigorous intellectual interrogation from a critical distance, *pied-noir* associations tend to present history as experience-based recollection in which authenticity is automatically accorded to witness testimony.

Whereas Stora argues that 'memory constitutes the object of study on which historical reflection rests', *pied-noir* associations take the view that memory is the source of history. They therefore place a greater store in personal accounts than in archives, believing that 'those who have not experienced this complex Algeria cannot truly represent it'.[93] This is not merely the sign of a healthy degree of scepticism towards archives and what they do or do not contain. If an official source can be found that supports a *pied-noir* reading of an event then this is often held to be sacrosanct as demonstrated by the ways in which the work of Faivre, who has explored military archives in great detail, is used. It is also reflected in the establishment of a series of *pied-noir* created and curated repositories to help ensure the preservation of materials relating to their past. The first such institution was the Centre de documentation historique sur l'Algérie (CDHA), which was founded in 1974 in Aix-en-Provence, where France's colonial archives are also housed. This was followed by the Centre d'études pied-noir (CEPN), which was located in Nice and, more recently, in 2012, by the Centre de documentation des Français d'Algérie (CDDFA) in Perpignan. Outlining its raison d'être, the CDHA noted that 'History is not written by the vanquished', going on to express the belief that 'we certainly must not count on anyone other than ourselves to recreate the climate [of French Algeria]'.[94] Such initiatives respond to the sense among certain *pieds-noirs* that 'history is made without them and in opposition to them' while simultaneously enabling activists to counter this by curating alternative narratives.[95]

The process of academic inquiry, especially the critical examination of a range of evidence, is often perceived by associations as personally motivated attack. In the wake of *Les Années algériennes,* Stora received abusive and threatening letters from members of the *pied-noir* community, while the obituary for Liauzu offered by the Cercle algérianiste described him as the 'relentless adversary of all expressions of *pied-noir* memory and pain'.[96] Such comments stem from the feeling that academic discourse constitutes a form of violation because it strips the *pied-noir* experience of 'its emotional singularity', reducing decolonisation to a subject like any other. As Stora correctly notes, *pieds-noirs* 'do not want their pain to be drowned in an ocean of footnotes at the bottom of the page'.[97] Yet, although attuned to the trauma suffered by *pieds-noirs* and its legacies, Stora has also made clear what he considers the limitations of consistently basing discussions about the Algerian War in the emotionally charged realm of personal memory.[98]

It is not the case that Stora, or indeed any historian, is seeking to deny a place to *pied-noir* memories, but rather to stress that this place is as one source among many. However, the idea that memory is not equivalent to history is anathema to many *pied-noir* associations who have based much of their discourse on precisely such an equation. This conflation of history and memory is indicative of a wider trend that has seen the status of testimony elevated from being 'second best to the archives', to a valuable source in its own right.[99] First-hand accounts are today, rightly, regarded as a vital component of contemporary history, offering insights into aspects of the past that would otherwise remain unknown. This heightened respect for bearing witness, which has its antecedents in the legacy of the Holocaust, has been given a further impetus by the growth in popularity of oral history. Together these have produced a greater willingness amongst people to divulge their experiences, helping to create a virtuous circle of testimony. These accounts, particularly when disseminated through the mass media, also appeal because they appear to democratise and enhance the accessibility of the past; the words of an anonymous bystander being regarded as equally valuable as those of a statesman. This is particularly true of the Internet, which, more than any other medium, breaks down the hierarchies of memories, while collapsing distinctions between different type of discourses.[100] As Eric Savarèse has suggested, one reason testimony is so valued by *pied-noir* associations is because it is seen as a way of levelling an otherwise unequal playing field, authenticating a counter-narrative that must compete against the institutional legitimacy accorded, as a matter of course, to academic experts such as Stora.[101]

Although not without its problems, the increasing acknowledgement of the value of testimony has enriched and broadened history immensely. However, in the hands of certain *pied-noir* groups, being an eyewitness has become the ultimate and, indeed, only criteria of historical authenticity. As such, it is less a tool through which to explore the past and more a weapon for excluding alternative sources and interpretations. This was the sense in which the editor of *La Lettre de Véritas* used it when she wrote the following:

> We are the witnesses. Living witnesses, often eye-witnesses, and, in this capacity, we represent a much more important source of information for those who want to objectively write history than the archives which they are authorised more and more to consult. Biased, truncated archives, falsified by their authors in order to better conceal their crimes![102]

This is not, of course, a phenomenon confined solely to the *pied-noir* community. During the studio discussion that followed the broadcast of his documentary *L'ennemi intime*, filmmaker Patrick Rotman engaged in a heated debate with General Maurice Schmitt who strongly objected to Rotman's portrayal of the army's involvement in torture. Responding to Schmitt's accusation that the documentary was inaccurate and unrepresentative, Rotman countered that he had interviewed dozens of people who corroborated the accounts that were shown in the final cut. Was Schmitt questioning the testimony relating to FLN attacks on civilians or the experiences of the *harki* who was tortured, Rotman asked, or just the veracity of those whose views he disagreed with?[103] Similarly, in expressing his objections to Kerchouche's memoire *Mon père, ce harki*, Faivre attributed the book's 'mistakes' to the fact that the author had no direct experience of camp life and was thus basing her interpretation on the testimony of others received forty years later. Instead, Faivre suggested, she should have relied on the evidence contained within official archives, as he does, rather than on 'negative judgements from those who've failed to integrate'.[104] Yet, tellingly, he sought to refute Kerchouche's claims by assembling testimonies from former social workers and others involved with the running of the camps, who could assert, based on personal observations, that 'Life in the camps was not inhumane as some claim'.[105]

For those who stand at the intersection between academia and activism, navigating between history and memory can be particularly complicated. As a scholar of the *harki* community, Hamoumou is dedicated to breaking with the simplified narratives of previous eras. 'It is time', he informed readers of *Le Figaro* in 1990, 'to refuse myths and hoaxes and to acknowledge the complexity of a civil war rooted in colonial history in order to understand who the *harkis* were'.[106] Yet as an activist, he is motivated by a sense of personal commitment to obtain justice for the community to which he belongs. These two imperatives do not always sit comfortably together. In lending his support to Boussad Azni's 2001 lawsuit indicting the French state for crimes against humanity with respect to their actions towards the *harkis* in 1962, Hamoumou claimed that it represented a necessary 'new mode of action', since demonstrations and hunger strikes 'have not been sufficient to obtain a just reparation'. He nonetheless remained aware of the potential problems of such an approach, warning against making 'hasty and abusive generalisations'.[107]

The tensions, between history and memory, between experience and other forms of knowledge, are neither new nor unique to the Algerian War. However, they have acquired a particular acuity since the 1990s owing to the commemorative context that now surrounds discussions of the conflict. As the various case studies in this chapter have shown, most often for the groups and individuals concerned, 'The issue is not to understand the past, but to be right'.[108] In pursuing this objective, groups have co-operated with those who they feel can assist them, while simultaneously pitting themselves against those perceived as enemies using a variety of tactics in an attempt to gain control over historical and commemorative narratives. The ultimate prize in terms of an ally is the French state because of its capacity to confer legitimacy upon particular interpretations. As the following chapter will show, competing for this coveted support has taken memory-based activism into new terrains. In the same way that the actions of other communities have influenced *pied-noir* and *harki* activists, so too have broader international developments. The result has been a convergence of activism around globally prominent themes such as judicialisation, victimhood and repentance as *pieds-noirs* and *harkis* alike sought to anchor their own campaigns within frameworks that transcended the borders of the nation.

Notes

1 Henry Rousso, 'Les Raisins verts de la guerre d'Algérie', in *La Guerre d'Algérie (1954–1962)*, ed. by Yves Michaud (Paris, 2004), p. 139.

2 For further discussion of this, see Mireille Rosello, *The Reparative in Narratives: Works of Mourning in Progress* (Liverpool, 2010), p. 4.

3 Benjamin Stora, *Les Guerres sans fin: un historien, la France et l'Algérie* (Paris, 2008), p. 103.

4 Pascal Blanchard and Isabelle Veyrat-Masson, 'Les Guerres de mémoires: un objet d'études, au carrefour de l'histoire et des processus de médiatisation', in *Les Guerres de mémoires: la France et son histoire*, ed. by Pascal Blanchard and Isabelle Veyrat-Masson (Paris, 2008), p. 24.

5   Georges Dillinger, 'Brève évocation de la fin de l'Algérie', *La Lettre de Véritas*, 93 (May 2005), 11.

6   Jim House and Neil MacMaster, *Paris 1961: Algerians, State Terror and Memory* (Oxford, 2006), p. 315.

7   Antoine Prost, 'The Algerian War in French Collective Memory', in *War and Remembrance in the Twentieth Century*, ed. by Jay Winter and Emmanuel Sivan (Cambridge, 1999), p. 166.

8   Florence Beaugé, 'Torturée par l'armée française en Algérie, "Lila" recherché l'homme qui l'a sauvée', *Le Monde* (20 June 2000), p. 1.

9   See, for example, Pierre-Henri Simon, *Contre la torture* (Paris, 1957); Henri Alleg, *La Question* (Paris, 1958); Pierre Vidal-Naquet, *L'affair Audin* (Paris, 1958).

10 Jacques Massu, *La Vrai bataille d'Alger* (Paris, 1971).

11 Paul Aussaresses, *Services spéciaux: Algérie 1955–1957* (Paris, 2001); Paul Aussaresses, *Je n'ai pas tout dit: ultimes révélations au service de la France* (Paris, 2008).

12 Stora's comments were made during an episode of *Arrêt sur images*, aired 7 January 2001 (La cinquième). Aussaresses was also present as a guest on the programme.

13 'Courrier des lecteurs', *France horizon*, 414–15 (September–October 2000), 17.

14 Louis Albertelli, Amar Boumaraf and Anne Cazal, 'Bouteflikabulations', *La Lettre de Véritas*, 45 (September 2000), 7.

15 See *La Voix du combatant – La Voix du djebel-flame* produced by the UNC-AFN; *L'ancien de l'Algérie*, published by FNACA since 1958.

16 Although Méliani is of Algerian origin, as a career soldier who trained at the prestigious Saint Cyr military academy and who has risen to the rank of Colonel, he has more in common with the likes of Moinet and Faivre than with the *harkis* on whose behalf he speaks.

17 No longer in Algeria in 1962, Moinet was unable to organise a similar act, although he did resign from the army in protest over the French state's treatment of the *harkis*.

18 Maurice Faivre, *Un village de harkis: des Babors au pays drouais* (Paris, 1994); Bernard Moinet, *Journal d'une agonie* (Paris, 1965; reprinted 1999); Bernard Moinet, *Ahmed? connais pas: le calvaire des harkis* (Paris, 1989); Abd-el-Aziz Méliani, *Le Drame des harkis* (Paris, 2001); François Meyer, *Pour l'honneur, avec les harkis: de 1958 à nos jours* (Tours, 2005).

19 *Harkis: soldats abandonnés* (Paris, 2012), p. 166.

20 *Harkis: soldats abandonnés*, p. 65.

21 Roger Fiorio, 'Hommage aux harkis, mes compagnons, mes frères', *L'Algérianiste*, 97 (March 2002), 4.

22 *Harkis: soldats abandonnés*, pp. 21, 86.

23 Thierry Rolando, 'Mémoire d'avenir', *L'Algérianiste*, 99 (September 2002), 3; Yves Sainsot, 'Grève de faim des enfants des harkis', *France horizon*, 384–5 (July–August 1997), 12.

24 Thierry Rolando, 'Le Temps de la justice et la vérité est-il enfin venu?', *L'Algérianiste*, 95 Supplement (September 2001), 1.

25 Jo Sohet, 'Les Harkis, ces oubliés de l'histoire 1962–1978', *L'Algérianiste*, 5 (15 March 1979), 27.

26 Clarisse Buono, *Pieds-noirs de père en fils* (Paris, 2004), p. 131.

27 Meyer, *Pour l'honneur*, p. 9.

28 For coverage of these protests in the national media, see Julien Martin, 'Des militants de la cause des harkis occupent le siège du PS', *Libération* (18 February 2006), p. 14; Benoît Hopquin, 'A Paris, les harkis manifestent pour retrouver une dignité bafouée', *Le Monde* (28 March 2006), p. 14.

29 Maurice Faivre, 'Désinformation de l'histoire des harkis par la télévision', *L'Algérianiste*, 117 (March 2007), 5.

30 Pierre Cattin, 'Un crime sans assassins', *La Lettre de Véritas*, 90 (February 2005), 4.

31 Cattin, 'Un crime', 4.

32 Maurice Faivre, *L'action sociale de l'armée en faveur des musulmans, 1830–2006* (Paris, 2007), p. 146.

33 The campaign sought to obtain 150,000 signatures on a petition demanding that homage be paid to what AJIR estimated to be the 150,000 victims of the postwar massacres. Mohand Hamoumou, 'AJIR pour les Harkis', *La Lettre de Véritas*, 54 (June 2001), 11.

34 AJIR, 'Point de vue: un traité d'amitié Franco-Algérien', *Pieds-noirs d'hier et d'aujourd'hui*, 135 (November 2005), 12.

35 For further discussion of this phenomenon, see Claire Eldridge, 'The *Pied-Noir* Community and the Complexity of "Coming Home" to Algeria', in *Coming Home? Vol. 2: Conflict and Postcolonial Return Migration in the Context of France and North Africa, 1962–2009*, ed. by Scott Soo and Sharif Gemie (Newcastle-upon-Tyne, 2013), pp. 12–32.

36 Among innumerable articles advancing this view a particularly good example is Michel Sanchez, 'Réfléxion: décolonisations bâclées: histoire ou actualité?', *Pieds-noirs magazine*, 22 (January 1992), 26.

37 Pierre Reveillaud, 'Le Feu en Algérie', *France horizon*, 343 (June–July 1993), 24; 'L'Algérie d'aujourd'hui', *France horizon*, 588–9 (January–February 1998), 12.

38 Jean Augeai, 'Rien n'a changé!', *France horizon*, 357 (December 1994), 24; Maurice Faivre, 'L'Algérie et les historiens', *L'Algérianiste*, 83 (September 1995), 100–2.

39 A. Bendetti, 'Pour qui sonne le glas?', *France horizon*, 372–3 (May–June 1996), 24.

40 This is also a pattern noted by Gert Oostindie with respect to repatriates from the Dutch East Indies. See 'Ruptures and Dissonance: Post-Colonial Migrations and the Remembrance of Colonialism in the Netherlands', in *Memories of Post-Imperial Nations: The Aftermath of Decolonization, 1945–2013*, ed. by Dietmar Rothermund (Cambridge, 2015), p. 42.

41 Eric Savarèse, 'Un regard compréhensif sur le "traumatisme historique". A propos de vote Front national chez les pieds-noirs', *Pôle Sud*, 34:1 (2011), 99–100.

42 'Le Terrorisme aveugle, lâche et inhumain', *La Lettre de Véritas*, 56 (October 2001), 1; Anne Cazal, 'Le coeur Américain', *La Lettre de Véritas*, 56 (October 2001), p. 3. For a broader discussion of this phenomenon, see Claire Eldridge, 'Returning to the "Return": Pied-Noir Memories of 1962', *Revue européenne des migrations internationals*, 29:3 (December 2013), 121–40.

43 Gérard Méulion, 'Lettre ouverte à Monsieur Tahar Ben Jelloun', *Pieds-noirs d'hier et d'aujourd'hui*, 90 (May 1998), 6; Jacky Pons, 'Tribune libre: la France prise en otage', *Pieds-noirs d'hier et d'aujourd'hui*, 54 (February 1995), 6.

44 Christopher Flood and Hugo Frey, 'Defending the Empire in Retrospect: The Discourse of the Extreme Right', in *Promoting the Colonial Idea: Propaganda and Visions of Empire in France*, ed. by Tony Chafer and Amanda Sackur (Basingstoke, 2002), p. 205.

45 Joseph Hattab Pacha, 'Le Mot du Président', *La Lettre de Véritas*, 7 (November 1996), 2.

46 Francette Mendosa, 'Editorial', *Aux échos d'Alger*, 72 (March 2001), 3.

47 The comments about 'burning cars' and 'attacking the police' refer to the periodic spates of urban unrest that wrack France's *banlieues*. Tellingly, Mendosa, like other *pieds-noirs* and many in the mainstream media, instinctively classed those committing such acts as immigrants, whereas in fact the vast majority are French citizens. Francette Mendosa, 'Editorial', *Aux échos d'Alger*, 91 (December 2003), 3. Emphasis in the original.

48 'Non à la Cité nationale de l'histoire de l'immigration', *L'Algérianiste*, 119 supplement (September 2007), 6.

49 Aïchoune, aged ten years old, participated in the women's demonstration of 20 October 1961 in protest against the events of the 17 October. For a comprehensive account of the memorial afterlives of 17 October, see House and MacMaster, *Paris 1961*, pp. 183–334.

50 Pierre Catin, 'Le Prétendu "massacre" des Algériens à Paris, le 17 octobre 1961', *La Lettre de Véritas*, 106 (October 2006), 4.

51 Nicole Ferrandis-Delaurre, 'Le 17 octobre dernier à Paris', *France horizon*, 425–6 (September-October 2001), 10.

52 Fatima Besnaci-Lancou, *Fille de harki*, with Marie-Christine Ray (Paris, 2003), p. 17, 119.

53 'Réconciliation algérienne', *TF1 20 heures*, aired 25 September 2004 (TF1).

54 Kerchouche and Hadjila Kemoum were also signatories to the manifesto. For the full text, see www.harki.net/article.php?id=6 [29 November 2013].

55 'Des enfants de harkis et d'immigrés commémorant samedi le 17 octobre 1961', *AFP Infos Françaises* (13 October 2004); 'Commémoration du 17 octobre 1961', *AFP Infos Françaises* (16 October 2004).

56 Mohamed Haddouche, 'Détournement de mémoire', *La Lettre de Véritas*, 89 (January 2005), 9. See also Faivre, *L'action sociale*, p. 145.

57 Géraldine Enjelvin and Nada Kovac-Kakabadse, 'France and the Memories of "Others": The Case of the *Harkis*', *History and Memory*, 24:1 (Spring/Summer 2012), 157.

58 Rosella Spina, *Enfants de harkis et enfants d'émigrés: parcours croisés, identités à recoudre* (Paris, 2012), p. 229.

59 Spina, *Enfants de harkis*, p. 196.

60 Spina, *Enfants de harkis*, p. 223.

61 For further discussion of 'mixed marriages' and the reactions they provoke, see Giulia Fabbiano, 'Mixité postcoloniale. Les unions des descendants d'émigrés algériens à l'épreuve de l'expérience migratoire parentale', *Diasporas*, 15 (2009), 99–110; Fatima Besnaci-Lancou, *Nos mères, paroles blessées* (Léchelle, 2006), p. 81.

62 Guilia Fabbiano, 'Mémoires postalgériennes: la guerre d'Algérie entre héritage et emprunts', in *La Concurrence mémorielle*, ed. by Geoffrey Grandjean and Jérôme Jamin (Paris, 2011), p. 137.

63 Fabbiano, 'Mémoires postalgériennes', p. 146.

64 Régis Pierret, *Les Filles et fils de harkis: entre double rejet et triple appartenance* (Paris, 2008), p. 147.

65 Arezki Amazouz cited in Sabrina Kassa, *Nos ancêtres les chibanis! Portrait d'Algériens arrivés en France pendant les Trente Glorieuses* (Paris, 2006), p. 132; 'Je ne regrette rien', *Les Années algériennes* [episode 3], prod. Benjamin Stora, aired 7 October 1991 (A2).

66 Kassa, *Nos ancêtres*, p. 120.

67 Kassa, *Nos ancêtres*, p. 76.

68 Kassa, *Nos ancêtres*, p. 132.

69 See *Mémoires d'immigrés: l'héritage maghrébin,* dir. Yamina Benguigui, aired 30 May 1997 (Canal+). Among Mehdi Lallaoui's outputs, see *Un siècle d'immigrations en France* (three episodes), aired 10 to 24 October 1997 (FR3); *Les Beurs de Seine* (Paris, 1986); *Du bidonville aux HLM* (Paris, 1993); *Exils, exodes, errances* (Bezons, 2003).

70 An interesting example of this was a three-part documentary that considered *harkis* and Algerians together as part of the history of a Muslim presence in France. See 'Immigrés, 1945–1981', *Musulmans de France*, aired 20 December 2009 (FR3).

71 'Les Harkis', *Planète chaude* (two episodes), aired 12 and 19 December 1993 (FR3).

72 See, for example, 'Les Harkis: les fils de l'oubli', *Les Cinq continents*, aired 8 November 1994 (FR3); 'Amère patrie', *Documents x3*, aired 13 October 2006 (FR5); 'Harkis: des français entièrement à part?', *Contre courant*, aired 25 April 2003 (FR2).

73 'La Blessure: la tragédie des harkis', *Hors série*, dir. Isabelle Clarke and Daniel Costelle, aired 20 September 2010 (FR3).

74 Pierre Dimech, *La Désinformation autour de la culture des pieds-noirs* (Paris, 2006), p. 9.

75 Dimech, *La Désinformation*, pp. 23, 32, 34; Jose Castano, 'Le lobby politico-médaitque de l'anti-France', *L'écho de l'Oranie*, 193 (November–December 1987), 4.

76 Jean-Marc Lopez in Danielle Michel-Chich, *Déracinés: les pieds-noirs aujourd'hui* (Paris, 2000), p. 170.

77 Dimech, *La Désinformation*, p. 93.

78 'Histoire Actualité', *L'Algérianiste*, 51 (September 1990), 3; Georges Bosc, 'Interdit aux chiens et aux pieds-noirs', *L'Algérianiste*, 51 (September 1990), 1.

79 Sanchez, 'Réflexion: décolonisations bâclées. 26.

80 'Les Années algériennes', *L'Algérianiste*, 56 (December 1991), 2.

81 Although other programmes had brought together a range of voices, the cast assembled to debate *Les Années algériennes* was notable for the presence of former members of the FLN, which was unique for the time.

82 'Spécial guerre d'Algérie', *Mardi soir*, aired 8 October 1991 (A2).

83 *La Guerre d'Algérie: malentendu ou absurdité?* aired 9 September 1990 (FR3).

84 Among the many examples, see, in particular, 'Guerre d'Algérie: la fin des mensonges', *Mots croisés*, aired 3 November 2003 (FR2); 'Spécial guerre d'Algerie', *Mots croisés*, aired 21 May 2001 (FR2); 'Harkis: la mémoire sacrifiée?', *Ripostes*, aired 7 December 2003 (FR5); 'Spécial Algérie', *Culture et dépendances*, aired 6 March 2002 (FR3).

85 See, for example, 'Pour ceux d'Algérie, que reste-t-il du passé?', *Les Dossiers de l'écran*, aired 5 April 1983 (A2); 'Droit de réponse aux pieds-noirs', *Droit de réponse*, aired 8 November 1986 (TF1); 'Rapatriés: 25 ans de nostalgie', *Camera 2*, aired 22 June 1987 (A2).

86 'Que reste-t-il de la culture pied-noir?', *Ça se discute*, aired 5 April 2000 (FR2); 'Ça se discute!', *L'Algérianiste*, 90 (June 2000), 2.

87 Geneviève de Ternant, 'Editorial', *L'écho de l'Oranie*, 221 (July–August 1992), 1.

88 *Les Pieds-noirs: histoires d'une blessure* (three episodes), dir. Gilles Perez, aired 24 and 31 March, 7 April 2007 (FR3).

89 Claire Mauss-Copeaux, *Appelés en Algérie: la parole confisquée* (Paris, 1999); Anne Cazal, 'Le Dernier mot à la barbarie', *La Lettre de Véritas*, 33 (May 1999), 3.

90 'Les Faussaires de l'Histoire', *La Lettre de Véritas*, 20 (February 1998), 5.

91 'Désinformation', *Pieds-noirs d'hier et d'aujourd'hui*, 66 (March 1996), 8; Benjamin Stora and Thierry Leclère, *La Guerre des mémoires: la France face à son passé colonial* (Paris, 2007), pp. 89–91.

92 See, in particular, Stora's trilogy of autobiographical histories which explore how his own experiences have informed his research trajectory. Benjamin Stora, *La Dernière génération d'octobre* (Paris, 2003); Benjamin Stora, *Les trois exils: juifs d'Algérie* (Paris, 2006); Benjamin Stora, *Les Guerres sans fin: un historien, la France et l'Algérie* (Paris, 2008).

93 Pierre Goinard, 'En finir avec la désinformation', *L'Algérianiste*, 52 (December 1990), 2.

94 'Témoignages du passé. Opérations souvenirs', *L'Algérianiste*, 100 (1977), 12.

95 Stora speaking as part of the documentary *Algérie, Montpellier: aller simple*, 25 May 2002 (FR5).

96 Stora, *Les Guerres sans fin*, p. 140; 'La Disparition de Claude Liauzu', *L'Algérianiste*, 111 (June 2007), 9.

97 Benjamin Stora, 'Maroc-Algérie: retour du passé et écriture de l'histoire', *Vingtième siècle*, 68 (October–December 2000), 113.

98 See Stora's comments on 'Spécial guerre d'Algerie', aired 21 May 2001.

99 Raphaëlle Branche, *La Guerre d'Algérie: une histoire apaisée?* (Paris, 2005), p. 245.

100 For further comment on this with respect to the *pied-noir* community, see Amy L. Hubbell, 'Viewing the Past through a "Nostalgeric" Lens', in *Textual and Visual Selves: Photography, Film and Comic Art in French Autobiography*, ed. by Natalie Edwards, Amy L. Hubbell and Ann Miller (Lincoln, NE, 2011), p. 182.

101 Eric Savarèse, 'Mobilisations politiques et posture victimaire chez les militants associatifs pieds-noirs', *Raisons politiques*, 30 (May 2008), 49.

102 Anne Cazal, 'Cette vérité qui fait si peur!', *La Lettre de Véritas*, 51 (March 2001), 2.

103 'Spécial Algérie', aired 6 March 2002.

104 Faivre, 'Désinformation', 5.

105 The assertion was made by Micheline Balhache, the assistant to Colonel d'Humières who was described as a frequent visitor to the Rivesaltes and Saint-Maurice-l'Ardoise camps. Faivre, *L'action sociale*, p. 166.

106 Mohand Hamoumou, 'Les Harkis, un trou de mémoire franco-algérien', *Esprit*, 161 (May 1990), 32.

107 Michel Henry, 'Les Fils de harkis s'interrogent', *Libération* (30 August 2001), p. 4. The use of lawsuits by *harki* activists and the debates associated with this strategy will be discussed further in Chapter 8.

108 Stora, *Les Guerres sans fin*, p. 145.

8

Champs de bataille

Each memory-carrying group connected to the War of Independence possesses a specific perspective and has followed a distinct trajectory, even if these have not been developed in isolation. What these groups share is the objective of obtaining official recognition for their community and for their understanding of the past. In the last decade, the attention of activists has converged on particular institutions, notably the courtroom. Campaigns have also increasingly gravitated around certain themes, namely victimhood, responsibility and repentance, all of which have experienced a heightened visibility both in France and globally. Exploring the *champs de bataille,* or 'battlefields', on which the 'memory wars' are currently being 'fought' helps to illuminate the interplay between the domestic and international contexts in which the communities concerned are operating. Binding together these different elements is an overarching preoccupation with the question of transmission as both *pied-noir* and *harki* activists consider how best to pass on the past to subsequent generations and thus ensure the longevity of their respective collective memories.

The courtroom

Recent years have witnessed a noticeable reorientation of memory activism towards the judicial system; the lengthy list of lawsuits lodged by various groups leading historian Rapahëlle Branche, in 2005, to describe the courtroom as becoming *the* privileged site for discussions of the Algerian War.[1] Oliver Lalieu traces this phenomenon back to 1987 and the first of the Vichy trials which saw the Gestapo officer Klaus Barbie, dubbed the 'Butcher of Lyon' for his torture of prisoners in that city during the Second World War, convicted of crimes against humanity. This and the prosecutions that followed over the next decade revealed 'the legitimacy, many years after the fact, of seeking redress and learning lessons'.[2] In order to bring to trial multiple people who had been involved with the Vichy regime in a range of capacities it was necessary to successively amend France's definition of a 'crime against humanity', the only legal charge without a statute of limitations, in 1985, 1992, 1995 and 1997.[3] These modifications were primarily designed to facilitate the prosecution of four individuals who had carried out very different roles during the Occupation: Barbie, the German Gestapo agent; the former Bordeaux Prefect, Maurice Papon; the *milicien* Paul Touvier;[4] and Vichy's chief of police, René Bousquet, who was assassinated in June 1993 shortly before his trial was due to commence. Following attempts by Barbie's lawyer, the always provocative Jacques Vergès, to qualify colonialism as a crime against humanity, legislators also sought to formulate these changes in order to ensure that they did not open the way to events in Algeria being brought under the legal spotlight, even though existing amnesty laws already made this an unlikely scenario.[5] Such legal obstacles have not, however, deterred groups connected to the Algerian conflict. In fact, it has been argued that amnesties, by depriving victims of any 'meaningful legal recourse', have fuelled such campaigns. In the light of this, the crimes against humanity charge offers an alternative means through which to retrospectively accuse and demand reparations, even if these are understood to be primarily symbolic.[6]

It was in this spirit that Véritas spearheaded a lawsuit in 1997 against General Joseph Katz. The association accused him of crimes against humanity for his failure to dispatch French troops garrisoned in Oran to protect the settlers when riots broke out amidst independence celebrations on 5 July 1962 resulting in the loss of multiple European lives. Calls for this kind of legal action were not new, but the specific commemorative climate in France at the time worked to solidify general demands into concrete action. Véritas was clearly inspired by the concurrently unfolding Papon trial, which the association regularly referenced. In particular, the successful conviction of Papon on 2 April 1998 was viewed as a positive omen for their own ongoing case.[7] Unfortunately for Véritas, on 21 January 2000 a judge ruled that the deaths in Oran did not fall under the rubric of crimes against humanity and that while illegal acts may have been committed on that day, these were subject to the normal statute of limitations, which had expired. Véritas launched an appeal, but Katz died before this could be heard; he was ninety-three. 'We can only regret', wrote Véritas president, Joseph Hattab Pacha, 'that he did not live to one hundred in order to face the victims' families.'[8] Reflecting the deep-seated animosity towards Katz within the *pied-noir* community, Geneviève de Ternant of AOCAZ opined that 'Without doubt he will have been welcomed in hell by de Gaulle and they will roast there together to atone for their crimes.'[9]

Hattab Pacha subtitled his editorial 'The Butcher of Oran before the divine tribunal, but civil action is not dead', suggesting, correctly, that further lawsuits would follow. The Mouvement contre le racisme et pour l'amitié entre les peuples supported Louise Ighilahriz in her lawsuit relating to the torture she experienced at the hands of Massu's paratroopers; the children of Larbi Ben M'hidi made a similar representation to the courts over the death of their father while in the army's custody in 1957; while the group Le 17 octobre contre l'oubli launched a case against the French state for its role in the deaths of Algerians during the Battle of Paris.[10] Within the *harki* community the idea of employing the legal system in this manner appears to have first been raised in 1991. Following the summer of protests, *Le Monde* reported that Hacène Arfi's next move would be to engage a lawyer to look into the possibility of bringing a case against the French and Algerian authorities for crimes against humanity, although even then it was appreciated that this would be difficult.[11] It took a further two decades for such ideas to be turned into concrete action when, on 30 August 2001, Boussad Azni, the son of a *harki* and president of the Comité national de liaison des harkis (CNLH), supported nine *harkis* in registering a lawsuit against the French state for crimes against humanity with respect to its treatment of its auxiliaries in 1962, and the lasting suffering this had produced. The initiative was undertaken in co-operation with Albdelkrim Klech's organisation, Justice pour les harkis.

Born in 1959, Azni, whose family came to France in 1963, spent almost a decade growing up in the Bias camp. In addition to the normal hardships of camp life, Azni suffered the additional trauma of witnessing his father forcibly removed to Candélie, the *harki* psychiatric asylum. Although he left the camp in 1971, Azni remained haunted by what he had experienced there writing that the camp would 'weigh on my shoulders all my life'.[12] As a young man, Azni struggled with his identity and place in French society, falling briefly, like Arfi and Klech, into delinquency. His activist conscience was developed through the protests of 1975 in which he felt the *harkis*, and also M'hamed Laradji, had been made into *pied-noir* stooges. In reaction to this experience Azni opted to found his own organisations, first of all, the Association des Français rapatriés d'origine algérienne in 1986 and, subsequently, the CNLH.[13]

The lawsuit filed by the CNLH emphasised the patriotism of the *harkis*, making frequent reference to the 'blood debt' owed by France to these men. Arguing that all those engaged with the French were entitled to the same protection and rights, whether they were career soldiers, conscripts or auxiliaries, the lawsuit focused on the failure of France to honour this duty of care in 1962. This allowed the crime against humanity charge to be levelled on the basis of non-assistance to persons in danger.[14] In essence, as Azni declared on many occasions, he and the plaintiffs were seeking acknowledgement from the French state of its responsibility for the abandonment of the *harkis* in 1962 and the violence they suffered as a result of this.[15] In his 2002 memoir, *Harkis, crime d'état,* which also served to publicise the lawsuit, Azni acknowledged that the crime against humanity charge might seem 'excessive' to some. But, he went on to ask, what else could one call 'the concerted massacre, realised on a grand scale, of a population defined by precise criteria as belonging to an actual or perceived community?'[16] Beyond convincing his readers of the validity of this definition, Azni faced the more difficult challenge of convincing the courts to agree with him. On 17 June 2003, the Cour de cassation, France's highest judicial authority, rejected the lawsuit, prompting Azni to turn his attention to the Europeans courts where the suit was also dismissed.

As with other similar cases, the symbolic value of the gesture was arguably more important than the outcome. Coming mere weeks before the inaugural Journée nationale d'hommage aux harkis, Azni's actions garnered significant media coverage. One news report made the observation that just as the *harkis* passed before a judge in 1962 in order to reclaim French nationality, so today they were going before the courts to reclaim justice.[17] The failure of the initial lawsuit did not deter Azni from launching another attempt in 2003, seeking this time to indict the former minister of the armies, Pierre Messmer, on the same charges. Nor has it stopped other *harki* activists from framing their demands in similarly legalistic and loaded language.[18] On a personal level, the lawsuit and the media opportunities it created considerably raised Azni's profile as an activist. In 2003, he was invited by Prime Minister Jean-Pierre Raffarin to serve as vice-president of the recently created Haut conseil des rapatriés (HCR), which, in liaison with the inter-ministerial commission on *rapatriés,* was tasked with formulating opinions and proposals on measures affecting *pieds-noirs* and *harkis,* especially in the domain of memory.[19] Following his support for Nicolas Sarkozy in the 2007 presidential election, Azni was given an advisory position attached to the secretary of state for veterans. A combative and often divisive figure, Azni's nascent political career was cut short when he abruptly resigned from this post, publicly accusing Sarkozy of having 'betrayed' his electoral promises. When Azni died at the end of 2012, aged just fifty-three, he was buried, as per his own request, in the Bias camp cemetery.[20]

Although effective in attracting attention to the *harki* cause, Azni's actions also aroused opposition. Much of the criticism he faced revived debates prevalent during the Vichy trials regarding the incompatibility of the complexities of history with the definitive and simplified nature of legal justice. Conforming to the restrictive format of the legal process, the story presented by Azni was, by necessity, less nuanced than accounts articulated in different contexts. Instead of the complicated allegiances of someone like Dalila Kerchouche's father who aided the FLN, while also serving as an auxiliary; in Azni's rendering, 'France was everything' for the *harkis*.[21] The lines between heroes and villains, perpetrators and victims, also needed to be drawn more sharply by Azni because the intended result of the lawsuit was to establish clear-cut guilt. Diversity and detail thus risked being sacrificed in the service of a master narrative that had to appear unambiguous in order to succeed in its objectives. In keeping with his previous statements, Mohand Hamoumou argued that the courtroom was too blunt an instrument to do justice to the intricacies of the *harki* experience.[22] In particular, Hamoumou expressed concerned about 'mistaking the guilty party' since it was 'not France that committed these massacres, but the Algerian authorities of the time'.[23] In response, Azni claimed that 'Algeria was the executioner of a sentence pronounced by France'.[24] Yet, for filmmaker and *harki* descendant Farid Haroud, it was precisely historical contortions of this nature that were the problem. 'I am not sure', he stated, 'that this will help the younger generations for whom the problem, quite simply, is narrating history and there is much to do in that regard.'[25]

In defending his combative style of activism, Azni claimed that 'we are still at war'.[26] Appearing alongside Azni in an episode of *C dans l'air* in 2002 dedicated to the Algerian conflict, Benjamin Stora described Azni's efforts as 'admirable', but went on to argue that it was necessary to find ways to move beyond 'perpetual accusations', so as to illuminate the past without moralising it, or casting it as a continual battle out of which only one victor could emerge. Azni countered that his goal was to gain recognition of the fact that neither himself nor his father were traitors; rather the real traitors were those in power on the other side of the Mediterranean.[27] Having endured for decades the stigmatisation of the *harkis* (including, most recently, witnessing them being branded as aggressors by President Bouteflika during his state visit to France), for Azni the imperative to establish a legally enshrined corrective to this clearly overrode Stora's advocacy of a dispassionate historical picture.

The ascendancy of victimhood

Azni's actions speak to the ascendancy of victimhood as a valued status within France. Indeed, the preface to *Harkis, crime d'état* defined the goal of the lawsuit as attributing to the *harkis* 'their true status, that of victims'.[28] For Henry Rousso, this trend is a clear offshoot of Annette Wieviorka's 'era of the witness', whereby: 'The figure of the hero fades little by little in favour of that of the victim, and the confrontation between former adversaries no longer rests on the question of knowing whether one side or the other led a war for "just" ends ... but on their ability to present themselves as victims.'[29] With respect to the Algerian War specifically, the fact that no one emerged unsullied from the conflict meant that the status of 'victim' was not definitively tied to any one group and has thus remained a prize to be fought over. The result has been a memorial landscape in France that is largely devoid of agency, but instead littered with groups seeking to present themselves as victims of factors beyond their control and, in the process, to devolve responsibility for their fate onto an external party or force.

Although always a crucial part of the *pied-noir* lexicon, the emphasis on suffering and victimisation has become more pronounced over time, both within this community and more broadly. For the *harkis*, mobilisation undertaken in recent decades has centred on transforming the community from victims of the constructions of external commentators into a body of agency reclaiming activists. Yet, paradoxically, the discourse many activists promote is fundamentally framed by the idea that *harkis* have been the casualty of a catalogue of betrayal and abandonment perpetrated by others. Irrespective of the group in question, claiming the status of victim and pressing for recognition on these grounds requires the identification and condemnation of an 'other', with the result that 'the memory of enmity is cultivated, sustained and transmitted'.[30] This in turn helps to explain the attraction of judicial pronouncements which are viewed as irrefutable indicators of who is the victim and who is the perpetrator. As Sylvie Thénault astutely asks, 'More than "the truth", are the French not searching for "certainties" about the legitimacy of current positions and of requests for reparations, about the wrongdoings of each other?'[31]

When tracing the origins of this judicially orientated mentality, the Vichy trials once again emerge as a central reference point.[32] Especially significant was the prosecution of Papon which, in addition to focusing on his service to the Vichy government, also highlighted his tenure as the chief of police in Paris during the Algerian War, including on the night of 17 October 1961. Bringing the histories of Vichy and Algeria together in a single individual, the Papon case validated the idea that these two unique periods were somehow comparable.[33] The media frequently made this connection, as did many *harki* activists. Concluding a documentary focused on Azni's lawsuit, the programme's voiceover stated: 'That which the Jews asked for, the *harkis*, like other victims of history, are calling for today'.[34] Azni himself not only made direct reference to the precedent set by Vichy, but did so in language rooted in the concepts of persecution and genocide strongly reminiscent of that which accompanied the reawakening of Jewish memory in the 1970s.[35] The Bias camp was thus referred to as 'a genuine concentration camp', with the employment offered by the government to the *harkis* in these spaces framed by the sentence: 'What did the Germans say? "Arbeit macht frei", work makes you free, that was written above the entrance to Buchenwald.'[36]

Pied-noir activists also regularly invoked Vichy and the Shoah, both as a point of comparison to underline the severity of their suffering, and as a model to emulate in terms of the recognition obtained by the Jewish community from the state. When discussing the prosecution of Katz, Véritas' Anne Cazal was therefore able to write:

> The blood of a Frenchman from Algeria counts as much as the blood of a metropolitan French person of Jewish origin. The tragedy of the Shoah was appalling and moves us profoundly, but historically other crimes against humanity are written in the blood of our compatriots that cannot and must not be concealed or forgotten.[37]

The contemporary international situation has furthermore influenced the way in which this courtroom-based quest is conceived of and justified. As the vice-president of Justice *pour les harkis* explained to reporters on the day Azni lodged his lawsuit, 'When you see Pinochet stuck in England, Ariel Sharon hunted by a Palestinian in Belgium, Milosevic in the Hague, we, the *harkis*, we're right in it.'[38] Yet, although international precedents were clearly important, their principal role seemed to be to add further weight and wider contemporary resonance to a pre-existing vocabulary developed, above all, in reference to recent French history.

A positive view of colonialism

The courtroom was seen as offering memory activists the opportunity to assign responsibility for their suffering to a specific individual or entity at the same time as establishing a definitive and legally binding interpretation of the past. These were equally the issues at stake in debates surrounding Article 4 of the 23 February 2005 law and the Journée nationale d'hommage aux harkis inaugurated in 2001. Both examples reflected not only the effectiveness of lobbying efforts by *pied-noir* and *harki* activists respectively, but also the growing role of the state as simultaneously an actor and an arbiter.

The 23 February 2005 law offered national recognition to the men and women who had 'participated in the work accomplished by France' in its former colonies, provided further financial allocations for *pieds-noirs* and *harkis,* and, through Article 4, stipulated that school curricula should 'acknowledge in particular the positive role of the French presence overseas, notably in North Africa'.[39] The law emerged out of a specific convergence of circumstances, of which perhaps the most significant was the 2002 presidential elections which saw the FN's Jean-Marie Le Pen secure enough votes to go through to the second round run-off against Jacques Chirac. Although Chirac ultimately defeated Le Pen comfortably with 82 per cent of votes cast, the shock of the first round result had lasting consequences. In particular, it prompted Chirac to engage in a more assiduous courtship of the *rapatrié* electorate in a bid to counter the appeal of Le Pen's overtly nostalgic and pro-colonial rhetoric.

Having affirmed his 'solidarity' with the *rapatrié* community verbally, once returned to power Chirac put his words into action through his prime minister, Raffarin, who, a mere three weeks after his appointment, created by decree an inter-ministerial task force for *rapatriés*. This was in keeping with Raffarin's declaration that policies in favour of the *rapatriés* were to be a government 'priority', as was his decision, in February 2003, to place Michel Diefenbacher, UMP deputy for the Lot-et-Garonne, in charge of producing a report on how best to complete efforts to recognise the *rapatriés*. Delivered in September 2003, following consultation with 100 individuals all of whom were either members of the HCR or linked to pied-noir associations, this report formed the basis of the 23 February 2005 law.[40]

Coming in the wake of several years of damaging revelations about the conduct of the French in Algeria, especially those centred on the use of torture by the army, *pied-noir* activists and their allies were eager to take advantage of this more favourable political climate. In addition to offering their views to Diefenbacher, *pied-noir* associations stepped up their protests to the Minster for Education over the impact that the continual public denigration of France's work in Algeria was having upon the school curriculum, foreshadowing the importance placed on education in the final draft of the law. Associations also lobbied right-wing politicians, many of whom were in any case very amenable to supporting narratives glorifying French imperial *grandeur* and global dominance under the Third Republic.[41] These efforts were given an added impetus by the sense among *pied-noir* activists and certain right-wing politicians that they needed to win back the ground lost through commemorative concessions granted by the previous prime minister, the socialist Lionel Jospin (1997–2002), particularly his public recognition of the fact that that there had been multiple victims on the night of 17 October 1961 which contradicted the long-standing official version of only two deaths.[42]

This wider context helps to explain why such importance was attached to Article 4. This single clause not only encapsulated the ethos of much *pied-noir* activism, but promised to promote it across the education system, regarded by associations as a crucial vector in their attempts to secure influence over the official historical narrative; an influence they feared had been on the wane in recent years. Even though many activists felt the law could have gone further in areas such as financial provision and the assignation of responsibility for the 'mistakes' committed between 1954 and 1962, it was nonetheless welcomed as 'an important step'.[43] In contrast to the current situation where children were taught a distorted version of history because of the 'stranglehold' on the educational apparatus by teachers 'impregnated' with theories 'close to Marxist-Leninism', *pied-noir* activists hoped that the record would now be set straight.[44]

By giving legal sanctity to a positive evaluation of France's colonial past, Article 4 provided *pied-noir* associations with a powerful weapon through which to defend the honour of their ancestors and also their own place within the nation's history. Tellingly, amidst the battle to retain this clause, assertions regarding the need to recognise the fully French status of the *pieds-noirs* assumed a renewed prominence, more than four decades after they had initially been brandished. Writing to the deputy mayor of Aix-en-Provence, one *pied-noir* association representative implored her to support Article 4, so that 'we can feel ourselves to be fully French anew'.[45] Finally, by providing a legally endorsed interpretation of history, Article 4 promised to open up a new channel through which *pied-noir* associations and activists could challenge alternative interpretations, potentially silence conflicting viewpoints and thus overturn the perceived dominance of the 'anti-colonial lobby'.

What *pied-noir* activists regarded as a long-overdue correction was, however, perceived by others as the unacceptable imposition of a unilateral official history and an affront to the neutrality of the educational establishment. *Harki* representatives were among those who mobilised to oppose Article 4 even though some, such as Hamoumou and AJIR, had been involved in drafting the original bill. In fact, AJIR denounced the

law before it made it onto the statute books, claiming that far from soliciting enthusiasm as the government had hoped, the law 'provokes only
deception, frustration and bitterness', while contributing nothing to healing the still open wounds of the community.[46] Fatima Besnaci-Lancou's
association was even more critical, strongly opposing both Article 4 and
Article 13, which rehabilitated former OAS members, including awarding
them financial compensation.[47] In response to these and other objections,
pied-noir activists formed 'Justice and Memory', a collaborative action
committee comprising, amongst others, Véritas, the Cercle algérianiste
and ANFANOMA, which dedicated itself to defending and protecting
the law.[48]

Following months of acrimonious exchanges and polemics, Chirac
used his presidential veto in January 2006 to rescind Article 4. Avoiding
further parliamentary debate on the matter reflected the President's
desire to move past the bitter divisions this specific clause had created,
while keeping intact the rest of the law's provisions. *Pied-noir* activists interpreted Chirac's decision not as an attempt to achieve national
reconciliation, but as another example of the discrimination to which
their community and its history were regularly subjected. Arguing that
'Absolutely nothing in the law prevents researchers from studying all
aspects of the French presence overseas', associations claimed the law was
not inflicting a unilateral interpretation of the past, but simply 'restoring balance'.[49] In their eyes, it was not supporters of the law who threatened intellectual neutrality and liberty, but rather their opponents who
'through dogmatism, deny the positive work of France in Algeria even
though evidence [of it] abounds'.[50] Regarded as yet another victory for
the strengthening forces of anti-colonialism and the associated discourse
of 'repentance', activists asked why it was that they were unable to secure
the kind of recognition afforded through memory laws to groups such as
Jews and Armenians, or to the history of slavery?[51] By confirming their
status as a beleaguered minority, failure over Article 4 in some senses gal-
vanised activists, leading to the creation of a new federative initiative, the
Coordination nationale des Français d'Algérie (CNFA). But, ultimately,
given the potential of Article 4 to legally enshrine the historical vision of
French Algeria long promoted by *pied-noir* associations, the overriding
sentiment when it was annulled was one of bitter disappointment.

The question of responsibility

Within the *harki* community, responsibility is the issue that has come to
dominate the agenda of activists. The desire for official acknowledgement

from the state of its role in the community's fate in 1962 provided a strong
unifying theme that is, once again, filtered through the prism of Vichy.[52]
When Besnaci-Lancou spoke of the need for *harkis* to receive from the
government 'a stronger gesture ... like for the Jewish community', she was
undoubtedly referring Chirac's speech of 16 July 1995 commemorating
the Vel d'Hiv *rafles* (round-ups) when the President directly acknowledged the role played by the French state in the deportation of tens of
thousands of Jews during the Second World War.[53] The most obvious
occasion for such a declaration with respect to the *harkis* was the inaugural Journée nationale d'hommage aux harkis on 25 September 2001, instigated by Chirac as part of his wider efforts to commemorate the Algerian
War and those who fought in it. Speaking on the day, Chirac reiterated
the gratitude of the nation towards the *harkis* for their loyal service, as
previous presidents had done. But, crucially, he went on to state that the
harkis and their families had been 'the victims of a terrible tragedy'. The
massacres of 1962 'must be recognised', he argued, along with the fact that
'France, by leaving Algerian soil, failed to prevent them. It failed to save
its children.'[54] This was the closest the French government had ever come
to admitting culpability. That such a concession was made in the context
of a specific day of commemoration devoted solely to the *harkis* greatly
enhanced the symbolic weight attached to Chirac's words, as did his own
status as a veteran of the Algerian War.

Reactions to Chirac's declaration were, however, mixed. The President
had gone further than any of his predecessors in acknowledging responsibility, albeit only responsibility for not protecting the *harkis* from violence committed by the FLN. He also appeared to endorse a move away
from the traditional presentation of the *harkis* as having fought loyally
for France. His line about more than 200,000 of them having 'taken up
arms for the Republic and for France, to defend their lands and to protect their families' implied a mix of motivations underlying engagement
as an auxiliary and was thus more in keeping with narratives being promoted by *harki* activists.[55] Yet, it was equally clear that the *harkis* were
to be kept within the narrow confines of an established discourse that
defined them as brave and loyal soldiers of the nation, rather than as
colonial subjects used for political and strategic ends by an imperial
power. A point reinforced by fact that the government's focus remained
firmly on the post-Evian period, ignoring anything prior to that date.[56]
It was on such grounds that Géraldine Enjelvin characterised Chirac's
speech as an exercise in symbolic power through which the state had
appropriated the collective history of the *harkis,* imposing in its place
an official version of the past that 'bore little resemblance' to what those

who experienced the war remembered.[57] Although she accepted that the speech represented a more inclusive public narrative of the Algerian War, Enjelvin went on to ask whether, by rewriting the 'master narrative' to include the *harkis,* the state was not in fact engineering a 'delegitimation' of the *harki* identity by, once again, seeking to speak *for* the community in a language that reflected its own priorities.[58] In Algeria, the Journée nationale d'hommage aux harkis was more consensual in the sense that, publicly at least, it was universally denounced as an attempt to falsify history as part of a bid by the French state to jettison their responsibilities onto the FLN. The argument was also made, with reference to the recent actions of Azni, that seeking legal recourse against the French state for their treatment of the *harkis* in 1962 was akin to the children of Second World War collaborators trying to file a lawsuit against de Gaulle. In the same vein, it was pointed out that the citizens of Algeria had had no opportunity to bring cases for crimes against humanity against figures such as Generals Massu and Bigeard.[59]

Within the *harki* community there was a general agreement that the Journée nationale d'hommage aux harkis marked an important step forward, but this was combined with the insistence that more remained to be done. Hamoumou perhaps summed it up best when he stated that 'the recognition due to the former *harkis* and other "French Muslims" is not a charitable recognition for suffering endured but, first of all, the acknowledgement of the wrongdoings of the governments of the era'.[60] That is to say, admitting fault was a welcome start, but what the *harkis* were really holding out for was acceptance of responsibility. 'We want the government and the National Assembly to finally have the courage to debate the *harki* problem starting by acknowledging the responsibility of France', asserted Klech. 'They did it for the Armenians, they recognised the genocide, why not for us?'[61] As with *pied-noir* reactions to the 23 February 2005 law, *harki* demands were couched in the language of memory equality, expressing a desire for the same level of recognition that had been accorded to other groups within the nation and in the same formats, be it a trial with national pedagogic dimensions, a 'memory law', or a specific commemorative gesture.[62]

The role of the state

Underlying these recent developments is a sense that only concrete gestures made at the highest levels are capable of 'healing the still open wounds' of the Algerian War.[63] This, in turn, relates to a growing intolerance of ambiguity as reflected in trends towards obtaining definitive statements about the past. The body most able to give such assurances is, of course, the state through its various apparatuses, which is why it has become such a focal point for activists. As historian Robert Berlot reminds us, citizens traditionally feel that 'the state must deplore, denounce and pronounce on the good and the bad, the true and the false, the commemorable and the non-commemorable'.[64] The problem, certainly with respect to the Algerian War, is that the state is the target of various claims at the same time as it is expected to be the arbiter of these.[65] Consequently, rather than the dominant pole, the state is reduced to being 'one of the competing voices', as well as 'the paradigmatic site within which conflicting tendencies are fought out'.[66]

Further complicating the situation is the reactive commemorative strategy pursued by the state. In general, successive governments have preferred not to engage with this divisive and controversial history at all, as indicated by several decades of successful resistance to grassroots commemorative pressure. The series of measures enacted since the 1990s for the most part reflect concessions granted in response to specific events and emergent situations rather than the enactment of any preconceived plan. The law of 14 June 1994, affirming the moral debt of the nation towards the *harkis,* can be read as a response to the 1991 protests; Lionel Jospin's promise to increase access to the archives came in the wake of revelations provoked by the Papon trial; and the 23 February 2005 law was first mooted as Chirac sought to secure *pied-noir* support in his 2002 run-off against Le Pen.[67]

Yet, attempts by the state to be proactive have proven equally unsuccessful as demonstrated by the fate of the HCR. Created by prime ministerial decree in December 2002, the HCR was intended to give official recognition to *pied-noir* and *harki* demands while simultaneously bringing their activism under the control of state institutions. In practice, however, the initiative foundered as a result of the unwillingness of the representatives involved to compromise, and their determination, instead, to pursue of their own, often radically different, agendas at all costs. Frustrated by a lack of progress on what they regarded as key issues, successive waves of *pied-noir* members resigned from the HCR in 2004, 2006 and 2009, fundamentally undermining the organisation. Summing up the sense of disillusionment within the community, ANFANOMA president Yves Sainsot asked: 'What good is the illusion of a dialogue between a powerless Haut conseil and blind and deaf senior figures [in government]?'[68] A further example of the state's attempts to manage the legacies of the conflict in order to promote a consensual, or at least uncontroversial, version of this past was the designation of 5 December, a date with no war-related significance, as the national day of homage to those who died for France in Algeria, Tunisia and Morocco; a move that, somewhat predictably, satisfied none of the interested parties.

Despite the aim of promoting harmony, in reality the state's ad hoc commemorative programme has only intensified the sense of competition between different activists. Each measure enacted only partially satisfies the group in question, motivating them to continue campaigning, while simultaneously encouraging other groups to agitate for similar attention. The absence of clarification of official responsibilities furthermore means that these competing claims exist in a 'political and ethical vacuum that encourages a dangerous relativism', whereby all commemorative demands are viewed as equally valid.[69] Consequently, even though far more is known today about the Algerian War and about French colonialism, the narrative that is presented for public consumption continues to contain distortions and omissions. The emergence of different postcolonial groups and their respective campaigns to secure space for themselves within the national historical imagination has certainly filled in many of the gaps that used to exist, which is to be welcomed. But, at the same time, this process has allowed other silences to persist and new ones to develop. An additional consequence is the perpetuation of the perception of Algeria as an unresolved issue which causes the war to return periodically to the public spotlight in dramatic episodes that temporarily rivet the nation. Outside of these incidents, however, no sustained attention is devoted to the conflict by the state or by the general public; only the activists themselves remain engaged. A phenomenon aptly illustrated by the torture controversy, which generated an immense amount of polemic in 2000 and 2001 before disappearing without any tangible commemorative legacy, or any real advance in the way the issue was publicly discussed or understood.[70]

The quest for permanence

Obtaining definitive and legally binding statements about the past are part of ongoing attempts by *pieds-noirs* and *harkis* to anchor their histories in permanent sites external to their communities and thus to ensure a presence beyond the lifespan of living witnesses. Pursuing this objective through other avenues, *harki* activists have recently begun pushing for the creation of physical *lieux de mémoire* as part of a process of reclaiming the spaces associated with their initial installation in France.[71] These efforts have seen commemorative plaques placed at the sites of the Rivesaltes and Saint-Maurice-l'Ardoise camps, while municipalities with significant concentrations of *harkis*, such as Dreux and Fréjus, have begun to name streets and roundabouts in recognition of the community. In 2003, the village of Ongles (Alpes-de-Haute-Provence), site of a former forest hamlet, created a permanent exhibit recalling the history of the community, followed by a museum of history and memory in 2008. More recently, as part of the fiftieth anniversary commemorations, a memorial to the *harkis* was unveiled near the Logis d'Anne site in Jouques (Bouches-du-Rhône).[72]

Physically inscribing the history of their community on the French landscape represents a relatively recent element within *harki* activism. In contrast, *pied-noir* associations have been engaged in such endeavours for many decades with the multiple edifices erected across France since the 1960s functioning as both permanent historical markers and gathering places for the contemporary community. In line with the more combative commemorative climate, the new millennium saw an increasing determination among certain activists to remember particularly contentious elements of the past, notably the OAS, and a concomitant strengthening of opposition to such moves. On 5 July 2003, the lengthily titled Association amicale pour la défense des intérêts moraux et matériels des anciens détenus politiques et exilés de l'Algérie française added plaques commemorating the deaths of OAS members Jean Bastien-Thiry, Roger Degueldre, Albert Dovecar and Roger Piegts to an existing stele in Marignane (Bouches-du-Rhône). The same year, a monument in the cemetery of Béziers (Hérault), erected in the 1960s to commemorate the civilian and military dead of the Algerian War, was also adorned with photographs of these four men. In November 2007, 8000 people attended the inauguration of the Cercle algérianiste's Mur des disparus in the grounds of the Sainte Claire convent in Perpignan, which, since 2012, has also housed the CDDFA. This 'wall of the disappeared', whose cost of €55,000 was covered primarily by donations from Cercle algérianiste members, consists of plaques bearing the names of Europeans killed or missing during the Algeria War who have no graves, controversially amalgamating civilian settlers with members of the OAS.[73]

These sites serve as an appropriate symbol of the 'memory wars' phenomenon, representing spaces that are literally being fought over by those with conflicting perspectives. Interestingly, the fault lines of these divisions are both intra as well as inter-communal. In response to the emergence of Perpignan as a key site for this new wave of *pied-noir* commemorations, former settler Jacky Malléa created the Association nationale des pieds-noirs progressistes et leurs amis (ANPNPA) in

2008.[74] The group opposes the Mur des disparus and the CDDFA arguing that together they represent the implantation of a distorted history that ignores the pre-1954 actions of the settlers, the inequalities of the colonial system, and what the ANPNPA regard as war crimes committed by *Algérie française* partisans during the conflict itself.[75] More generally, there has been an upsurge in opposition to *pied-noir*-led physical commemorations from a variety of quarters. The Marignane stele was removed in 2008 following years of escalating confrontations involving the LDH, the PCF and various local officials; an act that only further motivated an already militant local *pied-noir* population who defiantly continued to gather at the now empty site.[76] The previous year, red paint was thrown over a stele in the Perpignan cemetery depicting Bastien-Thiry being put to death by firing squad. In denouncing this act, *Véritas* noted the lack of press coverage accorded to the vandalism, in contrast to the usual media outcry generated by cemetery desecrations. Hattab Pacha attributed this to a revival of hostility towards *pieds-noirs* stemming from the abrogation of Article 4 which had emboldened the community's 'enemies'.[77] Exemplifying this perceived animosity was the Prefect of Béziers who, in 2006, banned *pied-noir* ceremonies to mark 5 July 1962, arguing these gatherings were a cover for rehabilitations of the OAS. But, it is also the case that local decisions have often been overturned by higher powers. An administrative tribunal in 2009 ruled that the Béziers ceremony should be allowed to go ahead, shortly before the Marignane municipality ordered that the disputed stele be reinstated, albeit without the plaques listing the anniversary of the deaths of the four OAS members.

The continued determination of *pied-noir* associations to propose and finance such monuments testifies to their willingness to fight to maintain a physical presence within the national landscape. 'It seems important for us to continue to mark "our territory" and to keep these witness accounts in memory of all our fallen or missing', ANFANOMA asserted following the news that ceremonies in Béziers would resume.[78] More than simply obtaining space within the physical memory of the nation, *pied-noir* associations have tied their actions to the issue of equality between different memories. In defending edifices to the OAS, militants argued that families had the right to commemorate their loved ones, irrespective of how they died. Denying any political dimension, these acts were therefore framed as purely commemorative.[79] Activists also emphasised the 'total rehabilitation' of former OAS members following de Gaulle's 1968 amnesty, Mitterrand's reinstatement of military ranks and decorations, and compensation measures extended via the 23 February 2005 law. In the light of this fact, to deny commemorative space to such men, while simultaneously supporting projects such as the monument to victims of the OAS unveiled in Paris in 2011, undercut any claims by the authorities to be pursuing a policy of national reconciliation.[80] Such arguments represent a new twist on long-standing attempts by *pied-noir* activists to depoliticise the actions of the OAS and to define them as victims in accordance with the increasingly valuable currency such a designation carries within current memory politics.

What the *pied-noir* community continue to lack, however, is a state-endorsed marker of their history. Various initiatives have been proposed over the years, but none have come to fruition. The most high profile of these failed attempts was the Mémorial national de la France d'outre-mer, which was to be located in Marseille. Its long gestation dates back to the early 1980s, although concrete measures to implement it, including deciding to locate it in Marseille, came only in the 1990s. A long-cherished objective of *pied-noir* associations, the project repeatedly floundered as agreement on the content and message of the site proved impossible to broker between the various representatives included in the advisory committee. In addition to the significance of the port city within the history of the empire, the Marseille memorial was important because it was state-sponsored, rather than simply an association-led project. It therefore contained the potential to afford the *pied-noir* community national recognition within a positively conceptualised and officially sanctioned historical narrative. Similar problems have beset the Fondation pour la mémoire de la guerre d'Algérie, a project included in the 23 February 2005 law, but which then lay dormant until Sarkozy's administration revived it in 2010. Widely criticised, the foundation has struggled to secure support from any group connected to the Franco-Algerian past.[81]

In many senses, the hopes attached to national projects like the Marseille memorial have been reorientated as *pied-noir* associations, in partnership with favourable municipalities, have sought instead to create local institutions whose character they can exercise a greater degree of control over. This was the impetus behind Perpignan's CDDFA, described by Suzy Simon-Nicoise as a space that would transmit 'large and small traces of what we were [in Algeria] and what we will preserve here'.[82] In a similar vein, plans were underway, until very recently, for a museum in Montpellier dedicated to the history of the French presence in North Africa. In the pipeline since 1996, the proposed Musée d'histoire de France et d'Algérie formed part of former mayor Georges Frêche's careful courtship of the *rapatrié* vote over many decades, a policy continued by

his immediate successor, Hélène Mandroux. Given Frêche's close relationship with the *pied-noir* community and their influence within the
municipality, the guarded hope among local activists was that museum
would reflect their vision of French colonisation as a beneficial and harmonious enterprise. Delays in gaining state approval pushed the original
2007 opening back to 2015. Then, in spring 2014, news broke that the project had been shelved by the city's new mayor, the PS dissident Philippe
Saurel, who announced that the space would instead be given over to
contemporary art.[83]

In spite of this particular outcome, the evidence in this and other
chapters points to the fact that, in general, local municipalities have
been both more proactive in soliciting and more successful in managing
memory communities than the state. Although a substantive discussion
of this issue is beyond the scope of this book, one possible reason for
this pattern is that local authorities see engagement with numerically
strong and active groups like the *pieds-noirs* in their immediate environs
as a way of de-politicising their activism. That is to say, by conceding to
demands for symbolic representation within the municipal space, such
as a monument, museum or archive, officials are able to focus the attention of activists on these projects and away from involvement in local
politics.[84] It is also worth noting the participation of prominent scholars
in both the Montpellier and Marseille initiatives. This suggests that there
is support within the academic community for a historical museum dedicated to France's colonial past, even if the realisation of such a project
remains problematic.

Towards a resolution?

In the light of the multiple terrains on which these 'memory wars'
are currently being fought and the conflicting agendas of the groups
involved, it is difficult to envisage what a 'resolution' would look like,
although various options have been proposed. For Stora, one of the
most vocal on this subject, it would require France to face its colonial
past in all its complexity, using a combination of recognition and reparation to bring about a reconciliation of memories between protagonists,
the state and wider society.[85] As others have highlighted, the challenge is
how to acknowledge this plurality of experiences in a way that 'reject[s]
feelings of revenge … without negating the suffering of others', before
then formulating these diverse memories into a cohesive and useable
national patrimony.[86] Although for the historian Peter Dunwoodie a fixa-
tion on the 'fantasy' of a single collective memory as an 'instrument of

national identity' is not the solution, but rather part of the problem.[87] Similar arguments have been advanced by bodies like ACHAC who have attacked what they regard as the stifling effects of attempting to shoehorn a wealth of different postcolonial identities into a single national framework, advocating instead the adoption of a more flexible and multilayered approach.[88]

Beyond these intellectual debates lies the issue of what *pieds-noirs, harkis* and other groups want. 'Recognition' and 'justice' are two of the most commonly articulated demands, but there is little sense of what, in practice, these would consist of or require. Each gesture from the state has been condemned either for falling short of the definitive act or statement that each group is holding out for, or as compromised by similar overtures made to other groups. Yet, if either *pied-noir* or *harki* representatives obtained what they claim to want, then they would lose their particularity along with their raison d'être. Both communities have now built collective identities based on unacknowledged suffering and on their exclusion from the nation. Removing these pillars would undermine the foundational elements of their communal specificity. This was recognised in the 1970s by *pied-noir* associations when they shifted their focus away from material compensation that had, in effect, been obtained, towards the open-ended task of protecting the legacy of their unique cultural and historical patrimony. As long as unsatisfied demands persist, there remains a reason for activists and associations to carry on campaigning which, in turn, helps to maintain the vitality of the group. Competition, as the case studies presented in this chapter demonstrate, fulfils a similar function, supporting Wieviorka's assertion that 'memory can exist only if it is kept in public space in a quasi-permanent fashion through agitation and conflicts'.[89]

The identities defended by *pied-noir* and *harki* activists are now well established. To depart from these would require considerable effort with no guarantee of success. As Giulia Fabbiano has pointed out, it is therefore easier to remain a victim, which gives one the right 'to complain, to protest and to demand', than to accept reparation for the offense committed and thus face the uncertainties inherent in the creation of a new communal identity. Not least because such acceptance may also entail acknowledging what the group in question did, as well as what was done to them.[90] Consequently, there is little incentive for the communities concerned to accept the inherently limited offers of a state trying to balance and unify a range of competing commemorative demands. Hence why those involved continue to advocate for unequivocal gestures, such as laws or courtroom verdicts, that would be sufficiently definitive to assure them and their memories of a secure and, crucially, distinctive place within the national narrative. The real question, therefore, is how long can this campaigning mentality be sustained?

Notes

1 Raphaëlle Branche, *La Guerre d'Algérie: une histoire apaisée?* (Paris, 2005), p. 111.

2 Olivier Lalieu, 'L'invention du "devoir de mémoire"', *Vingtième siècle*, 69 (January–March 2001), 93.

3 For further discussion of the issues raised by these trials, see Henry Rousso, *The Haunting Past: History, Memory and Justice in Contemporary France*, trans. R. Schoolcraft (Philadelphia, PA, 1998); Richard J. Golsan (ed.), *The Papon Affair: Memory and Justice on Trial* (New York and London, 2000).

4 The *milice* was a paramilitary organisation created by the Vichy regime to help defeat the French Resistance, which employed tactics including torture, summary executions and assassinations. The group also participated in the rounding up and deportation of Jews. In 1994, Touvier became the first Frenchman to be convicted of crimes against humanity when he was found guilty of murdering seven Jewish hostages in Rilieux-la-Pape, near Lyon, on 29 June 1944.

5 A crime against humanity is defined in French law as the 'massive and systematic practice of executions, tortures or abductions', committed 'in the name of a state practicing a politics of ideological hegemony'. It is this latter stipulation that is designed to confine the charge's application to the Vichy years.

6 Branche, *La Guerre d'Algérie*, p. 112; Jim House and Neil MacMaster, *Paris 1961: Algerians, State Terror and Memory* (Oxford, 2006), p. 317.

7 René Blanchot, 'Katz, le boucher d'Oran', *La Lettre de Véritas*, 22 (April 1998), 6.

8 Joseph Hattab Pacha, 'Le mot du Président', *La Lettre de Véritas*, 51 (March 2001), 2.

9 Geneviève de Ternant, 'Tolérance zéro', *L'écho de l'Oranie*, 274 (May-June 2001), 1.

10 Branche, *La Guerre d'Algérie*, p. 116.

11 François Xavier Reymond, 'Un an après la révolte des enfants de harkis. Le nouveau combat de Hacène', *Le Monde* (25 July 1992), p. 7.

12 Boussad Azni, *Harkis, crime d'état: généalogie d'un abandon* (Paris, 2002), p. 124.

13 Azni, *Harkis*, p. 129.

14 Azni, *Harkis*, p. 25.

15 See, for example, Azni's statements on 'Communauté harki', *ARTE info*, aired 29 August 2001 (ARTE); 'La Mémoire des harkis', *Edition nationale*, aired 30 August 2001 (FR3); 'Souvenirs: les harkis', *Le Six minutes*, aired 30 August 2001 (M6).

16 Although not an official part of the lawsuit, Azni believed the crimes against humanity charge was equally applicable to way the French state treated the *harkis* after 1962. In particular, he viewed the Bias camp as part of a deliberate government plan to ensure the gradual disappearance of the *harkis* because they were living reminders of France's humiliation in Algeria. Azni, *Harkis*, pp. 103–19, 147–8.

17 'La Mémoire des harkis', aired 30 August 2001. The most extended treatment of the lawsuit was provided by the documentary *Harkis: le crime*, aired 12 February 2002 (ARTE).

18 See, for example, Fatima Besnaci-Lancou, 'Introduction. En finir aves toutes les légendes', in *Les Harkis dans la colonisation et ses suites*, ed. by Fatima Besnaci-Lancou and Gilles Manceron (Ivry-sur-Seine, 2008), pp. 23–4.

19 The official Web page for the HCR, which has not been updated since 2005, can be found at: http://archives.gouvernement.fr/villepin/acteurs/premier_ministre/les_services_premier_ministre_195/haut_conseil_rapatries_284/index.html [31 January 2015].

20 Abderahmen Moumen, 'De l'absence aux nouveaux porte-parole: évolution du mouvement associatif harki (1962–2011)', *Les Temps modernes*, 666 (November–December 2011), 168; Bessy Selk, 'Disparition de Boussad Azni', *La Dépêche du Midi* (29 December 2012), p. 34.

21 Dalila Kerchouche, *Mon père, ce harki* (Paris 2003), p. 254; Azni, *Harkis*, p. 154.

22 Mohand Hamoumou, 'Les Harkis, un trou de mémoire franco-algérien', *Esprit*, 161 (May 1990), 32.

23 Henry Michel, 'Les Fils de harkis s'interrogent', *Libération* (30 August 2001), p. 4.

24 Azni, *Harkis*, p. 153.

25 Michel, 'Les Fils de harkis', p. 4.

26 *Harkis*, aired 12 February 2002.

27 'Les Cicatrices françaises', *C dans l'air*, aired 12 March 2002 (FR5).

28 Azni, *Harkis*, p. 8.

29 Henry Rousso, 'La Guerre d'Algérie et la culture de la mémoire', *Le Monde* (5 April 2002), p. 17.

30 House and MacMaster, *Paris 1961*, p. 352.

31 Sylvie Thénault, 'France-Algérie: pour un traitment commun du passé de la guerre d'indépendance', *Vingtième siècle*, 85 (January–March 2005), 127. This view is shared by Resistance expert Robert Berlot; see his 'Préface' in Francis Jeanson, *Notre guerre* (Paris, 2001), p. 9.

32 William B. Cohen, 'The *Harkis*: History and Memory', in *Algeria and France 1800–2000: Identity, Memory, Nostalgia*, ed. by Patricia M.E. Lorcin (New York, 2006), p. 178.

33 For a summary of the problems with such a comparison, see Branche, *La Guerre d'Algérie*, p. 95.

34 *Harkis*, aired 12 February 2002.

35 *Harkis*, aired 12 February 2002; Cohen, 'The *Harkis*', pp. 176–7. Although Cohen's observation was in reference to the *harki* community in general, it seems particularly appropriate to Azni.

36 Azni, *Harkis*, pp. 79, 104.

37 Anne Cazal, 'Dernier minute: procès Katz', *La Lettre de Véritas*, 40 (February 2000), 11.

38 Michel, 'Les Fils de harkis', p. 4.

39 For the full text of the law, see www.legifrance.gouv.fr/affichTexte.do?cidText e=JORFTEXT000000444898&dateTexte [25 January 2016].

40 Valérie Esclangon-Morin, François Nadiras and Sylvie Thénault, 'Les Origines et la genèse d'une loi scélérate', in *La Colonisation, la loi et l'histoire*, ed. by Claude Liauzu and Gilles Manceron (Paris, 2006), pp. 31–6.

41 Esclangon-Morin et al., 'Les Origines', pp. 52–3.

42 For further information on this, see Joshua Cole, 'Entering History: The Memory of Police Violence in Paris, October 1961', in *Algeria and France 1800–2000: Identity, Memory, Nostalgia*, ed. by Patricia M.E. Lorcin (New York, 2006), p. 121.

43 Yves Sainsot, 'Une loi en demi-teinte', *France horizon*, 458–9 (February 2005), 1.

44 Pierre Dimech, *La Désinformation autour de la culture des pieds-noirs* (Paris, 2006), p. 27.

45 www.babelouedstory.com/thema_les/associations/845/845.html [13 December 2013]. Also cited in Eric Savarèse, 'Mobilisations politiques et posture victimaire chez les militants associatifs pieds-noirs', *Raisons politiques*, 30 (May 2008), 55.

46 Cited in Michèle Baussant, 'Ni mémoire, ni oubli: la France à l'épreuve de son histoire coloniale', in *Du vrai au juste: la mémoire, l'histoire et l'oubli*, ed. by Michèle Baussant (Saint-Nicolas, Québec, 2006), p. 180.

47 The association's online statement can be found at www.harki.net/article. php?id=50 [21 December 2013].

48 Esclangon-Morin, et al., 'Les Origines', p. 56.

49 Faberon, 'La Loi', 6; 'As before', *France horizon*, 460–1 (April 2005), 4.

50 'Colonisation', *Pieds-noirs d'hier et d'aujourd'hui*, 137 (January 2006), 12.

51 It is a crime in France to deny the Holocaust under the 1990 Gayssot law. It was also, until February 2012, a crime to deny that the 1915–16 killing of Armenians was a 'genocide'. The law was struck down by the Constitutional Court on the grounds that it infringed freedom of speech, although President François Hollande has vowed to create new legislation in its place. In 2001, the Taubira law, named after politician Christiane Taubira, recognised slavery as a crime against humanity.

52 A particularly good illustration of this is the consensus that prevailed among Kerchouche, Besnaci-Lancou and Hamoumou during the televised discussion following the broadcast of the documentary *La Blessure: la tragédie des harkis*. See *Hors série*, aired 20 September 2010 (FR3).

53 For the full text of the speech, see: www.jacqueschirac-asso.fr/les-grands-discours-de-jacques-chirac/?post_id=2326 [25 January 2016].

54 For the full speech, see: www.jacqueschirac-asso.fr/les-grands-discours-de-jacques-chirac/?post_id=2336 [25 January 2016].

55 See: www.jacqueschirac-asso.fr/les-grands-discours-de-jacques-chirac/?post_id=2336 [25 January 2016].

56 For further discussion of this framing of the history of the *harkis,* see Sung Choi, 'Les Anciens combattants musulmans dans la France postcoloniale: la politique d'intégration des harkis après 1962', *Les Temps modernes* 666 (November-December 2011), 139.

57 Géraldine Enjelvin, 'The Harki Identity: A Product of Marginalisation and Resistance to Symbolic Violence?', *National Identities*, 8:2 (June 2006), 114–15.

58 Enjelvin, 'The Harki Identity', 123–4.

59 *Harkis,* aired 12 February 2002.

60 Mohand Hamoumou, 'Les Harkis ont soif de vérité', *La Croix* (20 September 2001), p. 27.

61 Guillaume Bonnet, 'La France rend mercredi un nouvel hommage national aux harkis', *AFP Infos Françaises* (23 September 2002).

62 For a discussion of this phenomenon with respect to campaigns surrounding 17 October 1961, see House and MacMaster, *Paris 1961,* p. 298.

63 Branche, *La Guerre d'Algérie,* p. 98.

64 Berlot, 'Préface', p. 8.

65 House and MacMaster, *Paris 1961,* p. 315.

66 Mirielle Rosello, *The Reparative in Narratives: Works of Mourning in Progress* (Liverpool, 2010), p. 5.

67 Branche, *La Guerre d'Algérie,* pp. 100–1; Esclangon-Morin et al., 'Les origines', p. 31.

68 Yves Sainsot, 'Démission collective du Haut Conseil des Rapatriés', *France horizon,* 496–497 (March–April–May 2009), 1.

69 House and MacMaster, *Paris 1961,* p. 315.

70 Jan C. Jansen, 'Politics of Remembrance, Colonialism and the Algerian War of Independence in France', in *A European Memory? Contested Histories and Politics of Remembrance,* ed. by Małgorzata Pakier and Bo Stråth (New York and Oxford, 2010), p. 284.

71 Abderahmen Moumen, 'Les Lieux de mémoire du groupe social "harki". Inventaire, enjeux et évolution', in *Les Harkis: histoire, mémoire et transmission,* ed. by Fatima Besnaci-Lancou, Benoit Falaize and Gilles Manceron (Ivry-sur-Seine, 2010), p. 139.

72 Laurent Muller, *Le Silence des harkis* (Paris, 1999), p. 226; Moumen, 'Les lieux', 140; 'Inauguration du Mémorial national des Harkis', *L'Algérianiste,* 140 (December 2012), 8.

73 'Le Mémorial des disparus ne fait pas le tri entre les victimes', *L'Algérianiste,* 136 supplement (December 2011), 5.

74 For further details, see www.anpnpa.org [10 May 2014]. A brief autobiography of Malléa, who was born in Guelma in 1940, can be found at www. ldh-toulon.net/Jacky-Mallea-de-Guelma-aux.html [15 January 2015].

75 Interview with Jacky Malléa in '50 ans d'Évian: portraits croisés des pieds-noirs', *Soir 3 journal,* aired 15 March 2012 (FR3).

76 'En guise de stèle', *La Lettre de Véritas,* 138 (15 December 2009), 1.

77 Joseph Hattab Pacha, 'Profanation à Perpignan', *Pieds-noirs d'hier et d'aujourd'hui,* 153 (June 2007), 23.

78 '5 juillet, interdiction de recueillement lévée?', *France horizon,* 498–9 (June–July–August 2009), 4.

79 'Droit au recueillement, une liberté fondamentale', *France horizon,* 522–3 (April–May–June 2012), 3.

80 Open letter to Pascal Matraji, head of the Bureau histoire et mémoire, in *Pieds-noirs d'hier et d'aujourd'hui,* 194 (March 2011), 22–3; Jean-François Collin, 'La Stèle de Marignane réimplantée!', *La Lettre de Véritas,* 152 (April 2011), 9.

81 www.fm-gacmt.org/fondation-algerie-maroc-tunisie/ [23 December 2014].

82 'À Perpignan', *L'Algérianiste,* 131 supplement (September 2010), 4.

83 Eric Bietry-Rivierre, 'Montpellier: un musée sans Histoire', *Le Figaro* (20 May 2014), p. 36.

84 I am grateful to Emile Chabal for prompting me to reflect on this question.

85 Benjamin Stora and Thierry Leclère, *La Guerre des mémoires: la France face à son passé colonial* (Paris, 2007), pp. 89–98.

86 House and MacMaster, *Paris 1961,* p. 333. One of the best discussions of the difficulties inherent in such a task is Baussant, 'Ni mémoire', pp. 165–97.

87 Peter Dunwoodie, 'Postface: History, Memory and Identity – Today's Crisis, Yesterday's Issue', *French History,* 20:3 (September 2006), 322–3.

88 www.achac.com [23 December 2014].

89 Annette Wieviorka, 'Le Vel d'Hiv: histoire d'une commémoration', in *Travail de mémoire 1914–1998. Une nécessité dans un siècle de violence,* ed. by Jean-Pierre Bacot (Paris, 1999), p. 165.

90 Guilia Fabbiano, 'Devenir-harki: les modes d'énonciation identitaire des descendants des anciens supplétifs de la guerre d'Algérie', *Migrations société,* 20:120 (November–December 2008), 170.

Conclusion

The year 2012 marked the half-century of Algerian independence and of the arrival of the *pieds-noirs* and *harkis* in France. In terms of the genealogies of memory that this book has sought to trace, anniversaries offer useful occasions on which to take stock: to step back and think about whose voices are being heard, which stories are being told and who is listening. They also enable us, in the words of Isabel Hollis, to identify 'key moments of fracture, division and reconciliation'.[1] The tenor of the 2012 commemorations did not quite stretch to reconciliation: no French officials were present for the 5 July independence day ceremonies in Algeria, although during his state visit in December the recently elected president, François Hollande, did officially acknowledge the 'suffering' imposed by colonialism on the Algerian people.[2] Nonetheless, there was a clear attempt by the French state to move beyond fracture and division in its handling of the anniversary year. Indicative of this was the very visible way in which the conflict was discussed and commemorated, including a series of prominent exhibitions and public debates in symbolic official spaces.[3]

Perhaps the most notable of these was the exhibition 'Algérie: 1830–1962', which was held in France's national military museum at the Hôtel des Invalides in Paris. Combining historical artefacts with illustrations produced by the Algeria-born *bande dessinée* artist Jacques Ferrandez, the exhibition attracted 44,000 visitors over the course of its three-month run.[4] Situated in the 7th *arrondissement*, a stone's throw from the National Assembly and other republican political institutions, the location of the exhibition exemplified how the War of Independence had progressively worked its way from the margins into the centre of French politics; a shift further underlined by the prominence of postcolonial social and cultural issues within the concurrently unfolding presidential election campaign.[5] In explaining his intentions, the exhibit's organiser Lieutenant-Colonel Christophe Bertrand stated that he was motivated by 'a wish to show everything' and to tackle a 'difficult subject' with rigour and honesty.[6] This stance was welcomed, not least by Sylvie Thénault, who felt that by placing the war within the broader historical context of French colonialism and through its willingness to engage with the complexities of the conflict, including openly confronting violence committed by the French Army as well as by the FLN, the exhibition represented a 'step forward'. It furthermore demonstrated for Thénault the emergence of a memory that had 'calmed', a process undoubtedly aided by the passing of those generations most directly implicated in the war.[7] Although there were limitations and some lingering biases, especially concerning the presentation of violence, overall 'Algérie: 1830–1962' reflected the 'increasing dialogue and understanding' surrounding Algeria and its historical relationship to France that gave the 2012 commemorations a different character to those of previous decades.[8]

This evolution was also evident in the extensive media coverage that spanned the entire anniversary year, but which peaked around the particularly significant dates of 19 March and 5 July. Even though no official ceremonies were held on either date, both occasions were marked in the media through glossy supplements, souvenir issues, or specially commissioned documentaries and debates.[9] Echoing the aim of the 'Algérie 1830–1962' exhibit organisers to concentrate on facts and avoid apportioning blame, media treatments focused on providing historical overviews of the conflict.[10] In keeping with wider commemorative trends, individual testimony was particularly prominent with the media taking care to elicit a range of voices, so as to represent all sides of the conflict. These perspectives were framed in a deliberately non-confrontational manner, so as to create, according to Fiona Barclay, 'not a cacophony of competing interests, but a comprehensive memorial mosaic which would contribute towards a holistic view of the war'.[11] Some raised concerns about the implications of such an approach, notably Benjamin Stora who repeated his long-standing warnings with regard to the risks of 'memory *communautarisme*', as a result of enabling each community to remain encased within their own recollections rather than entering into dialogue with others.[12] But, on the whole, 2012 was marked by a concerted effort in the public domain to discuss the war in ways that were historically grounded, open, and inclusive of the different communities affected by these events.

The last *pied-noir*?

Such attitudes were not, however, to the fore among *pied-noir* associations for whom the fiftieth anniversary represented an attack rather than an opportunity. In contrast to the twenty-fifth anniversary in 1987, which was seized upon as an occasion to demonstrate the vitality and value of the *pied-noir* community to the wider nation, activists were on the defensive in 2012. A national gathering was held in Marseille at the end of June, but on a much smaller scale than its inaugural sister event in Nice in 1987, receiving little publicity or commentary from associations. This was in keeping with the tone of association coverage more generally which, rather than encouraging *pieds-noirs* to come together and positively proclaim a collective identity or robustly defend their vision of the past, centred on listing the suffering and injustices that continued to be inflicted upon the community. Convinced that 'from now on anti-colonialism is the official doctrine of the Republic', associations focused on denouncing the recognition being given to other communities through gestures such as a monument to victims of the OAS unveiled in Paris and the presence of Hollande at the 17 October 1961 ceremonies, while their own wishes were consistently ignored.[13]

For ANFANOMA's Yves Sainsot, 2012 had simply provided an occasion for 'our most stubborn enemies to keep harping on about their old resentments and to keep trying to dishonour our memory'.[14] The heightened atmosphere of the anniversary year seemed only to underline the sense among *pied-noir* associations that since 2005 they had been on the losing side of the commemorative battle. Epitomising this loss of ground was the decision by the Senate to enshrine 19 March, the date of the signature of the Evian ceasefire accords, as the national day of commemoration for the victims of the Algerian War. The 'lively' debate surrounding this decision demonstrated the ongoing sensitivity of the topic and its continuing ability to arouse significant passions across the political spectrum. Indeed, the subject had previously been broached in 2002, during the fortieth anniversary, only to be shelved because it remained too controversial. That the final decision in 2012 was contentious was of little comfort to *pied-noir* associations forced to confront the defeat, at the highest level, of one of their longest running and most unifying campaigns.[15]

As the Senate debated, a small group of elderly *pied-noir* protestors gathered outside with their trademark 'No to 19 March' placards. Both the size of the demonstration and the advanced age of its participants fuelled the sense that *pied-noir* activism is winding down as militants are increasingly unable to maintain the vigour of previous years, let alone decades. Although the rhetoric of associations continues to centre on their 'unfailing devotion' to the cause of preserving *pied-noir* history and memory, the reality is that of a community which, fifty years on from its inception, is losing both its energy and its members.[16] Reflecting a growing preoccupation with the question of who will take over from existing activists, it seems no coincidence that the Cercle algérianiste chose 'transmission' as the theme of its annual conference in 2009. Although not a new concern – the Cercle algérianiste had been debating how to 'prepare our children to take the helm' since 1977, only a few years after the association formed – the question of how to ensure the successful transmission of the past to subsequent generations is becoming increasingly acute.[17]

It is important not to forget, however, that there has already been one successful inter-generational transfer of memory within the *pied-noir* community: current spokespeople being of a different generation to those who led and participated in associations in the immediate aftermath of 1962. The most obvious marker of this change was the shift in focus from material to commemorative concerns in the mid-1970s and the arrival of self-consciously 'young' activists like Cercle algérianiste founders Jacques Villard and Maurice Calmein. However, this process was not experienced as a dramatic rupture because both cohorts shared the common denominator of having lived in French Algeria and lived through the identity-forming exodus of 1962. Historical commonalities thus created a sense that all belonged to the same community with the continuation of national associations such as ANFANOMA, RANFRAN and USDIFRA from one era into the other further strengthening this perception.

The commitment of what one might call the 'third generation', however, seems less assured. Several factors are at play, including the simple passage of time. Ironically, the rapid socio-economic integration of the *rapatriés* often distanced descendants born in France from their familial heritage, making it difficult for children of *pieds-noirs* to appreciate the experiences of their parents in the 1960s. The wider context in which colonialism, the Algerian War and the settlers are discussed in France also makes it hard for younger generations to position themselves with respect to these histories. They are caught, as Michèle Baussant explains, between wishing to remain loyal to their family history, while also being surrounded by official, educational and media discourses that present an increasingly critical image of that same history and its actors.[18]

It is not the case, as some within *pied-noir* associations have complained, that their children are simply not interested in the past. Interviews conducted by the sociologist Clarisse Buono demonstrated a strong attachment among *pied-noir* descendants to Algeria as an ancestral land and a place about which many of them wished to know more.[19] What this generation appear less concerned with is participating in the kind of commemorative battles being waged by associations. This may be because many feel actively excluded by the insistence of existing activists on the importance of lived experience, particularly as a source of legitimacy and the best weapon through which to combat competing perspectives. By making first-hand knowledge the touchstone of authenticity, *pied-noir* associations have created a transmission cul-de-sac, whereby future generations, no matter how committed to activism, will always be limited by the fact that they themselves did not live through the events they are charged with preserving. This leaves the community vulnerable to the collective memory curse of the shelf life that was first outlined by Maurice Halbwachs, risking a scenario in which 'the last European born in Algeria on the eve of independence will also be the last *pied-noir*'.[20]

Harkis and the elusive 'official gesture'

The response of the *harki* community to 2012 was different to that of the *pieds-noirs,* as are the concerns of activists regarding the future. The visibility of *harkis* within the anniversary year commemorations, whether in exhibits, conferences, publications or documentaries, confirmed the status of the community as integral to contemporary French understandings of the War of Independence. Although *harkis* continue to be problematically cast in official and popular discourses as 'soldiers of France', ignoring the colonial dimensions of their enrolment and service, it is difficult to argue that they are still 'the forgotten of history'. Yet, the meaningful 'official gesture' that so many activists have called for continued to elude them, even in 2012. As a participant in the televised debate 'Après la déchirure' in March following the broadcasting of Stora's documentary of the same name,[21] Dalila Kerchouche was passionately insistent that what was still needed was 'an official acknowledgement by the President of the Republic of the French state's responsibility for the abandonment of the *harkis*'.[22]

This was a particular sensitive issue within the *harki* community because, five years previously, Nicholas Sarkozy, had promised precisely such a declaration when he was campaigning for the presidency. After Sarkozy's declaration on 31 March 2007 that, if elected, he would 'recognise France's responsibility for the abandonment and massacre of the *harkis* ... so that oblivion does not murder them once more', activists were surprised that he did not then attend any of the Journée nationale d'hommage aux harkis ceremonies, until the tenth such commemoration in 2011.[23] Yet, even on this date, no statement was issued relating to his 2007 pledge. In fact, it was only during the final frantic weeks of his 2012 re-election bid that Sarkozy saw fit to make a brief pit stop, between campaign engagements, at Rivesaltes where he presented General François Meyer with the Légion d'Honneur before briefly speaking in order to acknowledge the responsibility of the Republic in not protecting the *harkis* in 1962. The fact that his opponent, Hollande, had written to *harki* associations ten days earlier promising to make the same official statement if elected prompted many to attribute rather cynical motives to Sarkozy's sudden gesture.[24]

Hollande kept to his word, using the 2012 Journée nationale d'hommage aux harkis to state: 'Fifty years ago, France abandoned its own soldiers, those who had put their trust in her, those who were under her protection, those who had chosen her and who had served her.'[25] This was the first time the state had officially used the word 'abandon' to describe its treatment of the *harkis*. On the surface, this speech therefore appeared to satisfy this long-standing demand of the community. However, the impact of this important moment was undermined by the fact that Hollande was unable to deliver his historic message in person. Instead, his words were read by the minister with special responsibility for veterans, Kader Arifat, at a ceremony outside the Hôtel des Invalides. Further compromising Hollande's statement in the eyes of many *harkis* was his high-profile support of 17 October 1961 commemorations. That same year, Hollande attended the fifty-first anniversary ceremony in Paris where, on behalf of the Republic, he acknowledged that Algerians had been killed as the result of a 'bloody repression' and paid homage to the memory of those victims.[26]

This pattern of potentially significant but ultimately compromised commemorative initiatives was to be repeated with the inauguration of a national memorial to the *harkis* in December 2012. Taking the form of an oriental door, the five-metre-high edifice was located in the Jocques commune (Bouches-du-Rhône), close to the site of the former Logis d'Anne camp and in an area still containing a large number of *harkis* and their descendants. Erected at the initiative of *harki* associations and with support from the local municipality, the memorial was arguably 'national' neither in inspiration nor significance. Far from the political and cultural centre, the *harkis*' memorial was, like the community itself, tucked away in a remote corner of France. While it was welcomed by those who gathered to witness its unveiling, the memorial nonetheless demonstrated the ongoing absence of a prominent physical marker with actual national resonance to the history of the *harki* community. The year thus closed with Ali Amrane of the Collectif de harkis des Alpes Maritimes, in the context of Hollande's official visit to Algeria, repeating the now well-worn hope that 'the current government will make a strong gesture' in favour of the community.[27]

Issues relating to transmission and continuing activism within the *harki* community are different to those faced by *pieds-noirs*, not least because the definition of 'community' is looser. Very early in its history, the term 'harki' lost its specific meaning, expanding first to incorporate all auxiliary roles, then those Algerians who served the French in other capacities, before finally being stretched in the post-1962 period to include the wives, families and descendants of these men. While many, rightly, insist that being a *harki* is not hereditary and thus figures such as Kerchouche, Fatima Besnaci-Lancou and Hacène Arfi are not *harkis* in a strict sense, they are nonetheless considered and consider themselves to be part of the wider *harki* community. This, in combination with the consequences of enrolment being felt far beyond the *harkis* themselves and the inversion of inter-generational transmission mechanisms, has created more fluid and complex notions of belonging. Legitimacy as a spokesperson is therefore not tied to first-hand experience. It stems rather from a shared and ongoing sense of injustice at the way in which the community as a collective entity has been treated, with members, irrespective of their generational status, feeling affected in some way by this. Such sentiments are further perpetuated by the absence of socio-economic success and integration on the scale enjoyed by *pieds-noirs*. This is not to suggest that all *harkis* and their descendants live in poverty; many within the community have established successful and financially stable lives and more attention needs to be paid to these individuals to counter the pernicious stereotype that the history of the *harki* community is synonymous with a failure to integrate. But it is equally true that some do continue to struggle with the legacies of the initial treatment to which the *harkis* were subjected in France. This was underlined by a 2003 broadcast that reunited participants from the 1976 *Les Dossiers de l'écran* documentary on the *harkis* to discuss how their lives had changed in the intervening years. Forty-year-old Mohamed, the son of Hocine Bouzidi, the grocer featured in the original programme, noted that for all the doctors and lawyers that had emerged from the *harki* community, many remained 'imprisoned in the neighbourhood'.

He furthermore pointed out that living alongside the 'native French' was not the same as being fully integrated.[28] The unresolved nature of the practical situation of some *harkis,* in combination with outstanding commemorative demands relating to the position of the community as a whole within the memory of the nation, provides a compelling motive for younger members to remain mobilised. Activism is therefore something in which multiple generations have a tangible stake, rather than being something they are primarily enjoined to carry on with for their parents' sake, as is often the case for *pied-noir* children.[29]

Domestic imprints

As has been consistently demonstrated in this book, the commemorative picture within individual communities differs from that projected through national and official channels; 2012 was no different in that respect. This is not to deny that what happens nationally is influenced by grassroots activism and vice versa. Instead, what this study has shown are the variety of relationships and interactions that have defined the landscape of postcolonial memory in France since 1962 and the ways in which these have altered over time. Awareness of these wider frames is necessary in order to anchor the discourses articulated by *pied-noir* and *harki* activists with respect to the particular institutions and social milieu that produced them. The purpose has not been to argue that *pieds-noirs* and *harkis* are unique in terms of their experiences; 1962 was traumatic for a range of different groups, while having a difficult relationship with Algeria and with France is not the sole preserve of any one community. Rather, the significance of the case studies presented here lies in the fact that they provide an empirically grounded demonstration of the ways in which postcolonial migrants have shaped French politics and society for many years, including during the supposedly 'silent' pre-1990 era. Mapping the behaviour and interactions of the *pieds-noirs* and *harkis* thus contributes to our understanding of the evolution of civil society in France since the 1960s.

Through their rapid and cohesive mobilisation, *pied-noir* activists helped define the shape of identity politics in postcolonial France, setting an agenda that other groups, including the *harkis*, were then compelled to engage with – whether by copying or contesting it – in line with their own priorities. The impact of this was still visible in 2012. For all *pied-noir* activists felt they were being ignored by the mainstream media, Barclay's research has shown that the community in fact occupied a prominent place in the anniversary coverage. While by no means the sole focus, events central to the *pied-noir* narrative, especially their departure from Algeria in 1962, featured heavily. Perhaps most telling was the attention paid to events on 26 March 1962 in the rue d'Isly and in Oran on 5 July 1962. Virtually unreported at the time in mainland France, both moments quickly became commemorative touchstones for *pied-noir* associations, not least because they facilitated a narrative of unrecognised suffering. That the two dates have now also risen to prominence within mainstream overviews of the war is testament to the impact of *pied-noir* activism upon metropolitan consciousness. Speaking about the Eurasian Dutch settlers thirty years after their arrival in the Netherlands, activist Ellen Derksen stated that 'The *Indisch* Dutch have not silently assimilated away, they have silently imprinted their mark on Dutch society.' Her comment could equally be applied to the *pieds-noirs* in ways that the current siege mentality of the community perhaps prevents them from appreciating.[30]

In a similar fashion, the conspicuous place accorded to the *harki* community in 2012, compared to previous anniversaries, reminds us that there is no single chronology of memory and that the respective power dynamics and contextual factors that determine which voices are or are not heard can and do change. Through their distinct but interconnected genealogies of memory, the *pied-noir* and *harki* communities therefore enable a more nuanced understanding to be advanced of the mechanisms of memory creation, articulation and transmission with respect to the Algerian War. As case studies, they challenge the notion of the stark absence/presence dichotomy and help to situate the current competitive commemorative climate within a broader historical trajectory.

International resonances

This is, however, more than just a French history. The Algerian War of Independence was an event with global significance. As its afterlives continue to play out, this wider resonance remains and perhaps has even been amplified. It should, for example, be remembered that the experiences of the *pieds-noirs* and *harkis* in 1962 were part of a much broader process of migration that accompanied the end of empires in Europe and beyond after the Second World War. The exact circumstances that prompted departure, the contexts into which they arrived, the levels of state support provided, the degree of familiarity with the metropole, the attitude of the metropolitan population, the homogeneity of the returning communities, and the extent to which those 'repatriated' chose to maintain a distinct identity or to assimilate as seamlessly as possible, all these things varied considerably from country to country. What was common across the board, however, was the importance of citizenship. At the most basic level, it granted entry to the metropole, a right of abode once there and then access to whatever level of state aid that was available. It was also symbolically significant, underscoring the cultural and linguistic affinities that bound repatriates to their metropolitan cousins in spite of surface differences produced by time spent abroad. As Chapter 2 demonstrated, lacking these cultural, linguistic and ethnic markers of belonging made it easier for the French government to paint the *harkis* and their families as 'not French', in spite of their status as citizens, and to confine them to the margins of society.

A further common denominator was the sense of non-belonging – of being an 'internal stranger' – that pervades repatriate testimonies irrespective of the empire in question.[31] 'I am Japanese and yet not Japanese', reported one *hikiagesha* (repatriate) from Manchuria, reflecting a sense of alienation that was often exacerbated by the less than warm reception accorded to repatriates by metropolitan populations, who, like the French in 1962, saw these men and women as unwanted economic burdens and unwelcome reminders of a painful and humiliating past.[32] Such sentiments were even more pronounced when the individuals in question were of mixed heritage as was the case for the Eurasian or *Indisch* Dutch and a considerable number of Portuguese *retornados* (returnees).[33] But whereas the Dutch government proactively sought to ensure that inclusion on the basis of citizenship was not undermined by ethnic differences among the various repatriate communities, in Portugal those of mixed or African origin reported suffering significant economic discrimination and social ostracism. In particular, many found themselves classed as 'external strangers' and amalgamated with postcolonial migrant populations who had never had a claim to citizenship such as the growing number of economic migrants from Cape Verde now present in Portugal.[34] This echoes the position of the *harkis* and their children, who regularly found themselves viewed as part of the Algerian immigrant population in spite of their French nationality.

In contrast to the Portuguese *retornados* who have largely eschewed organisation around any distinct cultural identity or political interests, the majority of other repatriate groups have mobilised collectively along similar lines to the *pieds-noirs* and *harkis*. As in the French case, campaigns have sought financial compensation alongside symbolic recognition for the communities concerned. Mirroring the kinds of demands advanced in France, Indo-Dutch repatriates, for example, have fought for and obtained a national day of remembrance, which has existed since 1988. They have also been successful in securing government subsidies for books on their community's history. This is something the Moluccan community have also been granted, alongside the creation, in 1990, of a state-sponsored museum in Utrecht to their past as soldiers of the Royal Dutch Indian Army.[35] Perhaps the best known parallel to the situation of the *pieds-noirs,* in organisational terms at least, are the German expellee or *Vertriebene* associations which, partly because of the size of the constituencies to which they could appeal, have enjoyed considerable prominence and impact in the post-1945 period, even if, like their *pied-noir* counterparts, that influence is today on the wane.[36]

What also unites these disparate migrant populations is the way in which they have all become foils for a range of postcolonial questions, anxieties and debates in their respective 'home' nations, particularly centred on issues of identity and belonging. As 'the embodiment of a colonial history brought home', repatriates and other postcolonial migrants serve as living reminders of the fact that the formal cessation of colonial rule was by no means the end of the story.[37] As the diversity of European nations has increased, so too has the pressure on governments to reformulate national narratives, in order to reflect better the changing composition of their citizenry while still maintaining some sense of cohesion and consensus. The French state is far from alone in finding it a challenge to balance a range of often contradictory and competing interests and communities all seeking inclusion and official recognition.

Underlining the point that this situation does not only pertain to the history of empire, the Dutch historian Gert Oostindie writes: 'The postwar rediscovery of the colonial past fits within a broader pattern of making room, often with a guilty conscience, for the descendants of the victims of people's history.'[38] The attempts of the Dutch, the French and others to process the problematic past represented by colonialism therefore need to be placed alongside the efforts of a range of countries to confront difficult and divisive events in their national histories, including the Holocaust in Germany, the Franco dictatorship in Spain, apartheid in South Africa, genocide in Rwanda and the 'stolen generations' of Australia. In 'working through' these complex and usually still controversial histories, often following lengthy but perhaps necessary periods of silence, memory has emerged as a central concern and site of contestation.[39] As groups and individuals affected by these events and their legacies have mobilised in order to find a place for their specific experiences within the national historical imagination they have raised a similar set of issues to those prompted by the activism of the *pied-noir* and *harki* communities. In particular, they have posed difficult questions about national identity, about inclusion and notions of belonging, and about who possesses the authority and the legitimacy to speak on behalf of the past and thus to determine its meaning in the present.

International comparisons and connections are further thrown into relief by the fact that the idea of tightly delimited national memories is increasingly being called into question, not least by the development of a global human rights agenda which has provided a transnational arena for memories related to conflict to be articulated, recognised and legitimated.[40] This is reflected in the increased salience of concepts such as reconciliation, repentance, reparations and victimhood, especially within a judicial context. Seeing the history of memories of the Algerian War offered here as part of this bigger picture – as part of a world that possesses a heightened memorial consciousness and an increasingly transnational vocabulary through which this is articulated – enables us to appreciate better the global resonances of the experiences of the *pieds-noirs* and *harkis*, without losing sight of the specific elements of their distinct yet interrelated postcolonial trajectories.

Notes

1   Isabel Hollis, 'Algeria in Paris: Fifty Years On', in *French Politics since the 1970s*, ed. by Emile Chabal (London, 2014), p. 129.

2   'Réactions aux propos de François Hollande sur la colonisation en Algérie', *JT 19/20 Edition nationale,* aired 21 December 2012 (FR3).

3   For a comprehensive list of national commemorations, see Michèle Bacholle-Bošković, 'Quelles commémorations pour les cinquante ans de la guerre d'Algérie?', *French Cultural Studies*, 25:2 (2014), 236–7.

4   A good sense of the content of the exhibition can be gained from the catalogue, see Christophe Bertrand, Sébastien Denis and Emmanuel Ranvoisy (eds.), *Algérie 1830–1962*, with Jacques Ferrandez (Paris, 2012).

5   Hollis, 'Algeria in Paris', pp. 129–35.

6   'Commémorations de l'indépendance de l'Algérie', *ARTE journal,* aired 5 July 2012 (ARTE).

7   'Commémorations', aired 5 July 2012 (ARTE).

8   Hollis, 'Algeria in Paris', p. 133. The chapter also discusses the problems with the ways in which violence committed by the French Army was depicted in relation to that of the FLN.

9   For further details, see Bacholle-Bošković, 'Quelles commémorations', 236–40.

10 Hollis, 'Algeria in Paris', p. 134.

11 Fiona Barclay, 'Reporting on 1962: the Evolution of *pied-noir* Identity across Fifty Years of Print Media', *Modern and Contemporary France*, 23:2 (2015), 206.

12 See, in particular, Stora's comments during '50 ans Accords d'Évian: portraits croisés de pieds-noirs', *Soir 3 journal*, aired 15 March 2012 (FR3).

13 Jean Monneret, 'Face à l'anticolonialisme d'État', *La Lettre de Véritas*, 163 (September–October 2012), 4.

14 Yves Sainsot, 'Année de tous les dangers', *France horizon*, 524–5 (July–August 2012), 1.

15 'Adoption au Sénat d'une journée de commémoration de la guerre d'Algérie', *20 heures*, aired 8 November 2012 (FR2).

16 Nicole Ferrandis, 'Chers lecteurs', *France horizon*, 526–7 (November–December 2012), 12.

17 Maurice Calmein, 'Appellation contrôlée', *L'Algérianiste* (1977), 10.

18 Michèle Baussant, *Pieds-noirs: mémoires d'exils* (Paris, 2002), p. 8.

19 Clarisse Buono, *Pieds-noirs de père en fils* (Paris, 2004), p. 152.

20 Michèle Baussant, 'Identité passagère: pied-noir, une figure de l'exil', in *La Guerre d'Algerie dans la mémoire et l'imaginaire*, ed. by Anny Dayan Rosenman and Lucette Valensi (Paris, 2004), p. 116.

21 'Déchirure' means to tear, rip or wrench, but it can also be used figuratively to mean heartbreak.

22 'Débat: après la déchirure', *Spéciale guerre d'Algérie*, aired 11 March 2012 (FR2)

23 The full text of Sarkozy's 2007 speech can be found at www.harkis.com/article .php3?id_article=286 [24 January 2015].

24 See, for example, 'Harkis, une reconnaissance à l'arraché!', *L'Algérianiste*, 138 (June 2012), 11; 'Le Président de la République à Rivesaltes', *Pieds-noirs d'hier et d'aujourd'hui*, 205 (May 2012), 13.

25 'Harkis. M. Hollande reconnaît les "fautes" de la France', *Le Monde* (27 September 2012), p. 10.

26 Thomas Wieder, 'François Hollande reconnaît la répression du 17 octobre 1961', *Le Monde* (19 October 2012), p. 10.

27 Réactions aux propos de François Hollande', aired 21 December 2012.

28 'Les Harkis', *Contre courant*, aired 25 April 2003 (A2).

29 For further discussion of the question of transmission, see Claire Eldridge, 'Passing the Torch: Memory Transmission and Activism within the *Pied-Noir* Community Fifty Years after Algerian Independence', in *Algeria Revisited: History, Culture and Identity, 1830 to the Present*, ed. by Rabah Aissaoui and Claire Eldridge (London, forthcoming).

30 Ellen Derksen cited in Gert Oostindie, 'Ruptures and Dissonance: Post-Colonial Migrations and the Remembrance of Colonialism in the Netherlands', in *Memories of Post-Imperial Nations: The Aftermath of Decolonization, 1945–2013*, ed. by Dietmar Rothermund (Cambridge, 2015), p. 43.

31 For further discussion of this concept, see Stephen K. Lubkemann, 'Race, Class and Kin in the Negotiation of "Internal Strangerhood" among Portuguese Retornados', in *Europe's Invisible Migrants*, ed. by Andrea L. Smith (Amsterdam, 2003), p. 75.

32 Lori Watt, 'Imperial Remnants: The Repatriates in Postwar Japan', in *Settler Colonialism in the Twentieth Century*, ed. by Caroline Elkins and Susan Pedersen (New York, 2005), p. 251.

33 This was in contrast to the *pieds-noirs* where historically low rates of inter-marriage with the other populations in colonial Algeria ensured an ethnically homogenous repatriate community in 1962, even if they were diverse in other respects, especially in socio-economic terms.

34 Hans van Amersfoot and Mies van Niekerk, 'Immigration as a Colonial Inheritance: Post-Colonial Immigrants in the Netherlands, 1945–2002', *Journal of Ethnic and Migration Studies*, 32:3 (2006), 326. Lubkemann, 'Race, Class and Kin', pp. 88–91.

35 However, state funding cuts have recently led to the closure of this institution. Oostindie, 'Ruptures and Dissonance', pp. 47–8.

36 For an overview of this mobilisation, see Pertti Ahonen, 'The German Expellee Organizations: Unity, Division, and Function', in *Vertriebene and Pieds-Noirs in Postwar Germany and France: Comparative Perspectives*, ed. by Manuel Borutta and Jan C. Jansen (Basingstoke, 2016), pp. 115–131.

37 Oostindie, 'Ruptures and Dissonance', p. 52.

38 Oostindie, 'Ruptures and Dissonance', p. 54.

39 Benjamin Stora sees periods of silence in the wake of traumatic national events as 'necessary' in order to enable 'citizens to continue their lives together'. See 'La France et ses guerres de mémoires', in *Les Guerres de mémoires: la France et son histoire*, ed. by Pascal Blanchard and Isabelle Veyrat-Masson (Paris, 2008), p. 7.

40 Jim House and Neil MacMaster, *Paris 1961: Algerians, State Terror and Memory* (Oxford, 2006), p. 93; Timothy Ashplant, Graham Dawson and Michael Roper., 'The Politics of War Memory and Commemoration: Contexts, Structures and Dynamics', in *The Politics of War Memory and Commemoration*, ed. by Timothy Ashplant et al. (London, 2000), p. 68.

Select bibliography

Primary sources

ASSOCIATION NEWSPAPERS, JOURNALS, MAGAZINES AND BULLETINS

L'Algérianiste (1975–2012)

L'Algérien en Europe (1965–82); becomes *La Semaine de l'émigration* (1982–85) becomes *L'actualité de l'émigration* (1985–91)

L'ancien de l'Algérie (1958–2012)

Baraka (1985–87)

Bulletin d'information du GNPI (1964–90, 1996–2000)

Les Cahiers de la nouvelle génération (1984–86)

Coup de soleil info (1990–91)

Différences (1980–2000)

L'écho d'Oran (1964–6); becomes *L'écho de l'Oranie* (1966–2007)

Aux échos d'Alger (1980–2007)

Ensemble: le journal Franco-Maghrébin (1997–98)

L'éveil des Français d'Algérie: bulletin d'information des harkis rapatriés d'Algérie et leurs amis (1995–97)

Exil: communautés algériennes (1983–84)

Les Français d'AFN et d'outre mer (1980–95)

Français musulmans (1980–2009)

France horizon: le cri du rapatrié (1957–2012)

FMR: le journal (1984)

FONDA: lettre d'information 1981–90); becomes *La tribune FONDA* (1990–2005)

Horizons-Maghrébins: le droit à la mémoire (1984–2003)

IM'média magazine (1984–88)

La Lettre jeune pied-noir (1981–85); becomes *Vocation française* (1985–86)

La Lettre de la maison des rapatriés de Cannes et leurs amis (1994–95)

La Lettre du RECOURS France (1995)

La Lettre de Véritas (1996–2012)

Méditerranée demain (1990–91)
Mémoire plurielle: les cahiers d'Afrique du Nord (1994–2003)
Mémoire vive: Algérie-Maroc-Tunisie (2004–6)
Midi: le magazine pieds-noirs (1965–67)
Pieds-noirs magazine (1990–93); becomes *Pieds-noirs d'hier et d'aujourd'hui* (1993–2000; 2003–12)
Le Rappel (1982–91)
RECOURS Infos (1985)
Sans frontière (1979–85)
Sétif de l'hexagone (1970–2006)
La Voix du combattant – La Voix du djebel-flame (1976–94)

MEMOIRS

Azni, Boussad, *Harkis, crime d'état: généalogie d'un abandon* (Paris, 2002).
Besnaci-Lancou, Fatima, *Fille de harki*, with Marie-Christine Ray (Paris, 2003).
Boualam, Saïd, *L'Algérie sans la France* (Paris, 1964).
——, *Les Harkis au service de la France*, (Paris: Editions France-Empire, 1963).
——, *Mon pays … la France* (Paris, 1962).
Bouzid, *La Marche: traversée de la France profonde* (Paris, 1984).
Chami, Abdelkader, Mehdi Chami and Geoffroy Sale, *Les Habits de mariage: itinéraire d'un harki* (Orléans, 2012).
Clément, Alain, *Quand la France a refusé de sauver le soldat Mohamed: mémoire d'un lieutenant sur la guerre d'Algérie* (Crest, 2011).
Cohen, Jean, *Chronique d'une Algérie révolue: comme l'ombre et le vent* (Paris, 1997).
Daniel, Jean, *L'ère des ruptures* (Paris, 1979).
Désir, Harlem, *SOS désirs* (Paris, 1987).
——, *Touche pas à mon pote* (Paris, 1985).
Dessaigne, Francine, *Déracinés!* (Paris, 1964).
——, *Journal d'une mère de famille pied-noir* (Paris, 1962).
Ferdi, Saïd, *Un enfant dans la guerre* (Paris, 1981).
Gadget, Roger, *Commando Georges: des harkis de feu* (Paris, 1990).
Garceau, Jean-Maurice, *Vive la France! L'odyssée des harkis du Commando Kodja* (Paris, 2002).
Hervo, Monique, *Chroniques du bidonville: Nanterre en guerre d'Algérie 1954–1962* (Paris, 2001).
Jammes, Patrick, *Médecin des harkis au camp de Bias, 1970–2000* (Paris, 2012).
Jouhaud, Edmond, *Serons-nous enfin compris?* (Paris, 1984).
——, *Ce que je n'ai pas dit* (Paris, 1977).
Katz, Jospeh, *L'honneur d'un général: Oran, 1962* (Paris, 1993).
Lenoir, René, *Mon Algérie tendre et violent* (Paris, 1994).
Loesch, Anne, *La Valise et le cercueil* (Paris, 1963).
Macias, Enrico, *Mon Algérie* (Paris, 2000).
——, *Non, je n'ai pas oublié* (Paris, 1982).
Méliani, Abd-el-Aziz, *Le Drame des harkis* (Paris, 2001).

Meyer, François, *Pour l'honneur, avec les harkis: de 1958 à nos jours* (Tours, 2005).

Moinet, Bernard, *Ahmed? connais pas: le calvaire des harkis* (Paris, 1980).

——, *Journal d'une agonie* (Paris, 1965, reprinted 1999).

Ortiz, Jo, *Mon combat pour l'Algérie française* (Helette, 2003).

Rey, Marie-Jeanne, *Mémoires d'une écorchée vive* (Paris, 1987).

Sadouni, Brahim, *Destin de harki*, with Alexandre Grigarigntz (Paris, 2001).

——, *Le Drapeau: écrit d'un harki* (Paris, 1990).

——, *Français sans patrie: la reconnaissance* (Rouen, 1985).

Salan, Raoul, *Mémoires 4: Fin d'un empire, l'Algérie, de Gaulle et moi, 7 juin 1958-10 juin 1960* (Paris, 1974).

——, *Mémoires 3: Fin d'un empire, Algérie française, 1er novembre 1954* (Paris, 1972).

Sutra, Josette, *Algérie mon amour: Constantine 1920–1962* (Paris, 1979).

Taleb, Eric, *La Fin des harkis* (Paris, 1972).

Telali, Saliha, *Les Enfants des harkis: entre silence et assimilation subie* (Paris, 2009).

Secondary sources

SELECTED AUDIOVISUAL SOURCES

1960s

'Les Rapatriés', *Faire face* (two episodes), aired 24 November and 8 December 1961 (Channel 1)

'Robert Boulin à Marseille', *JT 13H*, aired 11 December 1961 (Channel 1)

'Algérie: la fin d'une guerre', *Cinq colonnes à l'une*, 6 April 1962 (Channel 1)

'Algérie: le mois de l'exode', *Cinq colonnes à la une*, aired 1 June 1962 (Channel 1)

'Des Français d'Afrique du Nord', *Cinq colonnes à la une*, aired 2 June 1962 (Channel 1)

'October 62: les Français d'Algérie', *Cinq colonnes à la une*, aired 5 October 1962 (Channel 1)

'Un an après: être français en Algérie', *Cinq colonnes à l'une*, 1 March 1963 (Channel 1)

'Où en sont les rapatriés?', *Cinq colonnes à la une*, aired 3 May 1963 (Channel 1)

'C'étaient les harkis', *Cinq colonnes à l'une*, aired 7 June 1963 (Channel 1)

'Un million de Français, les rapatriés d'Algérie: L'île du Rhône', *Sept jours du monde*, aired 15 May 1964 (Channel 1)

'1965: des Français en Algérie', *Cinq colonnes à l'une*, aired 3 March 1965 (Channel 1)

'Naissance d'un village: Carnoux', *Cinq colonnes à l'une*, aired 7 October 1966 (Channel 1)

1970s

'Les Harkis de Saint-Valérien', *Panorama*, aired 17 April 1970 (Channel 1)

'L'Algérie dix ans après: les rapatriés', *Quatrième mardi* (two episodes), aired 23, 30 May 1972 (Channel 1)

'Algérie dix ans après: la rencontre de l'apaisement: Algérie', *Plein cadre*, aired 23 June 1972 (Channel 2)

'Les Harkis', *Les Dossiers de l'écran*, aired 17 May 1977 (A2)

'Et pourtant ils sont Français', *Les Dossiers de l'écran*, aired 17 May 1977 (A2)

1980s

'Les Pied-noirs vingt ans après', *La Rage de lire*, aired 5 March 1980 (TF1)

'La Guerre d'Algérie', *Apostrophes*, aired 11 September 1981 (A2)

Montpellier: 20 ans accords d'Evian, aired 19 March 1982 (A2)

'Le Fils du harki', *Pour changer aller simple*, aired 20 March 1982 (TF1)

Guerre d'Algérie, dir. Yves Courrière, aired 21 October 1982 (FR3)

'Guerre d'Algérie. Mémoire enfouie d'une génération', *Moeurs en direct* (three episodes), dir. Denis Chegaray, aired 7, 14 and 21 November 1982 (A2)

'Pour ceux d'Algérie, que reste-t-il du passé?', *Les Dossiers de l'écran*, aired 5 April 1983 (A2)

'Droit de réponse aux pieds-noirs', *Droit de réponse*, 8 November 1986 (TF1)

Grève des harkis, aired 20 February 1987 (TF1)

'Mohammed et Jacques', *Sept sur sept*, aired 22 March 1987 (TF1)

'Encadré rapatriés', *JT 13 heures*, aired 29 April 1987 (TF1)

'Rapatriés: 25 ans de nostalgie', *Camera 2*, aired 22 June 1987 (A2)

'Les Pieds-noirs, ça va?', *Les Dossiers de l'écran*, aired 20 October 1987 (A2)

Drame harkis, aired 25 December 1988 (TF1)

1990s

'Retour à la terre natale', *Du côté de chez Fred*, aired 31 May 1990 (A2)

La Guerre d'Algérie (five episodes), dir. Peter Batty, aired 12, 19 and 26 August, 2 and 9 September 1990 (FR3)

La Guerre d'Algérie: malentendu ou absurdité? aired 9 September 1990 (FR3)

'Revolte jeunes harkis', *JT 20 heures*, aired 10 October 1990 (TF1)

De Gaulle et l'OAS: L'Algérie c'est la France, aired 2 January 1991 (TF1)

'Benjamin Stora', *Le Divan*, 10 February 1991 (FR3)

'Arlette Laguiller', *Ciel, mon mardi!*, aired 4 June 1991 (FR3)

Les Années algériennes (four episodes), prod. Benjamin Stora, aired 23 and 30 September, 7 and 8 October 1991 (A2)

'Spécial guerre d'Algérie', *Mardi soir*, aired 8 October 1991 (A2)

'Algérie, mémoires d'une guerre', *Caractères*, 22 November 1991 (FR3)

'La Guerre sans nom', *La Marche du siècle*, aired 12 February 1992, (FR3)

Récits d'Algérie. aired 24 June 1992 (TF1)

Rester là-bas, dir. Dominuqe Cabrera, aired 13 December 1992 (ARTE)

'Être pied-noir trente ans après', *Français si vous parliez*, aired 1 February 1993 (FR3)

'Les Harkis': *Planète chaude* (two episodes), aired 12 and 19 December 1993 (FR3)

'Les Harkis: les fils de l'oubli', *Les Cinq continents*, aired 8 November 1994 (FR3)

'France-Algérie: la blessure ouverte', *7 et demi*, aired 17 December 1996 (ARTE)

'Peut-on échapper à la haine ordinaire?', *Ça se discute*, aired 28 May 1997 (A2).

Mémoires d'immigrés: L'héritage maghrébin, aired 30 May 1997 (Canal+)

'35 ans Pieds-noirs', *TF1 20 heures*, aired 14 June 1997 (TF1)

'Premier novembre 1954, la Toussaint rouge, les débuts de la guerre d'Algérie', *Les Brûlures de l'histoire*, aired 3 July 1997 (FR3)

Un siècle d'immigrations en France (three episodes), aired 10 to 24 October 1997, (FR3)

'Pas de regrets pour les Algériens', *8 et demi*, aired 17 October 1997 (ARTE)

'La Situation des harkis', *7 et demi: Sous dossier*, aired 13 November 1997 (ARTE)

'Polémique événement du 17 octobre 1961', *Le Vrai journal*, aired 14 February 1999 (Canal+)

2000s

'D'une rive à l'autre', *La Case de l'oncle Doc*, aired 6 March 2000 (FR3)

'Que reste-t-il de la culture pied-noir?', *Ça se discute*, aired 5 April 2000 (FR2)

'La Cité des pieds-noirs', *La Cinquième rencontre*, aired 6 June 2000 (La cinquième)

'Duplex à Bouteflika', *JA2 20 heures*, aired 16 June 2000 (FR2)

Arrêt sur images, aired 7 January 2001 (La cinquième)

'Spécial guerre d'Algerie', *Mots croisés*, aired 21 May 2001 (FR2)

'17 octobre 1961: une journée portée disparue', *Les Mercredis de l'Histoire*, aired 17 October 2001 (ARTE)

'Fils de harkis', *Chroniques d'ici*, aired 8 November 2001 (FR3)

Harkis: le crime, aired 12 February 2002 (ARTE)

L'ennemi intime (three episodes), dir. Patrick Rotman, aired 4, 5 and 6 March 2002 (FR3)

'Spécial Algérie', *Culture et dépendances*, aired 6 March 2002 (FR3)

'Les Cicatrices françaises', *C dans l'air*, aired 12 March 2002 (FR5)

'Algérie: réveils de mémoires', *Saga cities*, 16 March 2002 (FR3)

'Il y a 40 ans déjà l'histoire déchirée des Français d'Algérie', *La Case de l'oncle Doc*, aired 18 March 2002 (FR3)

Harki: un traître mot, aired 29 April 2002 (FR5)

Les Algériens de Lyon: Français d'ici, peuples d'ailleurs, 2 May 2002 (FR5)

'Spécial Algérie', *Culture et dependences*, aired 6 May 2002 (FR3)

Algérie, Montpellier: aller simple, 25 May 2002 (FR5)

'Le Mouchoir de mon père', *La Case de l'oncle Doc*, aired 21 September 2002 (FR3)

'Le Drame algérien', *C dans l'air*, aired 5–6 December 2002 (FR5)

'Les Jardiniers de la rue des martyrs', *Grand format*, aired 10 February 2003 (ARTE)

'Retour au pays', *Sept à huit*, aired 20 March 2003 (TF1)

'Harkis: des français entièrement à part?', *Contre courant*, aired 25 April 2003 (FR2)

Un parcours algérien (three episodes), aired 27 June, 4 July and 30 November 2003 (FR2)

'La Communauté harki, toujours indésirable en Algérie et mal intégrée en France', *Soir 3 journal*, aired 24 September 2003 (FR3)

'Guerre d'Algérie: la fin des mensonges', *Mots croisés*, aired 3 November 2003 (FR2)

'Massacres pieds-noirs et harkis en 1962', *Mots croisés*, aired 3 November 2003 (FR2)
'Harkis: la mémoire sacrifiée?', *Ripostes*, aired 7 December 2003 (FR5)
'Réconciliation algérienne', *TF1 20 heures*, aired 25 September 2004 (TF1)
'Une autre guerre d'Algérie', *La Case de l'oncle Doc*, 2 November 2004 (FR3)
L'émotion: retour de pieds-noirs en Algérie, aired 6 June 2005 (M6)
'L'adieu aux larmes', *Strip tease*, aired 21 August 2005 (Fr3)
'Réactions et souvenirs de 150 pieds-noirs de retour en Algérie', *20 heures le journal*, aired 19 March 2006 (FR2)
France Algérie: L'amour impossible, aired 12 April 2006 (ARTE)
1830–1962 Quand l'Algérie était française, aired 16 May 2006 (M6)
France-Algérie: une histoire d'amour, aired 16 May 2006 (M6)
'Retour en Algérie 40 ans après', *1310 le magazine*, aired 17 May 2006 (M6)
'Passé recomposé', *Envoyé special*, aired 22 June 2006 (FR2)
Harkis, dir. Alain Tasma, aired 10 October 2006 (FR2)
'Amère patrie', *Documents*, 13 October 2006 (FR5)
Les Pieds-noirs: histoires d'une blessure (three episodes), dir. Gilles Perez, aired 24 and 31 March, 7 April 2007 (FR3)
France-Algérie: les cicatrices de l'hisoire', *Ripostes*, aired 9 September 2007 (FR5)
'Le Choix de mon père', *La Case de l'oncle Doc*, aired 27 September 2008 (FR3)
'Immigrés, 1945–1981', *Musulmans en France*, aired 20 December 2009 (FR3)

2010s

'La Blessure: la tragédie des harkis', *Hors série*, dir. Isabelle Clarke and Daniel Costelle, aired 20 September 2010 (FR3)
'Débat: après la déchirure', *Spéciale guerre d'Algérie*, aired 11 March 2012 (FR2)
'Algérie, notre histoire', *Histoire*, aired 13 March 2012 (ARTE)
'Une histoire algérienne', *La Case du siècle*, aired 18 March 2012 (FR5)
Nos guerres d'Algérie, aired 26 June 2012 (FR3)
'Spéciale Algérie', *Vivement dimanche*, aired 2 September 2012 (FR2)
'L'amère patrie: le retour des Français d'Algérie', *Docs interdits*, aired 10 September 2012 (FR2)

SELECTED BOOKS AND ARTICLES

Abdallah, Mogniss H., 'La Marche pour l'égalité, une mémoire restaurer', *Hommes et migrations*, 1247 (January–February 2004), 99–104.
Abdellatif, Saliha, 'Le Français musulman ou une entité préfabriqué', *Hommes et migrations*, 1135 (1990), 28–33.
——, 'Les Français-musulmans ou le poids de l'histoire à travers la communauté picarde', *Les Temps modernes*, 452:4 (1984), 1812–38.
Abrial, Stéphanie, *Les Enfants de harkis: de la révolte à l'intégration* (Paris, 2002).
Ageron, Charles Robert, 'Le "Drame des harkis": mémoire ou histoire?' *Vingtième siècle*, 68 (October-December 2000), 3–15.
——, 'Les Supplétifs algériens dans l'armée française pendant la guerre d'Algérie', *Vingtième siècle*, 48 (October–December 1995), 3–20.

Amato, Alain, *Monuments en exil* (Paris, 1979).

Ashplant, T.G., Graham Dawson and Michael Roper (eds.), *The Politics of War, Memory and Commemoration* (London, 2000).

Ayoun, Monique, and Jean-Pierre Stora, *Mon Algérie: 62 personnalités témoignent* (Paris, 1989).

Azéma, Jean-Pierre, Jean-Pierre Rioux, and Henry Rousso, 'Les Guerres franco-françaises', *Vingtième siècle*, 5 (January–March 1985), 3–6.

Baillet, Pierre, 'L'intégration des rapatriés d'Algérie en France', *Population*, 2 (1975), 303–14.

Bancel, Nicolas, Pascal Blanchard and Sadrine Lemaire (eds.), *Culture coloniale en France: de la Révolution française à nos jours* (Paris: Editions Autrement, 2008).

Bancel, Nicolas, *Culture postcoloniale: traces et mémoires coloniales en France* (Paris, 2006).

——, *La Fracture coloniale: la société française au prisme de l'héritage coloniale* (Paris, 2005).

Bancel, Nicolas, Pascal Blanchard and Françoise Vèrges, *La République coloniale: essai sur une utopie* (Paris, 2003).

Barclay, Fiona, 'Reporting on 1962: The Evolution of *pied-noir* Identity across Fifty Years of Print Media', *Modern and Contemporary France*, 23:2 (2015), 197–211.

Barsali, Nora, François-Xavier Freland and Anne-Marie Vincent, *Générations beurs: français à part entière* (Paris, 2008).

Batty, Peter, *La Guerre d'Algérie* (Paris, 1989).

Baussant, Michèle, 'Caught between Two Worlds: The Europeans of Algeria in France after 1962', in *History, Memory and Migration: Perceptions of the Past and the Politics of Incorporation*, ed. by Irial Glynn and J. Olaf Kleist (Basingstoke, 2012), pp. 87–105.

——, 'Ni mémoire, ni oubli: la France à l'épreuve de son histoire coloniale. L'exemple des pieds-noirs et des harkis', in *Du vrai au juste: la mémoire, l'histoire et l'oubli*, ed. by Michèle Baussant (Saint-Nicolas, Québec, 2006), pp. 165–97.

——, 'Identité passagère: pied-noir, une figure de l'exil', in *La Guerre d'Algérie dans la mémoire et l'imaginaire*, ed. by Anny Dayan Rosenman and Lucette Valensi (Paris, 2004), pp. 103–16.

——, *Pieds-noirs: mémoires d'exils* (Paris, 2002).

Benguigui, Yamina, *Mémoires d'immigrés: l'héritage maghrébin* (Paris, 1997).

Bernardot, Marc, 'Être interné au Larzac', *Politix*, 69 (2001), 39–61.

Besnaci-Lancou, Fatima, *Des Harkis envoyés à la mort: le sort des prisonniers de l'Algérie indépendante (1962–1969)* (Ivry-sur-Seine, 2014).

Besnaci-Lancou, Fatima, with Benoit Falaize and Gilles Manceron, *Les Harkis: histoire, mémoire et transmission* (Ivry-sur-Seine, 2010).

Besnaci-Lancou, Fatima (ed.), *Des vies: 62 enfants de harkis racontent* (Ivry-sur-Seine, 2010).

Besnaci-Lancou, Fatima, and Gilles Manceron (eds.), *Les Harkis dans la colonisation et ses suites* (Ivry-sur-Seine: Editions de l'Atelier, 2008).

Besnaci-Lancou, Fatima, *Treize chibanis harkis* (Paris, 2006).

——, *Nos mères, paroles blessées: une autre histoire de harkis* (Léchelle, 2006).

Blanchard, Pascal and Isabelle Veyrat-Masson (eds.), *Les Guerres de mémoires: la France et son histoire* (Paris, 2008).

Bouamama, Saïd, *Héritiers involontaires de la guerre d'Algérie: jeunes Manosquins issus de l'immigration algérienne* (Manosque, 2003).

——, *Dix ans de marche des beurs: chronique d'un mouvement avorté* (Paris, 1994).

——, *Contribution à la mémoire des banlieues* (Paris, 1994).

Bouba, Philippe, *L'arrivée des pieds-noirs en Roussillon en 1962* (Canet, 2009).

Boulhaïs, Nordine, *Histoire des harkis du nord de la France* (Paris, 2005).

Boym, Svetlana, *The Future of Nostalgia* (New York, 2001).

Branche, Raphaëlle, *La Guerre d'Algérie: une histoire apaisée?* (Paris, 2005).

Brière, Camille, *Qui sont les harkis?* (Versailles, 1986).

——, *Ceux qu'on appelle les pieds noirs ou 150 ans de l'histoire d'un peuple* (Paris, 1984).

Brillet, Emmanuel, 'A Remarkable Heritage: The "Daily Round" of the Children of the Harkis, between Merger and Vilification', *Immigrants and Minorities*, 22:2–3 (July/November 2003), 333–45.

——, 'La Contingence et la geste: le harki, l'indicible du "mouvement de l'histoire"', in *L'époque de la disparition: politique et esthétique*, ed. by Alain Brossat and Jean-Louis Déotte (Paris, 2000), pp. 125–54.

Buono, Clarisse, *Pieds-noirs de père en fils* (Paris, 2004).

Calmein, Maurice, *Dis, c'était comment, l'Algérie française? 20 questions et réponses à l'intention des jeunes pieds noirs* (Friedberg, Bayern, 2002).

——, *Les Associations pieds-noirs* (Carcassonne, 1994).

Cazal, Anne, *Contes de ma province sanglante* (Hélette, 1997).

Chabal, Emile, 'Managing the Postcolony: Minority Politics in Montpellier, c.1960-c.2010', *Contemporary European History*, 23:2 (2014), 237–58.

——, 'La République postcoloniale? Making the Nation in Late Twentieth Century France', in *France's Lost Empires: Fragmentation, Nostalgia and la fracture coloniale*, ed. by Kate Marsh and Nicola Frith (Lanham, MD, 2010), pp. 137–52.

Chapsal, Julien, *Harkis à vie?* (Trézélan, 2006).

Charbit, Tom, 'La genèse sociale d'une crise "raciale": l'Installation des harkis dans le Gard rhodanien (1962–1975)', in *Vivre dans la différence d'hier et d'aujourd'hui*, ed. by Gabriel Audiso and François Pugnière (Avignon, 2007), pp. 31–55.

——, 'Un petit monde colonial en métropole: le camp de harkis de Saint-Maurice-l'Ardoise (1962–1976)', *Politix*, 76 (2006), 31–52.

——, 'Saint-Maurice-l'Ardoise: socio-histoire d'un camp de harkis (1962–1976)', *Migrations études*, 130 (September 2005), 1–12.

——, 'Sociographie des familles de harkis de Saint-Maurice-l'Ardoise', *Migrations études*, 128 (September 2005) 2–19.

Chauvin, Stéphanie, 'Des appelés pas comme les autres? Les conscrits "Français de souche nord-africaine" pendant la guerre d'Algérie', *Vingtième siècle*, 48 (October–December 1995), 21–30.

Choi, Sung, 'Les anciens combattants musulmans dans la France postcoloni-ale: la politique d'intégration des harkis après 1962', *Les Temps modernes* 666 (November–December 2011), 120–39.

——, 'The Muslim Veteran in Postcolonial France: The Politics of the Integration of Harkis after 1962', *French Politics, Culture and Society*, 29:1 (Spring 2011), 24–45.

Chossat, Michèle, 'In a Nation of Indifference and Silence: Invisible Harkis or Writing the Other', *Contemporary French and Francophone Studies*, 11:1 (2007), 75–83.

Cohen, William B., 'The *Harkis*: History and Memory', in *Algeria and France 1800–2000: Identity, Memory, Nostalgia*, ed. by Patricia M. E. Lorcin (New York, 2006), pp. 164–80.

——, 'Pied-Noir Memory, History and the Algerian War', in *Europe's Invisible Migrants*, ed. by Andrea L. Smith (Amsterdam, 2003), pp. 129–45.

——, 'The Algerian War, the French State and Official Memory', *Historical Reflections/Réflexions historiques*, 28:2 (2002), 219–39.

Comtat, Emmanuelle, *Les Pieds-noirs et la politique quarante ans après le retour* (Paris, 2009).

Confino, Alon, 'Collective Memory and Cultural History: Problems of Method', *American Historical Review*, 102:5 (December 1997), 1386–403.

Crapanzano, Vincent, *The Harkis: The Wound that Never Heals* (Chicago, IL and London, 2011).

Crespo, Gérard and Christain Fenech, *Les Grandes dates de la mémoire pieds-noirs: "souvenons-nous!"* (Carnoux-en-Provence, 2003).

Cubitt, Geoffrey, *History and Memory* (Manchester, 2007).

Daum, Pierre, *Le Dernier tabou: les harkis restés en Algérie après l'indépendance* (Arles, 2015).

——, *Ni valise ni cercueil: les pieds-noirs restés en Algérie après l'indépendance* (Arles, 2012).

Delorme, Christian, 'Le "Mouvement beur" a une histoire', *Les Cahiers de la nou-velle génération*, 1 (1984), 18–46.

Derrieu, Bernard and Habib Kadi, *La Cité de tapis: une communauté de rapatriés d'Algérie* (Pézenas, 1997).

Dessaigne, Francine and Marie-Jeanne Rey, *Un crimes sans assassins: Alger 26 mars 1962* (Perros-Guirec, 1994).

Dimech, Pierre, *La Désinformation autour de la culture des pieds-noirs* (Paris, 2006).

——, *Si jamais je t'oublie l'Algérie…25 ans d'Algérianisme* (Saint Esteve, 1998).

Domergue, René, *L'intégration des pieds-noirs dans les villages du Midi* (Paris, 2005).

Donadey, Anne, '"*Une certaine idée de la France*": The Algerian Syndrome and Struggles Over French Identity', in *Identity Papers: Contested Nationhood in Twentieth Century France*, ed. by Steven Unger and Tom Conley (Minneapolis, MN, 1996), pp. 215–33.

Dubois, Colette, 'La Nation et les français d'outre-mer: rapatriés ou sinistrés de la décolonisation?', in *L'Europe retrouvée: les migrations de la décolonisation*, ed. by Jean-Louis Miège and Colette Dubois (Paris, 1994), pp. 75–135.

Eldridge, Claire, 'Returning to the "Return": *Pied-Noir* Memories of 1962', *Revue européenne des migrations internationales*, 29:3 (December 2013), 121–40.

——, 'The *Pied-Noir* Community and the Complexity of "Coming Home" to Algeria', in *Coming Home? Vol. 2: Conflict and Postcolonial Return Migration in the Context of France and North Africa, 1962–2009*, ed. by Scott Soo and Sharif Gemie (Newcastle-upon-Tyne, 2013), pp. 12–32.

——, 'Le Symbole de l'Afrique perdue: Carnoux-en-Provence and the *Pied-Noir* Community', in *France's Lost Empires: Fragmentation, Loss and la fracture coloniale* ed. by Kate Marsh and Nicola Frith (Lanham, MD, 2011), pp. 125–36.

——, 'Blurring the Boundaries Between Perpetrators and Victims: *Pied-noir* Memories and the *Harki* Community', *Memory Studies*, 3:2 (April 2010), 123–36.

——, '"We've never had a voice": Memory Construction and the Children of the *Harkis*, 1962–1991', *French History*, 23:1 (March 2009), 88–107.

Enjelvin, Géraldine and Nada Kovac-Kakabadse, 'France and the Memories of "Others": The Case of the *Harkis*', *History and Memory*, 24:1 (Spring/Summer 2012), 152–77.

Enjelvin, Géraldine, 'A *Harki*'s Daughter's Offline and Online "parole cicatrisante"', *Australian Journal of French Studies*, 45:2 (2008), 136–49.

——, 'The Harki Identity: A Product of Marginalisation and Resistance to Symbolic Violence?', *National Identities*, 8:2 (June 2006), 113–27.

——, 'Les Harkis en France: carte d'identité française, identité harkie à la carte?', *Modern and Contemporary France*, 11:2 (May 2003), 161–73.

Esclangon-Morin, Valérie, *Les Rapatriés d'Afrique du Nord de 1956 à nos jours* (Paris, 2007).

——, 'La Mémoire déchirée des pieds-noirs', *Hommes et migrations*, 251 (September–October 2004), 99–109.

Evans, Martin, *Algeria: France's Undeclared War* (Oxford, 2012).

——, 'The *Harkis*: the Experience and Memory of France's Muslim Auxiliaries', in *The Algerian War and the French Army 1954–1962: Experiences, Images, Testimonies*, ed. by Martin S. Alexander, Martin Evans and J. F. V Keiger (Basingstoke, 2002), pp. 117–37.

——, *The Memory of Resistance: French Opposition to the Algerian War (1954–1962)* (Oxford, 1997).

Eveno, Patrick and Jean Planchais (eds.), *La Guerre d'Algérie: dossiers et témoignages* (Paris, 1989).

Fabbiano, Giulia, 'Être là. Les voyages au pays d'origine des familles harkies entre expérience mémorielle et situations d'apprentissage', in *Apprentissages en situation touristique*, ed. by Gilles Brougère and Giulia Fabbiano (Villeneuve d'Ascq, 2014), pp. 143–54.

——, 'Mémoires postalgériennes: la guerre d'Algérie entre héritage et emprunts', in *La Concurrence mémorielle*, ed. by Geoffrey Grandjean and Jérôme Jamin (Paris, 2011), pp. 131–47.

——, 'Mixité postcoloniale. Les unions des descendants d'émigrés algériens à l'épreuve de l'expérience migratoire parentale', *Diasporas*, 15 (2009), 99–110.

——, 'Devenir-harki: les modes d'énonciation identitaire des descendants des anciens supplétifs de la guerre d'Algérie', *Migrations société*, 20:120 (November–December 2008), 155–71.

——, 'De l'indigène colonial aux générations postalgériennes: procès d'identification et de différenciation des descendants de harkis et d'immigrés', *Migrations société*, 19:113 (September–October 2007), 95–110.

Faivre, Maurice, *L'action sociale de l'armée en faveur des musulmans, 1830–2006* (Paris, 2007).

——, *Les Combattants musulmans de la guerre d'Algérie: des soldats sacrifiés* (Paris, 1995).

——, *Un village de harkis: des Babors au pays drouais* (Paris, 1994).

Fargues, Dominique, *Mémoires de pieds-noirs* (Paris, 2008).

Fenouillet, Marcel, 'Naissance et histoire de l'ANFANOMA', in *Mémoires de la colonisation: relations colonisateurs-colonisés*, ed. by Régine Goutalier (Paris, 1994), pp. 105–11.

Fleury, Georges, *Le Combat des harkis* (Versailles, 1989).

Fleury-Vilatte, Béatrice, *La Mémoire télévisuelle de la guerre d'Algérie 1962–1992* (Paris, 2000).

Fritzsche, Peter, 'The Case of Modern Memory', *Journal of Modern History*, 73 (2001), 87–117.

——, 'Spectres of History: On Nostalgia, Exile and Modernity', *American Historical Review*, 106:5 (December 2001), 1587–618.

Gladieu, Stéphan and Dalila Kerchouche, *Destins de harkis: aux racines d'un exil* (Paris, 2003).

Gordon, Daniel A., *Immigrants and Intellectuals: May '68 and the Rise of Anti-Racism in France* (Pontypool, 2012).

Halbwachs, Maurice, *Les Cadres sociaux de la mémoire* (Paris, 1994).

——, *On Collective Memory*, trans. Lewis A. Coser (Chicago, IL, 1992).

——, *The Collective Memory*, trans. Francis J. Ditter and Vita Yazdi Ditter (New York, 1980).

Hamoumou, Mohand, with Abderahmen Moumen, 'L'histoire des harkis et Français musulmans: la fin d'un tabou?', in *La Guerre d'Algérie: 1954–2004, la fin de l' amnésie*, ed. by Mohammed Harbi and Benjamin Stora (Paris, 2004), pp. 317–44.

——, *Et ils sont devenus harkis* (Paris, 1993).

——, 'Les Harkis: une double occultation', in *Intégration et exclusion dans la société française contemporaine*, ed. by Gilles Ferréol (Lille, 1993), pp. 79–104.

——, 'Les Harkis, un trou de mémoire franco-algérien', *Esprit*, 161 (May 1990), 25–46.

Harbi, Mohammed and Benjamin Stora (eds.), *La Guerre d'Algérie: 1954–2004, la fin de l' amnésie* (Paris, 2004).

'Harkis, 1962–2012: les mythes et les faits' [Special issue], *Les Temps modernes*, 666 (November–December 2011), 1–315.

Harkis: soldats abandonnés (Paris, 2012).

Hautreux, François-Xavier, *La Guerre d'Algérie des harkis, 1954–1962* (Paris, 2013).

——, 'L'engagement des harkis (1954–1962): essai de périodisation', *Vingtième siècle*, 90 (April-June 2006), 33–45.

Hmed, Choukri, '"Tenir ses hommes": la gestion des étrangers "isolés" dans les foyers SONACOTRA après la guerre d'Algérie', *Politix*, 76 (2006), 11–30.

Hogue, Jeanine de la, *Mémoire écrite de l'Algérie depuis 1950: les auteurs et leurs oeuvres* (Paris, 1992).

House, Jim and Neil MacMaster, *Paris 1961: Algerians, State Terror and Memory* (Oxford, 2006).

Hureau, Joëlle, *La Mémoire des pieds-noirs de 1830 à nos jours* (Paris, 2001).

——, 'Associations et souvenir chez les Français rapatriés d'Algérie', in *La Guerre d'Algérie et les Français*, ed. by Jean-Pierre Rioux (Paris, 1990), pp. 517–25.

Jansen, Jan C., 'Politics of Remembrance, Colonialism and the Algerian War of Independence in France', in *A European Memory? Contested Histories and Politics of Remembrance*, ed. by Małgorzata Pakier and Bo Stråth (New York and Oxford, 2010), pp. 275–91.

Jasseron, Georges, *Les Harkis en France, scènes et témoignages* (Paris, 1965).

Jordi, Jean-Jacques, 'Khélifa Haroud: harki 1957–1967', in *Des hommes et des femmes en guerre d'Algérie*, ed. by Jean-Charles Jauffret (Paris, 2003), pp. 360–1.

——, 'Les Pieds noirs: constructions identitaires et réinvention des origines', *Hommes et migrations*, 1236 (March–April 2002), 14–25.

——, 'Les rapatriés, une histoire en chantier', *Le Mouvement sociale* 197 (October-December 2001), 3–7.

——, 'Archéologie et structure du réseau de sociabilité rapatrié et pied-noir', *Provence Historique*, 47 (1997), 177–88.

——, *1962, l'arrivée des pieds-noirs* (Paris, 1995).

——, *De l'exode à l'exil. Rapatriés et pieds noirs en France: l'exemple marseillais, 1954–1992* (Paris, 1993).

Jordi, Jean-Jacques, and Mohand Hamoumou, *Les Harkis, une mémoire enfouie* (Paris, 1999).

Jordi, Jean-Jacques and Emile Temime (eds.), *Marseille et le choc des décolonisations: les rapatriements 1954–1964* (Aix-en-Provence, 1996).

Jubineau, Emilien, *L'énigme Roseau: la parole pied-noir assassinée* (St Georges d'Orques, 1997).

Kaberseli, Ahmed, *Le Chagrin sans pitié* (Paris, 1988).

Kansteiner, Wulf, 'Finding Meaning in Memory: A Methodological Critique of Collective Memory Studies', *History and Theory* 41 (May 2002), 179–97.

Kara, Mohamed, *Les Tentations du repli communautaire: le cas des franco-maghrébins en général et des enfants de harkis en particulier* (Paris, 1997).

Kassa, Sabrina, *Nos ancêtres les chibanis! Portrait d'Algériens arrivés en France pendant les Trente Glorieuses* (Paris, 2006).

Kerchouche, Dalila, *Leïla: avoir dix-sept ans dans un camp de harkis* (Paris, 2006).

——, *Mon père, ce harki* (Paris, 2003).

Kettane, Nacer, *Droit de réponse à la démocratie française* (Paris, 1986).

Khellil, Mohand, *L'intégration des maghrébins en France* (Paris, 1991).

Khellil, Mohand and Jules Maurin (eds.), *Les Rapatriés d'Algérie en Languedoc-Roussillom 1962–1992* (Montpellier, 1992).

Koubi, Richard M., *Pieds-noirs belle pointure* (Paris, 1979).

Langelier, Elise, *La Situation juridique des harkis (1962–2007)* (Paris and Poitiers, 2009).

Leconte, Daniel, *Les Pieds-noirs: histoire et portrait d'une communauté* (Paris, 1980).

Lefeuvre, Daniel, *Pour en finir avec la repentance colonial* (Paris, 2006).

Lepoutre, David with Isabelle Cannoodt, *Souvenirs de familles immigrées* (Paris, 2005).

Liauzu, Claude (ed.), *Violence et colonisation: pour en finir avec les guerres de mémoire* (Paris, 2003).

Liauzu, Claude, and Gilles Manceron (eds.), *La Colonisation, la loi et l'histoire* (Paris, 2006).

Lindenberg, Daniel, 'Guerres de mémoire en France', *Vingtième siècle* 42 (April–June 1994), 77–96.

Lorcin, Patricia M. E., *Historicizing Colonial Nostalgia: European Women's Narratives of Algeria and Kenya 1900-Present* (New York, 2012).

——, (ed.), *Algeria and France 1800–2000: Identity, Memory, Nostalgia* (New York, 2006).

Manceron, Gilles and Hasan Remaoun, *D'une rive à l'autre: la guerre d'Algérie de la mémoire à l'histoire* (Paris, 1993).

Manes, Rosemary Averell, *The Pieds-Noirs 1960-2000: A Case Study in the Persistence of Subcultural Distinctiveness* (Bethesda, MD, 2005).

Mauro, Francis and Bathoche Mahious, *Compiègne, terre d'accueil pour les Harkis* (Agincourt, 2004).

McCormack, Jo, *Collective Memory: France and the Algerian War (1954–1962)* (Lanham, MD, 2007).

Mercier, Cécile, *Les Pieds-noirs et l'exode de 1962 à travers la presse franaise* (Paris, 2003).

Mettay, Joël, *L'archipel du mépris: histoire du camp de Rivesaltes de 1939 à nos jours* (Canet, 2008).

Michel-Chich, Danielle, *Déracinés: les pieds-noirs aujourd'hui* (Paris, 2000).

Miller, Jeannette E., 'A Camp for Foreigners and "Aliens": The Harkis' Exile at the Rivesaltes Camp (1962–1964)', *French Politics, Culture and Society*, 31:2 (Winter 2013), 21–44.

Molénat, Jacques, *Le Marigot des pouvoirs: systèmes, réseaux, communautés, notables et francs-maçons en Languedoc-Roussillon* (Castelnau-le-Lez, 2004).

Morelle, Chantal, 'Les Pouvoirs publics français et le rapatriement des harkis en 1961–1962', *Vingtième siècle*, 83 (July–September 2004), 109–19.

Morin, Valérie, 'Les "Pieds-noirs": des immigrés de la décolonisation', in *Histoire de l'immigration et question coloniale en France*, ed. by Nancy L. Green and Marie Poinsot (Paris, 2008), pp. 111–16.

——, 'Quel devoir de mémoire pour les rapatriés? Réflexion sur la loi du 23/02/05', *Confluences méditerranée*, 53 (Spring 2005), 105–20.

Mougenot, Ourdia, *Trois femmes kabyles: histoire d'une relation entre la France et l'Algérie* (Paris, 2004).

Moumen, Abderahmen (ed.), *Ils arrivent demain… Ongles, village d'accueil des familles d'anciens harkis* (Ongles, 2008).

Moumen, Abderahmen, *Entre histoire et mémoire: les rapatriés d'Algérie diction-naire bibliographique* (Nice, 2003).

——, *Les Français musulmans en Vaucluse 1962–1991: installation et difficultés d'intégration d'une communuaté de rapatriés d'Algérie* (Paris, 2003).

Muller, Laurent, 'Enfants d'immigrés, enfants de harkis', *Confluences*, 34 (Summer 2000), 141–51.

——, *Le Silence des harkis* (Paris, 1999).

——, 'Le Silence des pères et l'identité problématique des enfants de harkis', *Cultures et sociétés*, 8 (Winter 1996), 39–48.

——, 'Les enfants de harkis et leurs parents: entre distance et proximité', *Cultures et sociétés*, 4 (Winter 1994), 7–16.

Muyl, Marie, 'Le Parti pied-noir: une opportunité européenne', *Pôle Sud*, 24 (2006), 59–73.

Nora, Pierre (ed.), *Realms of Memory*, 3 vols. (New York, 1996–98).

Olick, Jeffrey K., 'Collective Memory: The Two Cultures', *Sociological Theory*, 17:3 (1999), 333–48.

Palacio, Léo, *Les Pieds-noirs dans le monde* (Paris, 1968).

Péju, Paulette, *Les Harkis à Paris* (Paris, 1961).

Pervillé, Guy, *Pour une histoire de la guerre d'Algérie* (Paris, 2002).

Peyrefitte, Alain, *C'était de Gaulle* (Paris, 1994).

Phaneuf, Victoria, 'Negotiating Culture, Performing Identities: North African and Pied-Noir Associations in France', *The Journal of North African Studies*, 17:4 (September 2012), 671–86.

Pierret, Régis, *Les Filles et fils de harkis: entre double rejet et triple appartenance* (Paris, 2008).

——, 'Les Enfants de harkis, une jeunesse dans les camps', *Pensée plurielle*, 14 (2007), 179–92.

Polac, Catherine, 'Quand "les immigrés" prennant la parole', in *L'engagement poli-tique décline ou mutation?* ed. by Pascal Perrineau (Paris, 1994), pp. 359–86.

Prost, Antoine, 'The Algerian War in French Collective Memory', in *War and Remembrance in the Twentieth Century*, ed. by Jay Winter and Emmanuel Sivan (Cambridge, 1999), pp. 161–76.

Ribs, Jacques, *Plaidoyer pour un million de victimes* (Paris, 1975).

——, *L'indemnisation des français dépossedés outre-mer* (Paris, 1971).

Rioux, Jean-Pierre (ed.), *La Guerre d'Algérie et les Français* (Paris, 1990).

Roblés, Emmanuel, *Ces minorités qui font la France: les pieds-noirs* (Paris, 1982).

Roche, Anne 'Pieds-noirs: le "retour"', *Modern and Contemporary France*, 2:2 (1994), 151–64.

——, 'Deuil et mélancolie dans quelques autobiographies "nostalgériques" de l' "après 1962"', *Cahiers de sémiotique textuelle*, 4 (1985), 95–110.

Rodolico, Thérèse, 'Carnoux-en-Provence. Cité nouvelle des rapatriés', *Bulletin de la Société de géographie de Marseille*, 76:5 (1966), 47–57.

Rosaldo, Renato, 'Imperialist Nostalgia', *Representations*, 26 (Spring 1989), 107–22.

Rosello, Mireille, *The Reparative in Narratives: Works of Mourning in Progress* (Liverpool, 2010).

Rosenman, Anny Dayan and Lucette Valensi (eds.), *La Guerre d'Algerie dans la mémoire et l'imaginaire* (Paris, 2004).

Rothberg, Michael, Debarati Sanyai and Max Silverman (eds.), '*Noueds de mémoire*: Multidirectional Memory in Postwar French and Francophone Culture', [Special issue], *Yale French Studies*, 118–9 (2010), 241.

Rothberg, Michael, *Multidirectional Memory: Remembering the Holocaust in the Age of Decolonization* (Stanford, CA, 2009).

Rousso, Henry, 'Les Raisins verts de la guerre d'Algérie', in *La Guerre d'Algérie (1954–1962)*, ed. by Yves Michaud (Paris, 2004), pp. 127–51.

——, *The Vichy Syndrome: History and Memory in France Since 1944*, trans. Arthur Goldhammer (Cambridge, MA, 1991).

Saïah, Ysabel, *Pieds-noirs et fiers de l'être* (Paris, 1987).

Savarèse, Eric, 'Un regard compréhensif sur le "traumatisme historique". À propos de vote Front national chez les pieds-noirs', *Pôle Sud*, 34:1 (2011), 91–104.

—— (ed.), *L'Algérie dépassionnée: au delà du tumulte des mémoires* (Paris, 2008).

——, 'Mobilisations politiques et posture victimaire chez les militants associatifs pieds-noirs', *Raisons politiques*, 30 (May 2008), 41–58.

——, *Algérie, la guerre des mémoires* (Paris, 2007).

——, 'Pieds-Noirs, harkis, rapatriés: la politicisation des enjeux', *Pôle Sud*, 24:1 (2006), 3–14.

——, 'Guerres de mémoires autour de la question algérienne', *Diasporas*, 2 (2005), 134–43.

——, *L'invention des pieds-noirs* (Paris, 2002).

——, 'Enjeu et usages d'une mémoire pied-noir', *Annuaire de l'Afrique du Nord*, 39 (2000–1), 85–104.

——, *Histoire coloniale et immigration: une invention de l'étranger* (Paris, 2000)

Sayad, Abdelmalek, *La Double absence: des illusions de l'émigré au souffrances de l'immigré* (Paris, 1999).

——, 'Le Mode de génération des générations "immigrés"', *L'Homme et la société*, 111–12 (January–June 1994), 155–74.

Schembre, Christian, 'La Deuxième génération ou naissance d'une identité', in *Les Rapatriés d'Algérie en Languedoc-Roussillon, 1962–1992*, ed. by Mohand Khellil and Jules Maurin (Montpellier, 1992), pp. 131–40.

Scioldo-Zürcher, Yann, 'The Cost of Decolonisation: Compensating the *Pieds-Noirs'*, in *France since the 1970s: History, Politics and Memory in an Age of Uncertainty*, ed. by Emile Chabal (London, 2014), pp. 99–114.

——, *Devenir métropolitain: politique d'intégration et parcours de rapatriés d'Algérie en métropole (1954-2005)* (Paris, 2010).

——, 'Des pratiques administratives inédites pour les français rapatriés d'Algérie (1961–1967)', in *Histoire de l'immigration et question coloniale en France*, ed. by Nancy L. Green and Marie Poinsot (Paris, 2008), pp. 99–104.

——, 'Faire des français d'Algérie des métropolitains', *Pôle Sud*, 24:1 (2006), 15–28.

Shepard, Todd, 'Excluding the *Harkis* from Repatriate Status, Excluding Muslim Algerians from French Identity', in *Transnational Spaces and Identities in the Francophone World*, ed. by Hafid Gafaiti, Patricia M. E. Lorcin and David G. Troyansky (Lincoln, NE, 2009), pp. 94–114.

——, *The Invention of Decolonization: The Algerian War and the Remaking of France* (Ithaca, NY and London, 2006).

Sirvente, Edmond, *Les Pieds-noirs: une histoire, un peuple, une culture* (Prades, 1988).

Slyomovics, Susan, 'Algeria Elsewhere: The Pilgrimage of the Virgin of Santa Cruz in Oran and in Nîmes, France', in *Folklore Interpreted: Essays in Honour of Alan Dundes*, ed. by Regina Bendix and Rosemary Lévy-Zumwalt (New York, 1995), pp. 337–54.

Smith, Andrea, 'Settler Sites of Memory and the Work of Mourning', *French Politics, Culture and Society*, 31:3 (Winter 2013), 65–92.

——, *Colonial Memory and Postcolonial Europe: Maltese Settlers in Algeria and France* (Bloomington IN, 2006).

——, 'Place Replaced: Colonial Nostalgia and Pied-Noir Pilgrimages to Malta', *Cultural Anthropology*, 18:3 (2003), 329–64.

——, 'Colonialism and the Poisoning of Europe: Towards an Anthropology of Colonists', *Journal of Anthropological Research*, 30 (1994), 383–93.

Soufi, Fouad, 'L'histoire face à la mémoire: Oran, le 5 juillet 1962', in *La Guerre d'Algérie dans la mémoire et l'imaginaire*, ed. by Anny Dayan Rosenman and Lucette Valensi (Saint-Denis, 2004), pp. 133–48.

——, 'Oran, 28 février 1962, 5 juillet 1962. Deux événements pour l'histoire, deux événements pour la mémoire', in *La Guerre d'Algérie au miroir des décolonisations françaises* (Paris, 2000), pp. 635–76.

Spina, Rosella, *Enfants de harkis et enfants d'émigrés: parcours croisés, identités à recoudre* (Paris, 2012).

Stora, Benjamin *Les Guerres sans fin: un historien, la France et l'Algérie* (Paris, 2008).

——, *Le Livre, mémoire de l'histoire: réflexions sur le livre et la guerre d'Algérie* (Paris, 2005).

——, *Imaginaires de guerre: les images dans les guerres d'Algérie et du Viet-nam* (Paris, 2004).

——, 'Guerre d'Algérie: 1999-2003, les accélérations de la mémoire', *Hommes et migrations*, 1244 (July–August 2003), 83–95.

——, 'Algérie: les retours de la mémoire de la guerre d'indépendence', *Modern and Contemporary France*, 10:4 (2002), 461–73.

——, *Le Transfert d'une mémoire: de l' "Algérie Française" au racisme anti-arabe* (Paris, 1999).

——, *Le Dictionnaire des livres de la guerre d'Algérie* (Paris, 1996).

——, *Ils venaient d'Algérie: l'immigration algérienne en France 1912–1992* (Paris, 1992).

——, *La Gangrène et l'oubli: la mémoire de la guerre d'Algérie* (Paris, 1991).

——, 'Guerre d'Algérie: la récupération des héritages de mémoires', *Cahiers d'Histoire*, 31:3–4 (1986), 357–67.

Stora, Benjamin, and Thierry Leclère, *La Guerre des mémoires: la France face à son passé colonial* (Paris, 2007).

Stora, Fernande, *L'Algérie pour mémoire* (Paris, 1978).

Sueur, James D. Le, 'Beyond Decolonization? The Legacy of the Algerian Conflict and the Transformation of Identity in Contemporary France', *Historical Reflections/Réflexions historiques*, 28:2 (2002), 277–91.

——, 'Decolonizing "French Universalism": Reconsidering the Impact of the Algerian War on French Intellectuals', in *North Africa, Islam and the Mediterranean World from the Almoravids to the Algerian War*, ed. By Julia Clancy–Smith (London, 2001), pp. 167–86.

Sutton, Homer B., 'Postcolonial Voices: Vindicating the Harkis', *Contemporary French Civilization*, 20:2 (1996), 231–39.

Ternant, Geneviève de, *L'agonie d'Oran 5 juillet 1962*, 3 vols. (Calvisson, 1991–2000).

Thénault, Sylvie, 'France-Algérie: Pour un traitment commun du passé de la guerre d'indépendance', *Vingtième siècle*, 85 (January–March 2005), 119–28.

Thomson, Alistair, *Anzac Memories: Living with the Legend* (Melbourne, 1994).

Titraoui, Taouès and Bernard Coll, *Le Livre des harkis* (Bièvres, 1991).

Tumblety, Joan (ed.), *Memory and History: Understanding Memory as a Source and Subject* (London and New York, 2013).

Valat, Rémy, *Les Calots bleus et la Bataille de Paris: une force de police auxiliaire pendant la guerre d'Algérie* (Paris, 2007).

Verdès-Leroux, Jeanine, *Les Français d'Algérie de 1830 à aujourd'hui: une page d'histoire déchirée* (Paris, 2001).

Veyrat-Masson, Isabelle, *Quand la télévision explore le temps. L'histoire au petit écran, 1953–2000* (Paris, 2000).

Wenden, Catherine Wihtol de, 'The Harkis: A Community in the Making?', in *French and Algerian Identities from Colonial Times to the Present*, ed. by Alec G, Hargreaves and Michael J Heffernan (Lewiston, 1997), pp. 189–201.

——, 'Harkis: le paradoxe identitaire', *Regards sur l'actualité*, 175 (November 1991), 33–45.

——, 'La Vie associatif des harkis', *Migrations société*, 1:5–6 (October–December 1989), 9–26.

Winter, Jay, 'Thinking about Silence', in *Shadows of War: A Social History of Silence in the Twentieth Century*, ed. by Efrat Ben Ze'ev, Ruth Ginio and Jay Winter (Cambridge, 2010), pp. 3–31.

——, *Sites of Memory, Sites of Mourning: The Great War in European Cultural History* (Cambridge, 1995).

Winter, Jay, and Emmanuel Sivan (eds.), *War and Remembrance in the Twentieth Century* (Cambridge, 1999).

Wood, Nancy, *Vectors of Memory: Legacies of Trauma in Postwar Europe* (Oxford and New York, 1999).

Wormser, André, 'En quête d'une patrie: les Français musulmans et leur destin', *Le Temps modernes*, 452–4 (March–April–May 1984), 1839–57.

Zanoun, Louisa (ed.), '1983. La Marche pour l'égalité et contre le racisme' [Special issue], *Migrance*, 41 (2013), 1–233.

UNPUBLISHED THESES AND DISSERTATIONS

Choi, Sung E., 'From Colonial Settler to Postcolonial Repatriate: The Integration of the French from Algeria, 1962 to the Present', unpublished doctoral dissertation, UCLA, 2007.

Sussman, Sarah Beth, 'Changing Lands, Changing Identities: The Migration of Algerian Jewry to France 1954–1967', unpublished doctoral dissertation, Stanford University, 2002.

Index

Notes: 'n' after a page reference indicates the number of the note on that page.